Finance Theory

Finance Theory

ROBERT A. JARROW

Associate Professor of Finance and Economics
Johnson Graduate School of Management
Cornell University

Prentice-Hall International, Inc.

© 1988 by Prentice-Hall, Inc.
A Division of Simon & Schuster
Englewood Cliffs, NJ 07632

1561490

Printed in the United States of America

10 9 8 9 6 5 4 3 2 1

ISBN 0-13-314923-4

Prentice-Hall International (UK) Limited, *London*
Prentice-Hall of Australia Pty. Limited, *Sydney*
Prentice-Hall Canada Inc., *Toronto*
Prentice-Hall Hispanoamericana, S.A., *Mexico*
Prentice-Hall of India Private Limited, *New Delhi*
Prentice-Hall of Japan, Inc., *Tokyo*
Simon & Schuster Asia Pte. Ltd., *Singapore*
Editora Prentice-Hall do Brasil, Ltda., *Rio de Janeiro*
Prentice-Hall, Inc., *Englewood Cliffs, New Jersey*

To my parents

CONTENTS

PREFACE

The title of this book, *Finance Theory,* is adopted from an MBA elective course at Cornell University's Johnson Graduate School of Management. My lecture notes for this course constitute the core of the book. Consistent with this origin, the book is targeted for advanced second-year MBA or first-year PhD candidates. It is hoped, however, that even the seasoned finance academic will obtain new insights after reading this book. This hope is fostered by the content of the book, 50 percent of which is new. It is new, not in what is covered but in how it is covered. The organization, structure, and even the derivations of many of the models are unique to this book.

The organization and structure of this book distinguish it from others in the field. Existing textbooks parallel the historical development of finance—i.e., the capital asset pricing model (CAPM) is the central topic, with arbitrage pricing theory delegated to an isolated chapter. The present book breaks with this tradition. The material is presented in a logical progression, from the simple to the complex, necessarily implying that arbitrage pricing theory comes first and equilibrium models (like the CAPM) second. Arbitrage pricing theory, therefore, constitutes half the text; equilibrium pricing theory constitutes the other half. The CAPM constitutes only two chapters. The material is presented in an integrated and unified fashion.

This text covers the major models in financial economics and is a theory book. The empirical literature is referenced, but not critically evaluated. In developing the theory, a number of themes are emphasized. First, an attempt is made to keep the book self-contained, especially with respect to theorems and their proofs. In this regard, the text can serve as a concise reference. Second, an attempt is also made to keep each chapter self-contained. In this way, later chapters can be read independently of earlier chapters. A consequence of this desire, however, is a greater repetition of the assumptions and the notation. It is arguable whether this is a positive or negative externality. Third, difficult material is delegated to starred sections, which can be skipped without loss of content. With the exception of starred sections, prerequisites for this text are calculus, introductory probability theory, and introductory statistics.

As in any project of this size, it could not have been accomplished without the aid and advice of many individuals. Special thanks are extended to Lawrence Glosten, Larry Hexter and his student Gary Powell, and Chris Leach. Thanks are also expressed to Barb Guile, whose speed and patience in typing this manuscript were greatly appreciated.

Finance Theory

1

INTRODUCTION
AND OVERVIEW

Finance theory, the title of this book, is a phrase that encompasses under its umbrella portfolio theory, the capital asset pricing model, call option pricing, and arbitrage pricing theory; in sum, it includes those models most often associated with financial economics.[1] In the late 1960s and early 1970s, the field was most closely associated with the capital asset pricing model (CAPM), as evidenced by the emergence of classic texts basically devoted to that topic (see Fama and Miller [1], Hirshleifer [2], Sharpe [3]). Since that time, finance theory has expanded and matured, and arbitrage pricing theory and such areas as option pricing have assumed increasing importance, both in research and applications. Consistent with these trends, this text provides a more contemporary treatment of finance, with arbitrage pricing theory receiving greater emphasis.

In this text the belief that arbitrage pricing and equilibrium pricing theories are complements rather than substitutes is emphasized. Arbitrage pricing theories are most useful for pricing contingent claims, i.e., financial claims whose cash flows depend on other traded securities. Alternatively, equilibrium pricing theories (like the CAPM) are most useful for pricing the primary traded securities, like common equity. Although each model can be invoked to apply to the other case, its assumptions and inherent limitations do not lead to a good fit.

[1]For the uninitated to finance or economics, a practical definition of financial economics is found in those topics that appear with some regularity in such publications as the *Journal of Finance, Journal of Financial and Quantitative Analysis, Journal of Financial Economics,* and *Journal of Banking and Finance.*

The book is divided into two parts: Part I studies certainty models, and Part II studies models with uncertainty. Part I, less than a third of the text, is included for pedagogical reasons. Most of the underlying concepts can be introduced without the added mathematical complexity of probability theory.

For easy reference, Parts I and II are structured in a similar fashion, with each part subdivided into two subsections. The first subsection examines arbitrage pricing theory (APT), and the second subsection builds on the first to study equilibrium pricing theory. Arbitrage pricing theory comes first because equilibrium pricing theory requires more structure than APT, especially with respect to preferences. Each pricing theory composes roughly half the text. The subsections themselves are divided into chapters, each chapter studying a specific topic.

Part I consists of six chapters. Chapters 2, 3, and 4 study arbitrage pricing models under certainty; Chaps. 5 and 6 study equilibrium pricing under certainty.

Chapter 2 introduces the basics of ordinal utility theory, a procedure needed to model a consumer's behavior. An axiomatic construction is presented, which is applied to the consumption-saving model employed throughout the remainder of the text. This chapter follows the standard presentation of this material.

Chapter 3 presents the basics of arbitrage pricing theory. An economy is constructed, and arbitrage opportunities are defined. The restrictions necessarily imposed on prices such that no arbitrage opportunities exist are studied, leading to the notions of value additivity and dominance. Finally, a utility theory based justification for the desirability of an arbitrage opportunity is explored. The presentation of this material is unique to this text.

Chapter 4 applies the abstract theory of arbitrage pricing to two standard topics in corporate finance. The first topic is dividend relevance: Does a higher dividend per share increase share value? The second topic is debt/equity relevance: Does the debt/equity ratio influence firm value? The approach this chapter takes to study these issues is familiar to financial economists; however, the proofs are new. Given the theory of Chap. 3, simpler proofs than the standard are available.

Chapter 5 initiates the study of equilibrium pricing theory by returning to the study of ordinal utility theory. The optimal consumption and portfolio decision is characterized through the use of calculus and Lagrangian multipliers. Much of this material is standard. One exception is a section that gives sufficient conditions on preferences (utility functions) such that no arbitrage opportunities exist in an economy. This is the rigorous justification for an assumption invoked earlier in Chap. 3.

Building on these insights, Chap. 6 introduces a competitive equilibrium, a concept fundamental to economics. A competitive equilibrium in both the consumption goods market and the bond market is explored. A section clarifying the differences and similarities between arbitrage pricing theory and equilibrium price theory follows. This section brings together all the material in Part I.

Although of little applicability to the actual economy, Part I provides the foundational insights needed for Part II.

Part II builds on the material presented in Part I to study how uncertainty influences investor behavior and therefore pricing. The sequential nature of the development fosters understanding by isolating the changes necessitated by uncertainty. The power of probability theory is revealed. Chapters 7 to 13 study arbitrage pricing theory, and Chaps. 14 to 19 examine equilibrium pricing theory. Much of this material is not available elsewhere in textbook form.

Cardinal utility theory is the content of Chap. 7. The axiomatic derivation contained herein is new and builds on the axiomatic structure of Chap. 2. The relationship between cardinal utility theory and the expected utility hypothesis is studied and clarified. As in Chap. 2, the abstract model is applied to the consumption-saving framework utilized in the remainder of the text.

Chapter 8 presents the generalized arbitrage pricing theory, which is the precursor to Ross's arbitrage pricing theory, discussed in Chap. 9. A single period economy is constructed and arbitrage opportunities defined. The restrictions on prices imposed by the absence of arbitrage opportunities are studied. The final section relates arbitrage opportunities to preferences. Chapter 8's material is not available elsewhere in textbook form.

Ross's arbitrage pricing theory is presented in Chap. 9. The approach taken here builds on the generalized arbitrage pricing theory of Chap. 8. This development clarifies the reasons for imposing the linear factor hypothesis and also provides an intuitive interpretation of the basic theorem. The APT is evaluated and its testability explored. Later, in Chap. 18, the APT is reconsidered to obtain an equilibrium version.

Chapters 10 and 11 provide corporate finance applications of the single period arbitrage pricing theory of Chap. 8. These chapters revisit the material of Chap. 4 to study dividend policy and debt/equity policy, respectively. The approach taken in these chapters is standard; however, the proofs are new and simpler. Consequently, the underlying structure is clarified. The last section in each chapter discusses the limitations of the arbitrage pricing theory approach. In particular, information and its signaling effects are explored.

Chapter 12 introduces the simplest multiperiod extension of the arbitrage pricing theory economy of Chap. 8. This extended economy is used to study default-free bonds and the term structure of interest rates. Chapter 13 complicates the arbitrage pricing economy of Chap. 12 even more to incorporate the sophisticated dynamic trading strategies needed to study the pricing of call and put options. The pricing of call and put options is fundamental to the study of financial economics. These chapters are introductory and are designed to expose the student to the underlying concepts and methodology. An exhaustive investigation is delegated to other sources.

The remaining chapters in the text, Chaps. 14 to 19, study equilibrium pricing theory. Cardinal utility theory is revisited in Chap. 14. As in Chap. 7, the optimal consumption and portfolio decision is characterized through the use of calculus. The concepts of certainty equivalence and risk aversion are presented, notions fundamental to the CAPM of Chap. 15 and the equilibrium version of Ross's APT in Chap. 18. The link between arbitrage pricing theory and the existence of an optimal investment portfolio is also contained in this chapter. This link provides sufficient conditions on preferences such that no arbitrage opportunities exist in an economy.

Chapters 15, 16, and 17 study the capital asset pricing model. Chapters 15 and 16 present the single period version, and Chap. 17 presents the multiperiod economy. Chapter 17 is starred because of the sophistication of the underlying mathematics. Although much of the material in Chaps. 15 to 17 is standard to existing texts, the perspective taken here differs. Consistent with contemporary research trends, this text places more emphasis on equilibrium and the development of a consumption beta. Similarly, less emphasis is placed on the derivation of the mean-variance frontier. This differing perspective is consistent with the multiperiod generalizations of the single period models.

An equilibrium version of Ross's APT is presented in Chap. 18. This model is compared to the Chap. 9 version of the APT and to the CAPM of Chap. 15. The similarities and differences between the models are contrasted and compared. Special emphasis is placed on the model's testability. This chapter completes the study of equilibrium pricing models under the assumptions of homogeneous beliefs and homogeneous information sets (across investors).

The final chapter of the book, Chap. 19, explores the relaxation of the homogenity restrictions. Investors are allowed to have differential beliefs and differential information sets. In this context, the meaning of an equilibrium price system and the concept of an efficient market are studied. The perspective taken by this chapter is adopted from microeconomics. It is the concept of a rational expectations equilibrium.

REFERENCES

1. Fama, Eugene, and Merton Miller, *The Theory of Finance*. Hinsdale, Ill.: Dryden Press, 1972.
2. Hirshleifer, J., *Investment, Interest, and Capital*. Englewood Cliffs, N.J.: Prentice-Hall, 1970.
3. Sharpe, William, *Portfolio Theory and Capital Markets*. New York: McGraw-Hill, 1970.

2

ORDINAL UTILITY THEORY

As stated in Chap. 1, the goal of this textbook is to understand how security prices are determined in the capital markets. Fundamental to this process are the investors, individuals who buy and sell the securities. The actions of these investors ultimately determine prices. Consequently, if we are to understand how prices are determined, we must first understand investor behavior—the purpose of this chapter.

In the context of an economy where there is no uncertainty, investor behavior is modeled. An axiomatic development of ordinal utility theory will be presented. The generalization of this theory to an uncertain economy is presented in Chap. 7. The logical structure of that theory, however, is identical to the theory presented here. Even though ordinal utility theory may first appear to be of limited use in understanding actual decision making under uncertainty, this is not true. In fact, it will be shown that decision theory under uncertainty has as its foundation the decision theory presented below.

2.1. AXIOMATIC STRUCTURE

Consider an individual faced with a decision problem. We will sometimes call this individual an investor and sometimes a consumer, depending on the decision problem at hand. This individual is faced with a set of alternatives, called the choice set and denoted by the symbol B, from which the person must choose a preferred element. For example, let the choice set B be the set consisting of one apple, one orange, one peach, and all fractional combinations of these three fruits. The individual's decision problem is to determine which of these fruits—or possibly even a fractional combination of them—he or she prefers. For example, the individual might choose half an apple and half an orange.

To model this process, we can imagine the individual's decision proceeding in a pairwise manner. That is, to determine which element of the choice set B is preferred, the individual first considers two arbitrary elements: $x, y \in B$. From these, the individual picks the preferred element, x, and discards the other, y (it is no longer considered). From B minus the two elements $\{x, y\}$, the individual picks a third element, z, and compares it to the previous winner x. From the new pair $\{x, z\}$, the preferred element is determined, say, x again. This element is now compared to a fourth element of B, and the process continues. Finally, at the end of the process, the preferred element of all B is identified.

We now formalize this process. First, let us consider the set of alternatives B. We assume that B is a *convex* subset of *n-dimensional Euclidean space*, denoted by $\mathbb{R}^n$. By convex, we mean that if $x, y \in B$, then $\alpha x + (1 - \alpha)y \in B$ for any $\alpha \in [0, 1]$. The interpretation is that we can fractionally combine elements in the choice set B to obtain new elements in B. Second, B being a subset of n-dimensional Euclidean space implies that any element $x = (x_1, \ldots, x_n) \in B$ can be viewed as being a vector of commodities, where x_i is the number of units of the ith commodity contained in x for $i = 1, \ldots, n$.

Next, we assume that each individual is endowed with a *preference relation*, denoted by $\underline{\pi}$.[1] Given two elements, x and $y \in B$, $x \underline{\pi} y$ means either that x is preferred to y or that x is indifferent to y. An individual's preference relation is assumed to satisfy the following three rationality axioms:

Axiom 2.1: Reflexivity

For any $x \in B$, $x \underline{\pi} x$.

Axiom 2.2: Comparability

For any $x, y \in B$, either $x \underline{\pi} y$ or $y \underline{\pi} x$.

Axiom 2.3: Transitivity

For any $x, y, z \in B$, if $x \underline{\pi} y$, and $y \underline{\pi} z$, then $x \underline{\pi} z$.

The first axiom, *reflexivity*, says that when x is compared to x, the investor is indifferent between the two choices. This axiom is included for technical reasons. The second axiom, *comparability*, says that every pair of elements from the choice set B can be compared. Without this axiom, an individual could not

[1]Formally, $\underline{\pi}$ is a subset of $\{(x, y) : x \in B$ and $y \in B\}$.

determine an optimal choice. This is because there would exist at least two elements of B between which the individual could not discriminate (i.e., decide which is best or whether they are indifferent). The third axiom, *transitivity*, ensures that choices are consistent. If x is preferred to y and y is preferred to z, then x is preferred to z.

Example 1   A Preference Relation

Let $B = \{(x, y): x \in [0, \infty) \text{ and } y \in [0, \infty)\}$ represent the set of alternatives. Let x represent ounces of orange soda and y represent ounces of grape soda. B is easily seen to be a convex subset of $\mathbb{R}^2$. Consider an individual with the following preference relation:

$$\text{Given} \quad (x_1, y_1), (x_2, y_2) \in B$$
$$(x_1, y_1) \; \underset{\sim}{\pi} \; (x_2, y_2) \quad \text{if and only if} \tag{2.1}$$
$$x_1 + y_1 \geq x_2 + y_2$$

The individual is concerned only with the total quantity of soda available—the more the better!

We now check to see if axioms 2.1–2.3 are satisfied. For reflexivity, take $(x_1, y_1) \in B$. Since $x_1 + y_1 = x_1 + y_1$, it is true that $(x_1, y_1) \; \underset{\sim}{\pi} \; (x_1, y_1)$. Next, choose $(x_1, y_1) \in B$ and $(x_2, y_2) \in B$. Either $x_2 + y_2 \geq x_1 + y_1$ or $x_1 + y_1 \geq x_2 + y_2$ is true. Hence either $(x_1, y_1) \; \underset{\sim}{\pi} \; (x_2, y_2)$ or $(x_2, y_2) \; \underset{\sim}{\pi} \; (x_1, y_1)$ must hold. Comparability is satisfied. Finally, consider (x_1, y_1), (x_2, y_2), $(x_3, y_3) \in B$ such that $(x_1, y_1) \; \underset{\sim}{\pi} \; (x_2, y_2)$ and $(x_2, y_2) \; \underset{\sim}{\pi} \; (x_3, y_3)$. Then, by definition (2.1), $x_1 + y_1 \geq x_2 + y_2$ and $x_2 + y_2 \geq x_3 + y_3$. Combined, these give $x_1 + y_1 \geq x_3 + y_3$, so $(x_1, y_1) \; \underset{\sim}{\pi} \; (x_3, y_3)$. The relation is transitive. $\square$

Example 2   Dictionary Order

As in example 1, let the choice set $B = \{(x, y): x \in [0, \infty) \text{ and } y \in [0, \infty)\}$. The alternative set is ounces of orange soda represented by x and ounces of grape soda represented by y. This time, let the individual's preference relation be given by

$$\text{Given} \quad (x_1, y_1) \in B \quad \text{and} \quad (x_2, y_2) \in B$$
$$(x_1, y_1) \; \underset{\sim}{\pi} \; (x_2, y_2) \quad \text{if and only if} \tag{2.2}$$
$$\text{either} \quad [x_1 > x_2]$$
$$\text{or} \quad [x_1 = x_2 \quad \text{and} \quad y_1 \geq y_2]$$

This is called the *dictionary order* because the preference relation ranks pairs of soda like a dictionary lists words starting with a and b. Orange soda comes first and grape second. If there is more orange soda in a pair, it is preferred. The individual prefers orange soda to the exclusion of grape soda. For example, 2 ounces of orange soda is preferred to 1 ounce of orange and any amount of grape soda. Only if the quantity of orange soda is equal across the two choices is grape considered. In this case, the pair with more grape soda is preferred.

We will now show that condition (2.2) satisfies axioms 2.1–2.3.

Reflexivity. Take $(x_1, y_1) \in B$. $x_1 = x_1$ and $y_1 \geq y_1$, so $(x_1, y_1) \, \underset{\sim}{\pi} \, (x_1, y_1)$.

Comparability. Take $(x_1, y_1) \in B$ and $(x_2, y_2) \in B$. Either $x_1 > x_2$ or $x_2 > x_1$ or $x_1 = x_2$. If $x_1 > x_2$, then $(x_1, y_1) \, \underset{\sim}{\pi} \, (x_2, y_2)$. If $x_2 > x_1$, then $(x_2, y_2) \, \underset{\sim}{\pi} \, (x_1, y_1)$. If $x_1 = x_2$, then consider the y's. Either $y_1 \geq y_2$ or $y_2 \geq y_1$. If $y_1 \geq y_2$, then $(x_1, y_1) \, \underset{\sim}{\pi} \, (x_2, y_2)$. If $y_2 \geq y_1$, then $(x_2, y_2) \, \underset{\sim}{\pi} \, (x_1, y_1)$.

Transitivity. Take $(x_1, y_1), (x_2, y_2), (x_3, y_3) \in B$, such that $(x_1, y_1) \, \underset{\sim}{\pi} \, (x_2, y_2)$ and $(x_2, y_2) \, \underset{\sim}{\pi} \, (x_3, y_3)$.

Hence there are four possibilities:

(i) $x_1 > x_2$ and $x_2 > x_3$

(ii) $x_1 > x_2$ and $x_2 = x_3$ and $y_2 \geq y_3$

(iii) $x_1 = x_2$ and $y_1 \geq y_2$ and $x_2 > x_3$

(iv) $x_1 = x_2$ and $y_1 \geq y_2$ and $x_2 = x_3$ and $y_2 \geq y_3$

Cases (i)–(iii) give $(x_1, y_1) \, \underset{\sim}{\pi} \, (x_3, y_3)$ since $x_1 > x_3$. Case (iv) gives $(x_1, y_1) \, \underset{\sim}{\pi} \, (x_3, y_3)$ since $x_1 = x_3$ and $y_1 \geq y_3$. $\square$

2.2. EXISTENCE OF AN ORDINAL UTILITY FUNCTION

For most modeling purposes, working with the preference relation $\underset{\sim}{\pi}$ as described above is difficult. Knowledge of $\underset{\sim}{\pi}$ effectively requires a complete listing of the preferences over all pairs of elements from the choice set B. It would be much simpler if we had a rule that assigned a numeric value to each element of the choice set such that larger numeric values implied higher preference. Such a rule is called a *utility function*. To obtain a utility function, we need to impose two additional axioms. Why? Because it can be shown that the preference relation (2.2) given in example 2 in Sec. 2.1 cannot be represented by a utility function.[2] Before we state the last axioms, we need a definition.

Given $x, y \in B$ and a preference relation $\underset{\sim}{\pi}$ satisfying axioms 2.1–2.3, we say x is indifferent to y, written as

$$x \sim y \quad \text{if and only if} \quad x \, \underset{\sim}{\pi} \, y \quad \text{and} \quad y \, \underset{\sim}{\pi} \, x$$

We also say x is strictly preferred to y, written as

$$x \, \pi \, y \quad \text{if and only if} \quad x \, \underset{\sim}{\pi} \, y \quad \text{and not} \quad x \sim y$$

We now state axiom 2.4:

[2] The proof of this statement can be found in Debreu [1, p. 72, footnote 2].

Axiom 2.4: Order Preserving

For any x, $y \in B$ where $x \, \pi \, y$ and α, $\beta \in [0, 1]$,
$[\alpha x + (1 - \alpha)y] \, \pi \, [\beta x + (1 - \beta)y]$ if and only if $\alpha > \beta$.

This axiom relates preferences between x and y in the choice set B to preferences between convex combinations of x and y. It says that if x is preferred to y, then in combinations involving α percent of x and $(1 - \alpha)$ percent of y, those combinations with a larger proportion of x are preferred. This axiom can be clarified by returning to the examples presented in Sec. 2.1.

Example 1   A Preference Relation: Revisited

The preference relation (2.1) satisfies the order-preserving axiom 2.4. To see this, take (x_1, y_1), $(x_2, y_2) \in B$ such that $(x_1, y_1) \, \pi \, (x_2, y_2)$. Then, by (2.1)

$$x_1 + y_1 > x_2 + y_2 \quad \text{or } x_1 + y_1 - x_2 - y_2 > 0$$

Take α, $\beta \in [0, 1]$ such that $\alpha > \beta$. Note that $\alpha(x_1 + y_1 - (x_2 + y_2)) > \beta(x_1 + y_1 - (x_2 + y_2))$. Adding $(x_2 + y_2)$ to both sides of this inequality and rearranging terms give

$$\alpha(x_1 + y_1) + (1 - \alpha)(x_2 + y_2) > \beta(x_1 + y_1) + (1 - \beta)(x_2 + y_2)$$

or

$$[\alpha(x_1, y_1) + (1 - \alpha)(x_2, y_2)] \, \pi \, [\beta(x_1, y_1) + (1 - \beta)(x_2, y_2)]$$

The reverse implication follows immediately since the steps in the stated proof are reversible.   □

Example 2   Dictionary Order: Revisited

The preference relation (2.2) also satisfies the order-preserving axiom 2.4. Take (x_1, y_1), $(x_2, y_2) \in B$ such that $(x_1, y_1) \, \pi \, (x_2, y_2)$. Then $[x_1 > x_2]$ or $[x_1 = x_2$ and $y_1 > y_2]$. First, take the case $x_1 > x_2$. Here $x_1 - x_2 > 0$. Hence $\alpha(x_1 - x_2) > \beta(x_1 - x_2)$ for α, $\beta \in [0, 1]$ and $\alpha > \beta$. Adding x_2 to both sides gives

$$\alpha x_1 + (1 - \alpha)x_2 > \beta x_1 + (1 - \beta)x_2$$

Using (2.2), this implies

$$[\alpha(x_1, y_1) + (1 - \alpha)(x_2, y_2)] \, \pi \, [\beta(x_1, y_1) + (1 - \beta)(x_2, y_2)]$$

Last, take the case $[x_1 = x_2$ and $y_1 > y_2]$. Here, using the same argument as above but this time for $y_1 > y_2$, we get

$$[\alpha y_1 + (1 - \alpha)y_2] > [\beta y_1 + (1 - \beta)y_2]$$

Since $\alpha x_1 + (1 - \alpha)x_2 = \beta x_1 + (1 - \beta)x_2$, by (2.2) we get

$$[\alpha(x_1, y_1) + (1 - \alpha)(x_2, y_2)] \, \pi \, [\beta(x_1, y_1) + (1 - \beta)(x_2, y_2)]$$

The converse direction follows similarly by reversing the steps in the preceding argument. □

This order-preserving axiom, 2.4, in combination with the previous three rationality axioms, is still not sufficient to generate a utility function. Still needed is axiom 2.5:

Axiom 2.5: Intermediate Value

For any $x, y, z \in B$, if $x \, \pi \, y \, \pi \, z$ then there exists a unique $\alpha \in (0, 1)$ such that $\alpha x + (1 - \alpha)z \sim y$.

This intermediate value axiom says that given three alternatives with rankings of $x \, \pi \, y \, \pi \, z$, there exists a fractional combination of x and z that is indifferent to y. Trade-offs between the alternatives exist.

Example 1 A Preference Relation: Revisited

The preference relation (2.1) satisfies the intermediate value axiom 2.5. To see this, take $(x_1, y_1), (x_2, y_2), (x_3, y_3) \in B$ such that $(x_1, y_1) \, \pi \, (x_2, y_2) \, \pi \, (x_3, y_3)$. Then, by condition (2.1), $x_1 + y_1 > x_2 + y_2 > x_3 + y_3$. Consider

$$\alpha = \frac{(x_2 + y_2) - (x_3 + y_3)}{(x_1 + y_1) - (x_3 + y_3)}$$

Multiplying both sides of this expression by $[(x_1 + y_1) - (x_3 + y_3)]$ and rearranging terms give us $\alpha(x_1 + y_1) + (1 - \alpha)(x_3 + y_3) = (x_2 + y_2)$. Hence $[\alpha(x_1, y_1) + (1 - \alpha)(x_3, y_3)] \sim (x_2, y_2)$ for the unique $\alpha \in (0, 1)$ specified above. □

Example 2 Dictionary Order: Revisited

The preference relation (2.2) does *not* satisfy the intermediate value axiom 2.5. To see this, suppose $(x_1, y_1), (x_2, y_2), (x_3, y_3) \in B$ such that $(x_1, y_1) \, \pi \, (x_2, y_2) \, \pi \, (x_3, y_3)$, and $x_1 > x_2 = x_3$ and $y_2 > y_3$.
Now for any $\alpha \in (0, 1)$, we have

$$\alpha(x_1, y_1) + (1 - \alpha)(x_3, y_3)$$
$$= \alpha(x_1, y_1) + (1 - \alpha)(x_2, y_3)$$
$$= (\alpha x_1 + (1 - \alpha)x_2, \alpha y_1 + (1 - \alpha)y_3)$$

But for $\alpha > 0$, we have $\alpha x_1 + (1 - \alpha)x_2 > x_2$, so $\alpha(x_1, y_1) + (1 - \alpha)(x_3, y_3) \, \pi \, (x_2, y_2)$ is true for all $\alpha \in (0, 1)$. Hence, there is no $\alpha \in (0, 1)$ such that $\alpha x + (1 - \alpha)z \sim y$.
It is the violation of this axiom that prevents the existence of a utility function for the dictionary order preference relation (2.2). □

To make the derivation simpler, we introduce one additional axiom. This axiom is imposed on the choice set B.

Axiom 2.6: Boundedness

There exists an x^*, $y^* \in B$ such that $x^* \underline{\pi} z \underline{\pi} y^*$ for all $z \in B$.

This axiom ensures the existence of a most preferred element $x^* \in B$ and a least preferred element $y^* \in B$. In terms of the preference relation π, these two elements bound the set of alternatives B. For most applications, this axiom is automatically satisfied, and so its imposition doesn't really limit the usefulness of the model. Consider the following example:

Example 3   A Bounded Choice Set

For example 1, the alternatives set is $B = \{(x, y):x \in [0, \infty)$ and $y \in [0, \infty)\}$. Given the preference relation π as defined in condition (2.1), the boundedness axiom 2.6 is not satisfied. To see this, given any $(z_1, z_2) \in B$, we have $(z_1 + 1, z_2) \pi (z_1, z_2)$ since $z_1 + z_2 + 1 > z_1 + z_2$. So a maximum element does not exist.

However, considering the example at hand, one might not believe that there is an unlimited quantity of orange soda (x) and grape soda (y) available. If the supply of these goods is limited, say, 1 billion ounces each for both orange and grape, then the axiom is satisfied.

Here redefine $B = \{(x, y):x \in [0, 10^9]$ and $y \in [0, 10^9]\}$, and now any $(z_1, z_2) \in B$ is such that $2(10^9) \geq z_1 + z_2 \geq 0$. So $(10^9, 10^9) \underline{\pi} (z_1, z_2) \underline{\pi} (0, 0)$ for all $(z_1, z_2) \in B$. □

Given axioms 2.1–2.6, we can now state and prove the theorem.[3]

Theorem 2.1: Existence of Ordinal Utility Functions

Given a preference relation π over the choice set B that satisfies axioms 2.1–2.6, there exists a utility function $U:B \rightarrow \mathbb{R}$ such that[4]

(a) $x \pi y$ if and only if $U(x) > U(y)$

and

(b) $x \sim y$ if and only if $U(x) = U(y)$

Proof

See Sec. 2.4. □

This theorem makes modeling consumer preference behavior easier. We need only know the utility function U to duplicate an individual's ranking of the elements in the choice set B.

---

[3]This theorem can be proven without the imposition of axiom 2.6. The proof, however, is more difficult (see Herstein and Milnor [4]).

[4]The symbol $U:B \rightarrow \mathbb{R}$ means that the function U maps elements of B into the real line, $\mathbb{R}$.

Example 4   A Bounded Choice Set: Revisited

Given that the preference relation (2.1) and the choice set B of example 3 satisfies axioms 2.1–2.6, we know by theorem 2.1 that a utility function exists. For example

$$U_1(x_1, y_1) = x_1 + y_1$$

$$U_2(x_1, y_1) = (x_1 + y_1)^2 + 15$$

$$U_3(x_1, y_1) = \log (x_1 + y_1)$$

are all valid utility functions representing the preference relation (2.1). To see this, note that

$$(x_1, y_1) \, \pi \, (x_2, y_2) \quad \text{if and only if}$$

$$x_1 + y_1 > x_2 + y_2 \quad \text{if and only if}$$

$$(x_1 + y_1)^2 + 15 > (x_2 + y_2)^2 + 15 \quad \text{if and only if}$$

$$\log (x_1 + y_1) > \log (x_2 + y_2)$$

This same logic also works with an equality to show $(x_1, y_1) \sim (x_2, y_2)$ if and only if $U_i(x_1, y_1) = U_i(x_2, y_2)$ for $i = 1, 2, 3$.   □

As the previous example shows, given that the hypotheses of theorem 2.1 hold, a utility function exists, but it need not be unique. In fact, let G be any function mapping $\mathbb{R}$ into $\mathbb{R}$, denoted $G:\mathbb{R} \to \mathbb{R}$ such that if $x > y$, then $G(x) > G(y)$. G is said to be a *strictly positive monotonic transformation*. Given the utility function U in theorem 2.1, define a new function $GoU:B \to \mathbb{R}$ by $GoU(x) \equiv G(U(x))$. This is a *composition* of the functions U and G. Here GoU is an acceptable utility function since

$$G(U(x)) > G(U(y)) \quad \text{if and only if}$$

$$U(x) > U(y) \quad \text{if and only if}$$

$$x \, \pi \, y$$

In fact, the converse is also true.[5] Consequently, we say the utility function guaranteed by theorem 2.1 is unique up to a strictly positive monotonic transformation. Such a utility function is called an *ordinal* utility function.

This nonuniqueness is important for two reasons. First, it implies one

---

[5]That is, if $U:B \to \mathbb{R}$ and $V:B \to \mathbb{R}$ are two utility functions representing the same preference relation, then there exists a positive monotonic transformation $G:\mathbb{R} \to \mathbb{R}$ such that $V = GoU$.

Proof
Since for all $x, y \in B$, $U(x) = U(y)$ implies $x \sim y$, which implies $V(x) = V(y)$ (by Gleason [3, p. 68, theorem 5-2.2]), there exists $G:\mathbb{R} \to \mathbb{R}$ such that $V(x) = GoU(x)$. Now G is strictly positively monotonic because if $U(x) > U(y)$, then $x \, \pi \, y$, so $G(U(x)) = V(x) > V(y) = G(U(y))$.   □

cannot compare utility levels across individuals. To see this, consider a person named Adam with utility function U_a and a person named Betty with utility function U_b. The alternative x is assigned the utility levels of $U_a(x) = 10$ for Adam and $U_b(x) = 20$ for Betty. This does not mean that Betty likes x twice as much as Adam does. Why? Because $U_a^*(x) = 2U_a(x)$ is also an acceptable utility function for Adam and $U_a^*(x) = 20$. Now Adam using U_a^* and Betty using U_b have the same utility level of 20 for x. Since it cannot be the case that Adam likes x both twice as much as Betty and also the same as Betty, we see that the absolute value of utility is unimportant. The only important property of utility is the relative rankings across elements within the choice set for each individual. Utility levels cannot be compared across individuals.

This leads to the second important implication of the nonuniqueness of the ordinal utility function. It implies that convexity or concavity of U does not discriminate between preferences. Going back to example 4, we see that both $U_2(x_1, y_1)$ and $U_3(x_1, y_1)$ are equivalent utility functions. Yet U_2 is convex and U_3 is concave. We will return to this observation in Chap. 5.

For the remainder of Part I of the text, unless otherwise stated, whenever an individual's preferences are employed, we will always assume they satisfy the rationality axioms 2.1–2.6 so that an ordinal utility function exists.

2.3. THE CONSUMPTION-SAVING MODEL

The development of the utility function given in Sec. 2.2 is very abstract and can be applied to numerous decision problems. The problem of fundamental concern to finance is the consumption-saving decision, which is explored in depth in Chaps. 3 to 6. To set the stage, we need to show how the consumption-saving problem can be cast into the format just presented. The following development (with minor modifications) will be consistently employed throughout the remainder of the text.

2.3.1. Preliminaries

We consider an economy that consists of only two time periods: today and tomorrow. These will be denoted by time 0 and time 1. An "instant" before time 0 all individuals appear and they all disappear an "instant" after time 1. An individual lives and consumes in both times 0 and 1.

We assume that there is only a single good available in the economy to consume—call it wheat. Instead of wheat, one could think of this single good as a basket of commodities, but it must be the same basket across individuals (see Fama and Miller [2, p. 19]).

The set of alternatives B available to the individual is defined as

$$B = \{(C_0, C_1) : C_0 \in [0, L_0] \quad \text{and} \quad C_1 \in [0, L_1]\} \qquad (2.3)$$

where C_0 represents the units of wheat consumed at time 0 by the individual;

C_1 represents the units of wheat consumed at time 1 by the individual;

L_0 is the limit on aggregate supply of wheat available at time 0; and

L_1 is the limit on aggregate supply of wheat available at time 1.

An individual has preferences over pairs of wheat at times 0 and 1. Note that, by assumption, the least amount of wheat the individual can consume in any period is 0 and the most is L_0 or L_1 in times 0 and 1, respectively. Assuming that the person's preferences satisfy the rationality axioms 2.1–2.6, by theorem 2.1, we know there exists an ordinal utility function $U:B \to \mathbb{R}$. We will let $U(C_0, C_1)$ denote the utility level of the pair (C_0, C_1) of units of wheat at times 0 and 1.

2.3.2. Monotonic Preferences

There is an additional property of preferences that will be assumed in the consumption-saving model called *monotonicity*. The idea is that a consumer always prefers more wheat to less wheat.

Assumption 2.1: Monotonicity

Given $\delta > 0$, $(C_0, C_1) \in B$, $(C_0 + \delta, C_1) \in B$, and $(C_0, C_1 + \delta) \in B$,

$$U(C_0 + \delta, C_1) > U(C_0, C_1)$$

and

$$U(C_0, C_1 + \delta) > U(C_0, C_1)$$

In words, assumption 2.1 states that increasing the level of consumption in any time period by $\delta > 0$ units of wheat increases the individual's utility level and, hence, welfare. This assumption is critical to the foundations of arbitrage pricing theory considered in Chap. 3.

2.4. PROOF OF THEOREM 2.1

The style of proof is similar to that of Herstein and Milnor [4]. For an alternative proof, under a modified set of assumptions, see Debreu [1].

Proof

To show the existence of a function $U:B \to \mathbb{R}$, we write down a candidate and show that it satisfies the stated conditions.

Choose, from axiom 2.6, x^*, $y^* \in B$ such that $x^* \; \pi \; z \; \pi \; y^*$ for all $z \in B$. Without loss of generality, let $x^* \; \pi \; y^*$. [Otherwise, $x^* \sim z \sim y^*$ for all $z \in B$, and $U(z) \equiv 0$ for all $z \in B$ is a trivial utility function that satisfies conditions (a) and (b).] Consider an arbitrary $z \in B$. By axioms 2.1–2.3, there are three possible cases:

$$1. \quad z \sim x^*$$

$$2. \quad x^* \; \pi \; z \; \pi \; y^*$$

$$3. \quad z \sim y^*$$

We define the function U by giving its value under all three cases:

Case 1. Define $U(z) = 1$.

Case 2. By axiom 2.5, there exists a unique $\alpha \in (0, 1)$ such that $[\alpha x^* + (1 - \alpha)y^*] \sim z$. Define $U(z) = \alpha$.

Case 3. Define $U(z) = 0$.

We now show that U satisfies properties (a) and (b).

Property (a)

Necessity. Suppose z_1, $z_2 \in B$ are such that $z_1 \; \pi \; z_2$. Show $U(z_1) > U(z_2)$. We do this by considering all possible cases. There are four cases, which we list:

$$N1. \quad z_1 \sim x^* \; \pi \; z_2 \; \pi \; y^*$$

$$N2. \quad z_1 \sim x^* \; \pi \; z_2 \sim y^*$$

$$N3. \quad x^* \; \pi \; z_1 \; \pi \; z_2 \; \pi \; y^*$$

$$N4. \quad x^* \; \pi \; z_1 \; \pi \; z_2 \sim y^*$$

Case N1. By definition, $U(z_1) = 1$ and $U(z_2) = \alpha$, where $\alpha \in (0, 1)$ uniquely satisfies $\alpha x^* + (1 - \alpha)y^* \sim z_2$. But $U(z_1) = 1 > \alpha = U(z_2)$.

Case N2. By definition, $U(z_1) = 1 > 0 = U(z_2)$.

Case N3. By definition, $U(z_i) = \alpha_i$, where $\alpha_i \in (0, 1)$ uniquely satisfies $\alpha_i x^* + (1 - \alpha_i)y^* \sim z_i$. Now, by axiom 2.3, $z_1 \sim [\alpha_1 x^* + (1 - \alpha_1)y^*] \; \pi \; [\alpha_2 x^* + (1 - \alpha_2)y^*] \sim z_2$. We claim $\alpha_1 > \alpha_2$. Suppose not; then $\alpha_1 \leq \alpha_2$, so by axiom 2.4, $[\alpha_2 x^* + (1 - \alpha_2)y^*] \; \pi \; [\alpha_1 x^* + (1 - \alpha_1)y^*]$. This is a contradiction. Hence $\alpha_1 > \alpha_2$ is true, or $U(z_1) = \alpha_1 > U(z_2) = \alpha_2$.

Case N4. By definition, $U(z_1) = \alpha_1$, where $\alpha_1 \in (0, 1)$ uniquely satisfies $\alpha_1 x^* + (1 - \alpha_1)y^* \sim z_1$ and $U(z_2) = 0$. But $U(z_1) = \alpha_1 > 0 = U(z_2)$. $\square$

This completes the necessity part.

Sufficiency. Suppose, given $z_1, z_2 \in B$, that $U(z_1) > U(z_2)$. Show $z_1 \pi z_2$. Again, we do this by considering all possible cases. There are four of them:

S1. $U(z_1) = 1$, where $z_1 \sim x^*$ and $U(z_2) = \alpha_2$, where $\alpha_2 \in (0, 1)$ uniquely satisfies $[\alpha_2 x^* + (1 - \alpha_2)y^*] \sim z_2$.

S2. $U(z_1) = 1$, where $z_1 \sim x^*$ and $U(z_2) = 0$, where $z_2 \sim y^*$.

S3. $U(z_i) = \alpha_i$, where $\alpha_i \in (0, 1)$ uniquely satisfies $[\alpha_i x^* + (1 - \alpha_i)y^*] \sim z_i$.

S4. $U(z_1) = \alpha_1$ as defined in case S3 and $U(z_2) = 0$, where $z_2 \sim y^*$.

Case S1. In this case, $z_1 \sim x^* \sim [1x^* + (1 - 1)y^*]$ and $z_2 \sim [\alpha_2 x^* + (1 - \alpha_2)y^*]$. By axiom 2.4, since $1 > \alpha_2$, $z_1 \pi z_2$. (Also use axiom 2.3.)

Case S2. Here $z_1 \sim x^* \pi y^* \sim z_2$.

Case S3. Here $z_1 \sim [\alpha_1 x^* + (1 - \alpha_1)y^*]$ and $z_2 \sim [\alpha_2 x^* + (1 - \alpha_2)y^*]$. Since $\alpha_1 > \alpha_2$, by axiom 2.4, $z_1 \pi z_2$. (Also use axiom 2.3.)

Case S4. Here $z_1 \sim [\alpha_1 x^* + (1 - \alpha_1)y^*]$ and $z_2 \sim y^* \sim [0x^* + (1 - 0)y^*]$. By axiom 2.4 and axiom 2.3, since $\alpha_1 > 0$, $z_1 \pi z_2$.   □

This completes the sufficiency part and the proof of property (a).

Property (b)

Necessity. Suppose $z_1 \sim z_2$ but $U(z_1) \neq U(z_2)$. Then $U(z_1) > U(z_2)$ or $U(z_2) > U(z_1)$. By property (a), this implies $z_1 \pi z_2$ or $z_2 \pi z_1$—a contradiction—hence $U(z_1) = U(z_2)$.   □

Sufficiency. Suppose $U(z_1) = U(z_2)$, but $z_1 \pi z_2$ or $z_2 \pi z_1$. By property (a), $U(z_1) > U(z_2)$ or $U(z_2) > U(z_1)$—a contradiction—hence $z_1 \sim z_2$ by axiom 2.2.   □

2.5. SUMMARY

This chapter presents an axiomatic development of ordinal utility theory under certainty. In its abstract form, it is assumed that an individual is confronted with a choice set B, a convex subset of $\mathbb{R}^n$, over which the individual has a preference relation π that satisfies six axioms. The six axioms are the following:

Reflexivity	For any $x \in B$, $x \pi x$.
Comparability	For any $x, y \in B$, either $x \pi y$ or $y \pi x$.
Transitivity	For any $x, y, z \in B$, if $x \pi y$ and $y \pi z$, then $x \pi z$.
Order preserving	For any $x, y \in B$ where $x \pi y$ and $\alpha, \beta \in [0, 1]$,

$[\alpha x + (1 - \alpha)y]\ \pi\ [\beta x + (1 - \beta)y]$ if and only if $\alpha > \beta$.

Intermediate value   For any x, y, $z \in B$, if $x\ \pi\ y\ \pi\ z$ then there exists a unique $\alpha \in (0, 1)$ such that $\alpha x + (1 - \alpha)z \sim y$.

Boundedness   There exists an x^*, $y^* \in B$ such that $x^*\ \pi\ z\ \pi\ y^*$ for all $z \in B$.

Under these six axioms, it is shown that the preference relation π can be represented by an ordinal utility function $U:B \rightarrow \mathbb{R}$ such that for any x, $y \in B$

$$x\ \pi\ y \quad \text{if and only if} \quad U(x) > U(y)$$

and

$$x \sim y \quad \text{if and only if} \quad U(x) = U(y)$$

Instead of modeling investor behavior with π, we can now use the utililty function U. This provides a vast simplification in terms of the mathematical analysis.

Unfortunately, although the existence of a utility function is guaranteed by theorem 2.1, it is not unique. This nonuniqueness implies that utility levels cannot be compared across individuals. Furthermore, it implies that convexity and concavity of an ordinal utility function U do not discriminate between preferences.

The consumption-saving model demonstrates how to fit this model into the utility theory framework previously developed. In this model, investors live two periods (time 0 to time 1) and choose among pairs of wheat to be consumed in both periods. Consumption choices are bounded above in each time period by the aggregate supply of wheat available and bounded below by 0. Assuming an individual's preferences satisfy axioms 2.1–2.6, by theorem 2.1 a utility function exists and is denoted by $U(C_0, C_1)$. For future analysis, it is also assumed that the preferences satisfy a monotonicity property that states that more consumption in any period, everything else constant, is strictly preferred to less consumption.

2.6. REFERENCES

1. Debreu, G., *Theory of Value*. New Haven, Conn.: Yale University Press, 1959.
2. Fama, Eugene, and Merton Miller, *The Theory of Finance*. Hinsdale, Ill.: Dryden Press, 1972.
3. Gleason, Andrew, *Fundamentals of Abstract Analysis*. Reading, Mass.: Addison-Wesley, 1966.
4. Herstein, I., and John Milnor, "An Axiomatic Approach to Measurable Utility," *Econometrica*, 21 (1953), 291–297.

3

THE ASSET MODEL

This chapter introduces the basic concepts used to value assets with the arbitrage pricing methodology. The results proven will seem obvious or trivial in the context of the model. This is intentional: Our purpose here is to expose the crucial concepts of arbitrage pricing theory without the added mathematical complications of probability theory or the complications inherent in a specific application. As such, this chapter is an exercise in abstract model building.

The utility theory developed in Chap. 2 will be used only once in this chapter, in a seemingly tangential manner, to motivate a crucial assumption. However, without this motivation, the asset model would be less relevant to the actual pricing of securities. Consequently, utility theory will be shown to enter into the arbitrage pricing method in a subtle, but important way.

Later, in Chap. 8, uncertainty will be introduced into this asset model. This requires the use of probability theory; however, the concepts and arguments will be identical to those presented here. The time spent studying this chapter is well worth the effort in terms of time saved later.

3.1. PRELIMINARIES

This section introduces the fundamentals of the asset model. This model has two time periods, represented by today (time 0) and tomorrow (time 1). We assume there are $K + 1$ assets trading in an organized market at time 0. An asset will be denoted by a subscript $j \in \{0, 1, \ldots, K\}$. An asset obtains its value (or price) at time 0 because it provides a cash flow *denominated in dollars* at time 1. The cash flow can be thought of as the "liquidating value" plus any "dividends" received on the security at time 1. This cash flow will be a given in the model, i.e., an assumption that is *exogenously* imposed. Before we state this assumption, we must introduce the investors. We assume that the economy is populated with a finite number of investors whose beliefs satisfy:

Assumption 3.1: Homogeneous Beliefs

All investors agree that the cash flow from asset j at time 1 is $x_j > 0$ for all $j = 0, 1, \ldots, K$.

This assumption states that every investor in the economy agrees that asset j pays positive x_j dollars at time 1. There is no uncertainty in an investor's beliefs.

Next we discuss the markets in which the assets trade. Every investor is assumed to have unlimited access to the asset market at time 0. The asset market is characterized as a *frictionless market*, i.e.:

Assumption 3.2: Frictionless Markets

The asset market has no transaction costs, no taxes, and no restrictions on short sales[1] (such as margin requirements), and assets are divisible.

This assumption is an idealization. It is introduced to simplify the analysis, which can be justified on two grounds. First, if traders who transact in large quantities and at very low cost, e.g., institutions, determine the market, it may be a reasonable first approximation. Second, and perhaps the most convincing, frictionless market models provide a benchmark against which actual markets can be compared. Unless we understand how the idealized market works, we cannot possibly understand how the more complex market works.

Luckily, for most models the frictionless market assumption 3.2 can be easily relaxed. More often than not, however, economic intuition will be sufficient to provide an understanding of particular frictions. Given the existing error inherent in any model, this qualitative sensitivity analysis may be sufficient. Now back to the model.

We assume that each investor believes he can buy and sell as many assets as desired without changing the market price. Each investor is said to act as a price taker. This also is an idealization, called *competitive markets*. Due to its importance, we separate out this condition as our next assumption.

---

[1]A *short sale* of an asset is equivalent to selling an asset one does not own. An investor can do this by borrowing the asset from a third party and selling the borrowed security. The net position is a cash inflow equal to the price of the security and a liability (borrowing) of the security to the third party. In abstract mathematical terms, a short sale corresponds to buying a negative amount of a security.

Assumption 3.3: Competitive Markets

Every investor acts as a price taker.

This assumption is standard to much of finance. It is a reasonable approximation when the number of investors is large in an economy, and no single investor has a substantial proportion of the economy's wealth.[2]

The price in *dollars* of one unit of asset j at time 0 is a function of the cash flow of asset j at time 1. Each individual asset has a price for one unit. Yet an investor can buy or sell multiple units of an asset as well. Hence there is a price for multiple units. Similarly, an investor may buy or sell preconstructed combinations of assets, which we will call *portfolios*, and these also have a price. A notation that simultaneously captures all of these possibilities is a *price function*, which maps cash flows at time 1 into a price at time 0. The price function will be denoted by the symbol p, mapping units of dollar cash flows into units of dollars at time 0, i.e.:

$$p: \mathbb{R} \rightarrow \mathbb{R}$$

For example, one unit of asset j has a price in dollars at time 0 of $p(x_j)$ since x_j is the cash flow in dollars to asset j at time 1. This is true for all assets $j \in \{0, 1, \ldots, K\}$. Continuing, N units of asset j selling as a package has a price of $p(Nx_j)$ at time 0 since the cash flow at time 1 is Nx_j. For a package consisting of N_1 units of asset 1 and N_2 units of asset 2, its price at time 0 is $p(N_1 x_1 + N_2 x_2)$ since the package's cash flow at time 1 is $N_1 x_1 + N_2 x_2$. Finally, if an investor shorts one unit of an asset, then the cash flow at time 1 is $-x_j$, and the time 0 price of this portfolio is $p(-x_j)$.

A difference in notation and interpretation should be noted. The package consisting of N_1 units of asset 1 and N_2 units of asset 2 is bought and sold as a *unit*, for a price of $p(N_1 x_1 + N_2 x_2)$. Yet an investor could also buy and sell the components *separately*. That is, an investor could buy N_1 separate units of asset 1 and also N_2 separate units of asset 2 for a price of $N_1 p(x_1) + N_2 p(x_2)$.

The astute reader should suspect a relationship between the prices of these two possibilities, especially under the frictionless market assumption 3.2. The relationship between the prices of these two possibilities is what arbitrage pricing theory studies. In fact, arbitrage pricing theory imposes various exogenous assumptions on this price relationship. This is the task to which we now turn.

With this market structure, we can now introduce the concept of an *arbitrage opportunity*. Before we do, let us formally define a portfolio. A *portfolio* is any collection of assets 0 through K. Hence a portfolio is represented by a $K + 1$ element vector $(N_0, N_1, \ldots, N_K)$, where

$$N_j = \text{the number of units of asset } j \text{ held}$$

Under the frictionless market assumption 3.2, the number of shares N_j could be

---

[2]A formal justification of this statement can be found in Hildenbrand and Kirman [1, Chap. 5] or Ichiishi [2, Chap. 5].

positive or negative. A positive N_j means a purchase of the asset, while a negative N_j means a short sale of the asset. A portfolio is considered to be formed at time 0 and to remain unchanged until time 1.

Definition: An Arbitrage Opportunity

An *arbitrage opportunity* is a portfolio $(N_0, N_1, \ldots, N_K)$ such that either

$$(1) \quad p\left(\sum_{j=0}^{K} N_j x_j\right) \neq \sum_{j=0}^{K} N_j p(x_j) \qquad \text{or}$$

$$(2) \quad (a) \quad \sum_{j=0}^{K} N_j p(x_j) \leq 0 \qquad \text{and}$$

$$(b) \quad \sum_{j=0}^{K} N_j x_j > 0 \qquad \text{or}$$

$$(3) \quad (a) \quad \sum_{j=0}^{K} N_j p(x_j) \geq 0 \qquad \text{and}$$

$$(b) \quad \sum_{j=0}^{K} N_j x_j < 0$$

An arbitrage opportunity is seen to correspond to a portfolio that satisfies one of three conditions. Condition (1) of the definition says that an arbitrage opportunity is a portfolio whose price differs from the prices of the assets combined separately. For example, suppose a portfolio consisting of N_1 units of asset 1 and N_2 units of asset 2 trades as a package. Its price is $p(N_1 x_1 + N_2 x_2)$. If this differs from $N_1 p(x_1) + N_2 p(x_2)$, say, $N_1 p(x_1) + N_2 p(x_2) < p(N_1 x_1 + N_2 x_2)$, then an industrious investor could perform the following strategy: Short sell the package $(N_1 x_1 + N_2 x_2)$, buy separately N_1 shares of asset 1, and buy separately N_2 shares of asset 2. The cash flow from this position at time 0 is $p(N_1 x_1 + N_2 x_2) - N_1 p(x_1) - N_2 p(x_2) > 0$, and the cash flow at time 1 is $-(N_1 x_1 + N_2 x_2) + N_1 x_1 + N_2 x_2 = 0$. This is a money pump! Section 3.3, in the context of the utility theory developed in Chap. 2, will show that every investor would jump at the opportunity to hold this strategic portfolio. In fact, each one would do so in unlimited quantities!

Conditions (2) and (3) of the definition are similar in interpretation. Let us concentrate on condition (2). Condition (2a) says the value of the portfolio $(N_0, \ldots, N_K)$ constructed by an investor buying and selling assets separately is nonpositive. This means that the construction of this portfolio generates a liability and therefore a zero or positive cash inflow. Condition (2b) states that this portfolio has positive cash flow at time 1. Hence it costs nothing (or generates cash at time 0) and it provides cash at time 1. This package would also be a money pump.

As justified in Sec. 3.3, an arbitrage opportunity represents a utility increasing opportunity (a free lunch) for everyone in the economy. An example will help clarify this statement.

Example 1   Arbitrage Opportunities

Consider a market consisting of three assets $\{0,1,2\}$ and a package consisting of 110 units of asset 0. The relevant information is contained in the accompanying table. The dollar cash flows at time 1 to the assets and the package are given in the second column. The prices in dollars of the assets and the package at time 0 are given in the third column.

	j	x_j	$p(x_j)$
asset	0	1	$1/1.10 \cong .91$
	1	110	100
	2	225	200
package ($N_0 = 110$)		110	85

There are two types of arbitrage opportunities in this market. First, condition (1) of the definition is satisfied, since

$$p(N_0 x_0) = p(110) = 85 \neq N_0 p(x_0) = 110(1/1.10) = 100$$

The package is cheaper than buying asset 0 separately and then combining. Hence, to make money, sell 110 units of asset 0 at time 0 while purchasing one package. The cash flow at time 0 is $100 - 85 = 15$ dollars. The cash flow at time 1 is 0 dollars. A clever investor would not stop with just this strategy. She would sell separately at least α times 110 units of asset 0 at time 0 and buy α packages. This strategy generates positive cash flows of $\alpha(15)$ at time 0. If we let α go to ∞, clearly unlimited dollars can be obtained.

In addition, condition (2) of the definition is also satisfied. Consider the portfolio given by the vector ($N_0 = 0$, $N_1 = -2$, $N_2 = 1$). Use of the numbers from the table gives

(a) $\displaystyle\sum_{j=0}^{2} N_j p(x_j) = 0(.91) - 2(100) + 1(200) = 0$

(b) $\displaystyle\sum_{j=0}^{2} N_j x_j = 0(1) - 2(110) + 225 = 5 > 0$

This portfolio is a money pump. It takes zero cash outflows to construct, but still provides 5 dollars for sure at time 1. An investor would desire to create this portfolio at least $\alpha > 0$ times and attempt to let α approach ∞. $\square$

One expects that under assumptions 3.1–3.3, a well-functioning economy would not contain any of these arbitrage opportunities. This statement will be partially justified in Sec. 3.3 in the context of the consumption-saving model. The idea is that if an arbitrage opportunity were present in an economy, everyone would rush to take advantage of it. In fact, everyone would desire to buy and sell the *same* securities in unlimited quantities. This cannot be a stable situation, and something must change. The something is prices (the price function). Prices would be expected to adjust until no arbitrage opportunities remained.

This line of reasoning is formalized in the following assumption (it is important to emphasize that the story just given is not part of the formal model but rather to motivate the next assumption):

Assumption 3.4: No Arbitrage Opportunities

The asset market contains no arbitrage opportunities.

This assumption allows us to determine prices in an economy such that no arbitrage opportunities are present. It puts structure on the price function. In particular, it implies that

$$\text{(i)} \quad p\left(\sum_{j=0}^{K} N_j x_j\right) = \sum_{j=0}^{K} N_j p(x_j) \quad \text{for all possible } N_j$$

and

$$\text{(ii)} \quad \text{if} \quad \sum_{j=0}^{K} N_j x_j > 0 \quad \text{then} \quad \sum_{j=0}^{K} N_j p(x_j) > 0$$

Condition (i) says that the price function is linear over cash flows. It allows us to value portfolios either as packages or by purchasing the parts separately. Sometimes condition (i) is called *value additivity*. Condition (ii) is important enough to separate out as a theorem.

Theorem 3.1: Dominance

Given assumptions 3.1–3.4

$$\text{if} \quad \sum_{j=0}^{K} N_j x_j > 0, \quad \text{then} \quad \sum_{j=0}^{K} N_j p(x_j) > 0$$

This theorem says that any asset or portfolio with positive cash flows at time 1 must have a positive price at time 0—an obvious result. Yet assumptions 3.1–3.4 are the minimal structure on an economy required to generate it.

In Chap. 8, this same type of result is generated in an economy with uncertainty. It is surprising, given its simplicity, how important this generalized theorem is in many applications (for example, see Chap. 13 on option pricing).

Value additivity (i) and the dominance condition (ii) have straight-forward but important implications for calculating portfolio returns.

Corollary 3.1: No Arbitrage Opportunities

(a) Returns on assets $j = 1, \ldots, K$ are well defined and equal

$$\frac{x_j - p(x_j)}{p(x_j)}$$

(b) The return on a portfolio $(N_0, N_1, \ldots, N_K)$ with $\sum_{j=0}^{K} N_j p(x_j) > 0$ can be written in percentage form as

$$\sum_{j=0}^{K} w_j \left(\frac{x_j - p(x_j)}{p(x_j)} \right) \quad \text{where} \quad w_j = \frac{N_j p(x_j)}{\sum\limits_{j=0}^{K} N_j p(x_j)}$$

represents the percentage of the portfolio value in asset j and $\sum_{j=0}^{K} w_j = 1$.

Proof

(a) Since $x_j > 0$ for $j = 0, \ldots, K$ by assumption 3.1, use of theorem 3.1 gives $p(x_j) > 0$. Hence we can divide by $p(x_j)$ to get meaningful returns.

(b) The return on the portfolio $(N_0, N_1, \ldots, N_K)$ is

$$\left(\sum_{j=0}^{K} N_j x_j - p \left(\sum_{j=0}^{K} N_j x_j \right) \right) \Big/ p \left(\sum_{j=0}^{K} N_j x_j \right)$$

Fortunately, by value additivity

$$p \left(\sum_{j=0}^{K} N_j x_j \right) = \sum_{j=0}^{K} N_j p(x_j)$$

So the return on $(N_0, \ldots, N_K)$ equals

$$\frac{\sum\limits_{j=0}^{K} N_j x_j - \sum\limits_{j=0}^{K} N_j p(x_j)}{\sum\limits_{j=0}^{K} N_j p(x_j)} = \sum_{j=0}^{K} w_j \left(\frac{x_j - p(x_j)}{p(x_j)} \right)$$

using step (a). This completes the proof.   □

This corollary states that a portfolio's return equals the weighted returns on the assets included in the portfolio. The weights equal the proportion of the initial portfolio's value that each asset represents. This corollary is often used in the literature without the realization that it is actually a consequence of an economy with no arbitrage opportunities. It need not hold otherwise. This insight will be important in subsequent chapters, especially in Chap. 9 in the discussion of the arbitrage pricing theory.

3.2. THEOREMS

This section uses the previous assumptions to prove an important theorem, a "converse" of theorem 3.1. We will state the theorem after introducing some additional notation. Let the zeroth asset have the following cash flow at time 1, $x_0 \equiv 1$. Define the *interest rate r* by

$$p(x_0) \equiv \frac{1}{1 + r}$$

The zeroth asset is a discount bond, each unit of which has a known cash flow of $x_0 = 1$ dollar at time 1. Its price today, $p(x_0)$, determines the interest rate r. This rate r is *exogenously* specified in this model. It is a given. This is a fundamental difference between the arbitrage pricing model studied here and the equilibrium pricing model studied in Chap. 6. In the equilibrium pricing model, the interest rate r (the price function) will be *endogenously* determined as part of the model. We will return to this issue at the end of Chap. 6.

The next theorem is the generalized arbitrage pricing theory. The generalization of this theorem in Chap. 8 forms the basis for Ross's arbitrage pricing theory.

Theorem 3.2: Generalized Arbitrage Pricing Theory

Given assumptions 3.1–3.4

(a) $p(x_j) = x_j/(1 + r)$ for all $j \in \{0, 1, \ldots, K\}$
(b) The return on every asset is equal to r, i.e. $(x_j - p(x_j))/p(x_j) = r$ for all $j \in \{0, 1, \ldots, K\}$

Proof

(a) Consider the portfolio composed of one unit of asset j and short x_j units of asset 0. We claim the price of this portfolio at time 0 is 0, i.e.

$$1p(x_j) - x_j p(x_0) =$$
$$1p(x_j) - x_j/(1 + r) = 0$$

Proving this claim will prove step (a). To prove the claim, suppose

$$1p(x_j) - x_j/(1 + r) > 0$$

Then

$$p(x_j) > x_j/(1 + r) \tag{3.1}$$

Consider the portfolio composed of $N_0 = +x_j$, $N_i = 0$ for all $i \neq j$, and $N_j = -1$. This portfolio has the following values:

at time 0: $\quad +x_j/(1 + r) - 1p(x_j) < 0 \quad$ by expression (3.1)

at time 1: $\quad +x_j 1 - 1x_j = 0$

By definition, this is an arbitrage opportunity that generates a contradiction of assumption 3.4. Hence $p(x_j) \leq x_j/(1 + r)$ is the only possibility. Suppose $p(x_j) < x_j/(1 + r)$. Reversing the above portfolio generates an arbitrage opportunity and another contradiction. The only remaining possibility is therefore

$$p(x_j) = x_j/(1 + r)$$

This completes the proof.

(b) Follows by algebra from step (a). $\quad\square$

Condition (a) of this theorem gives a method for pricing any asset that trades at time 0. Simply take its cash flow at time 1, x_j, and discount at the rate r.

Example 1 Arbitrage Opportunities: Revisited

The proper no arbitrage opportunity prices for the assets and the package are (given the interest rate is .10)

$$p(x_0) \;=\; 1/1 + r = 1/1.10$$
$$p(x_1) \;=\; 110/1.10 = 100$$
$$p(x_2) \;=\; 225/1.10 \cong 204.55$$
$$p(110x_2) \;=\; 110/1.10 = 100$$

These prices differ from those in the table. We see that both asset 2 and the package are underpriced there. This accounts for the arbitrage opportunities. $\quad\square$

Condition (a) also provides the converse to theorem 3.1. If, for example, the price of any asset is positive, $p(x_j) > 0$, then by condition (a), $x_j = (1 + r)p(x_j) > 0$. This "converse" property of theorem 3.1 does not hold in an economy containing uncertainty. It will be seen that given uncertainty, it is possible for time 0 prices to be positive, but time 1 cash flows to be negative with positive probability.

Condition (b) of this theorem states that in a world of certainty there is really only one type of asset. It earns the return r. All other assets are just multiples of it. This theorem is a special case of Ross's arbitrage pricing theory, to be developed in Chap. 9.

It should be pointed out that although the previous theory was developed for a two-period economy (times 0 and 1), it is easily extended to a multiperiod economy. The same type of theorem holds. In the multiperiod economy, one discounts at the rate appropriate for the particular period in which the cash flow is obtained. These rates must be exogenously specified.

3.3. ARBITRAGE OPPORTUNITIES AND PREFERENCES

This section embeds our asset model into the consumption-saving model developed in Chap. 2. The point of this exercise is to show that every investor will want to add an arbitrage opportunity to his portfolio. Why? Because by doing so, utility will increase. This will give a utility theory based support for the nonexistence of arbitrage opportunities (assumption 3.4).

Recall the consumption-saving model of Sec. 2.3 in Chap. 2. In that model, investors consume a single consumption good in both times 0 and 1. Under the preference axioms, an arbitrary investor's preferences over consumption can be represented by a utility function $U(C_0, C_1)$. Assumption 2.1 in that section also endowed this function with the property of monotonicity, i.e., consumers always prefer more consumption in any period to less.

The first issue we must address in combining the two models is that preferences are defined over units of the consumption good and the assets are defined as paying off in dollars. We need a common unit of measurement. This is done by introducing the concept of a *price level*. A price level at time 0 is simply the number of dollars it takes to purchase one unit of the consumption good at time 0, say, $\rho_0 > 0$.

Similarly, the price level at time 1 is the number of dollars it takes to purchase one unit of the consumption good at time 1, say, $\rho_1 > 0$. The *inflation rate* is defined to be $(\rho_1 - \rho_0)/\rho_0$, which is the percentage change in dollars over the time period needed to buy the same consumption good. We can now use the price level to obtain the value in consumption goods of the asset's cash flows at either time 0 or time 1. For example, the price in units of the consumption good of asset j's cash flows x_j at time 1 is x_j/ρ_1. Similarly, the time 0 price of asset j in terms of units of the consumption good is $p(x_j)/\rho_0$.

The asset market will play a fundamental role in the consumption-saving model. By assumption, it will provide the only way a consumer can transfer consumption goods across time. By investing in assets, she can increase (or decrease) her consumption at time 1. To formalize this description, we assume that the consumer enters time 0 with an endowment of units of the consumption good in both times 0 and 1, say, $(\overline{C}_0, \overline{C}_1)$. In addition, she is endowed at time 0 with shares of assets 0 through K, i.e., $(\overline{N}_0, \ldots, \overline{N}_K)$. This endowment can be consumed and invested at times 0 and 1 exactly as given. However, part of the time 0 endowment can be invested in a portfolio of assets to be consumed at time 1. Also available is the option to liquidate some of the endowed shares and consume them at time 0. These are the only ways the consumer can alter her consumption in time 1.

Let $(N_0, N_1, \ldots, N_K)$ be the portfolio the investor constructs. This portfolio is constrained in the following way:

$$\overline{C}_0 + \sum_{j=0}^{K} \overline{N}_j p(x_j)/\rho_0 = C_0 + \sum_{j=0}^{K} N_j p(x_j)/\rho_0 \qquad (3.2)$$

The endowed consumption units at time 0, $\overline{C}_0$, and the portfolio wealth, $\sum_{j=0}^{K} \overline{N}_j p(x_j)/\rho_0$, is split between the actual consumption units at time 0, $\overline{C}_0$, and the units of the consumption good invested in assets 0 through K, represented by $\sum_{j=0}^{K} N_j p(x_j)/\rho_0$. Note that the dollar price of the assets at time 0 is converted into units of the consumption good by the price level ρ_0. Condition (3.2) is called the investor's time 0 *budget constraint*. By definition, the consumption at time 1 in consumption goods is the cash flow from the portfolio at time 1 in dollars $(\sum_{j=0}^{K} N_j x_j)$ after adjusting by the price level, and the endowed time 1 consumption units, $\overline{C}_1$, i.e.

$$C_1 \equiv \sum_{j=0}^{K} N_j x_j/\rho_1 + \overline{C}_1 \qquad (3.3)$$

By definition, this is the consumer's time 1 budget constraint.

Given expressions (3.2) and (3.3), we can rewrite the preference relation and budget constraints as

$$U(C_0, \sum_{j=0}^{K} N_j x_j/\rho_1 + \overline{C}_1) \qquad (3.4)$$

subject to

$$\overline{C}_0 + \sum_{j=0}^{K} \overline{N}_j p(x_j)/\rho_0 = C_0 + \sum_{j=0}^{K} N_j p(x_j)/\rho_0$$

where N_j represents the number of units of asset j held by the investor.

We will now show that if an arbitrage opportunity exists, an investor can increase his utility level by holding a strategic portfolio. The *same* portfolio will work for every investor. For space considerations, we will do the analysis only for an arbitrage opportunity of the type given by expression (2) in the definition of an arbitrage opportunity. The same analysis holds for the other cases as well.

Suppose there exists an arbitrage portfolio $(M_0, M_1, \ldots, M_K)$ such that

$$\sum_{j=0}^{K} M_j p(x_j) = 0 \qquad (3.5)$$

and

$$\sum_{j=0}^{K} M_j x_j > 0 \qquad (3.6)$$

This condition is in dollars. Most important, note that since the price levels are positive ($\rho_0 > 0$ and $\rho_1 > 0$), this also represents an arbitrage opportunity in terms of units of the consumption good:

$$\sum_{j=0}^{K} M_j p(x_j)/\rho_0 = 0 \tag{3.7}$$

and

$$\sum_{j=0}^{K} M_j x_j/\rho_1 > 0 \tag{3.8}$$

Suppose the investor adds this arbitrage opportunity to his portfolio. His new portfolio will be

$$(N_0 + M_0, N_1 + M_1, \ldots, N_K + M_K)$$

First, by (3.7) his budget constraint at time 0 is still satisfied, since

$$\overline{C}_0 + \sum_{j=0}^{K} \overline{N}_j p(x_j)/\rho_0 = C_0 + \sum_{j=0}^{K} N_j p(x_j)/\rho_0$$

$$= C_0 + \sum_{j=0}^{K} (N_j + M_j) p(x_j)/\rho_0 \tag{3.9}$$

So the arbitrage portfolio plus the original portfolio is still a feasible strategy.
Second, by (3.8)

$$\sum_{j=0}^{K} (N_j + M_j) x_j/\rho_1 > \sum_{j=0}^{K} N_j x_j/\rho_1 \tag{3.10}$$

So the utility level for this new portfolio is

$$U(C_0, \sum_{j=0}^{K} (N_j + M_j) x_j/\rho_1 + \overline{C}_1) > U(C_0, \sum_{j=0}^{K} N_j x_j/\rho_1 + \overline{C}_1) \tag{3.11}$$

The left-hand side of condition (3.11) represents the utility of the consumption pair generated by the new portfolio. It exceeds the right-hand side of (3.11) by the monotonicity assumption. The right-hand side of condition (3.11) is the original level of utility given by expression (3.4). This completes the proof of the assertion.

This relationship between preferences and arbitrage opportunities explains why arbitrage opportunities should not exist in an economy. Although this explanation is not a formal part of the model's structure, it is a utility-based interpretation for the assumption of no arbitrage opportunities.

It should be noted that the above argument really only depends on preferences being monotonic, assumption 2.1. It does not require the existence of an ordinal utility function; hence preferences need not satisfy the order-preserving axiom, the intermediate value axiom, or the boundedness axiom. This is the reason why the arbitrage pricing methodology is so robust.

3.4. SUMMARY

This chapter presents the theory of arbitrage pricing in an economy with no uncertainty. The economy is characterized by trading in $K + 1$ assets whose known cash flows are agreed upon by all investors (assumption 3.1). These assets trade in markets that are frictionless (assumption 3.2) and competitive (assumption 3.3). An arbitrage opportunity is defined to be a portfolio of the $K + 1$ assets, which provides either positive cash inflows at time 0 and zero cash inflows or outflows at time 1 or a portfolio that has zero or positive cash inflows at time 0 and positive cash inflows at time 1. We exclude the existence of these arbitrage opportunities by assumption 3.4.

The implications of these four assumptions result in two theorems. The first theorem, theorem 3.1, states that any portfolio with a positive cash flow at time 1 must have a positive price at time 0. Conversely, the second theorem, theorem 3.2, states that any portfolio with a positive price at time 0 must have a positive cash flow at time 1—indeed, this cash flow must equal the time 0 price compounded by the return on the zeroth asset.

The last section of this chapter utilizes the utility theory developed in Chap. 2 to justify the no arbitrage opportunity assumption 3.4. It is shown here that the monotonicity of preferences is sufficient to guarantee that an investor's utility is increased by adding a feasible arbitrage opportunity to his existing portfolio. By feasible, we mean that the portfolio with the arbitrage opportunity included still satisfies the investor's budget constraints.

3.5. REFERENCES

1. Hildenbrand, W., and A. P. Kirman, *Introduction to Equilibrium Analysis*. Amsterdam: North-Holland, 1976.
2. Ichiishi, Tatsuro, *Game Theory for Economic Analysis*. Orlando, Fla.: Academic Press, 1983.

4

CORPORATE FINANCE

This chapter presents an application of the arbitrage pricing theory developed in Chap. 3. The application involves two issues in corporate finance: dividend policy and debt/equity policy. The dividend policy issue relates to the quantity of dividends per share a firm pays out on its common equity—i.e., is there an optimal dividend per share? The debt/equity policy issue relates to the financing of the firm's investment activities—i.e., should investment be financed with debt or equity or both? In other words, is there an optimal ratio of debt to equity in the firm? This chapter studies these questions in the context of the asset model developed in Chap. 3.

Given the restrictive nature of an economy under certainty, this chapter's results cannot be extrapolated to the actual (and uncertain) economy. This, however, is not the goal of the model developed here. This chapter only introduces the key concepts and arguments utilized in studying these corporate finance policy questions. Later, in Chaps. 10 and 11, the arguments introduced here will be expanded to include uncertainty in the economy. It will be surprising to see how little the model structure and the arguments change. Unlike the model of this chapter, those of Chaps. 10 and 11 are intended to be applied to the actual economy.

4.1. DIVIDEND POLICY

This section studies the dividend policy issue—i.e., is there an optimal amount of dividends per share of common equity that maximizes the share's price? In the context of the asset model introduced in Chap. 3, we claim that the answer to this question is no. Dividends to be paid per share are irrelevant to the share's price. At first, this result may seem counterintuitive. But it is the type of result that "grows on you." The more one thinks about it, the more intuitive it becomes. The following model aids in this exercise by providing the proper structure for sorting things out. Let us now prove the claim.

Consider the single period economy introduced in Chap. 3. There are two time periods, times 0 and 1. The two-period aspect of this model, however, is not crucial to the subsequent result. It is utilized only for the simplicity of the presentation. Assume there are $K + 1$ assets trading in this economy satisfying assumptions 3.1–3.4. That is, all the investors have homogeneous beliefs about the known cash flows from the assets at time 1, the markets for the assets are frictionless and competitive, and there are no arbitrage opportunities.

Let two of the assets that trade represent the common equity of two distinct firms, firm A and firm B. We will impose sufficient structure on these firms so that they are *identical*, with the exception of dividends paid per share. This identical structure is necessary to answer the dividend policy question. To see why this is true, one should realize that we are performing a "controlled experiment." Everything but dividends needs to be held constant. We then change dividends paid per share and see if share value changes. If something else were allowed to change, then we would be unable to tell whether dividends per share or this other factor caused the results. Therefore, all of the effort involved in proving the dividend irrelevance claim is contained in constructing the controlled experiment, i.e., the identical firm hypothesis. This is the task to which we now turn.

To motivate this hypothesis, consider what it takes for the two firms (A and B) to be identical. At time 0, they need to have the same assets (buildings, machines, management), the same investment projects (present and future), and the same liabilities (bonds, leases, common equity). The assets and liabilities in place at time 0, if the same, will generate the same cash flows at time 1 and in the future.

To investigate the dividend decision, we let these two identical firms differ in only one respect: in the dividends paid per share at time 1. At all other future dates, dividends per share are (implicitly) presumed equal. This structure provides the "controlled experiment." A comparison of the common equity values at time 0 will reveal the answer. If the common equity values are the same, dividend policy is irrelevant. If the common equity values differ, dividend policy matters.

We now introduce the notation. Let

x_A = The remaining dollar cash flows to firm A at time 1 after (i) all refinancing of liabilities except common equity is completed and (ii) all investments (new and continuing) are made;

d_A = dividends paid per share on firm A's common equity at time 1;

n = the number of common equity shares of firm A outstanding at time 0;

$$\Delta n_A = \text{the change in the number of firm A's common equity shares outstanding at time 1; and}$$

$$s_A = \text{firm A's common equity value per share in dollars at time 1.}$$

The terms x_B, d_B, n, Δn_B, and s_B are defined similarly, with firm B replacing firm A in each of the definitions. Note that by construction, both firms have n shares of common equity outstanding at time 0. This is a trivial part of the identical firm hypothesis.

At time 1 each firm's cash flows must satisfy the following accounting identity:

$$x_A = nd_A - \Delta n_A s_A$$
$$x_B = nd_B - \Delta n_B s_B$$

(4.1)

For firm A, this identity states that the remaining cash flow at time 1 after investments and refinancing (except with respect to equity) is either paid out as dividends (nd_A) or used to refinance equity ($\Delta n_A s_A$). The negative sign appears before the refinancing equity term since if equity is retired, Δn_A is negative; yet the cash outflow is positive. The negative sign preceding Δn_A corrects for this, i.e., $-\Delta n_A > 0$. A similar cash flow identity holds for firm B. This accounting identity is really just an analytic restatement of the definitions of x_A and x_B, making precise which cash flow decisions are fixed and which are free to be chosen.

We now turn to the identical firm hypothesis underlying the controlled experiment. This takes two assumptions:

Assumption 4.1: Identical Cash Flows at Time 1

$$x_A = x_B$$

Assumption 4.2: Identical Cash Flows to Equity in the Future

$$(n + \Delta n_A)s_A = (n + \Delta n_B)s_B$$

Assumption 4.1 says that the remaining time 1 cash flows to both firms, *prior* to the equity refinancing and the dividend decision, are identical.[1] This is the first condition required for our controlled experiment. If this assumption were not included, the firms would not be identical except for dividend policy, and consequently one could not differentiate changes in share value due to dividends versus changes in share value due to differences in the asset cash flows.

---

[1] This assumption implies that the investment projects undertaken by either firm are independent of dividend policy.

Assumption 4.2 ensures that both firms' cash flows and dividend policies are identical *after* time 1. This assumption is necessitated by the single period nature of the model. To understand this assumption, consider the term $(n + \Delta n_A)s_A$. This represents the *total* value of all of firm A's common equity outstanding at time 1. Alternatively stated, this represents the time 1 present value of all future dividends and any liquidating value to the existing common equity shares. By letting this present value equal $(n + \Delta n_B)s_B$, this assumption implies that all the future dividends and any liquidating value are identical across firms. In a multiperiod version of this model, assumption 4.2 could be derived from these more basic assumptions. In the context of our single period model, we assume this result directly.

Finally, we need to specify the difference in the dividend policies across the two firms. Let the dividend per share paid by firm A exceed the dividend per share paid by firm B, i.e., $d_A > d_B$. We will now compare the value of each firm's equity at time 0 and see if there is any difference.

Using the notation introduced in Chap. 3, recall that $p(d_A + s_A)$ represents the time 0 per share price (in dollars) of firm A's common equity. Each share of firm A's common equity gets a dividend, d_A, and a liquidating value, s_A. The price functional $p(\cdot)$ is applied to the time 1 dollar cash flow per share of common equity. Similarly, $p(d_B + s_B)$ represents the time 0 per share price of firm B's common equity.

Theorem 4.1: Dividend Irrelevance

Given assumptions 4.1 and 4.2,

$$p(d_A + s_A) = p(d_B + s_B) \tag{4.2}$$

Proof

To prove this theorem, we need only show that

$$d_A + s_A = d_B + s_B \tag{4.3}$$

This expression is derived as follows. Using assumption 4.1 and the cash flow identity (4.1), we get

$$x_A = x_B$$

$$nd_A - \Delta n_A s_A = nd_B - \Delta n_B s_B$$

or

$$nd_A - nd_B = +\Delta n_A s_A - \Delta n_B s_B$$

Now assumption 4.2 states that $\Delta n_A s_A - \Delta n_B s_B = ns_B - ns_A$. Substitution gives

$$nd_A - nd_B = ns_B - ns_A$$

Dividing by $n > 0$ and rearranging terms generate condition (4.3). $\qquad \square$

This theorem shows that the share price of firm A's common equity equals the share price of firm B's common equity. The difference in dividends paid per share is irrelevant. Dividend policy does not matter.

To understand what is really happening, note that the capital gains to firm A, $[s_A - p(s_A + d_A)]$, plus the dividends, d_A, equals the capital gains to firm B, $[s_B - p(s_A + d_B)]$, plus the dividends, d_B. If $d_A > d_B$, then $[s_A - p(s_A + d_A)] < [s_B - p(s_B + d_B)]$. Dividends replace capital gains.

Inspection of the above argument shows that its crucial aspects are the identical firm hypotheses (assumptions 4.1 and 4.2) and the exclusion of arbitrage opportunities. The first hypotheses are needed as part of the controlled experiment. The second condition is the arbitrage pricing methodology. If either of these conditions does not hold, the argument falls apart. Hence if one is a skeptic and still believes that dividends do matter, then the reason must be because either of these two conditions does not hold. Perhaps there are frictions in the markets, like taxes. Perhaps the identical firm hypothesis, assumption 4.2, cannot hold due to information asymmetries and the informational content of dividends. Whatever the specific cause, the model developed here is useful in that it focuses the argument on the relevant issues. In essence, if dividends do matter, the model tells us what cannot be the cause. We will return to these issues in Chap. 10.

4.2. DEBT/EQUITY POLICY

In studying the issue of whether debt/equity policy influences firm value, we will use a similar approach to that employed in the discussion of dividend policy. We consider the single period economy of Chap. 3 with times 0 and 1. There are $K + 1$ assets trading in this economy, and it is populated with investors, both of which satisfy assumptions 3.1–3.4. That is, all the investors have homogeneous beliefs about the known cash flows from the assets at time 1, the markets for the assets are frictionless and competitive, and there are no arbitrage opportunities.

Four of the assets that trade are related to two distinct firms, firm A and firm B. Firm A's liabilities (right-hand side of its balance sheet) are composed of debt and common equity. The debt consists of m_A bonds each with a cash flow of x_A^b at time 1. These bonds trade at time 0 and have a price per share of $p(x_A^b)$. The common equity consists of n_A shares each with a cash flow of x_A^e at time 1. The common equity also trades at time 0, and the value per share is $p(x_A^e)$. The total value of firm A's liabilities at time 0, or *firm value*, is defined to be

$$V_A \equiv m_A p(x_A^b) + n_A p(x_A^e)$$

The quantity $m_A p(x_A^b)$ equals the market value of firm A's debt at time 0, and the quantity $n_A p(x_A^e)$ equals the market value of firm A's equity at time 0. The debt/equity ratio for firm A in market value terms is

$$m_A p(x_A^b)/n_A p(x_A^e)$$

The quantity V_A is called the firm's value, since to own all of the firm's assets one must own all of its liabilities. V_A represents the market price of these liabilities.

The corresponding quantities for firm B are

$$
\begin{aligned}
m_B &= \text{number of bonds of firm B trading at time 0;} \\
x_B^b &= \text{cash flow in dollars at time 1 per bond;} \\
n_B &= \text{number of shares of firm B's common equity trading at time 0;} \\
x_B^e &= \text{cash flow in dollars at time 1 per common equity share; and} \\
V_B &\equiv m_B p(x_B^b) + n_B p(x_B^e) \text{ is the value of firm B at time 0.}
\end{aligned}
$$

As in Sec. 4.1, to study the debt/equity issue we need to set up another controlled experiment. That is, we need to consider two firms, both of which are *identical* with the exception that their debt/equity ratios differ. We then want to see if their firm values differ. If the firm values differ, then debt/equity policy matters. If the firm values are identical, then debt/equity policy is irrelevant. All the effort in studying this issue is spent in setting up the controlled experiment through the construction of an identical firm hypothesis.

To motivate the assumption, consider what it means for two firms to be identical, with the exception of their debt/equity ratios. It means that the firms at time 0 need to have the same assets, the same management, and the same investment projects. The only difference is their liability structure, i.e., how they finance the assets. Now if the firms have the same assets, sales force, and so on, then the total cash flows at time 1 to both firms should be the same.[2]

Assumption 4.1: Identical Cash Flows at Time 1

$$ x_A = x_B $$

where

$$ x_A \equiv m_A x_A^b + n_A x_A^e $$

$$ x_B \equiv m_B x_B^b + n_B x_B^e $$

Assumption 4.1 states that the total cash flow to firm A at time 1, x_A, equals the total cash flow to firm B at time 1, x_B. The total cash flows from the assets of firm A at time 1, by construction, are distributed either to the bondholders, $m_A x_A^b$, or to the equity holders, $n_A x_A^e$. The sum of these two cash flows equals x_A (similarly for firm B).

Let firm A have more debt than firm B. Suppose the firm's debt/equity ratios differ at time 0, i.e., $m_A p(x_A^b)/n_A p(x_A^e) > m_B p(x_B^b)/n_B p(x_B^e)$.

---

[2] This assumption implies that the investment projects undertaken by either firm are independent of debt/equity policy.

Theorem 4.2: Debt/Equity Irrelevance

Given assumption 4.1

$$V_A = V_B$$

Proof

Consider the following equalities:

$$
\begin{aligned}
V_A &= m_A p(x_A^b) + n_A p(x_A^e) \\
&= p(m_A x_A^b + n_A x_A^e) && \text{(by assumption 3.4)} \\
&= p(m_B x_B^b + n_B x_B^e) && \text{(by assumption 4.1)} \\
&= m_B p(x_B^b) + n_B p(x_B^e) && \text{(by assumption 3.4)} \\
&= V_B \qquad \square
\end{aligned}
$$

This theorem states that firm value is independent of a firm's debt/equity ratio, i.e., debt/equity policy is irrelevant. This conclusion follows directly from the identical firm hypothesis, assumption 4.1, and the absence of arbitrage opportunities, assumption 3.4.

An alternative proof could be given as follows (in most texts, this is the standard proof of this proposition and was first provided by Modigliani and Miller [1, 2]).

Proof

Suppose $V_A \neq V_B$, say $V_A > V_B$. Under assumption 4.1, an arbitrage opportunity would exist. To construct the arbitrage opportunity, buy α percent of firm B's bonds and equity at a time 0 price of $\alpha(m_B p(x_B^b) + n_B p(x_B^e)) = \alpha V_B$ and sell short α percent of firm A's bonds and equity at a time 0 price of $\alpha(m_A p(x_A^b) + n_A p(x_A^e)) = \alpha V_A$. The immediate time 0 cash inflow is $\alpha V_A - \alpha V_B = \alpha(V_A - V_B) > 0$ (recall by assertion $V_A > V_B$). The time 1 cash flow is $\alpha(m_B x_B^b + n_B x_B^e) - \alpha(m_A x_A^b + n_A x_A^e)$, which is zero by assumption 4.1. This is an arbitrage opportunity—but a contradiction. Hence $V_A \leq V_B$ must be true. If one supposes $V_A < V_B$, then reversing the strategy again gives an arbitrage opportunity. The only remaining possibility is $V_A = V_B$. $\square$

This alternative proof clarifies the crucial arguments employed. If $V_A \neq V_B$, an industrious investor could (on his own account) purchase the undervalued firm and sell the overvalued firm, generating positive cash flows at time 0 and no liabilities at time 1. This investment strategy is the same one we used to justify *value additivity* in Chap. 3.

The debt/equity irrelevance theorem was proven under frictionless markets, and therefore it ignores both personal and corporate taxes. These frictions can be shown to change the irrelevance proposition, but these issues are postponed until Chap. 11.

4.3. SUMMARY

This chapter applies the arbitrage pricing theory to investigate corporate dividend policy and corporate debt/equity policy. It is shown that in frictionless and competitive markets, the absence of arbitrage opportunities implies that both dividend policy (theorem 4.1) and debt/equity policy (theorem 4.2) are irrelevant. The crucial part of these arguments involved setting up a controlled experiment, where only the policy issue under question was allowed to vary. Given the proper controlled experiment, the proof of the two theorems followed in a straightforward fashion. Generalizations of these theorems are left to Chaps. 10 and 11.

4.4. REFERENCES

1. Modigliani, Franco, and Merton Miller, "The Cost of Capital, Corporation Finance, and the Theory of Investment," *American Economic Review*, 48 (June 1958), 261–297.
2. ———, "Reply to Heins and Sprenkle," *American Economic Review*, 59 (September 1969), 592–595.

5

ORDINAL UTILITY THEORY
The Optimal Consumption and Portfolio Decision

The last three chapters developed the arbitrage pricing theory in a certain economy. This chapter begins the development of equilibrium pricing theory. The equilibrium pricing methodology utilizes more sophisticated arguments and also imposes additional assumptions on the economy and the investors within it. This extra structure has a cost in that it limits the applicability of the results. However, it also has a benefit: More substantial results are obtained. This is especially true with respect to investor behavior. This chapter introduces the additional assumptions needed on preferences. To simplify the presentation, we will limit our discussion to the asset model embedded in the consumption-saving framework as in Sec. 3.3 of Chap. 3.

5.1. PRELIMINARIES

Recall that in the consumption-saving model, the investor's preferences are modeled in an economy with only two time periods, times 0 and 1. The set of alternatives, denoted by $B = \{(C_0, C_1): C_0 \in [0, L_0], C_1 \in [0, L_1]\}$ represents all consumption pairs at times 0 and 1. Consumption at time 0 is bounded below by 0 and above by L_0, the aggregate supply of consumption good units at time 0. Similar bounds hold for the consumption units available at time 1.

We are given a preference relation π on the choice set B that satisfies axioms 2.1–2.6 of Chap. 2. The purpose of these axioms is to guarantee the existence of an ordinal utility function $U(C_0, C_1)$ mapping B into $\mathbb{R}$. It exists by theorem 2.1. This utility function is unique up to a strictly positive monotonic transformation.

We assume that consumers prefer more to less, i.e.

Assumption 5.1: Monotonic Preferences

Given $\quad \delta > 0, (C_0, C_1) \in B, (C_0 + \delta, C_1) \in B, \quad$ and $\quad (C_0, C_1 + \delta) \in B,$

$U(C_0 + \delta, C_1) > U(C_0, C_1) \quad$ and

$U(C_0, C_1 + \delta) > U(C_0, C_1)$

The consumption decision is made in the context of an asset market. There are $K + 1$ assets trading in an asset market at time 0. The asset market and investors satisfy assumptions 3.1–3.4 of Chap. 3. Briefly, these assumptions state that all investors agree that the jth asset, $(j \in \{0, 1, \ldots, K\})$, has a positive cash flow in dollars of $x_j > 0$ at time 1. The jth asset's price at time 0 in dollars is $p(x_j)$. The asset market is frictionless and competitive, and there are no arbitrage opportunities.

To denominate the dollar cash flows in terms of units of the consumption good, an exogenous price level is given by $\rho_0 > 0$ at time 0 and $\rho_1 > 0$ at time 1. The price level ρ_0 represents the number of dollars needed to purchase one unit of the consumption good at time 0. A similar definition applies to ρ_1.

An investor is assumed to enter time 0 with an endowment of consumption goods, denoted $(\overline{C}_0, \overline{C}_1)$ and a time 0 endowment of asset shares $(\overline{N}_0, \overline{N}_1, \ldots, \overline{N}_K)$. The investor can rearrange her consumption by investing or borrowing with the assets $0, \ldots, K$; however, her investment is constrained by her endowment.

Analytically, the investor's decision problem is to choose C_0, C_1 to maximize

$$U(C_0, C_1) \tag{5.1}$$

subject to

$$\overline{C}_0 + \sum_{j=0}^{K} \overline{N}_j p(x_j)/\rho_0 = C_0 + \sum_{j=0}^{K} N_j p(x_j)/\rho_0 \tag{5.1a}$$

and

$$C_1 = \overline{C}_1 + \sum_{j=0}^{K} N_j x_j/\rho_1 \tag{5.1b}$$

$$(C_0, C_1) \in B \tag{5.1c}$$

The choice variables are consumption at time 0, C_0, and consumption at time 1, C_1. From the constraints, however, we see that C_1 is determined by the shares of assets 0 through K, i.e., $\{N_0, \ldots, N_K\}$.

The consumption at time 0 is constrained to satisfy condition (5.1a), the time 0 budget constraint. Consumption at time 1 is constrained by condition (5.1b). Of course, the actual consumption pair chosen must remain in the set B; this is condition (5.1c). Note that in expressions (5.1a) and (5.1b) the dollar cash flow from the portfolios are converted to units of the consumption good by the price level at time 0 and time 1, respectively.

Conditions (5.1a)–(5.1c) can be simplified to

$$(C_0, C_1) \in A \equiv \{(C_0, C_1) \in B : \overline{C}_0 + \sum_{j=0}^{K} \overline{N}_j p(x_j)/\rho_0 = C_0 + \sum_{j=0}^{K} N_j p(x_j)/\rho_0$$

$$\text{and} \quad C_1 = \overline{C}_1 + \sum_{j=0}^{K} N_j x_j/\rho_1\}$$

The constrained choice set A is a subset of the choice set B, and it represents the reduced set of consumption possibilities due to the budget constraints at both times 0 and 1. The equilibrium pricing methodology is concerned with characterizing an individual's optimal choice element (C_0^*, C_1^*) from the prespecified subset A of B. The constrained choice set A is introduced to streamline the notation.

5.2. OPTIMALITY

The first issue we must address is the existence of an optimal element (C_0^*, C_1^*) in the constrained choice set A. We assume it directly.

Assumption 5.2: Existence of an Optimal Consumption Pair

There exists a (C_0^*, C_1^*) in the constrained choice set A that maximizes utility $U(C_0, C_1)$.

Assumption 5.2 can be restated as follows: There exists a (C_0^*, C_1^*) in A such that

$$U(C_0^*, C_1^*) \geq U(C_0, C_1) \quad \text{for all } (C_0, C_1) \text{ in } A \tag{5.2}$$

There is a substantial literature on the assumptions one could impose upon preferences π and the constrained choice set A directly in order for our existence assumption 5.2 to become a theorem.[1] These technicalities, although interesting, are incidental to the purpose of this text.[2]

[1]Given our assumptions, one only needs the existence of a continuous utility function U. A is seen to be a closed and bounded subset of Euclidean space $\mathbb{R}$. Hence we can apply Rudin [3, Theorem 4.16, p. 89]. Sufficient conditions on π to guarantee the continuity of U, in addition to axioms 2.1–2.6, can be found in Debreu [2, pp. 55–57].

[2]This is true as long as the assumptions introduced are logically consistent with the previous assumptions of the model. There is always the danger, when one imposes an assumption on a derived quantity of a model, that a contradiction arises. This is not the case with assumption 5.1 or 5.2 because these assumptions could be equivalently written in terms of π.

The second issue we must address is the characterization of the optimal element of the constrained choice set A. The identification of this element is to be obtained through standard calculus techniques. To apply these techniques, still more structure on preferences needs to be imposed.

Assumption 5.3: Regularity of the Utility Function U

There exists a utility function U continuous on $[0, L_1] \times [0, L_2]$ whose second-order partial derivatives exist and are continuous on $(0, L_1) \times (0, L_2)$.

This assumption allows the use of differentiation, which is essential in identifying a maximizing element of the utililty function through the use of calculus.

It is important to emphasize the distinction between the regularity assumption 5.3 and the implication of theorem 2.1. From theorem 2.1, we know there exists a utililty function. In fact, there exist many utility functions that are equivalent up to a positive monotonic transformation. Yet none of these need be continuous or have continuous second-order partial derivatives. Assumption 5.3 guarantees that there exists at least one of these very "regular" utility functions. From now on, the utility function under consideration will always have continuous second-order partial derivatives.

5.3. CONVEXITY

To identify uniquely the optimal consumption pair, an additional assumption is required. We impose the additional structure on the preference relation π over the choice set B.

Assumption 5.4: Strict Convexity of Preferences

Given $x, y \in B$, where $x \neq y$, if $x \, \pi \, y$, then $[\alpha x + (1 - \alpha)y] \, \pi \, y$ for all $\alpha \in (0, 1)$.

This assumption says that the preference relation π is such that if x is preferred or indifferent to y, then $\alpha x + (1 - \alpha)y$ is strictly preferred to y.

Using the order-preserving property of the utility function, we can restate assumption 5.4 as

Given $\quad (x_0, x_1), (y_0, y_1) \in B \quad$ where $(x_0, x_1) \neq (y_0, y_1)$,

if $\quad U(x_0, x_1) \geq U(y_0, y_1), \quad$ then $\hfill (5.3)$

$\quad U(\alpha x_0 + (1 - \alpha)y_0, \alpha x_1 + (1 - \alpha)y_1) > U(y_0, y_1) \quad$ for all

$\quad \alpha \in (0, 1)$

This is called *strict quasi-concavity* of the utility function U. This assumption has the interpretation that diversification in the goods consumed is preferred, i.e., combinations of pairs of goods are preferred to the original pairs. Assumption 5.4 guarantees the uniqueness of the optimal consumption pair.[3] In addition, it guarantees that the Lagrangian multiplier techniques are both necessary and sufficient for determining the maximum element.[4] This is the result we were after.

It should be noted that strict concavity of the utility function U might appear to be a plausible replacement for condition (5.3). However, this is not the case. Concavity of an ordinal utility function is not a property preserved under positive monotonic transformations (see Chap. 2). Hence its imposition would be inconsistent with the axiomatic structure used in Chap. 2. This is not the case for strict quasi-concavity, expression (5.3). It is preserved under positive monotonic transformations.

5.4. GRAPHICAL REPRESENTATION OF THE MONOTONICITY AND THE CONVEXITY ASSUMPTIONS

To aid us in our understanding of the monotonicity assumption 5.1 and the convexity assumption 5.4, this section employs standard calculus techniques for a graphical representation. The graphical representations will prove useful in Chap. 6 when studying equilibrium.

Recall that, by the regularity assumption 5.3, we are guaranteed the existence of a smooth utility function, $U(C_0, C_1)$. Its graph, in three-dimensional space, might resemble the diagram in Fig. 5.1. The axes on the floor of the diagram are consumption at time 0, C_0, and consumption at time 1, C_1. The value of the function, $U(C_0, C_1)$, is the set of points vertically above the (C_0, C_1) plane. In this particular graph, it resembles a dome, starting at $(0, 0)$ and ending at $(0, L_1)$ and $(L_0, 0)$.

One representation of the monotonicity assumption can be obtained as follows. Hold C_1 fixed at c_1. The vertical cross section of the graph of $U(C_0, c_1)$ would appear as in Fig. 5.2. Monotonicity (assumption (5.1)) implies that the slope of the cross section in Fig. 5.2 is positive. To see this, recall that the monotonicity assumption states that

$$U(C_0 + \delta, C_1) - U(C_0, C_1) > 0 \quad \text{for all } \delta > 0$$

Given the regularity assumption 5.3 and dividing by δ and taking the limit as $\delta \to 0$, we get

$$\frac{\partial U(C_0, C_1)}{\partial C_0} > 0 \tag{5.4a}$$

---

[3]To see this, suppose both x^* and y^* maximize U. By assumption 5.4, $U(\alpha x^* + (1 - \alpha)y^*) > U(y^*)$ for all $\alpha \epsilon (0, 1)$. This contradicts y^* as a maximum. Hence there can be at most one maximum element.

[4]For a reference, see Arrow and Enthoven [1].

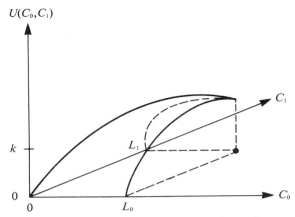

FIGURE 5.1: Representative graph of $U(C_0, C_1)$.

Expression (5.4a) represents the slope of the graph in Fig. 5.2 at an arbitrary point (C_0, C_1). The slope is positive, implying that if consumption is increased in time 0, everything else constant, then utility will increase. Similarly, holding C_0 fixed, the same arguments give

$$\frac{\partial U(C_0, C_1)}{\partial C_1} > 0 \qquad (5.4b)$$

Next we need to introduce the concept of an indifference curve. An *indifference curve* (or *iso-utility curve*) for $U(C_0, C_1) = k$ is the set of pairs (C_0, C_1) that generates the same level of utility, $U(C_0, C_1) = k$. For example, in Fig. 5.1, horizontally slice the utility function's graph at height k. This generates the dotted curve on the graph of $U(C_0, C_1)$. The projection of this dotted curve onto the (C_0, C_1) plane below would be an indifference curve for $U(C_0, C_1) = k$. This is diagrammed in Fig. 5.3. This curve gives those (C_0, C_1) that generate $U(C_0, C_1) = k$.

FIGURE 5.2: Representative graph of $U(C_0, C_1)$, where C_1 is fixed at c_1.

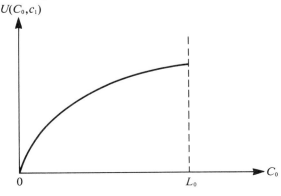

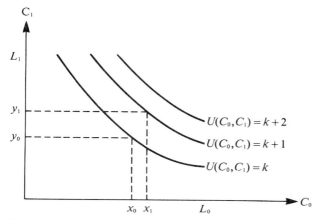

FIGURE 5.3: Representative indifference curves.

The monotonicity assumption has two additional implications for the indifference curves. The first implication is that indifference curves have higher utility levels as one moves upward and to the right in Fig. 5.3. To see why this is true, consider a move from (x_0, y_0) to (x_1, y_1), where both $x_1 > x_0$ and $y_1 > y_0$. This corresponds to a movement upward and to the right. Now, by monotonicity applied twice

$$U(x_1, y_1) > U(x_0, y_1) > U(x_0, y_0)$$

Hence (x_1, y_1) is on a higher indifference curve than is (x_0, y_0).

The second implication of mononicity involves the slope of an indifference curve. The slope is always negative. This follows by the implicit function theorem[5,6] since

$$\frac{dC_1}{dC_0}(x_0, x_1)\Bigg|_{U(C_0, C_1) \,=\, k} = -\frac{\partial U(x_0, x_1)/\partial C_0}{\partial U(x_0, x_1)/\partial C_1} < 0 \qquad (5.5)$$

This is negative by conditions (5.4a) and (5.4b). The negative slope of the indifference curve can be understood as follows. Consider the indifference curve $U(C_0, C_1) = k$. If we increase C_0, then, by monotonicity, $U(C_0, C_1)$ will increase. To keep $U(C_0, C_1) = k$ constant, we must therefore decrease C_1. This

---

[5]This theorem can be found in Rudin [3, p. 225].
[6]The symbol

$$\frac{dC_1}{dC_0}(x_0, x_1)\Bigg|_{U(C_0, C_1) \,=\, k}$$

means the slope of the indifference curve $U(C_0, C_1) = k$ evaluated at an arbitrary point (x_0, x_1) on this indifference curve, i.e., $U(x_0, x_1) = k$.

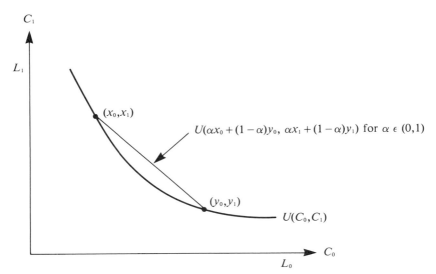

FIGURE 5.4: Representation of the convexity assumption 5.4.

positive shift in C_0 and a negative shift in C_1 to keep utility constant corresponds to a negative slope for the indifference curve.

Now the convexity assumption 5.4 can be studied. It is graphically represented in Fig. 5.4. If a chord is drawn between any two points on an indifference curve, say, (x_0, x_1) and (y_0, y_1), then any point on the interior of the chord lies on a higher indifference plane than $U(x_0, x_1) = k$. This is the graphical description of the convexity assumption 5.4 corresponding to condition (5.3).

5.5. TIME PREFERENCE

By examining the slope of a consumer's indifference curve, information is revealed about a consumer's preferences for consumption at time 0 versus consumption at time 1. This leads to the concept of *time preference*.

Definition: Positive Time Preference

An individual has *positive time preference* at $(C_0, C_1) \in B$ if and only if

$$U(C_0 + \delta, C_1) > U(C_0, C_1 + \delta) \quad \text{for all } \delta > 0$$

where

$$(C_0 + \delta, C_1) \in B \text{ and } (C_0, C_1 + \delta) \in B$$

(5.6)

In words, if the consumer would rather have $\delta > 0$ extra units of the consumption good today instead of the same δ tomorrow, he has positive time preference. This concept relates the desire for consumption goods *across* time.

It differs from monotonicity in that the monotonicity assumption 5.1 only considers consumption goods at a *fixed* point in time.

Similarly, we define *zero time preference* when $U(C_0 + \delta, C_1) = U(C_0, C_1 + \delta)$ replaces condition (5.6) and *negative time preference* when $U(C_0 + \delta, C_1) < U(C_0, C_1 + \delta)$ replaces condition (5.6). An investor with zero time preference is indifferent between δ units of additional consumption today or tomorrow. An investor with negative time preference prefers the additional δ units of consumption tomorrow.

The slope of the indifference curve at a particular point reflects positive, zero, or negative time preference. The rule is

If there is positive time preference at (x_0, x_1)

$$\left. \frac{dC_1}{dC_0}(x_0, x_1) \right|_{U(C_0, C_1) = U(x_0, x_1)}$$

$$< -1$$

If there is zero time preference at (x_0, x_1)

$$= -1 \quad (5.7)$$

If there is negative time preference at (x_0, x_1)

$$> -1$$

Proof

Positive time preference at (x_0, x_1) implies for $\delta > 0$

$$U(x_0 + \delta, x_1) - U(x_0, x_1) > U(x_0, x_1 + \delta) - U(x_0, x_1)$$

This implies

$$\frac{U(x_0 + \delta, x_1) - U(x_0, x_1)}{\delta} > \frac{U(x_0, x_1 + \delta) - U(x_0, x_1)}{\delta}$$

Taking the limit as $\delta \to 0$ under assumption 5.3 gives

$$\frac{\partial U(x_0, x_1)}{\partial C_0} > \frac{\partial U(x_0, x_1)}{\partial C_1}$$

By the monotonicity assumption, $(\partial U(x_0, x_1)/\partial C_1) > 0$, so we can divide by it, obtaining

$$-\frac{\dfrac{\partial U(x_0, x_1)}{\partial C_0}}{\dfrac{\partial U(x_0, x_1)}{\partial C_1}} < -1$$

With the use of the implicit function theorem, the left-hand side of this last expression equals the slope of the indifference curve $U(x_0, x_1)$. This completes the proof. $\square$

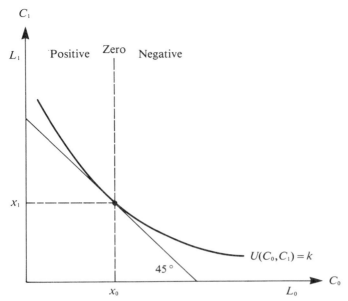

FIGURE 5.5: Representation of positive, zero, and negative time preferences.

To interpret a slope of -1, we draw a 45° line diagonally, as in Fig. 5.5. This line has a slope of -1. Its tangency to the indifference curve will therefore give the zero time preference point (x_0, x_1). To the left of this tangency point gives positive time preference points, while to the right of this tangency point gives negative time preference points. A point to the left of the tangency point represents a consumption pair more heavily weighted toward consumption at time 1 (in terms of the person's preferences). At this point, given the choice of $\delta > 0$ more units of consumption at time 1 versus at time 0, the consumer would choose to increase consumption at time 0. An analogous argument holds for points to the right of the tangency point.

For future comparison with the interest rate, it is convenient to rescale the slope of the indifference curve and to change its sign. The resulting quantity, now a percent, is known as the *time preference rate*.

Definition: Time Preference Rate

The time preference rate at (x_0, x_1), denoted $\ell(x_0, x_1)$, is

$$\ell(x_0, x_1) = -\left(\left. \frac{dC_1}{dC_0}(x_0, x_1) \right|_{U(C_0, C_1) = U(x_0, x_1)} + 1 \right) \qquad (5.8)$$

Using condition (5.7) we see that

If $\ell(x_0, x_1) > 0$, then the consumer has positive time preference.
If $\ell(x_0, x_1) = 0$, then the consumer has zero time preference.
If $\ell(x_0, x_1) < 0$, then the consumer has negative time preference.

An example will help solidify these notions.

Example 1 The Time Preference Rate

Suppose a consumer's utility function is

$$U(C_0, C_1) = \log C_0 + \frac{1}{(1 + \psi)} \log C_1$$

where $\psi > 0$. This utility function satisfies monotonicity, since

$$\frac{\partial U(C_0, C_1)}{\partial C_0} = \frac{1}{C_0} > 0$$

and

$$\frac{\partial U(C_0, C_1)}{\partial C_1} = \frac{1}{(1 + \psi)} \frac{1}{C_1} > 0$$

The slope of the indifference curve at (x_0, x_1) is

$$\frac{dC_1}{dC_0}(x_0, x_1) \bigg|_{U(C_0, C_1) = U(x_0, x_1)}$$

$$= -\frac{\dfrac{\partial U(x_0, x_1)}{\partial C_0}}{\dfrac{\partial U(x_0, x_1)}{\partial C_1}} = -\frac{\dfrac{1}{x_0}}{\dfrac{1}{(1 + \psi)}\dfrac{1}{x_1}} = -\frac{x_1}{x_0}(1 + \psi)$$

The time preference rate is

$$\ell(x_0, x_1) = -\left(\frac{dC_1}{dC_0}(x_0, x_1) \bigg|_{U(C_0, C_1) = U(x_0, x_1)} + 1 \right)$$

$$= +\frac{x_1}{x_0}(1 + \psi) - 1$$

If $x_1 = 75$, $x_0 = 50$, $\psi = .10$, then

$$\ell(75, 50) = (1.5)(1.1) - 1$$

$$= .65 > 0$$

and the consumer has positive time preference. ☐

5.6. THE OPTIMAL PORTFOLIO DECISION

This section studies the optimal portfolio decision in the context of the preference assumptions 5.1–5.4. Two theorems are derived investigating the characteristics of the optimal investment portfolio: Theorem 5.1 deals with its existence and theorem 5.3 with its uniqueness. Theorem 5.2 provides a set of sufficient conditions for the exclusion of arbitrage opportunities in this economy.

The consumption-saving decision as stated by condition (5.1) is repeated here for convenience: Choose C_0, C_1 to maximize

$$U(C_0, C_1) \tag{5.9}$$

subject to

$$\overline{C}_0 + \sum_{j=0}^{K} \overline{N}_j p(x_j)/\rho_0 = C_0 + \sum_{j=0}^{K} N_j p(x_j)/\rho_0 \tag{5.9a}$$

and

$$C_1 = \overline{C}_1 + \sum_{j=0}^{K} N_j x_j/\rho_1 \tag{5.9b}$$

$$(C_0, C_1) \in B \tag{5.9c}$$

By the existence assumption 5.2 we know an optimal (C_0^*, C_1^*) *exists* to the decision problem (5.9). Furthermore, by the convexity assumption 5.4, it is *unique*. Hence we are ensured the existence of a unique optimal consumption pair (C_0^*, C_1^*).

We now need to investigate the existence and uniqueness of an optimal investment portfolio.

Theorem 5.1: Existence of an Optimal Investment Portfolio

There exists an optimal investment portfolio $\{N_0^*, \ldots, N_K^*\}$.

Proof

By assumption 5.2, we are guaranteed the existence of an optimal investment portfolio. Indeed, this follows from condition (5.9b), since the optimal time 1 consumption, C_1^*, exists if and only if an optimal investment $\{N_0^*, \ldots, N_K^*\}$ exists. Recall that the investment portfolio completely determines C_1. □

The existence of an optimal investment portfolio is the existence assumption 5.2 transformed. We now show that this assumption implies that arbitrage opportunities do not exist. Alternatively stated, the existence assumption 5.2 can replace the no arbitrage opportunity assumption 3.4 in the context of the model developed above.

Theorem 5.2: Optimality Implies No Arbitrage Opportunities

In the above model the preference assumptions 5.1–5.4 and the market assumptions 3.1–3.3 imply the no arbitrage opportunity assumption 3.4; i.e., the existence of an optimal investment portfolio implies that no arbitrage opportunities exist.

Proof

This is a proof by contradiction. Let $(N_0^*, \ldots, N_K^*)$ represent an optimal investment portfolio. Suppose an arbitrage opportunity exists. For one type of arbitrage opportunity, condition 3.11 shows that $(N_0^*, \ldots, N_K^*)$ plus the arbitrage opportunity lies in the constrained choice set A and also increases the utility level. This contradicts $(N_0^*, \ldots, N_K^*)$ being the optimal investment portfolio. The other types of arbitrage opportunities can be handled similarly.   □

Given the existence of an optimal investment portfolio in the asset market (i.e., assumptions 5.1–5.4 and assumptions 3.1–3.3), the no arbitrage opportunity assumption 3.4 is redundant. This set of basic assumptions involving preferences and market conditions generates the exclusion of arbitrage opportunities.

It is now possible to show that there does *not* exist a unique optimal investment portfolio unless there is only one asset trading, i.e., $K \equiv 0$. In fact we show that unless $K \equiv 0$, the investor can construct an optimal investment portfolio utilizing any individual asset j. This implies that an investor views each asset as a perfect substitute for every other asset.

Theorem 5.3: Uniqueness of the Optimal Portfolio

(a) There exists a unique investment portfolio if and only if $K \equiv 0$.

(b) For each $j \in \{0, 1, \ldots, K\}$, there is an optimal investment portfolio consisting of only asset j.

Proof

Statement (b) proves statement (a). To prove statement (b), let $\{N_0^*, \ldots, N_K^*\}$ be an optimal investment portfolio. It exists by theorem 5.1. Consider

$$M_i = 0 \quad \text{for } i \neq j$$
$$M_j = (N_0^* x_0 + \ldots + N_K^* x_K)/x_j$$

First

$$\sum_{j=0}^{K} M_j x_j = \left(\sum_{i=0}^{K} N_i^* x_i / x_j \right) x_j$$

$$= \sum_{i=0}^{K} N_i^* x_i$$

and the portfolio $\{M_0, \ldots, M_K\}$ duplicates $\{N_0^*, \ldots, N_K^*\}$ at time 1. Second

$$\sum_{j=0}^{K} M_j p(x_j) = p\left(\sum_{j=0}^{K} M_j x_j \right) = p\left(\sum_{i=0}^{K} N_i^* x_i \right) = \sum_{i=0}^{K} N_i^* p(x_i)$$

by value additivity applied twice. So the portfolio $\{M_0, \ldots, M_K\}$ duplicates $\{N_0^*, \ldots, N_K^*\}$ at time 0. But $(M_0, \ldots, M_K)$ is the portfolio consisting of only asset j. □

Another way to state the result in theorem 5.3 is to say that there exists an optimal portfolio consisting of a *basis set* of assets. A *basis set* of assets is a collection of assets $\{0, \ldots, n\}$, where $n \leq K$ such that a portfolio of $\{0, \ldots, n\}$ can duplicate any portfolio involving $\{0, \ldots, K\}$, i.e., we say span $\{x_0, \ldots, x_n\}$ = span $\{x_0, \ldots, x_K\}$. Theorem 5.3 states that in a world of certainty, a basis set of assets consists of only one element. This result generalizes in Chap. 8. Given theorem 5.3, we are now justified in letting the certain economy consist of only one asset. This simplification will be the initial step of the equilibrium model of Chap. 6.

5.7. SUMMARY

This chapter introduces the additional structure on preferences in the asset model economy to ensure that in the context of the consumption-saving decision there exists a unique optimal consumption choice and a unique optimal portfolio choice. The additional assumptions required on preferences are the existence of an optimum, assumption 5.2, and convexity, assumption 5.4. Assumption 5.3, regular utility functions, is included in order to utilize calculus to get necessary and sufficient conditions for the optimal consumption-saving decision.

In the context of the model, a unique investment portfolio obtains if and only if one asset trades. This is becuase investors view all assets as perfect substitutes in a certain economy. Finally, we proved in theorem 5.2 that the existence of an optimal investment portfolio precludes the existence of arbitrage opportunities. This is a utility based justification for the no arbitrage opportunity assumption 3.4 of Chap. 3.

5.8. REFERENCES

1. Arrow, Kenneth, and Alain Enthoven, "Quasi-Concave Programming," *Econometrica*, 29 (October 1961), 779–800.
2. Debreu, G., *Theory of Value*. New Haven, Conn.: Yale University Press, 1959.
3. Rudin, Walter, *Principles of Mathematical Analysis*. New York: McGraw-Hill, 1976.

6

THE PURE EXCHANGE ECONOMY

This chapter completes Part I of the book, certainty models, with an examination of a pure exchange economy. A pure exchange economy is an economy where there is no production and there is only exchange of existing assets. The purpose of studying such an economy is to understand the mechanism through which assets are traded and prices determined. The mechanism we study here is called a competitive equilibrium. The concept of a competitive equilibrium is central to finance and economics. In a competitive equilibrium, individuals acting independently and in their own best interests trade after observing prices. A set of trades and prices such that aggregate demand equals aggregate supply is a competitive equilibrium. This is a static concept, nonetheless, if a competitive equilibrium is achieved in an economy, there is no reason for change. All investors are satisfied and there are no forces in the economy to generate dissatisfaction. The economy is in a stable position, i.e., an equilibrium. This chapter studies the trades and prices that result from such an equilibrium.

6.1. PRELIMINARIES

The pure exchange economy studied here was presented in Sec. 5.1 of Chap. 5. For ease of reference, we briefly summarize the major aspects of that model. For a detailed description of the assumptions and their interpretation, refer to the preceding chapters.

The economy consists of two dates, times 0 and 1. The economy is populated by I investors, which are indexed by $i = 1, \ldots, I$. Each investor's preferences are over units of consumption at times 0 and 1, i.e., over the choice set $B = \{(C_0, C_1) : C_0 \in [0, L_0], C_1 \in [0, L_1]\}$. Consumption at time 0 is bounded below by 0 and above by L_0, a limit on aggregate supply. Similar bounds hold for consumption at time 1. Preferences are representable by an ordinal utility function denoted by $U^i(C_0, C_1)$. The superscript i corresponds to the ith individual. This representation exists because of the imposition of the rationality axioms 2.1–2.6, discussed in Chap. 2.

Without loss of generality, we let the asset market consist of a single asset, a bond, which trades at time 0 and has a unit payoff in units of the consumption good at time 1.[1]

Assumption 3.1: Homogeneous Beliefs

All investors agree that the payoff in units of consumption from the bond at time 1 is one unit.

The market for this bond is frictionless (assumption 3.2) and competitive (assumption 3.3). Furthermore, there are no arbitrage opportunities in the economy (assumption 3.4). With only one asset trading, this implies that the price (in units of consumption goods) for the bond is positive and N units of the bond sells for N times the price of one bond.[2] For convenience, we denote the time 0 price of the bond to be $1/(1 + R)$ units of the consumption good. Consequently, R denotes the real rate of interest on the bond.[3] For brevity, we have denoted all prices and all returns in units of the consumption good. In the

---

[1] This is the same as the homogeneous beliefs assumption 3.1 of Chap. 3. To see this, by Sec. 5.6 of Chap. 5, we can examine only a one-asset economy. The bond defined in assumption 3.1 corresponds to a *package* consisting of ρ_1 units of asset 0, where ρ_1 is the time 1 price level for a consumption good in terms of dollars. Recall that $x_0 = 1$ dollar, hence $\rho_1 x_0 = \rho_1 1$ represents the time 1 cash flow in dollars from the bond. This payoff in units of the consumption good is $\rho_1 x_0 / \rho_1 = x_0 = 1$.

[2] We have under the no–arbitrage opportunity assumption 3.4 of Chap. 3 that

$$p(x_0) = \frac{1}{(1 + r)} > 0 \quad \text{and}$$

$$p(Nx_0) = Np(x_0)$$

Hence

$$\frac{p(x_0)}{\rho_0} = \left(\frac{1}{1 + r}\right)\frac{1}{\rho_0} > 0 \quad \text{and}$$

$$\frac{p(Nx_0)}{\rho_0} = Np(x_0)/\rho_0$$

[3] The nominal return on the bond plus one is

terminology of Chap. 3, we have transformed dollars into units of the consumption good through the price levels at time 0 and time 1.[4]

The ith consumer enters time 0 with an endowment of $(\overline{C}_0^i, \overline{C}_1^i)$ units of the consumption good and $\overline{N}^i$ shares of the bond. We assume that $\overline{C}_0^i > 0$ or $\overline{C}_1^i + \overline{N}^i > 0$ for all i, i.e., each investor has an endowment containing a positive amount of the consumption good. Their consumption decision is to choose (C_0, C_1) to maximize $U^i(C_0, C_1)$ subject to

$$\overline{C}_0^i + \overline{N}^i \frac{1}{(1 + R)} = C_0 + N \frac{1}{(1 + R)} \tag{6.1a}$$

and

$$C_1 = \overline{C}_1^i + N \tag{6.1b}$$

$$(C_0, C_1) \in B \tag{6.1c}$$

Expressions (6.1a)–(6.1c) correspond to the investor's budget constraints.

We assume that U^i satisfies monotonicity (assumption 5.1), that there exists an optimal consumption pair for each investor (assumption 5.2), that U^i is a smooth function with continuous second-order partial derivatives (assumption 5.3), and that preferences are strictly convex (assumption 5.4). These assumptions imply that the optimal consumption pair is unique and that the optimal investment in bonds is unique (by theorem 5.3 of Chap. 5).

The next section of this chapter will characterize these optimal consumption and investment choices using calculus. Before proceeding to that analysis, however, it is convenient to combine the budget constraints into one equality. To do this, we first solve for $N = C_1 - \overline{C}_1^i$ in (6.1b) and then substitute into expression (6.1a) to get (after rearranging terms)

$$\overline{C}_0^i + \frac{\overline{C}_1^i}{(1 + R)} + \frac{\overline{N}^i}{(1 + R)} = C_0 + \frac{C_1}{(1 + R)} \tag{6.2}$$

The left-hand side of expression (6.2) represents the time 0 present value of the ith investor's endowment in units of the consumption good. The right-hand side of expression (6.2) represents the time 0 present value of the *desired* or *actual* units of the consumption good demanded.

The budget constraint (6.2) is graphed in Fig. 6.1. The budget constraint is a straight line that goes through the endowment point $(\overline{C}_0^i + \overline{N}^i/$

$$\frac{\rho_1 x_0}{p(\rho_1 x_0)} = \frac{1}{p(x_0)} = (1 + r)$$

The real return plus one is

$$(1 + R) \equiv \frac{1}{p(\rho_1 x_0)/\rho_0} = \frac{(1 + r)}{\rho_1/\rho_0} = \frac{(1 + r)}{(1 + \Pi)}$$

where $\Pi = (\rho_1 - \rho_0)/\rho_0$ is the inflation rate.

[4] See footnotes 1 through 3.

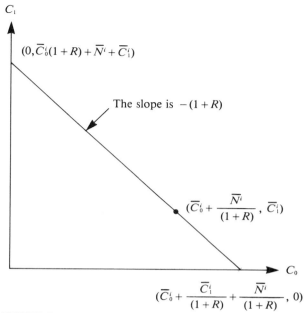

FIGURE 6.1: The budget constraint.

$(1 + R)$, $\overline{C}_1^i$) and intersects the C_0 axis at a position equal to the present value of consumption $[\overline{C}_0^i + \overline{N}^i/(1 + R) + \overline{C}_1^i/(1 + R), 0]$. The intersection of the budget constraint with the C_1 axis has a height that corresponds to the future value of consumption $(0, \overline{C}_0^i(1 + R) + \overline{N}^i + \overline{C}_1^i)$. The budget constraint has a slope of $-(1 + R)$. This means that for each unit of the consumption good at time 0 that the investor adds to his demand, he loses $(1 + R)$ units of consumption at time 1.

Utilizing this budget constraint we rewrite the consumer's decision problem as the following: Choose (C_0, C_1) to maximize $U^i(C_0, C_1)$ subject to

$$\overline{C}_0^i + \overline{C}_1^i/(1 + R) + \overline{N}^i/(1 + R) = C_0 + C_1/(1 + R)$$

and

$$(C_0, C_1) \in B \tag{6.3}$$

6.2. CHARACTERIZING THE OPTIMAL CONSUMPTION CHOICE

This section characterizes the optimal consumption choice (C_0^i, C_1^i) of the ith consumer, i.e., we solve the consumer's decision problem given in expression (6.3). This solution will be studied in two ways: graphically and analytically. Both approaches to solving the problem will add to our understanding of the issues involved.

We start with the graphical analysis. Consider the diagram in Fig. 6.2.

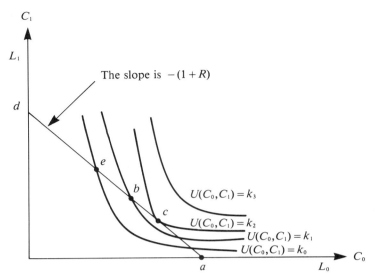

FIGURE 6.2: The consumption pair.
The points are

$$a = (\overline{C}_0^i + \overline{C}_1^i/(1 + R) + \overline{N}^i/(1 + R), 0)$$

$$b = (\overline{C}_0^i + \overline{N}^i/(1 + R), \overline{C}_1^i)$$

$$c = (C_0^i, C_1^i), \text{ the optimal consumption pair}$$

$$d = (0, \overline{C}_0^i(1 + R) + \overline{C}_1^i + \overline{N}^i)$$

$$[a, d] = \text{budget constraint (slope equal to } - (1 + R))$$

$$k_0 < k_1 < k_2 < k_3$$

Point b represents the endowment point, and thus the line segment $[a, d]$ is the consumer's budget constraint, since it has a slope of $-(1 + R)$. These represent the consumption pairs the investor can afford.

Four indifference curves are graphed on the figure: $U(C_0, C_1) = k_0$, $U(C_0, C_1) = k_1$, $U(C_0, C_1) = k_2$, and $U(C_0, C_1) = k_3$. The indifference curves are convex, negative sloping, and increasing in value as they move in the northeast direction. The indifference curve represented by the utility value k_1 goes through the endowment point b. This utility level, therefore, represents the level of utility the investor would attain by not trading and just consuming her endowment in the ordering of $\overline{C}_0^i$ units at time 0 and $(\overline{N}^i + \overline{C}_1^i)$ units at time 1.

By trading bonds, the investor can move anywhere along the budget constraint $[a, d]$. Suppose she decides to consider a movement to point e. This represents a reduction of consumption at time 0 from her endowment point b, and therefore it represents an additional purchase of bonds at time 0. These bonds will increase the time 1 consumption at point e above that given by her endowment point b. Unfortunately, this movement will put the investor on the indifference curve with a value of k_0. This is *below* her endowment point utility level k_1. Because this movement decreases the investor's utility level, it will not be made. The investor will not buy additional bonds.

Consider a movement to point c. This represents an increase in consumption at time 0 from the endowment point b. Therefore, it represents a sale of bonds at time 0 and possibly borrowing (e.g., if $\overline{N}^i = 0$). This sale of bonds or borrowing will decrease consumption at time 1 from that contained in the endowment point. This time the movement has placed the investor on a higher indifference curve, i.e., the utility level k_2 exceeds the utility level at the endowment point k_1. The investor will want to make this change.

By construction, any change from point c, either buying or selling (borrowing) bonds, will decrease the investor's utility level. Hence point c represents the investor's optimal consumption choice pair (C_0^i, C_1^i).

The optimal consumption choice pair is seen to occur at the tangency point of the indifference curve with the budget constraint. This fact will always be true unless the investor's optimum consumption at time 0 or time 1 is zero (see Fig. 6.3). In Figure 6.3, the optimal consumption at time 1 is zero, and the slope of

FIGURE 6.3: Optimum consumption at time 1 is zero.

$$a = (\overline{C}_0^i + \overline{C}_1^i/(1 + R) + \overline{N}^i/(1 + R), 0)$$
$$b = (\overline{C}_0^i + \overline{N}^i/(1 + R), \overline{C}_1^i)$$
$$c = (C_0^i, C_1^i)$$
$$d = (0, \overline{C}_0^i(1 + R) + \overline{C}_1^i + \overline{N}^i)$$

$[a, d]$ = budget constraint

$$k_0 < k_1 < k_2 < k_3$$

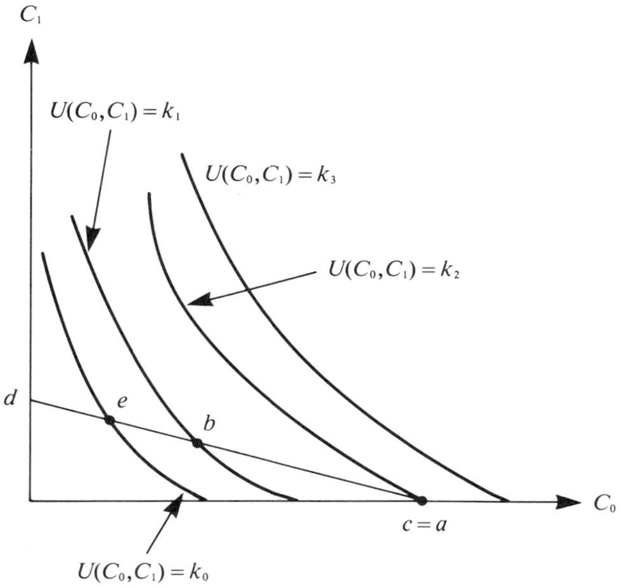

the indifference curve at the optimum consumption pair (negative) is less than or equal to the slope of the budget constraint, $-(1 + R)$. An analogous condition holds if the optimal consumption at time 0 is zero. In this case, the slope of the budget constraint will be less than or equal to the slope of the indifference curve at the optimal consumption pair.

One final observation needs to be made: If the slope of the budget constraints changes (say, to $R^* > R$), then the optimal consumption pair will change (unless either consumption at time 1 is zero or consumption at time 1 is zero and $-(1 + R^*)$ is still less than or equal to the slope of the indifference curve at the optimal consumption pair). See Fig. 6.4.

Recall from Chap. 5 that the slope at (C_0^i, C_1^i) of the indifference curve equals $-(1 + \ell^i(C_0^i, C_1^i))$, where $\ell^i(C_0^i, C_1^i)$ is the ith person's time preference rate at (C_0^i, C_1^i); see expression (5.8). We can therefore summarize the graphical analysis by saying that the optimal consumption pair (C_0^i, C_1^i) on the budget constraint satisfies the following:

$$\ell^i(C_0^i, C_1^i) = R \quad \text{if } C_0^i > 0, C_1^i > 0 \tag{6.4a}$$

$$\ell^i(C_0^i, C_1^i) \geq R \quad \text{if } C_1^i = 0 \tag{6.4b}$$

$$\ell^i(C_0^i, C_1^i) \leq R \quad \text{if } C_0^i = 0 \tag{6.4c}$$

At an optimal consumption pair (C_0^i, C_1^i) interior to $[0, L_0] \times [0, L_1]$, (6.4a), the investor's time preference rate equals the interest rate. At zero time

FIGURE 6.4: Sensitivity of the optimal consumption choice to changes in the interest rate.

$a = (\overline{C}_0^i + \overline{N}^i/(1 + R), \overline{C}_1^i)$

$b =$ optimum consumption pair at interest rate R^*

$c =$ optimum consumption pair at interest rate R

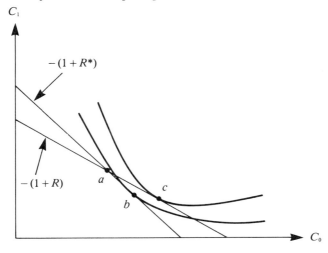

1 consumption, $C_1^i = 0$, the time preference rate exceeds or equals the interest rate, while at zero time 0 consumption, $C_0^i = 0$, (6.4b), the interest rate exceeds or equals the time preference rate, (6.4c).

We can interpret the time preference rate at (C_0^i, C_1^i) as the "utility"-determined interest rate at which the ith investor is indifferent between borrowing or lending.

Condition (6.4a) says that at the optimum consumption pair (C_0^i, C_1^i), the investor is indifferent to borrowing and lending at the rate R. If, for example, her borrowing and lending rate $\ell^i(C_0^i, C_1^i)$ exceeded R, the investor would not lend. She requires a return of $\ell^i(C_0^i, C_1^i)$ but can only get R. She would borrow since she is willing to pay an interest rate of $\ell^i(C_0^i, C_1^i)$ but only has to pay R. This borrowing decreases $\ell^i(C_0^i, C_1^i)$. She continues borrowing until either $\ell^i(C_0^i, C_1^i)$ equals R or there is no more to borrow against and $C_1^i = 0$.

The analytic solution duplicates the graphical analysis. For simplicity, let us make the following assumption:[5]

Assumption 6.1: Interior Optimal Consumption

For any $R > 0$, the optimal consumption pair (C_0^i, C_1^i) satisfies $C_0^i > 0$ and $C_1^i > 0$.

This excludes the constraints $C_0^i \in [0, L_0]$ and $C_1^i \in [0, L_1]$ from further consideration. Under assumption 6.1, to solve the decision problem, (6.3), we set up the Lagrangian function:

$$L(C_0, C_1, \lambda) = U^i(C_0, C_1) + \lambda(-\overline{C}_0^i - \overline{C}_1^i/(1 + R)$$
$$-\overline{N}^i/(1 + R) + C_0 + C_1/(1 + R))$$

where λ is the Lagrangian multiplier corresponding to the budget constraint. Under the convexity assumption 5.4, necessary and sufficient conditions for characterizing the optimum consumption pair (C_0^i, C_1^i) and Lagrangian λ^i are

$$\frac{\partial L}{\partial C_0} (C_0^i, C_1^i, \lambda^i) = 0$$

$$\frac{\partial L}{\partial C_1} (C_0^i, C_1^i, \lambda^i) = 0 \tag{6.5}$$

$$\frac{\partial L}{\partial \lambda} (C_0^i, C_1^i, \lambda^i) = 0$$

Evaluation of the partial derivatives gives

---

[5] Without assumption 6.1, we would give the necessary and sufficient equations using Kuhn-Tucker conditions (see Arrow and Enthoven [1]) rather than with Lagrangian multipliers.

$$\frac{\partial U^i(C_0^i, C_1^i)}{\partial C_0} + \lambda^i = 0 \qquad (6.6a)$$

$$\frac{\partial U^i(C_0^i, C_1^i)}{\partial C_1} + \frac{\lambda^i}{(1 + R)} = 0 \qquad (6.6b)$$

$$-\overline{C}_0^i - \overline{C}_1^i/(1 + R) - \overline{N}^i/(1 + R) + C_0^i + C_1^i/(1 + R) = 0 \qquad (6.6c)$$

Condition (6.6c) is the budget constraint. Conditions (6.6a) and (6.6b) can be simplified. Solving for λ^i in condition (6.6a) and substituting into (6.6b) yield (after some algebra)

$$-\frac{\dfrac{\partial U^i(C_0^i, C_1^i)}{\partial C_1}}{\dfrac{\partial U^i(C_0^i, C_1^i)}{\partial C_0}} = -(1 + R) \qquad (6.7)$$

This says that at an interior optimum (C_0^i, C_1^i), the slope of the indifference curve at (C_0^i, C_1^i), the left-hand side of (6.7), equals the slope of the budget constraint, the right-hand side of (6.7).

Further, (6.7) and (6.6c) are two equations in two unknowns (C_0^i, C_1^i). In general these solutions, (C_0^i, C_1^i), will depend on the parameters R, $\overline{C}_0^i$, and $\overline{C}_1^i$. This analytic analysis duplicates the graphical analysis. From expression (6.7) and the definition of the ith investor's time preference rate, $\ell^i(C_0^i, C_1^i)$, we obtain expression (6.4a) as well.

6.3. COMPETITIVE EQUILIBRIUM

The previous section characterized the ith consumer's consumption decision, assuming (assumption 3.3) that the consumer takes prices (the interest rate R) as given. Each consumer believes he cannot influence prices, yet all consumers acting simultaneously do determine prices. This process of price determination is the subject of this section.

The equilibrium process of price determination is most easily explained by utilizing a (Walrasian) auctioneer. The process starts with the auctioneer calling out an interest rate R. The consumers hearing this rate act as price takers and calculate their optimal consumption demands $(C_0^i(R), C_1^i(R))$, which, of course, depend on the interest rate. The consumers submit these demands to the auctioneer. The auctioneer attempts to match these demands with the available supply of goods at time 0, $\Sigma_{i\in I}\, \overline{C}_0^i$, and the available supply of goods at time 1, $\Sigma_{i\in I}\,(\overline{C}_1^i + \overline{N}^i)$. If the total demand at time 0, $\Sigma_{i\in I}\, C_0^i(R)$, and the total demand at time 1, $\Sigma_{i\in I}\, C_1^i(R)$, can be satisfied, i.e., equals total supply, then the process ends. The interest rate R and the satisfied demands $(C_0^i(R), C_1^i(R))$ for all $i \in I$ would be the equilibrium price and consumption pairs. If the total demand *cannot* be satisfied, then the economy is said to be in *disequilibrium*.

If a disequilibrium interest rate is called out, the auctioneer then asserts that no trades take place at the old interest rate, and he calls out a new interest rate. The new interest rate called out is designed by the auctioneer to reduce the existing discrepancy between aggregate supply and aggregate demand. Once this rate is called out, the process continues as before. Consumers submit their new optimal demands and the auctioneer again attempts to match these with aggregate supply. The hope is, of course, that an equilibrium interest rate exists and that the auctioneer will eventually call it out.

This story of the auctioneer does not match reality. It is introduced only to facilitate our understanding of the concept of an equilibrium. It does *not* correspond to the actual trading mechanism existing in security markets today. Nonetheless, it should make the following definition seem more reasonable.

Definition: A Competitive Equilibrium

A *competitive equilibrium* is an interest rate R and a set of consumption pairs $(C_0^i(R), C_1^i(R))$ for all $i = 1, \ldots, I$ such that

(i) $(C_0^i(R), C_1^i(R))$ represent the optimal consumption choice of the ith consumer [i.e., satisfy (6.7) and (6.6c)] and

(ii) aggregate supply equals aggregate demand, i.e.

$$\sum_{i=1}^{I} C_0^i(R) = \sum_{i=1}^{I} \overline{C}_0^i$$

$$\sum_{i=1}^{I} C_1^i(R) = \sum_{i=1}^{I} (\overline{C}_1^i + \overline{N}^i)$$

This concept of a competitive equilibrium corresponds to the everyday use of the word "equilibrium." If such a position is reached in the economy, there is no desire for change on the part of any individual. Everyone's demands are satisfied and everyone is at his or her highest utility level. Furthermore, the demands are exactly fulfilled by the existing supply of consumption goods. Everyone gets exactly what he or she desires, given budget constraints. No one is turned away or given too much.

A graphical description of the equilibrium interest rate can now be given. Given the optimal demands $(C_0^i(R), C_1^i(R))$, the equilibrium interest rate is that R which satisfies condition (ii). Condition (ii) contains two equations in one unknown. Fortunately, one of the equations is redundant. This is known as the *Walras law*.

Theorem 6.1: The Walras Law

For the previous economy

$$\sum_{i=1}^{I} C_0^i(R) = \sum_{i=1}^{I} \overline{C}_0^i \quad \text{if and only if} \quad \sum_{i=1}^{I} C_1^i(R) = \sum_{i=1}^{I} [\overline{C}_1^i + \overline{N}^i]$$

Proof

By the ith investor's budget constraint (6.3)

$$\overline{C}_0^i + (\overline{C}_1^i + \overline{N}^i)/(1 + R) = C_0^i + C_1^i/(1 + R)$$

Summing this expression across all investors and rearranging terms give

$$\sum_{i=1}^{I} \overline{C}_0^i - \sum_{i=1}^{I} C_0^i = \frac{1}{(1 + R)} \left[-\sum_{i=1}^{I} (\overline{C}_1^i + \overline{N}^i) + \sum_{i=1}^{I} C_1^i \right]$$

The left side of this expression is zero if and only if the right side is zero. ☐

The redundancy in the definition of a competitive equilibrium is due to the investor's budget constraint. Given the optimal consumption at time 0, consumption at time 1 is completely determined; i.e., it is a residual decision. It is residual due to the budget constraint. So if aggregate supply in the time 0 consumption goods market equals aggregate demand, then this will also be true in the time 1 consumption goods market.

With the Walras law, Fig. 6.5 represents the equilibrium interest rate R. The interest rate R is determined by the intersection of the aggregate supply curve with the aggregate demand curve. This diagrammatic representation is familiar to that often seen in standard macroeconomic analysis (e.g., see Branson [2]).

The key theorem of this section is now stated.

FIGURE 6.5: The equilibrium interest rate R^*.

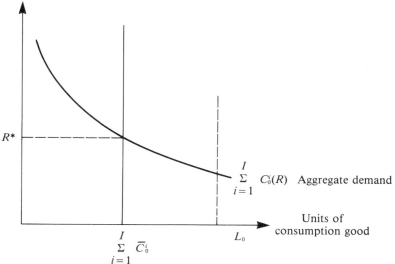

Theorem 6.2: Existence and Characterization of a Competitive Equilibrium

Under the economy of Secs. 6.1 and 6.2, a competitive equilibrium $[R, (C_0^i, C_1^i)$ for $i = 1, \ldots, I]$ exists and satisfies

$$\ell^i(C_0^i, C_1^i) = R \quad \text{for all } i = 1, \ldots, I$$

Proof

The competitive equilibrium can be seen to exist by referring to Ichiishi [3, p. 62, theorem 4.4.2] and noting that the economy of Secs. 6.1 and 6.2 satisfies the hypotheses of this theorem. A more detailed proof of this assertion is left to advanced courses.

The second part of the theorem follows from the interior optimum assumption 6.1 and condition (6.4a), which holds for all i investors. $\square$

This theorem asserts that a competitive equilibrium exists for this economy and that at the equilibrium, everyone's time preference rate equals the equilibrium interest rate. Consumers trade off consumption at time 0 for consumption at time 1 until the marginal rate of transformation just equals the interest rate. In this fashion, actual consumption is smoothed across time to reflect both specific preferences and the opportunity to trade with other investors.

This theorem also provides the first rationale for the existence of markets. Markets exist to increase the consumers' welfare. The ability to borrow or lend (in general) enables consumers to reach a higher level of utility (see Fig. 6.2) than they could obtain without markets. Without markets they must consume their endowment.

6.4. THE BOND MARKET

The previous section analyzed a competitive equilibrium in the consumption goods market at times 0 and 1. There is another way to study the equilibrium determination of interest rates that is dual to the above approach but equivalent to it. This method is to examine equilibrium in the bond market and to determine the interest rate that equates the aggregate supply of bonds to the aggregate demand. Surprisingly, this alternative approach determines the *same* equilibrium interest rate as in the preceding section. This approach to the determination of equilibrium prices is that most often used in finance (see the CAPM in Chap. 15 and/or the equilibrium version of Ross's APT in Chap. 18).

Definition: The Bond Market Equilibrium

A *bond market equilibrium* is an interest rate R and a set of bond demands $(N^i(R))$ for $i = 1, \ldots, I$ such that

(i) $N^i(R)$ represents the optimal demand for bonds of the ith consumer subject to the budget constraint, and

(ii) $\sum_{i=1}^{I} N^i(R) = \sum_{i=1}^{I} \overline{N}^i$

This definition is analogous to the definition of a competitive equilibrium in the preceding section, except that it is with respect to the bond market. An equilibrium occurs when the interest rate is such that every investor's optimal demand for bonds is satisfied and the aggregate supply of bonds equals the aggregate demand.

The following theorem compares the two equilibrium concepts.

Theorem 6.3: Equivalence of Equilibrium Interest Rates

In the above economy, the bond market equilibrium–determined interest rate is identical to the consumption good market competitive equilibrium–determined interest rate.

Proof

Note that by condition (6.1a), the time 0 budget constraint

$$\overline{C}_0^i - C_0^i = [N^i - \overline{N}^i]\frac{1}{(1 + R)}$$

Summing this expression over all i gives

$$\sum_{i=1}^{I} \overline{C}_0^i - \sum_{i=1}^{I} C_0^i(R) = \frac{1}{[1 + R]}\left[\sum_{i=1}^{I} N^i(R) - \sum_{i=1}^{I} \overline{N}^i\right]$$

Hence R makes the left-hand side of this expression zero if and only if it makes the right-hand side of this expression zero. $\square$

This theorem essentially states that these two equilibrium concepts are just different ways of viewing the same equilibrium economy. If the bond market is in equilibrium, then so is the consumption good market, and vice versa. In fact, the same interest rate clears both markets. It is a matter of convenience which market we study.

This equivalence is again due to the budget constraint. The consumption decision at time 0 is seen to be dual to the saving decision at time 0. What is left over after one consumes from his or her time 0 endowment is the investment in the bond market. This is just an alternate way of looking at the same decision.

6.5. EQUILIBRIUM PRICING VERSUS ARBITRAGE PRICING

The previous four sections analyzed equilibrium pricing in an economy under certainty. This section contrasts this approach to the arbitrage pricing approach in Chap. 3.

Chapter 3 utilized only assumptions 3.1–3.4 concerning the asset markets. Given these assumptions, and an exogenous interest rate R, arbitrage pricing theory implied that all assets must have the same return.[6] Equilibrium pricing, in contrast, uses assumptions 3.1–3.4 *plus* additional assumptions about investor preferences (axioms 2.1–2.6, assumptions 5.1–5.4, and assumption 6.1), as well as an equilibrium concept. The equilibrium concept is a static concept that requires aggregate demand to be equal to aggregate supply. Much more structure is imposed, yet more results are implied by the equilibrium analysis. First, the interest rate R is *endogenously* determined as part of the system. It is not a given. Second, this theory implies results about investor behavior. We see that at an equilibrium, everyone's time preference rates are equal, and equal to the interest rate.

Hence equilibrium pricing requires more inputs than arbitrage pricing, but is also generates more outputs. Which approach is preferred depends on the application under study. Some examples of these trade-offs and applications are provided in subsequent chapters.

6.6. SUMMARY

This chapter studied the equilibrium pricing of bonds in a certain economy. The purpose of the analysis was to introduce the concept of a competitive equilibrium and explore its consequences. A pure exchange economy was chosen for this exercise. Consumers live for two dates, times 0 and 1. They enter life with an endowment and must decide how much to consume at times 0 and 1. Bond markets provide a choice. The optimal demand is characterized as the tangency point of an indifference curve with the budget constraint. Any other demand provides a utility increasing change.

A competitive equilibrium is defined as an interest rate and optimal consumption demands by all consumers such that aggregate demand for consumption goods equals aggregate supply. Such an equilibrium exists. It was shown that an equivalent way to define an equilibrium is to use the bond market. The interest rate that equates aggregate demand for bonds with the aggregate supply is also the equilibrium interest rate. This alternative approach is more fruitful in multiple security markets.

Finally, arbitrage pricing theory was contrasted with equilibrium pricing

---

[6] Recall from footnote 3 that $R = ((1 + \Pi)/(1 + r)) - 1$, where r and Π are exogenously given.

theory. Although equilibrium pricing generates more results, it requires more assumptions. The choice of approach is dictated by the application.

6.7. REFERENCES

1. Arrow, Kenneth, and Alain Enthoven, "Quasi-Concave Programming," *Econometrica*, 29 (October 1961), 779–800.
2. Branson, William, *Macroeconomic Theory and Policy*. New York: Harper & Row, 1972.
3. Ichiishi, Tatsuro, *Game Theory for Economic Analysis*. Orlando, Fla.: Academic Press, 1983.

7

CARDINAL
UTILITY THEORY

This chapter begins Part II of the book, pricing models in an economy under uncertainty–the proper domain of finance theory. In this part of the book we shall study utility theory, Ross's arbitrage pricing theory, the capital asset pricing model, and numerous applications and extensions of these paradigms. Our efforts in Chaps. 1 through 6 will now pay off, since these earlier chapters have built up our economic intuition and have given us a running start. Surprisingly, most of the fundamental economic concepts and issues to be introduced will simply repeat the previous ideas but this time incorporate uncertainty. This extension requires the use of probability theory, the branch of mathematics dealing with the modeling of uncertainty through the use of random variables and probability distributions. Only the most basic ideas from probability theory will be employed but with far-reaching consequences.

The first example of this generalization from certainty to uncertainty is utility theory, the content of this chapter. The development will parallel the presentation used for utility theory in Chap. 2. This parallel development should aid our understanding and facilitate a comparison of the previous ideas.

7.1. AXIOMATIC STRUCTURE

Consider an arbitrary individual confronted with a decision problem. The individual is faced with a set of alternatives, denoted by the symbol $\bar{B}$, from which he must choose a preferred element. This time, however, the alternatives are not

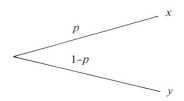

FIGURE 7.1: A lottery ticket involving outcomes x and y with probability $p \in [0, 1]$.

just different combinations of known goods like oranges, apples, or peaches. The alternatives will include gambles, which we will call *lottery tickets*. A lottery ticket will be analogous in concept to the everyday use of the phrase. A lottery ticket will represent a "risky" security whose outcomes occur with fixed or *objective* probabilities.

The first task in developing the theory is to formalize this expansion in the set of alternatives.[1] To start, let x and y be two alternatives in $\tilde{B}$. A *lottery ticket* involving the outcomes x and y with probability p and $(1 - p)$, respectively, $0 \leq p \leq 1$, can be represented on a tree diagram, as in Fig. 7.1. Each branch of the tree is associated with an outcome. The top branch in Fig. 7.1 is associated with the outcome x. The probability that a particular outcome occurs is written above the corresponding branch of the tree. For example, in Fig. 7.1, outcome x occurs with probability p.

This representation is too cumbersome to manipulate algebraically. Consequently we introduce the notation

$$[px \ \& \ (1 - p)y] \tag{7.1}$$

to represent the lottery ticket. The notation should be read as $[px \ \& \ (1 - p)y]$ is the lottery ticket involving outcome x with probability p and outcome y with probability $1 - p$.

The alternatives set $\tilde{B}$ can be characterized by the following four postulates:

Postulate 1

If $x, y \in \tilde{B}$, then $[px \ \& \ (1 - p)y] \in \tilde{B}$ for all $p \in [0, 1]$.

Postulate 2

For every $x, y \in \tilde{B}$ and $p \in [0, 1]$, $[px \ \& \ (1 - p)x] = x$ and $[1x \ \& \ 0y] = x$.

Postulate 3

For every $x, y \in \tilde{B}$ and $p \in [0, 1]$, $[px \ \& \ (1 - p)y] = [(1 - p)y \ \& \ px]$.

[1]This presentation partly follows Owen [7, pp. 116–121]. A more analytic development can be found in Jarrow [5].

Postulate 4

For every $x, y \in \bar{B}$ and $p, q, r \in [0, 1]$, $[p[rx \ \& \ (1 - r)y] \ \&$
$(1 - p)[qx \ \& \ (1 - q)y]] = [(pr + (1 - p)q)x \ \& \ (1 - pr - (1 - p)q)y]$.

These postulates are best visualized in tree diagram form. See Fig. 7.2.

We assume the individual agrees with these postulates. Postulates 1, 2, and 3 are technical in nature. Postulate 1 says that the alternatives set $\bar{B}$ contains all lottery tickets involving elements x and y in $\bar{B}$. This is a closure condition. Postulate 2 identifies the alternative x with two lottery tickets: a lottery ticket, both of whose outcomes are x, and another lottery ticket with probability one of getting outcome x and probability zero of getting outcome y. Postulate 3

FIGURE 7.2: Tree diagram representation of postulates 2–4 for characterizing $\bar{B}$.

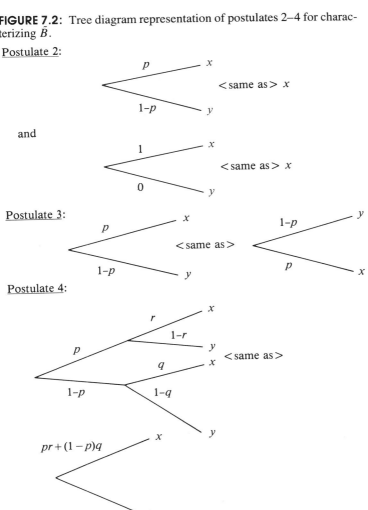

identifies an algebraic operation on lottery tickets that preserves the lottery ticket. It doesn't matter which order the branches occur in the tree diagram. Finally, postulate 4 shows the equivalence between a compound lottery ticket (i.e., a lottery ticket where an outcome is a lottery ticket) and a simple lottery ticket. To obtain the simple lottery ticket, look at all the branches of the compound lottery ticket involving outcome x. Find the probability that a single branch occurs by multiplying probabilities and then sum these probabilities across all branches generating outcome x. This sum is the new probability associated with outcome x in the simple lottery ticket.

A set $\tilde{B}$ that satisfies these four postulates is called a *mixture set*. We have interpreted $\tilde{B}$ as lottery tickets with p, the associated probability. It is revealing to note that the alternatives set B considered under certainty in Chap. 2 is also a mixture set. Here, given alternatives x, $y \in B$ and a fraction $p \in [0, 1]$, the combination $[px + (1 - p)y]$ is interpreted as a new element composed of p percent of the goods vector x and $(1 - p)$ percent of the goods vector y. The symbol $+$ replaces $\&$. The four postulates are satisfied for the set B of Chap. 2.

We assume that each individual is endowed with a preference relation on $\tilde{B}$ denoted by $\underset{\sim}{\pi}$. We use the same symbol for this preference relation as we did in Chap. 2, although in principle a different symbol should be employed.

Given two elements x, $y \in \tilde{B}$, the notation $x \underset{\sim}{\pi} y$ means either that x is preferred to y or that x is indifferent to y. We define indifference by $x \sim y$ if and only if $x \underset{\sim}{\pi} y$ and $y \underset{\sim}{\pi} x$. We define strict preference by $x \underset{\sim}{\pi} y$ if $x \underset{\sim}{\pi} y$ and not $x \sim y$.

The preference relation is assumed to satisfy the same six axioms given in Chap. 2. (See Chap. 2 for a detailed explanation of these axioms.)

Axiom 7.1: Reflexivity

For any $x \in \tilde{B}$, $x \underset{\sim}{\pi} x$.

Axiom 7.2: Comparability

For any x, y, $\in \tilde{B}$, either $x \underset{\sim}{\pi} y$ or $y \underset{\sim}{\pi} x$.

Axiom 7.3: Transitivity

For any x, y, $z \in \tilde{B}$, if $x \underset{\sim}{\pi} y$ and $y \underset{\sim}{\pi} z$, then $x \underset{\sim}{\pi} z$.

Axiom 7.4: Order Preserving

For any x, y, $\in \tilde{B}$ where $x \underset{\sim}{\pi} y$ and α, $\beta \in [0, 1]$, $[\alpha x \& (1 - \alpha)y] \underset{\sim}{\pi}$ $[\beta x \& (1 - \beta)y]$ if and only if $\alpha > \beta$.

Axiom 7.5: Intermediate Value

For any x, y, $z \in \tilde{B}$ if $x \, \pi \, y \, \pi \, z$ then there exists a unique $p \in (0, 1)$ such that $[px \, \& \, (1 - p)z] \sim y$.

Axiom 7.6: Boundedness

There exist an x^*, $y^* \in \tilde{B}$ such that $x^* \, \underline{\pi} \, z \, \underline{\pi} \, y^*$ for all $z \in \tilde{B}$.

Although these are the same six axioms, the alternatives set differs. The alternatives set is now composed of lottery tickets, *not* known outcomes. As in Chap. 2, we can now prove the following theorem:

Theorem 7.1: Existence of an Ordinal Utility Function

Given a preference relation π over the mixture set $\tilde{B}$ that satisfies axioms 7.1–7.6, there exists a utility function $U{:}\tilde{B} \to \mathbb{R}$ such that

(a) $x \, \pi \, y$ if and only if $U(x) > U(y)$ and

(b) $x \sim y$ if and only if $U(x) = U(y)$

Proof

Apply the proof of theorem 2.1 with & replacing +. We deal with lottery tickets $\tilde{B}$ instead of fractional combinations of elements of B. The mixture set postulates allow the use of the algebra employed on + to apply to &.   □

7.2. EXISTENCE OF CARDINAL UTILITY FUNCTIONS

If we stopped with the existence of an ordinal utility function, theorem 7.1, we could work through equilibrium pricing theory. Unfortunately, the resulting theory is not rich enough in terms of results. To develop the theory further, we impose an additional axiom:

Axiom 7.7: Strong Independence

For x, $y \in \tilde{B}$, if $x \, \pi \, y$ then for any $p \in (0, 1)$ and any $z \in \tilde{B}$ $[px \, \&(1 - p)z] \, \pi \, [py \, \& \, (1 - p)z]$.

Essentially, the strong independence axiom states that the introduction of uncertainty (through a lottery ticket) will not change preferences.[2] If an individual is indifferent between outcomes x and y, then she will be indifferent between a lottery ticket with probability p of getting outcome x and probability $1 - p$ of getting outcome z versus a lottery ticket with the same probabilities p and $1 - p$ with outcomes y and z, respectively. The only difference between the two lottery tickets is that the outcome x is replaced by an indifferent outcome y.

The strong independence axiom 7.7 is similar in appearance to the order-preserving axiom 7.4. However, the strong independence axiom is stronger. It can be shown that the strong independence axiom (together with axioms 7.1–7.3 and 7.5) actually implies the order-preserving axiom 7.4. So the order-preserving axiom 7.4 is now redundant.[3] For the subsequent analysis, we will assume the strong independence axiom 7.7 holds. Given this new axiom, we can obtain more than only the existence of an ordinal utility function as in theorem 7.1.

[2]This axiom implies that if $x \sim y$, then for all $p \in (0, 1)$ and any $z \in \bar{B}$

$$[px \ \& \ (1 - p)z] \sim [py \ \& \ (1 - p)z]$$

Proof

Suppose not. Suppose $[px \ \& \ (1 - p)z] \ \pi \ [py \ \& \ (1 - p)z]$. Then let $z = x$ and $p = r$ to get $x \ \pi \ [ry \ \& \ (1 - r)x]$ using postulate 2. Let $z = y$ and $p = (1 - r)$ to get $[(1 - r)x \ \& \ ry] \ \pi \ y$ using postulate 2. Use of postulate 3 gives $[ry \ \& \ (1 - r)x] \ \pi \ y$. By the transitivity axiom 7.3, $x \ \pi \ y$. Contradiction. $\square$

This fact will be used in the proof in Sec. 7.4.

[3]The proof that the strong independence axiom 7.7 implies the order-preserving axiom 7.4 follows. Let $x, y \in B$ be such that $x \ \pi \ y$. First, let $\alpha, \beta \in [0, 1]$ be such that $\alpha > \beta$. By postulate 2

$$y = \left[\left(\frac{\alpha - \beta}{1 - \beta} \right) y \ \& \ \left(\frac{1 - \alpha}{1 - \beta} \right) y \right]$$

Given $x \ \pi \ y$, by axiom 7.7

$$\left[\left(\frac{\alpha - \beta}{1 - \beta} \right) x \ \& \ \left(\frac{1 - \alpha}{1 - \beta} \right) y \right] \ \pi \ \left[\left(\frac{\alpha - \beta}{1 - \beta} \right) y \ \& \ \left(\frac{1 - \alpha}{1 - \beta} \right) y \right]$$

By substitution

$$\left[\left(\frac{\alpha - \beta}{1 - \beta} \right) x \ \& \ \left(\frac{1 - \alpha}{1 - \beta} \right) y \right] \ \pi \ y \qquad (\#)$$

By postulate 4

$$[\alpha x \ \& \ (1 - \alpha)y] = \left[\beta x \ \& \ (1 - \beta) \left[\frac{(\alpha - \beta)}{(1 - \beta)} x \ \& \ \frac{(1 - \alpha)}{(1 - \beta)} y \right] \right]$$

By axiom 7.7, since (#) is given

$$\left[\beta x \ \& \ (1 - \beta) \left[\left(\frac{\alpha - \beta}{1 - \beta} \right) x \ \& \ \left(\frac{1 - \alpha}{1 - \beta} \right) y \right] \right] \ \pi \ [\beta x \ \& \ (1 - \beta)y]$$

By substitution

Theorem 7.2: Existence of a Cardinal Utility Function[4]

Given a preference relation π over the mixture set $\tilde{B}$ that satisfies axioms 7.1–7.7, there exists a utility function $U:\tilde{B} \rightarrow \mathbb{R}$ such that

(a) $x \ \pi \ y$ if and only if $U(x) > U(y)$

(b) $x \sim y$ if and only if $U(x) = U(y)$

(c) Given $x, y \in \tilde{B}$ and $p \in [0, 1]$

$$U([px \ \& \ (1 - p)y]) = pU(x) + (1 - p)U(y)$$

Proof

See Sec. 7.4. □

The crux of the theorem is condition (c). In an abstract mathematical sense, it says that the utility function U is a linear function from $\tilde{B}$ to $\mathbb{R}$. Let us give condition (c) an economic interpretation. To do this, consider the lottery ticket $[px \ \& \ (1 - p)y]$. The utility measure of this lottery ticket is $U([px \ \& \ (1 - p)y])$, which is given by the left-hand side in (c). The right-hand side in (c) says that this is equal to $pU(x) + (1 - p)U(y)$, which is the *expected utility* of getting outcome x with probability p and outcome y with probability $(1 - p)$. Hence, to evaluate the utility of a lottery ticket, first the individual must rank each outcome using utilities. Second she must take the expected value of these utilities using the given probabilities. It is this property of the utility function that distinguishes it from an ordinal utility function derived without the use of the strong independence axiom.

The importance of this property can be made clearer if we put more structure on the alternatives set $\tilde{B}$.

Example 1   Discrete Probability Distribution

This example considers as the alternatives set all probability distributions over a finite set of outcomes, $\{x_1, \ldots, x_n\}$. Such probability distributions are often called *discrete* probability distributions. Formally, let

$$[\alpha x \ \& \ (1 - \alpha)y] \ \pi \ [\beta x \ \& \ (1 - \beta)y]$$

This is axiom 7.4.

Second, let $[\alpha x \ \& \ (1 - \alpha)y] \ \pi \ [\beta x \ \& \ (1 - \beta)y]$. Suppose $\beta \geq \alpha$. Then, by the previous step, $[\beta x \ \& \ (1 - \beta)y] \ \pi \ [\alpha x \ \& \ (1 - \alpha)y]$. Contradiction. Hence $\alpha > \beta$.

□

[4]In fact, the boundedness axiom 7.6 can easily be dropped at this point (see Owen [7, p. 120] for the proof). We include axiom 7.6 to make the derivation easier.

$$\bar{B} = \{\text{all probability distributions over the range}$$

$$X = \{x_1, \ldots, x_n\}\}$$

$$= \{\text{functions } q:X \to [0, 1] \quad \text{such that}$$

$$q(x_i) \geq 0 \quad \text{and} \quad \sum_{i=1}^{n} q(x_i) = 1\}$$

An alternative $q \in \bar{B}$ is seen to be a function mapping the outcomes $\{x_1, \ldots, x_n\}$ into a real number that is nonnegative and sums to one; i.e., q is a discrete probability density function. The individual chooses over these probability distributions.

In this situation, given $q_i, q_j \in \bar{B}$ and $p \in [0, 1]$, we define $[pq_i \& (1 - p)q_j] \equiv pq_i + (1 - p)q_j$. This definition specifies the operation $\&$ and the meaning of a lottery ticket. It is easy to show that this set $\bar{B}$, along with the operation $\&$, is a mixture set satisfying postulates 1–4.

Suppose we are given a preference relation π defined over $\bar{B}$ satisfying axioms 7.1–7.7; then, by theorem 7.2, there exists a utility function $U:\bar{B} \to \mathbb{R}$ such that for $q_i, q_j \in \bar{B}$ and $p \in [0, 1]$

$$U(pq_i + (1 - p)q_j) = pU(q_i) + (1 - p)U(q_j) \tag{7.2}$$

We now want to give this preference function U an alternative characterization, based on condition (7.2). Consider the elements $\delta_i \in \bar{B}$ defined by

$$\delta_i(x) = \begin{cases} 1 & \text{if } x = x_i \\ 0 & \text{otherwise} \end{cases} \tag{7.3}$$

for $i = 1, \ldots, n$. These discrete probability distributions are degenerate in that they isolate the certain outcome x_i with probability one. Next define $V:X \to \mathbb{R}$ by $V(x_i) \equiv U(\delta_i)$. This function V has as its domain the certain outcomes $X = \{x_1, \ldots, x_n\}$. Since $V(x_i)$ is the utility value of the lottery ticket with certain outcome x_i, this new function V is interpreted as the utility of the certain outcomes. It corresponds in an intuitive sense to the utility function studied in Chap. 2 in an economy under certainty.

Consider an arbitrary alternative $q \in \bar{B}$. Using the definition of the degenerate probability distributions in condition (7.3), we can rewrite the alternative q as

$$q(x) = \sum_{i=1}^{N} q(x_i)\delta_i(x)$$

To verify this expression, substitute x_j for x and use condition (7.3). We rewrite this expression as the sum of two terms:

$$q(x) = (1 - q(x_n))\left[\sum_{i=1}^{n-1} \frac{q(x_i)\delta_i(x)}{[1 - q(x_n)]}\right] + q(x_n)\delta_n(x)$$

Property (7.2) of the utility function can now be applied to give an alternate expression for the utility value of the alternative q.

$$U(q) = (1 - q(x_n))U\left(\sum_{i=1}^{n-1} \frac{q(x_i)}{(1 - q(x_n))} \delta_i\right) + q(x_n)U(\delta_n)$$

This represents the expected utility of the outcome $\sum_{i=1}^{n-1} (q(x_i)/(1 - q(x_n)))\delta_i$ and the outcome δ_n.

Now the outcome $\sum_{i=1}^{n-1} (q(x_i)/(1 - q(x_n)))\delta_i$ can also be rewritten as the sum of two terms:

$$(1 - q(x_{n-1}))\left[\sum_{i=1}^{n-2} \frac{q(x_i)}{(1 - q(x_n))(1 - q(x_{n-1}))} \delta_i\right] + \frac{q(x_{n-1})}{(1 - q(x_n))} \delta_{n-1}$$

Applying property (7.2) again yields another equivalent expression for the utility of the alternative q:

$$U(q) = (1 - q(x_n))(1 - q(x_{n-1})) U\left(\sum_{i=1}^{n-2} \frac{q(x_i)}{(1 - q(x_n))(1 - q(x_{n-1}))} \delta_i\right)$$
$$+ q(x_{n-1}) U(\delta_{n-1}) + q(x_n) U(\delta_n)$$

Applying this trick over and over again until there are no terms left gives

$$U(q) = \sum_{i=1}^{n} q(x_i) U(\delta_i)$$

The purpose of this procedure is to extend condition (7.2), the pairwise linearity of U, to finite sums (for $i = 1, \ldots, n$). The definition of the utility function over certain outcomes V gives the final characterization:

$$U(q) = \sum_{i=1}^{n} q(x_i) V(x_i) \tag{7.4a}$$
$$= E_q(V(x)) \tag{7.4b}$$

where $E_q(\cdot)$ is expectation with respect to the discrete probability distribution $q \in \tilde{B}$.

The right side of condition (7.4) is the expected utility using the utility function V over the certain outcomes. This identity, called the *expected utility hypothesis*, asserts that we can view utility theory under uncertainty as a two-stage process:

(i) first take the utility function V of the certain outcomes $\{x_1, \ldots, x_n\}$, and

(ii) then take the expectation of these utility values using the probabilities associated with the probability distribution $q \in \tilde{B}$.

Step (i) reduces the problem to a world of certainty, and step (ii) introduces the probabilities in a convenient manner. This procedure will give the identical ranking of the alternatives $q \in \tilde{B}$ as using the utility function U, which is defined directly over the probability distributions $\tilde{B}$. So, to evaluate preferences, sufficient information is the preferences over certain outcomes $V: X \to \mathbb{R}$ and the probabilities of the lottery tickets $q \in \tilde{B}$.   □

A specific application of example 1 may clarify the usefulness of the expected utility hypothesis.

Example 2   Numeric Application of Example 1

Let $\bar{B}$ = {all probability distributions over {\$10, \$1, \$15, \$$-$5}}, and let the individual's utility function defined over the certain outcomes be a quadratic function:

$$V(x) = 20x - (1/2)x^2$$

Now consider the two lottery tickets;

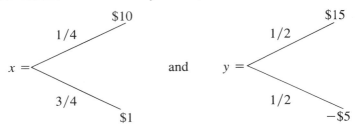

The utility levels for these two lottery tickets are determined by knowing {$V(10)$, $V(1)$, $V(15)$, $V(-5)$} and the stated probabilities of the two lottery tickets. The expected values of the utility outcomes rank the tickets.

$$U(x) = 1/4 \ V(10) + 3/4 \ V(1)$$
$$= 1/4 \ (150) + 3/4 \ (19.5) = 52.125$$
$$U(y) = 1/2 \ V(15) + 1/2 \ V(-5)$$
$$= 1/2 \ (197.5) + 1/2 \ (-112.5) = 42.5$$

Since $U(x) > U(y)$, the investor prefers x to y.   □

Examples 1 and 2 provide all the intuition underlying the theory and applications of the expected utility hypothesis. For the applications in this text, however, discrete probability distributions as the choice set is too restrictive. For this reason, the next example generalizes the expected utility hypothesis to general probability distributions. The example is starred because the mathematics employed is more difficult than that used elsewhere in this chapter. It can be omitted without loss of content.

*Example 3   General Probability Distributions

Example 3 generalizes example 1 from discrete distributions to arbitrary distributions over the range space $\mathbb{R}$. These include discrete as well as continuous probability distributions.

Let $\bar{B}$ = {all probability distributions over the range $X = \mathbb{R}$}. Given q_i, $q_j \in \bar{B}$ and $p \in [0, 1]$, define $[pq_i \ \& \ (1 - p)q_j] \equiv pq_i + (1 - p)q_j$. This defines the operation & on $\tilde{B}$ as corresponding to ordinary addition and multiplication by constants. The set $\tilde{B}$, together with this definition for & on $\tilde{B}$, is easily seen to be a mixture set.

Given a preference relation π over $\tilde{B}$ satisfying axioms 7.1–7.7, by theorem 7.2, we know there exists a utility function $U:\tilde{B} \rightarrow \mathbb{R}$ such that for $q_i, q_j \in \tilde{B}$ and $p \in [0, 1]$

$$U(pq_i + (1 - p)q_j) = pU(q_i) + (1 - p)U(q_j) \qquad (7.5)$$

Because the set $X = \mathbb{R}$ underlying $\tilde{B}$ contains an uncountably infinite number of elements, the same argument utilized in example 1 to generate the expected utility hypothesis will not go through. For this reason, we need an additional axiom. This axiom will essentially generate the expected utility hypothesis. This axiom states that if q_n converges to q in distribution, then $U(q_n)$ converges to $U(q)$; i.e., U is continuous over $\tilde{B}$.[5]

Axiom 7.8: Continuity

If q_n converges in distribution to q where $q_n, q \in \tilde{B}$, then $\lim_{n \to \infty} U(q_n) = U(q)$.

Convergence in distribution means that Prob $[x \le a:q_n]$ converges to Prob $[x \le a:q]$ for all continuity points $a \in \mathbb{R}$ of Prob $[x \le a:q]$ (see Billingsley [1, p. 17]). Informally, convergence in distribution tells us when two lottery tickets are approximately the same. The continuity axiom 7.8 therefore states that if two lottery tickets are approximately the same, then they are given approximately the same value in terms of utility. It is a continuity assumption on preferences. Under this assumption it can be shown that the expected utility hypothesis holds.[6]

---

[5]Technically, $\tilde{B}$ is the set of all probability measures defined over the measure space:

$$(\mathbb{R}, \text{Borel } \sigma\text{-algebra over } \mathbb{R})$$

Let $\tilde{B}$ have the topology of weak convergence (see Billingsley [1, p. 236]). This continuity axiom could be replaced by

$$\text{for} \qquad p \in [0, 1] \quad \text{and} \quad x, y \in \tilde{B},$$

$$\{z \in \tilde{B} : px + (1 - p)y \ \pi \ z\} \quad \text{and}$$

$$\{z \in \tilde{B} : z \ \pi \ px + (1 - p)y\}$$

are closed in the topology of $\tilde{B}$ (see Debreu [3]).

[6]A sketch of the proof of condition (7.6) now follows. The details are omitted. Take an arbitrary $q \in \tilde{B}$. By Billingsley [1, theorem 4, p. 236], there exists a sequence $y_n \in \tilde{B}$ such that

$$y_n(x) = \sum_{i=1}^{n} \lambda_i \delta_{x_i}(x) \quad \text{where}$$

$$U(q) = E_q(V(x)) \quad \text{for all } q \in \tilde{B} \tag{7.6}$$

where $E_q(\cdot)$ equals the expectation operator using the probability distribution q. The utility function V over the certain outcomes in x, $V:\mathbb{R} \to \mathbb{R}$, is defined by

$$V(x) \equiv U(\delta_x(y)) \quad \text{for all } x \in \mathbb{R}$$

where

$$\delta_x(y) = \begin{cases} 0 & \text{if } y < x \\ 1 & \text{if } y \geq x \end{cases}$$

The degenerate cumulative probability distribution $\delta_x(y)$ gives the outcome x probability one of occurring. Hence the function $V(x) = U(\delta_x(y))$ is the utility function for the certain outcome $x \in \mathbb{R}$. The continuity axiom 7.8 also implies that V is continuous.[7]

In summary, under the continuity axiom 7.8, the utility function $U:\tilde{B} \to \mathbb{R}$ can be characterized through expression (7.6) as the expected utility $E_q(V(x))$ over the certain outcomes $x \in \mathbb{R}$. This result generalizes easily to arbitrary probability distributions over n-dimensional spaces $\mathbb{R}^n$. We will utilize the result for $n = 2$ in subsequent chapters. $\square$

The last issue to be addressed in this section is the nonuniqueness of the utility function U. Glancing back at example 2, it is easily seen that the utility function V defined over the certain outcomes is not unique. For example, $V^*(x) = 5[20\,x - (1/2)x^2]$ will also duplicate the individual's rankings. This implies that the utility function U defined over the alternatives set $\tilde{B}$ also is not unique. In fact, it can be shown that the utility function is only unique up to multiplication by a positive constant plus addition of another arbitrary constant. Such a transformation is called an *affine transformation*. This observation is formalized in the following corollary.

Corollary 7.2

If $U:\tilde{B} \to \mathbb{R}$ and $W:\tilde{B} \to \mathbb{R}$ are two utility functions for the preference $\underline{\pi}$, then there exist real numbers $\delta > 0$ and α such that

$$U(x) = \delta W(y) + \alpha$$

$$\delta_{x_i}(x) = \begin{cases} 0 & \text{if } x < x_i \\ 1 & \text{if } x \geq x_i \end{cases}$$

for $i = 1, \ldots, n$, $x_i \in \mathbb{R}$, $\sum_{i=1}^{n} \lambda_i = 1$, $\lambda_i > 0$ and $\lim_{n \to \infty} y_n = q$ in distribution. Now $\lim_{n \to \infty} U(y_n) = U(q)$ by axiom 7.8. But $U(y_n) = \sum_{i=1}^{n} \lambda_i U(\delta_{x_i}) = \int_{\mathbb{R}} V(x) dy_n$. V is bounded by axiom 7.6 since $V(x) = U(\delta_x)$ and U is bounded. Since V is continuous (see footnote 7) and bounded, by the definition of weak convergence, $\lim_{n \to \infty} U(y_n) = \int_{\mathbb{R}} V(x) dq(x)$ (see Billingsley [1, p. 11]). So $E_q(V(x)) = U(q)$. $\square$

[7]To show this, take $x_n \in \mathbb{R}$ to converge to $x \in \mathbb{R}$. Then $\delta_{x_n}(y)$ converges in distribution to $\delta_x(y)$, so by axiom 7.8, $U(\delta_{x_n}) \to U(\delta_x)$ or $V(x_n) \to V(x)$.

Proof

See Sec. 7.4.   □

The relation between the two utility functions U and W can be represented by a function $G:\mathbb{R} \rightarrow \mathbb{R}$ given by $G(r) = \delta r + \alpha$, which transforms the utility function W to U. This transformation is a positive monotonic transformation like that employed in Chap. 2 with ordinal utilities. The introduction of the strong independence axiom 7.7, however, further restricts the class of possible transformations to those given in the corollary. An element from this resulting class of equivalent utility functions is called a *cardinal* utility function.

This nonuniqueness of the utility function is important because it implies that utility levels cannot be compared across individuals. Indeed, if a person called Ann has a utility level $U_a(x) = 10$ for lottery ticket x, while a person called Bob has a utility level $U_b(x) = 20$, it does not mean Bob likes x twice as much as Ann. The reason is that $U_a^* = 2U_a$ is also an acceptable utility function for Ann where $U_a^*(x) = 20$. Using U^* for Ann instead of U, a comparison of utilities of Ann and Bob again would imply that Ann also likes x the same as Bob. Both assertions cannot be true.

There is a utility-based measure that can be compared across individuals. Consider the situation where the utility function's value over certain outcomes, V, maps the real line into itself (as in example 3). Given $V:\mathbb{R} \rightarrow \mathbb{R}$, define $A_h:\mathbb{R} \rightarrow \mathbb{R}$ as the ratio

$$A_h(x) = -\frac{V(x + h) + V(x - h) - 2V(x)}{V(x + h) - V(x)} \quad \text{for any } h > 0$$

This ratio can be compared across individuals. To prove this, note that given a positive affine transformation $G(r) = \delta r + \alpha$, as in corollary 7.2

$$-\frac{GoV(x + h) + GoV(x - h) - 2GoV(x)}{GoV(x + h) - GoV(x)}$$

$$= -\frac{\delta[V(x + h) + V(x - h) - 2V(x)]}{\delta[V(x + h) - V(x)]} = A_h(x)$$

Hence this ratio is *unique* for a class of cardinal utility functions because it is independent of the transformation given in corollary 7.2. If V is twice differentiable, then this ratio (after normalizing) simplifies by taking a limit:[8]

---

[8]To prove this

$$\lim_{h \to 0} A_h(x)/h = \lim_{h \to 0} -\frac{\dfrac{V(x + h) + V(x - h) - 2V(x)}{h^2}}{\dfrac{V(x + h) - V(x)}{h}} = -\frac{V''(x)}{V(x)}$$

We use the fact that

$$A(x) \equiv \lim_{h\to 0} A_h(x)/h = -\frac{V''(x)}{V(x)} \tag{8.4}$$

We will return to this measure in Chap. 14. At that time it will be shown that $A(x)$ is a local measure of an individual's aversion to risk.

7.3. THE CONSUMPTION-SAVING MODEL

This section applies the utility theory under uncertainty to the consumption-saving decision. This model forms the basis for both the arbitrage and equilibrium pricing theories explored in the remainder of the text. The approach is analogous to the consumption-saving model developed in Sec. 2.3. There is one generalization, however: Instead of choosing known quantities of consumption at time 1, the individual will now choose probability distributions over consumption at time 1. The purpose of this section is to clarify the meaning of this statement.

7.3.1. Preliminaries

We consider an economy that consists of only two time periods: today (denoted by time 0) and tomorrow (denoted by time 1). Individuals appear an "instant" before time 0, consume at both times 0 and 1, and then disappear an "instant" after time 1. Only a single consumption good is available in the economy. We think of this single consumption good as a composite basket of commodities where the same basket is consumed by all individuals.

The set of alternatives $\tilde{B}$ that the individual has preferences over is defined to be the set of all probability distributions over consumption at times 0 and 1. Formally

$\tilde{B} = \{$all joint probability distributions over (C_0, C_1) where $C_0 \in \mathbb{R}$ and $C_1 \in \mathbb{R}\}$

In this definition

C_0 represents the units of the consumption good consumed at time 0, and
C_1 represents the units of the consumption good consumed at time 1.

$$\lim_{h\to 0} \frac{V(x+h) + V(x-h) - 2V(x)}{h^2} = V''(x)$$

(See Rudin [8, Example 11, p. 115].)

The alternatives set $\tilde{B}$ is easily seen to be a mixture set, given that we define the operation & by

$$[pq_1 \ \& \ (1-p)q_2] \equiv pq_1 + (1-p)q_2$$

for $p \in [0, 1]$ and $q_1, q_2 \in \tilde{B}$. This operation corresponds to forming "compound" lottery tickets from "simple" lottery tickets.

Assuming that the preferences π of the individual over the choice set $\tilde{B}$ satisfy the rationality axioms 7.1–7.7, by theorem 7.2, there exists a cardinal utility function $U:\tilde{B} \to \mathbb{R}$. Given that the strong independence axiom holds, we now characterize the utility function U in terms of the expected utility criterion.

Consider the function $V:\mathbb{R}^2 \to \mathbb{R}$ representing the value of U under the certain outcomes $\{(C_0, C_1):C_0 \in \mathbb{R} \text{ and } C_1 \in \mathbb{R}\}$. This function will be denoted by $V(C_0, C_1)$. We now add one final assumption.

Axiom 7.8: Continuity

If q_n converges in distribution to q, where $q_n, q \in \tilde{B}$, then $\lim_{n \to \infty} U(q_n) = U(q)$.

This axiom essentially asserts that the utility function U is continuous with respect to convergence of probability distributions. Given this continuity axiom and condition (c) of theorem 7.2, it can be shown[9] that the utility function U over the lottery tickets $\tilde{B}$ is representable as in the expected utility hypothesis:

$$U(b) = E_b(V(C_0, C_1)) \quad \text{for all } b \in \tilde{B} \tag{7.8}$$

where $E_b(\cdot)$ represents expectation with respect to the probability distribution $b \in \tilde{B}$. The continuity axiom is added solely to obtain condition (7.8). Condition (7.8) need not hold without the continuity axiom. Its economic interpretation is discussed in example 3 in Sec. 7.2.

The utility rank $U(b)$ is seen to be equal to the quantity $E_b(V(C_0, C_1))$, which is the expected utility V of the certain outcomes (C_0, C_1), given a specified probability distribution $b \in \tilde{B}$. Recall that each lottery ticket $b \in \tilde{B}$ is identified with a unique probability distribution over the certain outcomes $C_0 \in \mathbb{R}$ and $C_1 \in \mathbb{R}$.

In contrast to the certainty model of Sec. 2.3 in Chap. 2, this chapter replaces known consumption at times 0 and 1 with a probability distribution over consumption at times 0 and 1. For the remainder of the text, we will work with the expected utility hypothesis representation as given in condition (7.8).

As an aside, it should be pointed out that this model could easily be generalized in a straightforward manner to a multiperiod model with consumption at each date. This observation will be relevant in Chap. 17, which discusses multiperiod capital asset pricing models.

[9]The same proof as in footnote 6 works.

7.3.2. Monotonic Preferences

Given the expected utility hypothesis, condition (7.8), we see that when modeling consumption-saving behavior, sufficient information is

(i) the cardinal utility function $V(C_0, C_1)$ over the certain outcomes (C_0, C_1), and

(ii) the probability distribution over consumption: Prob $[C_0 \leq z_0, C_1 \leq z_1; b]$ for $z_0, z_1 \in \mathbb{R}$. This probability distribution depends on the chosen $b \in \tilde{B}$.

We will impose an additional property on the utility function called *monotonicity*. The belief is that a consumer always prefers more to less. We apply the assumption directly on $V(C_0, C_1)$.

Assumption 7.1: Monotonicity

Given $\delta > 0, C_0 \in \mathbb{R}$ and $C_1 \in \mathbb{R}$

then

$$V(C_0 + \delta, C_1) > V(C_0, C_1)$$

and

$$V(C_0, C_1 + \delta) > V(C_0, C_1)$$

Increasing the known consumption in any time period increases the individual's welfare. This assumption, surprisingly enough, is identical to that given in Sec. 2.3. Fortunately, the ability to transform the model of uncertainty to one under certainty by taking expectations allows the knowledge developed for the certainty case to carry forward.

7.4. PROOFS OF THEOREM 7.2 AND COROLLARY 7.2

This section contains the proofs of theorem 7.2 and corollary 7.2. The original proof can be found in Herstein and Milnor [4], which drops the boundedness axiom 7.6. For another proof under a slightly modified set of assumptions, see Debreu [3].

7.4.1. Proof of Theorem 7.2

Both parts (a) and (b) follow by theorem 7.1, which was proved in the text. We will utilize the utility function constructed in the proof of theorem 7.1. For easy reference, we repeat it here.

Let $x^*, y^* \in \tilde{B}$ be such that $x^* \pi y^*$ and $x^* \underset{\sim}{\pi} z \underset{\sim}{\pi} y^*$ for all $z \in \tilde{B}$. $U:\tilde{B} \rightarrow \mathbb{R}$ was defined by

$$U(z) = \begin{cases} 1 & \text{if } z \sim x^* \\ \alpha & \text{if } x^* \ \pi \ z \ \pi \ y^*, \text{ where } \alpha \ \epsilon \ (0, 1) \\ & \text{uniquely satisfies } [\alpha x^* \ \& \ (1 - \alpha)y^*] \sim z \\ 0 & \text{if } z \sim y^* \end{cases}$$

where U satisfies conditions (a) and (b).

Proof of Part (c)

Consider arbitrary $z_1, z_2 \ \epsilon \ \bar{B}$ such that $z_1 \ \pi \ z_2$. (If $z_1 \sim z_2$, then $[pz_1 \ \& \ (1 - p)z_2] \sim [pz_1 \ \& \ (1 - p)z_1] = z_1$ by the strong independence axiom 7.7 and postulate 2. Hence

$$U([pz_1 \ \& \ (1 - p)z_2]) = U(z_1) = pU(z_1) + (1 - p)U(z_1)$$
$$= pU(z_1) + (1 - p)U(z_2)$$

since $U(z_1) = U(z_2)$).

There are four cases to be considered.

Case N1. $z_1 \sim x^* \ \pi \ z_2 \ \pi \ y^*$. Now $[pz_1 \ \& \ (1 - p)z_2] \sim [px^* \ \& \ (1 - p)z_2]$ by the strong independence axiom 7.7. Also, $z_2 \sim [\alpha_2 x^* \ \& \ (1 - \alpha_2)y^*]$ for a unique $\alpha_2 \ \epsilon \ (0, 1)$ by the intermediate value axiom 7.5. Applying axiom 7.7 again gives

$$[pz_1 \ \& \ (1 - p)z_2] \sim [px^* \ \& \ (1 - p)[\alpha_2 x^* \ \& \ (1 - \alpha_2)y^*]]$$

Using postulate 4

$$[pz_1 \ \& \ (1 - p)z_2] \sim [(p + (1 - p)\alpha_2)x^* \ \& \ (1 - (p + (1 - p)\alpha_2))\,y^*]$$

Hence, by definition of U

$$U([(p + (1 - p)\alpha_2)x^* \ \& \ (1 - (p + (1 - p)\alpha_2))\,y^*]) = p + (1 - p)\alpha_2$$

But

$$U(z_1) = 1 \quad \text{and} \quad U(z_2) = \alpha_2$$

Hence

$$U([pz_1 \ \& \ (1 - p)z_2]) = U([(p + (1 - p)\alpha_2)x^* \ \& \ (1 - (p + (1 - p)\alpha_2))y^*])$$
$$= p + (1 - p)\alpha_2 = pU(z_1) + (1 - p)U(z_2)$$

Case N2. $z_1 \sim x^* \ \pi \ z_2 \sim y^*$. Given $\beta \ \epsilon \ [0, 1]$, $[\beta z_1 \ \& \ (1 - \beta)z_2] \sim [\beta x^* \ \& \ (1 - \beta)y^*]$ by two applications of axiom 7.7. Hence

$$U([\beta z_1 \ \& \ (1 - \beta)z_2]) = U([\beta x^* \ \& \ (1 - \beta)y^*])$$
$$= \beta = \beta U(z_1) + (1 - \beta)U(z_2)$$

since $U(z_1) = 1$ and $U(z_2) = 0$.

Case N3. $x^* \; \pi \; z_1 \; \pi \; z_2 \; \pi \; y^*$. By axiom 7.5

$$z_1 \sim [\alpha_1 x^* \; \& \; (1 - \alpha_1) y^*] \quad \text{for a unique } \alpha_1 \in (0, 1)$$

$$z_2 \sim [\alpha_2 x^* \; \& \; (1 - \alpha_2) y^*] \quad \text{for a unique } \alpha_2 \in (0, 1)$$

Consider $[\beta z_1 \; \& \; (1 - \beta) z_2]$ for $\beta \in (0, 1)$. By axiom 7.7 and postulate 4

$$[\beta z_1 \; \& \; (1 - \beta) z_2] \sim [(\beta \alpha_1 + (1 - \beta) \alpha_2) x^* \; \& \; (1 - (\beta \alpha_1 + (1 - \beta) \alpha_2) y^*])$$

So

$$U([\beta z_1 \; \& \; (1 - \beta) z_2])$$

$$= U([(\beta \alpha_1 + (1 - \beta) \alpha_2) x^* \; \& \; (1 - \beta \alpha_1 - (1 - \beta) \alpha_2) y^*])$$

$$= \beta \alpha_1 + (1 - \beta) \alpha_2 \quad \text{by definition of } U$$

$$= \beta U(z_1) + (1 - \beta) U(z_2)$$

Case N4. $x^* \; \pi \; z_1 \; \pi \; z_2 \sim y^*$. Consider for $\beta \in [0, 1]$, $[\beta z_1 \; \& (1 - \beta) z_2]$. Now $z_1 \sim [\alpha_1 x^* \; \& \; (1 - \alpha_1) y^*]$ for a unique $\alpha_1 \in (0, 1)$ by axiom 7.5. By axiom 7.7 and postulate 4

$$[\beta z_1 \; \& \; (1 - \beta) z_2] \sim [(\beta \alpha_1) x^* \; \& \; (1 - \beta \alpha_1) y^*]$$

So

$$U([\beta z_1 \; \& \; (1 - \beta) z_2]) = U([(\beta \alpha_1) x^* \; \& \; (1 - \beta \alpha_1) y^*])$$

$$= \beta \alpha_1$$

$$= \beta U(z_1) + (1 - \beta) U(z_2)$$

since $U(z_2) = 0$.

This completes the proof of part (c). □

7.4.2 Proof of Corollary 7.2

Suppose $W : \tilde{B} \to \mathbb{R}$ and $U : \tilde{B} \to \mathbb{R}$ are two functions satisfying (a), (b), and (c). Let $W : \tilde{B} \to \mathbb{R}$ be the function constructed in the proof of theorem 7.2. We claim there exists $\delta_u > 0$ and $\alpha_u \in \mathbb{R}$ such that

$$U(z) = \delta_u W(z) + \alpha_u \quad \text{for all } z \in \tilde{B}$$

Proof of Claim

Define $\delta_u \equiv U(x^*) - U(y^*)$ and $\alpha_u = U(y^*)$, where x^*, y^* are identified in the boundedness axiom 7.6. Note that $\delta_u > 0$, since $x^* \; \pi \; y^*$. We will show that $U(z) = \delta_u W(z) + \alpha_u$ for any $z \in \tilde{B}$. There are three cases.

Case 1. $z \sim x^*$. Here $W(z) = 1$ and $U(z) = U(x^*)$, so

$$U(z) = [U(x^*) - U(y^*)] + U(y^*)$$
$$= [U(x^*) - U(y^*)]W(z) + U(y^*)$$
$$= \delta_u W(z) + \alpha_u$$

Case 2. $x^* \pi z \pi y^*$. By definition, $W(z) = \alpha$, where $[\alpha x^* \& (1 - \alpha)y^*] \sim z$ for a unique $\alpha \epsilon (0, 1)$. Now

$$U(z) = \alpha U(x^*) + (1 - \alpha)U(y^*) \quad \text{by part (c) of theorem 7.2}$$
$$= [U(x^*) - U(y^*)]\alpha + U(y^*)$$
$$= \delta_u W(z) + \alpha_u$$

Case 3. $z \sim y^*$. Here $W(z) = 0$ and $U(z) = U(y^*)$, so

$$U(z) = 0 + U(y^*)$$
$$= \delta_u W(z) + \alpha_u$$

This completes the proof. $\square$

7.5. SUMMARY

This chapter constructs cardinal utility theory under uncertainty using a parallel development to that in Chap. 2. The set of alternatives $\tilde{B}$ consists of lottery tickets whose outcomes occur with known probabilities. Assuming the alternatives set is a mixture set, i.e., satisfying postulates 1–4, and that the individual's preferences defined over $\tilde{B}$ satisfy the same six rationality axioms as in Chap. 2, we obtain the existence of an ordinal utility function.

To generate a richer theory, however, we add another axiom. This axiom is called the strong independence axiom and asserts that for $x, y \epsilon \tilde{B}$, if $x \pi y$, then for any $p \epsilon (0, 1)$ and $z \epsilon \tilde{B}$, the lottery ticket $[px \& (1 - p)z]$ is preferred to $[py \& (1 - p)z]$. In essence, uncertainty itself doesn't change preferences. This additional axiom leads to the existence of a cardinal utility function.

Two concrete examples are provided to emphasize the richness of this additional axiom. The first is where the choice set consists of all distributions over a finite set of outcomes. The second example consists of all distributions over the real line $\mathbb{R}$. It is shown that for the first example, under no additional assumptions, the utility function has an expected utility representation. For the second example, however, we need to add the additional axiom of continuity to get the expected utility hypothesis.

Finally, the construction of a cardinal utility function is specialized to the consumption-saving model. The consumption-saving model generalizes the model of Chap. 2 by introducing uncertainty over the possible consumption pairs. This model forms the basis of the arbitrage pricing and equilibrium pricing models formulated in subsequent chapters.

7.6. REFERENCES

1. Billingsley, Patrick, *Convergence of Probability Measures*. New York: John Wiley, 1968.
2. Breiman, Leo, *Probability*. Reading, Mass.: Addison-Wesley, 1968.
3. Debreu, G., *Theory of Value*. New Haven, Conn.: Yale University Press, 1959.
4. Herstein, I., and John Milnor, "An Axiomatic Approach to Measurable Utility," *Econometrica*, 21 (1953), 291–297.
5. Jarrow, Robert, "An Integrated Axiomatic Approach to the Existence of Ordinal and Cardinal Utility Functions," *Theory and Decision*, 22 (1987).
6. Kelley, John, *General Topology*. New York: Springer-Verlag, 1955.
7. Owen, Gulliermo, *Game Theory*, 2nd ed. Orlando, Fla.: Academic Press, 1982.
8. Rudin, Walter, *Principles of Mathematical Analysis*. New York: McGraw-Hill, 1976.

8

THE ASSET MODEL

This chapter presents the arbitrage pricing methodology in an uncertain environment, generalizing the theory presented in Chap. 3. It is surprising how similar the two analyses are. The same concepts and arguments are employed, the only difference being the introduction of uncertainty and the use of probability theory.

The arbitrage pricing methodology has a very simple objective: to price a set of traded assets using the prices of another set of traded assets. This chapter presents the theory in its most general form. Consequently, this chapter forms the basic insights underlying numerous areas of study in finance, including Ross's arbitrage pricing theory (Chaps. 9 and 18), dividend policy theory (Chap. 10), debt/equity policy theory (Chap. 11), bond pricing (Chap. 12), and option pricing theory (Chap. 13). In order that the development be rich enough to incorporate these numerous applications, we introduce from probability theory the concepts of a state space and an event set. These ideas are motivated through numeric examples. Footnotes will keep the presentation rigorous.

The utility theory of Chap. 7 enters the arbitrage pricing methodology only indirectly. It motivates the crucial assumption that excludes the existence of arbitrage opportunities. Later, in Chap. 14, a series of alternative assumptions on preferences and market structures is presented that implies the absence of

---

The material in this chapter on arbitrage pricing theory is based on ideas contained in Jarrow [4], Ross [5, 6], and Harrison and Kreps [2].

arbitrage opportunities in the asset model. Chapter 14 also serves as the link to the equilibrium pricing theory, discussed in subsequent chapters.

8.1. PRELIMINARIES

This model will have two time periods, represented by today (time 0) and tomorrow (time 1). The economy is uncertain at time 1. The uncertainty in the economy is characterized by a set of possible states, denoted by Ω, any one of which could occur. A state should be thought of as a complete description of the conditions prevailing in the economy at time 1. This set of states, Ω, is called the *state space*. A particular state is indicated by $\omega \in \Omega$. The states and their descriptions are unrestricted.

Assets will be assumed to trade in an organized market at time 0. An asset obtains its value (or price) at time 0 because it provides a cash flow *denominated in dollars* at time 1 under each possible state $\omega \in \Omega$. This cash flow can be interpreted as the "liquidating value" plus any "dividends" received on the asset at time 1 under state $\omega \in \Omega$. The notation for an arbitrary asset is $x(\omega)$, which represents the cash flow in dollars to asset x at time 1 given state ω occurs. Therefore, an asset can be characterized as a function mapping the state space Ω into cash flows; i.e., $x : \Omega \to \mathbb{R}$. The set of assets trading in the market at time 0 is indicated by the symbol M, for *marketed* assets. Formally, M is a subset of the set of functions mapping the state space Ω into the real numbers (which represent the cash flow in dollars at time 1). We assume the following:

Assumption 8.1: Marketed Assets

If x, $y \in M$ and α, $\beta \in \mathbb{R}$, then $\alpha x + \beta y \in M$.

This assumption puts structure on the set of assets that trade. It states that if assets x and y trade, then a portfolio consisting of α units of asset x and β units of asset y also trades as a *package*.[1] This assumption and the next correspond to the homogeneous beliefs assumption 3.1 of Chap. 3. The difference here is that we must condition on the uncertain state ω; otherwise, the structure is identical.

We assume that the economy is populated with a finite number of investors who satisfy:

Assumption 8.2: Conditioned Homogeneous Beliefs

Given a traded asset $x \in M$, every investor agrees that $x(\omega)$ is the time 1 dollar cash flow to asset x under state ω.

---

[1] M is a linear subspace of $\mathbb{R}^{\Omega} = \{$functions mapping $\Omega \to \mathbb{R}\}$.

Conditioned upon a particular state $\omega \in \Omega$, all investors agree on the time 1 cash flows to all the assets that trade.

The assets that trade, through their cash flows, reveal partial information about the actual state of Ω that has occurred at time 1. This happens because knowledge of how an asset's cash flow differs across states, combined with the actual cash flows at time 1, yields by backward deduction which state or set of states occurred. This information set, denoted by $\sigma(M)$, represents the collections of states that the assets' time 1 cash flows can discriminate.[2] An example will help clarify this concept.

Example 1   Description of the Information Set $\sigma(M)$

Let the state space consist of four possible states, $\Omega = \{1, 2, 3, 4\}$. They represent the four relevant conditions of the economy's health, perhaps $1 = $ "poor," $2 = $ "fair," $3 = $ "good," and $4 = $ "excellent."

Let x_i for $i = 1, 2$ be two different traded assets with payoffs as given in the accompanying table. Asset 1 pays \$5 in states 1 and 2 and \$10 in states 3 and 4. Asset 2 pays \$3 in states 1, 3, and 4 but \$6 in state 2. The set of marketed assets is $M = \{\alpha x_1 + \beta x_2 : \alpha, \beta \in \mathbb{R}\}$ and equals all portfolios consisting of α shares of asset 1 and β shares of asset 2. An $\alpha < 0$ or $\beta < 0$ represents a short sale or liability, whereas an $\alpha > 0$ or $\beta > 0$ represents a purchase.

states (ω)	$x_1(\omega)$	$x_2(\omega)$
1	5	3
2	5	6
3	10	3
4	10	3

To construct the information set generated by M, consider yourself standing at time 1. Suppose that you observe the cash flows of $x_1 = \$5$ and $x_2 = \$6$. This information tells you that state 2 must have occurred, since it is the only state yielding these two cash flows. So $\{2\} \in \sigma(M)$. Suppose, instead, that you observe the cash flows of $x_1 = \$5$ and $x_2 = \$3$. This implies that state 1 has occurred, so $\{1\} \in \sigma(M)$. Finally, suppose that you observe the cash flows of $x_1 = \$10$ and $x_2 = \$3$. This implies that either state 3 or state 4 has occurred, so $\{3, 4\} \in \sigma(M)$. You cannot discriminate, however, between states 3 and 4 by using only the knowledge of the time 1 cash flows. Furthermore, additional knowledge about portfolio cash flows at time 1 will not increase your ability to discriminate which states have actually occurred. Hence the information set constructed is

$$\sigma(M) = \{\varnothing, \{1, 2, 3, 4\}, \{1\}, \{2\}, \{3, 4\}, \{1, 2\}, \{1, 3, 4\}, \{2, 3, 4\}\}$$

These represent the *events* (collections of states) that we know at time 1 whether

---

[2] $\sigma(M)$ is the smallest σ-algebra of Ω generated by the functions $M \subset \mathbb{R}^\Omega$.

or not they occurred. We include the sets $\{1, 2, 3, 4\}$, $\{1, 3, 4\}$, and $\{2, 3, 4\}$ since we know whether these events have occurred because they represent unions of the sets analyzed earlier. Finally, the empty set $\varnothing$ is included for technical reasons. $\square$

The set of *events* $\sigma(M)$ is introduced in order to discuss the investor's probability beliefs. It is included to handle "paradoxical" situations where the state space Ω consists of an uncountably infinite number of states (like the real line); a single state by itself has a zero probability of occurring, and yet some state must occur. The method of dealing with this paradoxical situation is to assign probabilities not to states but to collections of states, or events. This approach underlies the distinction between discrete probability distributions and continuous probability distributions. Since most of the models in this text concern state spaces with more than a finite number of states, we employ this generalized technology.

We assume, therefore, that each investor has a probability distribution over the events H contained in $\sigma(M)$, denoted by $\text{Prob}_i(H)$. This stands for individual i's *subjective* probability that the event $H \in \sigma(M)$ will occur.[3]

We need to impose some homogeneity on these probability beliefs across investors:

Assumption 8.3: Unconditioned Beliefs

Given an event $H \in \sigma(M)$, $\text{Prob}_i(H) = 0$ if and only if $\text{Prob}_j(H) = 0$ for all investors i, j.

This assumption states that investors agree on zero probability events. They need not agree, however, on the absolute magnitudes of the probabilities for nonzero probability events. Consequently, investors need not agree about expected values or variances of the assets' cash flows. It will be seen later that this assumption guarantees that all investors agree on the identification of "arbitrage opportunities." This is the motivation underlying the imposition of assumption 8.3.

Example 1   Probability Beliefs: Revisited

Recall from example 1 that the relevant events deducible from the traded assets' time 1 cash flows are $\{1\}$, $\{2\}$, and $\{34\}$. Consider introducing investors a and b with the probability beliefs given in the accompanying table. The column under $\text{Prob}_a(H)$ gives person a's probability beliefs over the states $H \in \sigma(M)$; person b's probability beliefs are given under the column $\text{Prob}_b(H)$. The investors disagree in their subjective probability beliefs about the relative like-

---

[3] $(\Omega, \sigma(M), \text{Prob}_i)$ is a probability space, where $\text{Prob}_i : \sigma(M) \to [0, 1]$ is a probability measure. We assume that $\sigma(M)$ is complete with respect to Prob_i for all i; i.e., $\sigma(M)$ includes all subsets of sets $H \in \sigma(M)$ of $\text{Prob}_i(H) = 0$.

lihood of the individual events. These beliefs satisfy the unconditional beliefs assumption 8.3, since if a's probability is nonzero, then so is b's.

H	$\text{Prob}_a(H)$	$\text{Prob}_b(H)$
{1}	.2	.1
{2}	.3	.7
{34}	.5	.2

Now consider the economy composed of investors a, b, and c, as indicated in the accompanying table. This economy does not satisfy the unconditioned beliefs assumption 8.3. Consider the event {1}. For this event, investor c has $\text{Prob}_c(\{1\}) = 0$, whereas both a and b have $\text{Prob}_a(\{1\}) > 0$ and $\text{Prob}_b(\{1\}) > 0$, respectively. ☐

H	$\text{Prob}_a(H)$	$\text{Prob}_b(H)$	$\text{Prob}_c(H)$
{1}	.2	.1	0
{2}	.3	.7	.5
{34}	.5	.2	.5

The asset market is characterized as a *frictionless market* and a *competitive market*.

Assumption 8.4: Frictionless Markets

The asset market has no transaction costs, no taxes, and no restrictions on short sales (such as margin requirements), and asset shares are divisible.

Assumption 8.5: Competitive Markets

Every investor acts as a price taker.

These assumptions are discussed at length in Chap. 3. The reader is referred to that discussion for further elaboration.

Each traded asset $x \in M$ has a price in dollars at time 0 for one unit. This price reflects the possible values of the cash flows at time 1, $x(\omega)$, given the various states $\omega \in \Omega$. There is also a price for multiple units of x, say, N units, selling as a *package*. This package trades because of assumption 8.1, which asserts that the marketed assets are closed under portfolios. In addition, consider the portfolio consisting of N_1 shares of asset x_1 and N_2 shares of x_2: $[N_1 x_1 + N_2 x_2]$. It has a price selling as a *package* as well.

A concept that captures the prices of all these different packages simultaneously is a *price functional* that maps assets in M into a price at time 0. The price functional is denoted by $p:M \to \mathbb{R}$. For example, one unit of asset x has a price in dollars at time 0 of $p(x)$. This is true for all $x \in M$. Next, N units of asset x selling as a package would have a time 0 price of $p(Nx)$. Finally, the portfolio of assets x_1 and x_2 given by $[N_1 x_1 + N_2 x_2]$ selling as a package would have a price of $p(N_1 x_1 + N_2 x_2)$.

A difference in notation and interpretation needs to be emphasized. The package given by $[N_1 x_1 + N_2 x_2]$ trades as a unit with a price of $p(N_1 x_1 + N_2 x_2)$. However, there is an alternate investment strategy that an investor could use to generate the same cash flows at time 1 (under all states) as the package $[N_1 x_1 + N_2 x_2]$. An investor could purchase N_1 separate units of asset x_1 and N_2 separate units of asset x_2, for a time 0 price of $N_1 p(x_1) + N_2 p(x_2)$. The relationship between the time 0 prices of these two alternatives is the theme underlying arbitrage pricing theory.

With this market structure we can now introduce the concept of an *arbitrage opportunity*. We define a *finite asset portfolio* to be a finite collection of the assets in M; hence a finite portfolio is represented by an element $(N_1 x_1 + N_2 x_2 + \ldots + N_K x_K)$, where N_j equals the number of units of asset x_j held for $j = 1, \ldots, K$. The number of shares of asset x_j, N_j could be either positive or negative. A positive N_j means a purchase; a negative N_j means a short sale of the asset. A portfolio is considered to be formed at time 0 and held until time 1.

Definition: A Finite Asset Arbitrage Opportunity

A *finite asset arbitrage opportunity* is a portfolio $(N_0 x_0 + \ldots + N_K x_K) \in M$ such that any one of the following four conditions is satisfied:

(1) $p(N_0 x_0 + \cdots + N_K x_K) \neq \sum_{j=0}^{K} N_j p(x_j)$

(2) For some i, $\text{Prob}_i \left(\sum_{j=0}^{K} N_j x_j = 0 \right) = 1$ and $p\left(\sum_{j=0}^{K} N_j x_j \right) \neq 0$

(3) (a) $\sum_{j=0}^{K} N_j p(x_j) \leq 0$ and for some i

  (b) $\text{Prob}_i \left(\sum_{j=0}^{K} N_j x_j \geq 0 \right) = 1$ and

  (c) $\text{Prob}_i \left(\sum_{j=0}^{K} N_j x_j > 0 \right) > 0$

(4) (a) $\displaystyle\sum_{j=0}^{K} N_j p(x_j) \geq 0$ and for some i

(b) $\displaystyle\mathrm{Prob}_i\left(\sum_{j=0}^{K} N_j x_j \leq 0\right) = 1$ and

(c) $\displaystyle\mathrm{Prob}_i\left(\sum_{j=0}^{K} N_j x_j < 0\right) > 0$

A finite asset arbitrage opportunity is seen to be a portfolio consisting of a finite number of assets that satisfies one of four conditions. From here on out, we will drop the prefix "finite asset."

Condition (1) of the definition says that an arbitrage opportunity is a portfolio whose price as a package differs from the prices of the assets purchased separately and then combined. For example, consider the portfolio $[N_1 x_1 + N_2 x_2]$ trading as a package. Its price is $p(N_1 x_1 + N_2 x_2)$. If this differs from $N_1 p(x_1) + N_2 p(x_2)$, say, $N_1 p(x_1) + N_2 p(x_2) < p(N_1 x_1 + N_2 x_2)$, then a clever investor could undertake the following strategy: Short sell the package $(N_1 x_1 + N_2 x_2)$ and buy separately N_1 shares of x_1 and N_2 shares of x_2. The cash flow at time 0 from this strategy is $p(N_1 x_1 + N_2 x_2) - N_1 p(x_1) - N_2 p(x_2) > 0$. At time 1 the cash flow is 0. This is a money pump! In Sec. 8.3 in the context of the cardinal utility theory developed in Chap. 7, we show that every investor would desire to undertake this trading strategy. An arbitrage opportunity is meant to capture the intuitive notion of a utility-increasing trading strategy that entails *no* risk. Condition (1) captures this idea similarly for conditions (2)–(4).

Conditions (2), (3), and (4) involve the subjective probability beliefs of some ith investor. Careful examination of conditions (2), (3b), (3c), (4b), and (4c) reveals that the events isolated in those conditions are all in the information set $\sigma(M)$. This is because knowledge of the cash flow of the assets at time 1 is sufficient to know whether the stated event in (2)–(4) occurs. For example, consider condition (3c). Given we know that $\Sigma_{j=0}^{K} N_j x_j > 0$, this implies that the actual state ω_0 is in the event $\{\omega \in \Omega: \Sigma_{j=0}^{K} N_j x_j(\omega) > 0\}$. This event is in $\sigma(M)$. Furthermore, conditions (2), (3b), (4b), and (4c) only involve restrictions where the probabilities are zero. (Note that $H \in \sigma(M)$ such that $\mathrm{Prob}_i(H) = 1$ is true if and only if $\mathrm{Prob}_i(\mathrm{not}\ H) = 0$.) Hence, by the unconditioned probability beliefs assumption 8.3, if one investor sees an arbitrage opportunity, then all investors agree it is an arbitrage opportunity!

Now, given these insights, we can return to the interpretation of conditions (2)–(4). Condition (2) is also a money pump at time 0. *All* investors believe the portfolio has zero cash flows at time 1 with probability 1. But the time 0 price of this portfolio, selling as a package, is nonzero. Suppose $p(\Sigma_{j=0}^{K} N_j x_j) > 0$. A clever investor would short this package, generating $p(\Sigma_{j=0}^{K} N_j x_j)$ as a cash flow at time 0. He is certain there is no liability (in terms of cash flow) at time 1.

We next consider conditions (3) and (4). Since these conditions are similar, we concentrate only on condition (3). Condition (3a) states that the cash flow to purchasing N_j separate units of x_j for $j = 0, \ldots, K$ at time 0 is zero or positive. Furthermore, the portfolio will never have a negative cash flow at time 1, (3b), and with positive probability it has a positive cash flow at time 1, (3c). This is a probabilistic money pump! In Sec. 8.3 we prove that undertaking this investment strategy will increase the investor's utility. In fact, the investor would attempt to replicate the strategy an unlimited number of times.

Consider the following example.

Example 1   Arbitrage Opportunities: Revisited

Recall the economy consisting of four states, two assets, and the two investors (a and b). Let us consider a package consisting of 11 units of asset 1. The accompanying table summarizes the relevant facts about the traded assets.

states (ω)	$x_1(\omega)$	$x_2(\omega)$	package ($N_1x_1 = 11x_1$)
1	5	3	55
2	5	6	55
3	10	3	110
4	10	3	110

The fundamental events in $\sigma(M)$ are $\{1\}$, $\{2\}$, and $\{34\}$. Let the two investors a and b have subjective beliefs given as in the table.

H	$\text{Prob}_a(H)$	$\text{Prob}_b(H)$
$\{1\}$	.2	.1
$\{2\}$	.3	.7
$\{34\}$	.5	.2

These satisfy the unconditioned probability beliefs assumption 8.3.

The prices of the specified assets at time 0 are (by assumption)

$$p(x_1) = 4 \text{ dollars}$$
$$p(x_2) = 2 \text{ dollars}$$
$$p(N_1x_1) = 40 \text{ dollars}$$

This completes the relevant information.

We claim that there are arbitrage opportunities in this economy. First, condition (1) is satisfied. To see this, consider the package $11x_1$. Note that

$$p(11x_1) = 40 \neq 11p(x_1) = 11(4) = 44$$

Eleven units of asset x_1 is cheaper to purchase as a package than to buy each share separately. To make money, buy the package and sell 11 units of asset x_1. The time 0 cash flow is $11p(x_1) - p(11x_1) = 44 - 40 = 4$. The time 1 cash flow is zero. Why stop? A clever investor could perform this strategy α times, making 4α dollars at time 0. Letting $\alpha \to \infty$ will generate unlimited wealth!

Condition (2) is also satisfied. For convenience, relabel the package as if it were a "new" element of M, denoted x_3, where $x_3 \equiv 11x_1$. Now consider the portfolio consisting of $N_1 = -11$ shares of asset x_1 and $N_3 = +1$ shares of asset x_3. At time 0 its price is

$$N_1 p(x_1) + N_3 p(x_3) = -11(4) + 1(40) = -4 \neq 0$$

At time 1, the accompanying table shows that the remaining part of condition (2) is satisfied.

state	$N_1 x_1(\omega) + N_3 x_3(\omega)$	$\mathbf{Prob}_a(H)$	$\mathbf{Prob}_b(H)$
1	$-11(5) + 1(55) = 0$	.2	.1
2	$-11(5) + 1(55) = 0$	.3	.7
3	$-11(10) + 1(110) = 0$	.5	.2
4	$-11(10) + 1(110) = 0$		

Hence

$$\text{Prob}_a(N_1 x_1 + N_3 x_3 = 0) = 1 \quad \text{and}$$

$$\text{Prob}_b(N_1 x_1 + N_3 x_3 = 0) = 1$$

Condition (3) is also satisfied. Again define the asset $x_3 \equiv 11x_1$ as the package. Now consider the portfolio consisting of $N_1 = -10$ shares of asset x_1 and $N_3 = +1$ shares of asset x_3. At time 0, condition (3a) is satisfied: $N_1 p(x_1) + N_3 p(x_3) = -10 p(x_1) + 1 p(x_3) = -40 + 40 = 0$. At time 1, consider the payoff table:

state	$N_1 x_1(\omega) + N_3 x_3(\omega)$	$\mathbf{Prob}_a(H)$	$\mathbf{Prob}_b(H)$
1	$-10(5) + 1(55) = 5$	.2	.1
2	$-10(5) + 1(55) = 5$	.3	.7
3	$-10(10) + 1(110) = 10$	.5	.2
4	$-10(10) + 1(110) = 10$		

For person a

$$\text{Prob}_a(N_1 x_1 + N_3 x_3 \geq 0) = 1 \quad \text{and}$$

$$\text{Prob}_a(N_1 x_1 + N_3 x_3 > 0) = 1 > 0$$

Similarly for person b. Both persons a and b would attempt to create this strategy α times and let $\alpha \to \infty$. $\square$

One expects that a "well-functioning" economy would not contain any of these arbitrage opportunities. This statement is partially justified in Sec. 8.3. The idea is that if an arbitrage opportunity were present in an economy, then to increase utility at no risk, everyone would rush to take advantage of it. In fact, everyone would desire to buy and sell the same securities in unlimited quantities. This would not be a stable situation. Prices should adjust until no arbitrage opportunities remained.

This story motivates the following assumption.

Assumption 8.6: No Arbitrage Opportunities

The asset market contains no finite asset arbitrage opportunities.

This assumption allows us to determine prices in an economy such that no arbitrage opportunities are present. It puts structure on the price functional. In particular, the assumption of no arbitrage opportunities is equivalent to

(i) $p(N_0 x_0 + \ldots + N_K x_K) = \sum_{j=0}^{K} N_j p(x_j)$ for all $x_1, \ldots, x_K \in M$ and

$N_0, \ldots, N_K \in \mathbb{R}$

and

(ii) if for some i, $\text{Prob}_i\left(\sum_{j=0}^{K} N_j x_j(\omega) \geq 0\right) = 1$ and

$\text{Prob}_i\left(\sum_{j=0}^{K} N_j x_j(\omega) > 0\right) > 0$ then

$\sum_{j=0}^{K} N_j p(x_j) > 0$

Condition (i) says that the price functional is linear and it is called *value additivity*. Condition (ii) is a *dominance* relationship, which is important enough to isolate as a theorem.

Theorem 8.1: Dominance

Given assumptions 8.1–8.6, if for some i

$$\text{Prob}_i\left(\sum_{j=0}^{K} N_j x_j \geq 0\right) = 1 \quad \text{and}$$

$$\text{Prob}_i\left(\sum_{j=0}^{K} N_j x_j > 0\right) > 0 \quad \text{then}$$

$$\sum_{j=0}^{K} N_j p(x_j) > 0$$

This theorem states that any portfolio with nonnegative cash flows at time 1 and with a positive probability of positive cash flows must have a positive price today. This result is "obvious." An everyday example that satisfies the conditions of this theorem is common stock. Since common stock is of *limited liability* (i.e., its value can never go below zero), it satisfies the first condition. As long as the common stock is not expected to be worthless (bankrupt) at time 1 with probability 1, then it satisfies the second condition. Most common stock meet these requirements. Then the dominance theorem 8.1 implies the common stock should sell for a positive price.

This theorem is extremely important in option pricing theory, discussed in Chap. 13, especially when studying early exercise strategies for American options. It also implies corollary 8.1. However, before stating the corollary, we need to define formally the concept of a *limited liability* asset.

Definition: Limited Liability Asset

An asset $x \in M$ is defined to be of *limited liability* if for some investor i

$$\text{Prob}_i(x \geq 0) = 1 \quad \text{and}$$
$$\text{Prob}_i(x > 0) > 0 \tag{8.1}$$

A limited liability asset is an asset where the investor can only lose his initial investment (purchase price). It is also not the trivial asset with zero cash flows. Examples of limited liability assets include common stock, bonds, and equity options.

Corollary 8.1: No Arbitrage Opportunities

(a) Returns over the time period 0 to 1 on limited liability assets are well defined. That is, given a limited liability asset $x \in M$, its return in state $\omega \in \Omega$ is

$$\frac{x(\omega) - p(x)}{p(x)}$$

(b) The return over the time period 0 to 1 in state $\omega \in \Omega$ on a portfolio $(N_0 x_0 + \ldots + N_K x_K)$ of limited liability assets with $\sum_{j=0}^{K} N_j p(x_j) > 0$ can be written as

$$\sum_{j=0}^{K} w_j \left(\frac{x_j(\omega) - p(x_j)}{p(x_j)} \right) \quad \text{where} \quad w_j = \frac{N_j p(x_j)}{\sum_{j=0}^{K} N_j p(x_j)}$$

represents the percentage of the portfolio value in asset j and $\sum_{j=0}^{K} w_j = 1$.

Proof

(a) If $x \in M$ is a limited liability asset, by theorem 8.1, $p(x) > 0$. Hence we can divide by $p(x)$ to get meaningful returns.

(b) To calculate the return on the portfolio $(N_0 x_0 + \ldots + N_K x_K) \in M$ form $(N_0 x_0(\omega) + \ldots + N_K x_K(\omega) - p(N_0 x_0 + \ldots + N_K x_K))/ p(N_0 x_0 + \ldots + N_K x_K)$ if $p(N_0 x_0 + \ldots + N_K x_K) \neq 0$. By assumption 8.6, $p(N_0 x_0 + \ldots + N_K x_K) = \sum_{j=1}^{K} N_j p(x_j) > 0$, so the return is well defined. Applying assumption 8.6 again shows this equals

$$\left[\sum_{j=0}^{K} N_j x_j(\omega) - \sum_{j=0}^{K} N_j p(x_j) \right] \Big/ \sum_{j=0}^{K} N_j p(x_j)$$

$$= \sum_{j=0}^{K} w_j (x_j(\omega) - p(x_j))/p(x_j)$$

using step (a). $\square$

Step (b) of this corollary states that a portfolio's return is equal to the weighted returns on the assets included in the portfolio. The weights equal the proportion of the initial portfolio's value that each asset represents. This corollary is often used in the literature without recognition that it follows from an economy with no arbitrage opportunities. It is not a tautology and it need not hold. For example, it would not hold in a world where there are economies of scale in purchasing large packages of securities (as with quantity discounts).

8.2. THE GENERALIZED ARBITRAGE PRICING THEOREM

This section proves the key theorem under assumptions 8.1–8.6, and it is called the *generalized arbitrage pricing theorem* (GAPT). It fulfills the objective of the arbitrage pricing methodology, which is to price some subset of the traded assets with the known prices of another subset of traded assets. All other arbitrage pricing theories to be presented in this text are special cases of this theorem. For example, it is the preliminary step in the development of Ross's arbitrage pricing theorem of Chap. 9. The GAPT also generalizes theorem 3.2 (Chap. 3), which states that in an economy with no uncertainty all assets earn the risk-free rate.

Before stating and proving this theorem, we need to introduce a concept from linear algebra called a "basis," in particular, an *algebraic basis* for the set of securities M. The assets in the algebraic basis will form the fundamental set of traded assets from which all other traded assets will be priced.

To motivate the concept of an *algebraic basis*, let us consider the marketed assets M. There are a lot of assets included in M. Given any two assets x_1, $x_2 \in M$, we can construct an *infinite* number of different assets in M by forming the portfolios $(N_1 x_1 + N_2 x_2)$, where N_1, N_2 represents the number of shares held of asset x_1, x_2, respectively. There are even more possibilities available by combining portfolios with more than two assets. Our goal is to describe all the assets in M in a succinct way. What we need is the smallest set of assets $\{x_g\}$ for g, an element of some set G (written $\{x_g\}_{g \in G}$),[4] such that given an arbitrary asset x in M, it can be constructed in a unique way as a *finite* asset portfolio of the minimal set $\{x_g\}_{g \in G}$. This *minimal* set of assets $\{x_g\}_{g \in G}$ is called an algebraic basis.[5] A set of assets $\{x_g\}_{g \in G}$ is said to be *linearly independent* if for any finite subset $\{x_1, \ldots, x_K\}$, there exist no portfolio $(N_1, \ldots, N_K)$ such that $\Sigma_{j=1}^{K} N_j x_j = 0$. That is, no element of the set can be constructed as a finite asset portfolio from other elements in the set. An algebraic basis must therefore be linearly independent.

It is a standard fact from mathematics that an algebraic basis always exists for a set of marketed assets M satisfying assumption 8.1, which asserts that all portfolios trade (see Friedman [1]). We isolate this observation:

Existence of an Algebraic Basis for *M*

There exists a set of linearly independent assets $\{x_g\}_{g \in G} \subset M$ such that for any $x \in M$

$$x = \sum_{g \in G} N_g(x) x_g \tag{8.2}$$

where $N_g(x) \neq 0$ for only a *finite* number of g. Furthermore, the $N_g(x)$ are uniquely identified with x.

This set of assets $\{x_g\}_{g \in G}$ allows us to describe the marketed assets in a very succinct manner. Given any asset $x \in M$, it can be written as a portfolio of the elements of $\{x_g\}_{g \in G}$. The portfolio is *unique*. The right-hand side of condition (8.2) gives the portfolio of elements of $\{x_g\}$, which duplicates x. Note that for each x, only a *finite* number of the elements of $\{x_g\}$ need to be considered. Furthermore, the portfolio weights are uniquely associated with the asset x. It is also important to point out that the algebraic basis is *not* unique; however, given a particular basis, the coefficients in expression (8.2) are unique.

Arbitrage pricing theory has as its goal the pricing of the assets in M, *relative* to the prices of the assets in the algebraic basis set $\{x_g\}_{g \in G}$. The prices of the algebraic basis set $\{x_g\}_{g \in G}$ are *exogenously* given, i.e., $\{p(x_g)\}_{g \in G}$, and the prices of all the other marketed assets M determined from these. This is accomplished using value additivity and expression (8.2):

$$\text{if} \quad x \in M, \text{ then } \quad p(x) = \sum_{g \in G} N_g(x) p(x_g) \tag{8.3}$$

---

[4] The set G is an index set. It allows us to "number" the elements of $\{x_g\}$. For example, if $G = \{1, 2, 3\}$, then $\{x_g\}_{g \in G} = \{x_1, x_2, x_3\}$ and $\Sigma_{g \in G} x_g = \Sigma_{g=1}^{3} x_g$.

[5] Formally, an algebraic basis is a maximal linearly independent set of elements of the linear space M (see Friedman [1, p. 131]).

An example of this procedure is given by theorem 3.2, where in an economy with no uncertainty the price of one asset is sufficient to price all the other assets.

Applying these insights to returns instead of to prices gives the generalized arbitrage pricing theorem. To make the statement of the theorem easier, let us define the *return* on an asset $x \in M$ over the time period 0 to 1 with $p(x) \neq 0$ by $r(x) = [x - p(x)]/p(x)$. Note that since the time 1 cash flows to asset x are uncertain, returns are uncertain as well.

Theorem 8.2: Generalized Arbitrage Pricing Theorem

Under assumptions 8.1–8.6, if all the $\{x_g\}_{g \in G}$ are limited liability securities (or have $p(x_g) > 0$), then given any traded asset $x \in M$

$$r(x) = \sum_{g \in G} \lambda_g(x) r(x_g) \quad \text{where} \tag{8.4}$$

$$\lambda_g(x) = [N_g(x)p(x_g)] \Big/ \sum_{g \in G} N_g(x)p(x_g) \quad \text{and}$$

$$\sum_{g \in G} \lambda_g(x) = 1$$

Proof

This is corollary 8.1(b) and condition (8.2). $\quad \square$

The generalized arbitrage pricing theorem expresses the return on any asset $r(x)$ as a weighted combination of the returns on the basis assets $r(x_g)$. There are only a finite number of the portfolio weights $\lambda_g(x) \neq 0$ in this expression.

We define the *riskless asset* as the asset that pays off \$1 at time 1 under all states $\omega \in \Omega$. Its payoff is certain. We denote it by $x_\Omega \equiv 1$ for all $\omega \in \Omega$. By the dominance theorem 8.1, we know that the price of the riskless asset is positive, i.e., $p(x_\Omega) > 0$ and its return $r(x_\Omega) = [x_\Omega - p(x_\Omega)]/p(x_\Omega)$ is well defined. A corollary to theorem 8.2 is the following:

Corollary 8.2: Excess Return Form of the GAPT

Under the hypothesis of theorem 8.2, if the riskless asset trades, i.e., $x_\Omega \in M$, then

$$r(x) = r(x_\Omega) + \sum_{g \in G} \lambda_g(x)(r(x_g) - r(x_\Omega)) \tag{8.5}$$

Proof

$$r(x) = \sum_{g \in G} \lambda_g r(x_g) = r(x_\Omega) + \sum_{g \in G} \lambda_g r(x_g) - \sum_{g \in G} \lambda_g r(x_\Omega) \quad \text{since}$$

$$\sum_{g \in G} \lambda_g = 1 \quad \square$$

This corollary says that if a riskless asset trades, then the return on any asset x can be written as a linear combination of the excess returns (above the risk-free rate) on a finite number of the *basis* assets. Each of the basis assets in $\{x_g\}_{g \in G}$ trades in the frictionless market M.

Given an investor's subjective probability beliefs $\text{Prob}_i[\cdot]$, this theorem implies the following:

Corollary 8.3: Expected Return versus Risk

If $E_i(r(x))$ exists, then

$$E_i(r(x)) = r(x_\Omega) + \sum_{g \in G} \lambda_g(x)[E_i(r(x_g)) - r(x_\Omega)] \tag{8.6}$$

where $\lambda_g(x) \neq 0$ for only a finite number of $g \in G$.

The notation $E_i(\cdot)$ means the expectation with respect to the probability distribution $\text{Prob}_i(\cdot)$. In summation form, for discrete density functions with state space $\Omega = \{1, \ldots, n\}$, we have $E_i(x) = \sum_{\omega=1}^{n} x(\omega) \text{Prob}_i(\omega)$.

Corollary 8.3 states that each asset's expected return can be written as a finite linear combination of the excess expected return on a set of basis assets $\{x_g\}_{g \in G}$. This expression is similar in form to Ross's APT and the capital asset pricing model. The generalized arbitrage pricing theorem is introduced to show the weakest set of assumptions needed to express the excess expected return on any asset as a finite linear combination of the excess expected return on the basis assets. The subsequent pricing theories put more structure on $\{x_g\}_{g \in G}$ in order to get a restricted form of condition (8.6). This restricted form is needed since the set of basis assets can be very large, and if it is large enough, expression (8.6) is not usable in practice. The prime example of this necessity is given by Ross's APT in Chap. 9, where the basis set itself consists of an infinite number of assets. An example where this is not the case follows:

Example 1   Generalized Arbitrage Pricing Theory: Revisited

Recall from example 1 in Sec. 8.1 that the space of marketed assets is

$$M = \{\alpha x_1 + \beta x_2 : \alpha, \beta \in \mathbb{R}\}$$

where x_1, x_2 are given in the following table.

states	$x_1(\omega)$	$x_2(\omega)$	$y_1(\omega)$	$y_2(\omega)$
1	5	3	1	2
2	5	6	1	3
3	10	3	2	3
4	10	3	2	3

Also included in the table are two other traded assets, y_1 and y_2.

A basis set for M is $\{y_1, y_2\}$. They are linearly independent and generate the traded assets; indeed

$$x_1 = 5y_1$$

and

$$x_2 = -3y_1 + 3y_2$$

This is not the only basis for M, however, since $\{x_1, x_2\}$ is also a basis.

Now given the prices $p(x_1) = 4$ and $p(x_2) = 2$, we can rewrite these assets in return form as

$$r(x_1) = \frac{5y_1 - p(5y_1)}{p(5y_1)}$$

$$= r(y_1)$$

$$r(x_2) = \frac{(-3y_1 + 3y_2) - p(-3y_1 + 3y_2)}{p(x_2)}$$

$$= \frac{-3p(y_1)}{p(x_2)} r(y_1) + \frac{3p(y_2)}{p(x_2)} r(y_2)$$

$$= \lambda_1 r(y_1) + \lambda_2 r(y_2)$$

where $\lambda_1 = -3p(y_1)/p(x_2)$, $\lambda_2 = 3p(y_2)/p(x_2)$, and $\lambda_1 + \lambda_2 = 1$. $\quad\square$

Example 1 is the finite dimensional case (i.e., each basis has a finite number of elements). Here the algebraic basis is just the ordinary basis defined in linear algebra. The power of the generalized arbitrage pricing theorem 8.2 and corollary 8.3 is for the infinite dimensional case. For an example of this, we will wait until Chap. 9 and Ross's APT. We remark, however, that the insights developed in the simpler finite dimensional case carries over to the infinite dimensional case.

8.3. ARBITRAGE OPPORTUNITIES AND PREFERENCES

This section combines the asset model of Secs. 8.1 and 8.2 with the consumption-saving model developed in Sec. 7.3. The purpose of this exercise is to show that an arbitrage opportunity, when added to an investor's existing portfolio, will increase her utility. Therefore, the existence of arbitrage opportunities will create a situation where all investors would initiate trading. The act of trading (by all investors) would tend to adjust prices until all arbitrage opportunities were eliminated. Hence this section provides further partial justification for assumption 8.6, no arbitrage opportunities.

Recall the consumption-saving model in Sec. 7.3. There are two time periods: today (time 0) and tomorrow (time 1). Individuals consume a single consumption good in both time periods. Their preferences are represented by the expected utility function

$$E_b(V(C_0, C_1)) \quad \text{for all } b \in \bar{B} \tag{8.7}$$

where   (i) $V(C_0, C_1)$ is a cardinal utility function defined over certain outcomes C_0, C_1, and

   (ii)   each $b \in \bar{B}$ determines an objective probability distribution over consumption at time 0 and time 1, $\text{Prob}[C_0 \le z_0, C_1 \le z_1; b]$, where z_0, $z_1 \in \mathbb{R}$.

Furthermore, preferences are monotonic by assumption 7.1, implying that more consumption in any time period is strictly preferred to less.

To combine the two models we need to incorporate an exogenously specified *price level* in times 0 and 1. This is needed because preferences are defined over consumption goods in the consumption-saving model while asset prices are denominated in dollars. The price level at time 0 is defined to be the number of dollars necessary to purchase one unit of the consumption good at time 0, denoted $\rho_0 > 0$. The price level at time 1 is defined to be the number of dollars necessary to purchase one unit of the consumption good at time 1, denoted $\rho_1 > 0$. Since the economy is uncertain at time 1, however, ρ_1 is a random variable depending on the state $\omega \in \Omega$. Hence $\rho_1 : \Omega \to \mathbb{R}$ and $\rho_1(\omega) > 0$ will indicate the price level at time 1 under state ω.

The price level provides the appropriate mechanism for converting dollars to units of the consumption good. For example, the price in units of the consumption good of asset x_j's dollar cash flows at time 1 under state ω is $x_j(\omega)/\rho_1(\omega)$. Similarly, the time 0 price of asset x_j in consumption goods is $p(x_j)/\rho_0$.

The asset market will play a fundamental role in the consumption-saving model. It will provide the only way a consumer can transfer consumption goods across time. By investing in assets, she can increase or decrease her consumption in either time 0 or time 1.

To formalize this process, we assume that the consumer enters time 0 with an endowment. The endowment consists of consumption goods in both times 0 and 1, denoted by $(\bar{C}_0, \bar{C}_1(\omega))$, as well as a portfolio of the basis assets $\{x_g\}_{g \in G}$, denoted by $(\bar{N}_g)_{g \in G}$, where $\bar{N}_g \neq 0$ for only a finite number of assets. The endowed consumption at time 1 depends on the state of nature $\omega \in \Omega$. This endowment is the basis for an investor's wealth. If she desires a different pattern of consumption or a different portfolio, she can trade in the market. The actual consumption in times 0 and 1 is denoted by $(C_0, C_1(\omega))$ and the actual portfolio is denoted by $(N_g)_{g \in G}$, where $N_g \neq 0$ for only a finite number of g.

The actual consumption in times 0 and 1 is constrained by the individual's budget constraints. The time 0 budget constraint is given by condition (8.8):

$$\overline{C}_0 + \sum_{g \in G} \overline{N}_g p(x_g)/\rho_0 = C_0 + \sum_{g \in G} N_g p(x_g)/\rho_0 \tag{8.8}$$

The left-hand side of condition (8.8) represents the value of the endowment at time 0 (consumption plus portfolio) in units of the consumption good. The right-hand side of (8.8) shows how the endowment is used. Part of it is consumed, C_0, and the remainder invested in the portfolio $\{N_g\}_{g \in G}$.

By construction, the time 1 budget constraint under state ω is

$$\overline{C}_1(\omega) + \sum_{g \in G} N_g x_g(\omega)/\rho_1(\omega) = C_1(\omega) \tag{8.9}$$

In state ω, the investor consumes the time 1 value of her portfolio in consumption goods as well as her initial endowment, $\overline{C}_1(\omega)$. We see from condition (8.9) that the portfolio $\{N_g\}_{g \in G}$ provides the only way an investor can alter her time 1 consumption under a given state.

To utilize the preference function given in condition (8.7), we need to specify a reduced set of alternatives $\tilde{A} \subset \tilde{B}$ and the probability distribution $\text{Prob}[C_0 \leq z_0, C_1 \leq z_1; b]$ for $b \in \tilde{A}$. The set of alternatives is reduced due to two restrictions. The first restriction is due to the investor's prespecified *subjective* probability beliefs. $\tilde{B}$ represents all possible probability distributions; however, the investor, with her subjective beliefs, feels that only some of these are possible. This restricts $\tilde{B}$ partially. The second restriction is due to the availability of the asset market and the budget constraints. Our next task is to spell out these relationships.

Recall that the investor has a subjective probability distribution, $\text{Prob}_i[\cdot]$ over the information revealed by prices, $\sigma(M)$. Since the time 1 price level and the time 1 endowed consumption are random, they could potentially reveal information not contained in $\sigma(M)$. For this reason, the subjective probability distribution needs to be defined over a larger set of events—the information set revealed by prices, the endowment, and the price level, denoted by $\sigma(M, \overline{C}_1, \rho_1)$.

Given this probability distribution $\text{Prob}_i[H]$ for $H \in \sigma(M, \overline{C}_1, \rho_1)$, the probability distribution over C_0 and C_1, as given in expression (8.9), is completely specified. In fact, conditions (8.8) and (8.9) along with the probability $\text{Prob}_i[H]$ completely specify the reduced set of alternatives $\tilde{A}$. First, note that consumption at time 0, C_0, is constant. Second, note that once $C_0, \{N_g\}_{g \in G}$ are specified, $\text{Prob}_i[C_1 \leq z]$ is completely determined by conditions (8.8) and (8.9). Hence

$$\tilde{A} = \{(C_0, \text{Prob}_i[C_1 \leq z; C_0, \{N_g\}_{g \in G}]): C_0, \{N_g\}_{g \in G} \text{ satisfy (8.8) and (8.9)}\}$$

The set $\tilde{A}$ is those probability distributions that are (i) consistent with the ith investor's subjective beliefs and (ii) feasible considering her endowment and budget constraints. An element $b \in \tilde{A} \subset \tilde{B}$ is completely determined by C_0, $\{N_g\}_{g \in G}$ and $\text{Prob}_i[H]$. So we can rewrite expression (8.7) and the budget constraints as

$$E_i(V(C_0, C_1); C_0, \{N_g\}_{g \in G}) \quad \text{for all} \quad C_0, \{N_g\}_{g \in G} \tag{8.10}$$

satisfying

$$\overline{C}_0 + \sum_{g \in G} \overline{N}_g p(x_g)/\rho_0 = C_0 + \sum_{g \in G} N_g p(x_g)/\rho_0 \quad \text{and}$$

$$\overline{C}_1(\omega) + \sum_{g \in G} N_g x_g(\omega)/\rho_1(\omega) = C_1(\omega)$$

The term $E_i(y; C_0, \{N_g\}_{g \in G})$ is the expectation of y using the probability distribution $\text{Prob}_i[y \le z; C_0, \{N_g\}_{g \in G}]$, which depends on C_0, $\{N_g\}_{g \in G}$, and $\text{Prob}_i[H]$. For convenience, we will often write $E_i(V(C_0, C_1); C_0, \{N_g\}_{g \in G})$ as $E(V(C_0, C_1))$ when there is no chance for confusion. This occurs, for example, if we rewrite (8.10) for the ith consumer as

$$E\left(V\left(C_0, \overline{C}_1(\omega) + \sum_{g \in G} N_g x_g(\omega)/\rho_1(\omega)\right)\right) \tag{8.11}$$

where

$$\overline{C}_0 + \sum_{g \in G} \overline{N}_g p(x_g)/\rho_0 = C_0 + \sum_{g \in G} N_g p(x_g)/\rho_0$$

We will now show that the existence of an arbitrage opportunity implies that there exists a strategic portfolio that can increase an investor's expected utility. For brevity, we will only consider an arbitrage opportunity as given by condition (3) in the definition. However, a similar argument is possible for the remaining cases as well.

Suppose there exists a finite asset arbitrage opportunity $(M_0 x_0 + \ldots + M_K x_K)$ such that

$$\sum_{j=0}^{K} M_j p(x_j) = 0 \tag{8.12a}$$

and

$$\text{Prob}_i\left(\sum_{j=0}^{K} M_j x_j \ge 0\right) = 1 \tag{8.12b}$$

$$\text{Prob}_i\left(\sum_{j=0}^{K} M_j x_j > 0\right) > 0 \tag{8.12c}$$

This arbitrage opportunity is in units of dollars. It is important to realize that this is also an arbitrage opportunity in units of consumption goods as well. Since $\rho_0 > 0$ and $\rho_1(\omega) > 0$ all $\omega \in \Omega$, we can divide to obtain

$$\sum_{j=0}^{K} M_j p(x_j)/\rho_0 = 0 \tag{8.13a}$$

$$\text{Prob}_i\left(\sum_{j=0}^{K} M_j x_j/\rho_1 \geq 0\right) = 1 \tag{8.13b}$$

$$\text{Prob}_i\left(\sum_{j=0}^{K} M_j x_j/\rho_1 > 0\right) > 0 \tag{8.13c}$$

Suppose the investor adds this portfolio to $\{N_g\}_{g \epsilon G}$. The new portfolio will be

$$\{N_g\}_{g \epsilon G} + \{M_0, \ldots, M_K\}$$

We claim this portfolio satisfies the budget constraints and increases the investor's expected utility. To show this, consider the time 0 budget constraint. By condition (8.13a)

$$\overline{C}_0 + \sum_{g \epsilon G} \overline{N}_g p(x_g)/\rho_0 = C_0 + \sum_{g \epsilon G} N_g p(x_g)/\rho_0 + \sum_{j=0}^{K} M_j p(x_j)/\rho_0 \tag{8.14}$$

Further, by conditions (8.13b) and (8.13c)

$$\sum_{g \epsilon G} N_g x_g(\omega)/\rho_1 + \sum_{j=0}^{K} M_j x_j(\omega)/\rho_1 \geq \sum_{g \epsilon G} N_g x_g(\omega)/\rho_1 \quad \text{for all } \omega \epsilon \Omega \tag{8.15}$$

and for some $H \epsilon \sigma(M, \overline{C}_1, \rho_1)$ where $\text{Prob}_i(H) > 0$,

$$\sum_{g \epsilon G} N_g x_g(\omega)/\rho_1 + \sum_{j=0}^{K} (M_j) x_j(\omega)/\rho_1 > \sum_{g \epsilon G} N_g x_g(\omega)/\rho_1 \quad \text{for } \omega \epsilon H$$

Since $V(C_0, C_1)$ is increasing, this implies

$$E\left(V\left(C_0, \overline{C}_1(\omega) + \sum_{g \epsilon G} N_g x_g(\omega)/\rho_1 + \sum_{j=0}^{K} M_j x_j(\omega)/\rho_1\right)\right)$$

$$> E\left(V\left(C_0, \overline{C}_1(\omega) + \sum_{g \epsilon G} N_g x_g(\omega)/\rho_1\right)\right) \tag{8.16}$$

which proves our claim.

This section utilizes the cardinal utility theory of Chap. 7 to provide a justification for an arbitrage opportunity being a utility-increasing strategic investment. Crucial to this argument is the monotonicity assumption, i.e., that more consumption in any period under any state is preferred to less. In fact, this is the only major assumption required. The above argument generalizes to preferences that do not satisfy all the rationality axioms of Chap. 7, in particular, the strong independence axiom 7.7 need not hold. The weakness of these conditions on preferences makes the no arbitrage assumption 8.6 very plausible.

8.4. SUMMARY

This chapter introduces the arbitrage pricing methodology in the context of an uncertain economy with two time periods. The uncertainty in the economy at time 1 is characterized by a state space Ω. Asset payoffs at time 1 are contingent on the state $\omega \in \Omega$ occurring. A set of marketed assets M trade at time 0. These generate an information set, $\sigma(M)$, over which beliefs $\text{Prob}_i[\cdot]$ are defined. We assume that the set of marketed assets include all portfolios (assumption 8.1), all investors agree on the state contingent payoffs to the traded assets (assumption 8.2), all investors agree on zero probability events (assumption 8.3), and the markets are frictionless (assumption 8.4) and competitive (assumption 8.5).

An arbitrage opportunity is defined as a finite asset portfolio that (1) costs different selling as a package as opposed to its cost when self-constructed, or (2) has positive or zero cash flows at time 0 yet positive cash flows at time 1 that are strictly positive with positive probability. We exclude these opportunities from the economy (assumption 8.6) and examine the structure it implies on prices and returns.

Crucial to arbitrage pricing is the existence of a basis set of securities against which all other traded assets can be priced. This basis set leads to the statement and proof of the generalized arbitrage pricing theory.

The last section of the chapter utilizes the preference theory of Chap. 7 to give a utility-based justification for the no arbitrage opportunity assumption.

This chapter did not discuss one important topic in arbitrage pricing theory: the existence of an "equivalent martingale probability measure" in terms of which the price functional can be written as an expectation operator. This topic is not included because it requires sophisticated mathematics and it is not needed for any of the included material, see Harrison and Kreps [2], Harrison and Pliska [3], and Jarrow [4].

8.5. REFERENCES

1. Friedman, Avner, *Foundations of Modern Analysis*. New York: Holt, Rinehart & Winston, 1970.

2. Harrison, J. Michael, and David Kreps, "Martingales and Arbitrage in Multiperiod Securities Markets," *Journal of Economic Theory*, 20 (1979), 318–408.

3. Harrison, J. Michael, and Stanley Pliska, "Martingales and Stochastic Integrals in the Theory of Continuous Trading," *Stochastic Processes and Their Applications*, 11 (1981), 215–260.

4. Jarrow, Robert, "A Characterization Theorem for Unique Equivalent Martingale Probability Measures," *Economics Letters*, 22 (1986), 61–65.

5. Ross, S., "The Arbitrage Theory of Capital Asset Pricing," *Journal of Economic Theory*, 13 (1976), 341–360.

6. ———, "A Simple Approach to the Valuation of Risky Streams," *Journal of Business*, 51 (1978), 452–475.

9

ROSS'S APT

This chapter presents Ross's arbitrage pricing theory (APT) as a special case of the generalized arbitrage pricing theory (GAPT) developed in Sec. 8.2 of Chap. 8, in particular, theorem 8.2. Ross's model specializes the GAPT by imposing four additional assumptions on the economy. The first of these assumptions is that the traded assets' time 1 cash flows have finite means and variances (assumption 9.4). The second is that the riskless asset trades and that a basis set of assets is at most countably infinite (assumption 9.8). The third is the crucial linear factor hypothesis (assumption 9.9), while the fourth is that there are no infinite asset arbitrage opportunities (assumption 9.10). The consequence of these additional assumptions is the APT, theorem 9.1. Although the form that this theorem takes may be confusing, a complete understanding of its subtleties is extremely important. It is these subtleties that underly the issues surrounding the testability of the APT, and it is these subtleties that motivate the equilibrium-based extension of the APT in Chap. 18. Consequently, an entire section of this chapter is devoted to understanding and interpreting the theorem.

Utility theory enters the APT in an analogous manner to the way it entered the arbitrage pricing model in Chap. 8. That is, utility theory is only needed to motivate the no arbitrage opportunity assumptions, assumptions 9.7 and 9.10. It will be argued that the structure on preferences required to motivate these assumptions is very weak, making the theory robust from this perspective.

The derivation of the APT used below is unique to this text. An expanding literature exists that contains alternative derivations of Ross's original model;

some excellent references include Ross [9], Huberman [6], Chamberlain and Rothschild [4], Ingersoll [7], and Admati and Pfleiderer [1].

9.1. PRELIMINARIES

Ross's APT is a special case of the model developed in Sec. 8.2. For easy reference, we briefly review the model's assumptions and notation. For contrast, the new assumptions are indicated with a dagger (†). New assumptions will be discussed in greater detail.

The model has two time periods, represented by today (time 0) and tomorrow (time 1). The uncertainty in the economy at time 1 is characterized by a state space, Ω, with an arbitrary state denoted by $\omega \in \Omega$. An asset is a random variable defined by its dollar cash flows across all states at time 1, $x(\omega)$, where $x : \Omega \to \mathbb{R}$. The set of all assets that trade in the organized market at time 0 is denoted by the set M. These are called the marketed assets.

Assumption 9.1: Marketed Assets

If $x, y \in M$ and $\alpha, \beta \in \mathbb{R}$, then $\alpha x + \beta y \in M$.

This assumption states that if assets x and y trade, then the *package* consisting of α units of asset x and β units of asset y also trades. The traded assets, M, reveal an information set at time 1 that is denoted by $\sigma(M)$. These are the subsets of Ω, *events*, from which knowledge of the time 1 cash flows to the assets can determine if the event occurred. (A detailed discussion of this set of events is contained in Chap. 8, Sec. 8.1.) Finally, the economy consists of a finite number of investors whose beliefs satisfy the following assumptions.

Assumption 9.2: Conditional Homogeneous Beliefs

Given a traded asset $x \in M$, every investor agrees that $x(\omega)$ is the time 1 dollar cash flow to asset x, given state ω occurs.

Assumption 9.3: Unconditional Beliefs

Given an event $H \in \sigma(M)$

$$\text{Prob}_i(H) = 0 \quad \text{if and only if} \quad \text{Prob}_j(H) = 0$$

for all investors i, j where $\text{Prob}_i(H)$ represents investor i's probability belief.

Investors agree on the state contingent payoffs to all the traded assets (assumption 9.2), and they agree on zero probability events (assumption 9.3). We still need to impose additional structure on the investors' probability beliefs.

Assumption 9.4: Finite Second Moments[†]

For any traded asset $x \in M$

$$E_i(x^2) < +\infty \quad \text{for all investors } i$$

This assumption asserts that every investor believes the marketed assets have finite second moments (therefore finite means and variances).[1] This is the first additional assumption required beyond those in Chap. 8. It is included more for technical reasons than for its economic content. It allows us to compare traded assets and portfolios by considering their variances, knowing they exist.

Assumption 9.5: Frictionless Markets

The asset market has no transaction costs, no taxes, and no restrictions on short sales (such as margin requirements), and assets are divisible.

Assumption 9.6: Competitive Markets

Every investor acts as a price taker.

These are the standard ideal assumptions employed as a first approximation to the actual economy.

We define a price functional over the traded assets in M, $p:M \to \mathbb{R}$, where $p(x)$ gives the time 0 price in dollars of the traded asset $x \in M$. This price functional satisfies the following assumption:

Assumption 9.7: No Finite Asset Arbitrage Opportunities

The asset market contains no finite asset arbitrage opportunities as defined in Chap. 8.

This assumption implies that the price functional p satisfies value additivity and that all limited liability assets have strictly positive prices. The fact that these

---

[1]$E_i(x^2) < +\infty$ implies $E_i(|x|) < +\infty$ and $\text{var}_i(x) < +\infty$. First, $E_i|x| = \int_\Omega |x| dP_i \leq \int_A |x| dP_i + \int_B |x| dP_i$, where $A = \{\omega \in \Omega : |x| < 1\}$ and $B = \{\omega \in \Omega : |x| \geq 1\}$. This is, in turn $\leq 1 + \int_B |x|^2 dP_i \leq 1 + E_i(x^2) < +\infty$. Second, $\text{var}_i(x) = E_i(x^2) - (E_i(x))^2 < +\infty$.

arbitrage opportunities contain only a *finite* number of traded assets in M is important. Infinite asset portfolios will play a special role in the development of the theory. An additional assumption is needed to handle these expanded portfolios. However, before we are ready to state this assumption, some additional structure is needed.

As shown in Chap. 8, the previous assumptions are sufficient to prove the GAPT, theorem 8.2. The GAPT states that the return on any traded asset can be written as a linear combination of the returns on a finite number of traded assets belonging to a set of basis assets. This theorem will aid us in our understanding of the purpose behind the additional structure underlying the APT. Recall that to price any traded asset using the GAPT, the price of the entire basis set of assets is needed. This set of basis assets can be very large (uncountably infinite). If the GAPT is to be of any practical use, additional structure must be imposed to reduce the size of this basis set of assets. This goal underlies the three subsequent assumptions.

The first assumption states that the traded assets M are composed of all possible *finite* asset portfolios constructed from a *countable* set of *limited liability* assets $\{x_j\}_{j=1}^{\infty}$. The assets $\{x_j\}_{j=1}^{\infty}$ generating M are called the *primary* assets. Furthermore, we assume that the riskless asset trades $x_{\Omega} \in M$, where $x_{\Omega}(\omega) = 1$ for all $\omega \in \Omega$.

Assumption 9.8: Countable Set of Primary Assets[†]

The traded assets M consist of all *finite* portfolios using the limited liability primary assets $\{x_j\}_{j=1}^{\infty}$ and $x_{\Omega} \in M$.

The significance of this assumption is that there is *at most* a countably infinite number of primary assets. All of these assets are assumed to be of limited liability so that their returns are well defined. The theory in Chap. 8 allowed M to be a much larger set; hence assumption 9.8 is a restriction. Nonetheless, for actual economies, this is still quite an abstraction. The idea of assumption 9.8 is to approximate the actual economy with an economy in which there are a countably infinite number of primary assets. Of course, the approximation is only reasonable if the actual economy itself contains a large number of traded assets. The degree to which the approximation is reasonable needs to be judged by the ultimate usefulness and reliability of the model itself.

It is important also to note the following subtle aspect of the above model: The assets that trade, M, need not include all assets. This allows the economy to consist of traded and nontraded assets. The traded assets are priced by the model; the nontraded are not. In fact, the traded assets studied, M, can even be a proper subset of all the "traded" assets. This is true as long as the set of assets studied, M, is closed under portfolio composition in the sense of assumption 9.1. This interpretation is useful when considering contingent claims on the primary assets, like call options. Given that contingent claims on M also trade, the APT does not have to price these securities. These contingent claims can be priced using the techniques developed in Chap. 13, on option pricing. The reason for partitioning the traded assets in this way will become clear once we detail the next assumption, which introduces a special structure on the primary asset returns. Contingent claims, being nonlinear functions of the primary asset time 1 cash flows, will almost always destroy this special structure, whereas portfolios of these primary assets will not.

The next assumption is introduced by examining how a countable set of primary assets, assumption 9.8, refines the GAPT, theorem 8.2. Recall that the GAPT implies that the return on asset x_j equals

$$r(x_j) = \sum_{g \in G} \lambda_g(x_j) r(z_g) \quad \text{for } j = 1, 2, \ldots, +\infty \tag{9.1}$$

where $\sum_{g \in G} \lambda_g(x_j) = 1$, $\lambda_g(x) = 0$ for all but a finite number of g, $\{z_g\}_{g \in G}$ is an algebraic basis for M, and $r(x) = [x - p(x)]/p(x)$ if $p(x) \neq 0$.

Assumption 9.8 allows us to make two refinements to expression (9.1). First, the algebraic basis $\{z_g\}_{g \in G}$ is at most countably infinite since the primary assets $\{x_j\}_{j=1}^{\infty}$ themselves span M. So the index set can be taken to be the positive integers, i.e., $\{z_g\}_{g \in G} = \{z_g\}_{g=1}^{\infty}$. Second, we can express the returns relative to the risk-free rate due to corollary 8.2, so writing $\lambda_g(x_j)$ as λ_{jg}, expression (9.1), becomes

$$r(x_j) = r(x_\Omega) + \sum_{g=1}^{\infty} \lambda_{jg}[r(z_g) - r(x_\Omega)] \tag{9.2}$$

where $\sum_{g=1}^{\infty} \lambda_{jg} = 1$, and $\lambda_{jg} \neq 0$ only for a finite number of g.

Expression (9.2) characterizes the returns on the primary assets x_j as a linear combination of the riskless return and a finite number of basis assets' returns.

It is convenient to rewrite expression (9.2) one more time. We introduce new symbols for the returns on the basis assets, i.e., define

$$f_g = r(z_g) \quad \text{for } g = 1, \ldots, K$$

and

$$u_{g-K} = r(z_g) \quad \text{for } g = K + 1, \ldots, \infty$$

The basis asset returns are split into two sets. The returns on basis assets $\{z_g\}_{g=1}^{K}$ are rewritten as $\{f_k\}_{k=1}^{K}$, and the returns on basis assets $\{z_g\}_{g=K+1}^{\infty}$ are rewritten as $\{u_g\}_{g=1}^{\infty}$. With this new notation, expression (9.2) can be rewritten as

$$r(x_j) = r(x_\Omega) + \sum_{k=1}^{K} \lambda_{jk}(f_k - r(x_\Omega)) + \sum_{g=1}^{\infty} \lambda_{j,K+g}(u_g - r(x_\Omega)) \tag{9.3}$$

where $\lambda_{jg} \neq 0$ for only a finite number of g.

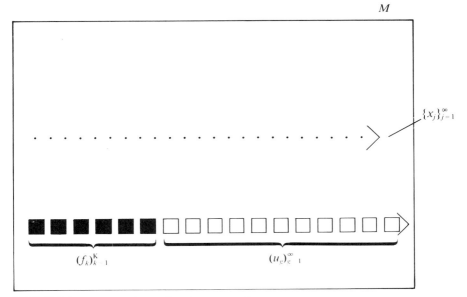

FIGURE 9.1: Relative sizes of various sets of assets.

The set of marketed assets M is represented by the entire square.

The set of primary assets $\{x_j\}_{j=1}^{\infty}$ is represented by the dotted line.

The set of basis assets $\{z_g\}_{g=1}^{\infty}$ is represented by the squared line.

The set of factors $\{f_k\}_{k=1}^{K}$ is represented by the darkened squares on the squared line.

The set of residuals $\{u_g\}_{g=1}^{\infty}$ is represented by the white squares on the squared line.

Expression (9.3) is still not very practical for pricing the assets traded in M. To price any asset in M (an uncountably infinite set), we need to know the prices (returns) of the basis assets $(f_k)_{k=1}^{K}$ and $(u_g)_{g=1}^{\infty}$. This is a countably infinite set. Some reduction has occurred going from an uncountable set of traded assets M to a countable infinite set. Yet, one still needs an infinite set of prices.

It would be nice if only a *finite* number of basis asset returns $(f_k)_{k=1}^{K}$ were needed to price "approximately" all the primary assets $(x_j)_{j=1}^{\infty}$.[2] This would be the significant reduction in the exogenous prices needed to utilize the theory (see Fig. 9.1). The next assumption partially attains this reduction in the size of the exogenously given prices.

---

[2] If M is infinite dimensional, i.e., an infinite number of the $\{x_j\}$ are linearly independent, then an approximation is the best we can ever obtain.

Assumption 9.9: Linear Factor Hypothesis[†]

$$r(x_j) = r(x_\Omega) + \sum_{k=1}^{K} \lambda_{jk} (f_k - r(x_\Omega)) + \lambda_{j,K+j} (u_j - r(x_\Omega))$$

$$\text{for } j = 1, 2, \ldots, \infty \qquad (9.4a)$$

where for all investors s

$$\text{cov}_s (u_i, u_j) = 0 \quad \text{if } i \neq j \qquad (9.4b)$$

and

$$\text{var}_s (\lambda_{j,K+j}(u_j - r(x_\Omega))) \leq \overline{\sigma}^2 \quad \text{for all } j \qquad (9.4c)$$

This assumption restricts the nonzero coefficients in expression (9.3). For each primary asset x_j, the coefficients preceding the returns $\{f_k\}_{k=1}^{K}$ are unrestricted, but only one of the remaining basis asset returns $\{u_g\}_{g=1}^{\infty}$ can have a nonzero coefficient. This coefficient is $\lambda_{j,K+j}$.

The returns $\{f_k\}_{k=1}^{K}$, which are *common* to all primary assets $\{x_j\}_{j=1}^{\infty}$, are called *factors*. The return u_j, which is *specific* to asset x_j, is called the *residual*.

The symbol $\text{cov}_s (u_i, u_j) = E_s[(u_i - E_s(u_i))(u_j - E_s(u_j))]$ is the covariance of the residual returns u_i and u_j using investor s's probability beliefs. Condition (9.4b) requires that all investors agree that the residual's returns are uncorrelated across assets; i.e., the covariance is zero. Finally, for technical reasons, condition (9.4c) requires that all investors agree that $\text{var}_s (\lambda_{j,K+j} u_j) = (\lambda_{j,K+j})^2 \text{var}_s (u_j)$ is uniformly bounded by $\overline{\sigma}^2$.

It needs to be emphasized that the linear factor hypothesis, assumption 9.9, is really the combination of two assumptions. The first is that there is a linear factor model [like expression (9.4)] generating asset returns, but the factors f_j need not correspond to the returns on traded assets. The second is that the factors f_j correspond to returns on traded assets in M, i.e., the factors trade. Although the second part of this assumption concerning the tradeability of the factors can be dropped, the resulting generality adds no additional insights. Furthermore, without the tradeability of the factors f_j, the resulting theory has less economic content. The interested reader can pursue this issue in the suggested references, especially Chamberlain and Rothschild [4] and Admati and Pfleiderer [1].

With the use of assumption 9.9, the expected return on any primary asset is (for investor s)

$$E_s(r(x_j)) = r(x_\Omega) + \sum_{k=1}^{K} \lambda_{jk} (E_s(f_k) - r(x_\Omega)) + \lambda_{j,K+j} (E_s(u_j) - r(x_\Omega)) \qquad (9.5)$$

The expected return is decomposable into three components: a riskless component earning the risk-free rate, $r(x_\Omega)$; a risky component due to the common factors earning an excess expected return of $\sum_{k=1}^{K} \lambda_{jk} (E_s(f_k) - r(x_\Omega))$; and a risky component due to the residual component earning an excess expected return of $\lambda_{j,K+j}(E_s(u_j) - r(x_\Omega))$.

In general, the residual expected excess return is nonzero. However, under conditions (9.4b) and (9.4c) of the linear factor hypothesis, there is reason to expect that this excess expected residual return should be small. Indeed, consider forming an equally weighted portfolio of the first n primary assets. The return on this portfolio is

$$\sum_{j=1}^{n} \frac{1}{n}(r(x_j)) = r(x_\Omega) + \sum_{j=1}^{n} \frac{1}{n} \sum_{k=1}^{K} (\lambda_{jk}(f_k - r(x_\Omega))) + \sum_{j=1}^{n} \frac{\lambda_{j,K+j}(u_j - r)}{n}$$

Now let the number of primary assets included get arbitrarily large ($n \to \infty$). The part of the portfolio return's risk that is due to the residual component, $\sum_{j=1}^{n}(\lambda_{j,K+j}(u_j - r(x_\Omega)))/n$, becomes very small. To see this, consider the following stream of equalities and inequalities:

$$\text{var}_s\left(\sum_{j=1}^{n} \frac{\lambda_{j,K+j}(u_j - r(x_\Omega))}{n}\right) = \frac{1}{n^2} \sum_{j=1}^{n} \text{var}_s(\lambda_{j,K+j} u_j) \leq \frac{\bar{\sigma}^2}{n}$$

As n gets large, the variance of this residual-based return goes to zero. Hence, in this sense, the residual's risk is *diversifiable* in a large portfolio.[3] One would expect, perhaps under additional assumptions, that the expected excess return on this residual should be approximately zero. Why? Because it can be diversified away in a large portfolio, and therefore no investor would ever bear this risk. This intuition is formalized precisely in the equilibrium version of the APT in Chap. 18. For now, we use it to motivate the following assumption.

Assumption 9.10: No Infinite Asset Arbitrage Opportunities[†]

If for some investor s

$$\sum_{j=1}^{n} w_j^n = 1 \quad \text{for all } n$$

and

$$\lim_{n \to \infty} \text{var}_s\left(\sum_{j=0}^{n} w_j^n r(x_j)\right) = 0$$

then

$$\lim_{n \to \infty} E_s\left(\sum_{j=0}^{n} w_j^n r(x_j)\right) = r(x_\Omega) < +\infty$$

This assumption states that if for some investor a sequence of portfolios exists with a positive investment ($\sum_{j=1}^{n} w_j^n = 1$) and a variance that goes to zero,

---

[3] This argument ignores the covariance between f_j and u_i. Since this argument is used only for motivation, this lack of rigor is acceptable. It can be made rigorous if we impose additional structure on the portfolio weights such that the portfolio (by construction) bears no factor risk as well.

then the limiting portfolio must earn the riskless rate. This assumption excludes *infinite asset arbitrage opportunities*. Indeed, suppose the expected return on the portfolio approached k, where $k > r(x_\Omega)$. Then an investor could borrow at the riskless rate $r(x_\Omega)$ and invest these borrowings into the above sequence of portfolios. The net investment is zero. The risk is zero (in the limit), but the return is a sure $k - r(x_\Omega) > 0$! Assumption 9.10 excludes these limiting arbitrage opportunities. This assumption extends the no finite asset arbitrage opportunities assumption 9.7 from finite asset portfolios to infinite asset portfolios.

This assumption is exogenously imposed in the above model. Sufficient conditions on preferences needed to motivate this assumption are studied in Sec. 9.4. Section 9.4 is starred because the mathematics required is beyond that used elsewhere in this chapter. It shows that the utility theory developed in Chap. 7 (axioms 7.1–7.8) are sufficient to generate this assumption. In fact, it can be shown that many of the rationality axioms can be dispensed with, in particular, the strong independence axiom (see Jarrow [8]). The required structure on preferences will be seen to be much weaker than that needed to generate the equilibrium models of subsequent chapters.

9.2. THE THEOREM

This section states the APT and discusses its interpretation. The form that the theorem assumes is particularly confusing, yet significant. Understanding its subtleties is important, since much of the controversy concerning the testability of the APT (discussed in Sec. 9.3) stems from its unusual structure. We now state the theorem.

Theorem 9.1: Ross's APT

Given assumptions 9.1–9.10

$$\lim_{n \to \infty} \sum_{j=1}^{n} [\lambda_{j, K+j} (E_s(u_j) - r(x_\Omega))]^2 < +\infty \tag{9.6}$$

for all investors s.

Proof

See Sec. 9.5. ☐

This theorem formally states that an infinite summation involving the expected residual returns of the primary assets, expression (9.6), is finite. To understand this result, one must realize that if an infinite sum of positive terms is finite, most of the terms in the sum must be close to zero. So expression (9.6) actually states that, "on average"

$$\lambda_{j,K+j}(E_s(u_j) - r(x_\Omega)) \approx 0 \tag{9.7}$$

where $\approx$ stands for approximately. But $\lambda_{j,K+j}(E_s(u_j) - r(x_\Omega))$ represents a constant, $\lambda_{j,K+j}$, times the excess expected return associated with the residual risk. Hence, loosely speaking, due to the ability to diversify in the limit, we see that the residual risk component receives "on average" zero excess expected return.

The following corollary further clarifies condition (9.6).

Corollary 9.1: Interpretation of the APT

Given a small $\epsilon > 0$, the assets can be divided into two groups $\{1, \ldots, n_\epsilon\}$ and $\{n_\epsilon + 1, \ldots, \infty\}$, such that

$$\text{for} \quad j \in \{1, \ldots, n_\epsilon\}, \, |\lambda_{j,K+j}(E_s(u_j) - r(x_\Omega))| \geq \epsilon$$

and

$$\text{for} \quad j \in \{n_\epsilon + 1, \ldots, \infty\}, \, |\lambda_{j,K+j}(E_s(u_j) - r(x_\Omega))| < \epsilon$$

Proof

Since $\sum_{j=1}^{\infty}(\lambda_{j,K+j}(E_s(u_j) - r(x_\Omega)))^2 < +\infty$ is absolutely convergent, the terms in the sum can be rearranged without changing the sum (see Rudin [10, p. 78]). Hence order $|\lambda_{j,K+j}(E_s(u_j) - r(x_\Omega))|^2$ from largest to smallest.

Given $\epsilon > 0$, assume there exists no $n_\epsilon > 0$ such that for $n \geq n_\epsilon$, $|\lambda_{j,K+j}(E_s(u_j) - r(x_\Omega))| < \epsilon$. Hence for all n, $|\lambda_{j,K+j}(E_s(u_j) - r(x_\Omega))| \geq \epsilon$; then

$$\lim_{n \to \infty} \sum_{j=1}^{n} \lambda_{j,K+j}^2 (E_s(u_j) - r(x_\Omega))^2 \geq \lim_{n \to \infty} n \, \epsilon^2 = +\infty$$

Contradiction. $\square$

The corollary states that for most assets $(n_\epsilon + 1, \ldots, \infty)$, the excess expected return on the residual component is near zero (less than a small ϵ). However, for a smaller group $(1, \ldots, n_\epsilon)$, the excess expected return on the residual component is large (greater than ϵ). In fact, for this group, the excess expected return for the residual can be quite large, for example, greater than 1000 percent! Fortunately, the ratio of the number of elements in this set to the total number of assets is infinitesimal—$(n_\epsilon/+\infty) = 0$. Nonetheless, the existence of this set of assets points out a limitation of the APT. The model only holds *on average*, not *uniformly*, for all primary assets. We will return to this observation in Sec. 9.3, when we discuss the testability of the APT.

Using expression (9.5), which breaks down the expected return on an asset into its component parts, we can rewrite the APT as

$$\lim_{n \to \infty} \sum_{j=1}^{n} \left(E_s(r(x_j)) - r(x_\Omega) - \sum_{k=1}^{K} \lambda_{jk}(E_s(f_k) - r(x_\Omega)) \right)^2 < +\infty \quad (9.8)$$

for all investors s; i.e.

$$E_s(r(x_j)) \approx r(x_\Omega) + \sum_{k=1}^{K} \lambda_{jk}(E_s(f_k) - r(x_\Omega)) \quad (9.9)$$

where $\approx$ means approximately in the sense that the infinite sum in expression (9.8) is finite.

Hence we have an *approximate* linear relationship between the return on any primary asset x_j, the risk-free rate, and the excess expected return on the factors $\{f_k\}_{k=1}^{K}$. This was the purpose for introducing the three assumptions: assumption 9.8, giving a countable basis; the linear factor hypothesis, assumption 9.9; and no infinite arbitrage opportunities, assumption 9.10. Expression (9.9) does not include the residual return's excess expected return as in the GAPT expression (9.5). Only a *finite* number of prices are needed to price approximately all traded primary assets. Since all the traded assets can be constructed as portfolios of the primary assets, assumption 9.8, we can use expression (9.9) to price all the traded assets (in M) as well. Expression (9.8) is the form most often referred to as the APT.

9.3. TESTABILITY

There is controversy in the literature concerning whether the APT, expression (9.8), is testable (see Shanken [11, 12], Dyvbig and Ross [5]). In the strictest sense, expression (9.8) is *not* testable. To understand why this is true, consider what is necessary to test the model. Formally, the experimenter must obtain estimates of the parameters $E_s(r(x_j))$, λ_{jk}, and $E_s(f_j)$ for all $k = 1, \ldots, K$ and $j = 1, \ldots, \infty$, and then calculate the sum in expression (9.8). If the sum is finite, the theory is validated. If the sum is infinite, the theory is rejected.

A dilemma now faces the experimenter. There is no way to obtain estimates of an infinite number of assets. At most, only a finite number of asset estimates can be obtained, say, $n_0 = 10^5$. So we can calculate the sum

$$\sum_{j=1}^{10^5} \left[E_s(r(x_j)) - r(x_\Omega) - \sum_{k=1}^{K} \lambda_{jk}(E_s(f_k) - r(x_\Omega)) \right]^2$$

But can this be used to validate or reject the model? The answer is no.

First, the sum

$$\sum_{j=1}^{10^5} \left[E_s(r(x_j)) - r(x_\Omega) - \sum_{k=1}^{K} \lambda_{jk}(E_s(f_k) - r(x_\Omega)) \right]^2$$

is always finite. Second, the infinite sum

$$\sum_{j=1}^{\infty} \left[E_s(r(x_j)) - r(x_\Omega) - \sum_{k=1}^{K} \lambda_{jk}(E_s(f_k) - r(x_\Omega)) \right]^2 < +\infty$$

if and only if

$$\sum_{j=10^5+1}^{\infty} \left[E_s(r(x_j)) - r(x_\Omega) - \sum_{k=1}^{K} \lambda_{jk}(E_s(f_k) - r(x_\Omega)) \right]^2 < +\infty$$

So, to validate expression (9.8) and the model, the observations we obtained for $(1, \ldots, 10^5)$ are irrelevant! It is the assets we have not estimated that decide the formal truth or falsity of the APT. In this sense, the model cannot be tested.

This same insight into testing the APT can be obtained from another perspective. First, take the reciprocal of expression (9.8):

$$\left[1 \bigg/ \sum_{j=1}^{n} (E_s(r(x_j)) - r(x_\Omega) - \sum_{k=1}^{K} \lambda_{jk}(E_s(f_k) - r(x_\Omega)))^2 \right] \qquad (9.10)$$

If this reciprocal approaches zero as $n \to \infty$, the APT, expression (9.8), will be contradicted, thereby rejecting the model. Yet for any finite n, this expression is always nonzero. So, in the strictest sense, the model is untestable.

There is an alternative point of view which starts with the assertion that no model is strictly valid since a model's assumptions are approximations and can be rejected out of hand. This is fundamental to the nature of models. In this point of view, testing a model really means testing the "goodness of fit" of the approximation to reality. This goodness of fit criteria necessarily reflects the end use of the model, i.e., the reason it was developed. For the APT, the purpose of the model is to price approximately the traded assets using only K factor prices. It seems that a reasonable method of testing this approximation is to examine whether the pricing relationships, $E_s(r(x_j)) - r(x_\Omega) - \sum_{k=1}^{K} \lambda_{jk}(E_s(f_k) - r(x_\Omega))$, are close to zero for the sample of assets under consideration. If so, it is consistent with the APT; if not, it is inconsistent. Unfortunately, many models will be developed with this same purpose in mind. The tests of the approximations will be effectively indistinguishable unless other uses (purposes for developing the model) are brought to bear for use in comparison testing. A list of references that empirically test the APT can be found at the end of Chap. 18.

*9.4. ALTERNATE SUFFICIENT CONDITIONS TO REPLACE ASSUMPTION 9.10

One can take two approaches to replace the no infinite asset arbitrage opportunity assumption 9.10 with alternate sufficient conditions. The first approach is to impose additional structure on investor preferences such that a violation of assumption 9.10 provides an opportunity to increase utility at no cost. The second approach is to impose more structure on the set of marketed assets. The second idea is to make the marketed assets "complete" enough so that no finite asset arbitrage opportunities, assumption 9.7, is sufficient to exclude infinite asset arbitrage opportunities. The second approach, not discussed below, is found in Jarrow [8]. This section is starred because it is more difficult than the preceding sections. It can be skipped without loss of content.

First, recall the consumption-saving model of Sec. 8.3 in Chap. 8. For brevity, we will repeat only the essential material. Recall from expression (9.1) that the basis set of assets is $\{z_j\}_{j=1}^{\infty}$. However, we can use the primary assets $\{x_j\}_{j=1}^{\infty}$ for the analysis since these also span the same set. For convenience, let $x_0 = x_{\Omega}$, the riskless asset. The time 0 budget constraint for an investor is

$$\overline{C}_0 + \sum_{j=0}^{\infty} \overline{N}_j p(x_j)/\rho_0 = C_0 + \sum_{j=0}^{\infty} N_j p(x_j)/\rho_0 \qquad (9.11)$$

where only a finite number of $\overline{N}_j$ and N_j are not equal to zero. Recall that $\overline{C}_0$ is the endowed consumption at time 0, $\overline{N}_j$ is the endowed portfolio shares in asset j, and $\rho_0 > 0$ is the exogenous time 0 price level for converting dollars to units of consumption. By construction, the time 1 budget constraint under state ω is[4]

$$\overline{C}_1(\omega) + \sum_{j=0}^{\infty} N_j x_j(\omega)/\rho_1(\omega) = C_1(\omega) \quad \text{for all } \omega \in \Omega \qquad (9.12)$$

where only a finite number of $N_j \neq 0$, $\overline{C}_1(\omega)$ is endowed time 1 units of consumption given state ω, and $\rho_1(\omega) > 0$ is the time 1 price level under state ω. The investor's preference function is

$$E\left(V\left(C_0, \overline{C}_1(\omega) + \sum_{j=0}^{\infty} N_j x_j(\omega)/\rho_1(\omega)\right)\right) \qquad (9.13)$$

subject to (9.11), where $V(C_0, C_1)$ is the cardinal utility function defined over consumption at times 0 and 1, and $E(\cdot)$ is the expectation operator. Formally, the expectation operator, utility function, and endowments should be subscripted to reflect a particular individual. We omit the subscript, however, to reduce the notational complexity of the subsequent expressions.

We introduce the following:

Assumption 9.11: Certain Inflation

$$\rho_1(\omega) \equiv \rho_1, \text{ a positive constant for all } \omega \in \Omega$$

This assumption makes dollar cash flows equivalent to a fixed proportion of the consumption good across all states $\omega \in \Omega$.

---

[4] It is sufficient for expression (9.12) to hold with probability one.

To interpret the certain inflation assumption 9.11 in the context of the above model, we must first transform conditions (9.11) and (9.12) into return form:

Define $\quad w_j \equiv \dfrac{N_j p(x_j)/\rho_0}{\left[\overline{C}_0 + \left(\displaystyle\sum_{j=0}^{\infty} \overline{N}_j p(x_j)/\rho_0\right) - C_0\right]} \quad$ for $j = 0, \ldots, \infty$ (9.14)

where $\Sigma_{j=0}^{\infty} w_j = 1$ and only a finite number of $w_j \neq 0$. The portfolio weight w_j represents the percentage of wealth in the portfolio represented by asset j.

Given expression (9.14), (9.12) takes the form

$$C_1(\omega) = \overline{C}_1(\omega) + W_0 \sum_{j=0}^{\infty} w_j(1 + R(x_j)) \tag{9.15}$$

where

$$R(x_j) \equiv \left[\frac{x_j}{\rho_1} - \frac{p(x_j)}{\rho_0}\right] \Big/ [p(x_j)/\rho_0]$$

and

$$W_0 \equiv \left[\overline{C}_0 + \left(\sum_{j=0}^{\infty} \overline{N}_j p(x_j) \Big/ \rho_0\right) - C_0\right]$$

Summarizing, in return form, expression (9.13) can be written as

$$E\left(V\left(C_0, \overline{C}_1 + W_0 + W_0 \sum_{j=0}^{\infty} w_j R(x_j)\right)\right) \tag{9.16}$$

subject to $\Sigma_{j=0}^{\infty} w_j = 1$.

Suppose there is a violation of assumption 9.10; i.e., there exists a sequence of asset portfolios $\{\delta_j(n)\}_{j=1}^{n}$ such that $\Sigma_{j=0}^{n} \delta_j(n) = 1$ for all n (we write $\delta_j(n) = \delta_j$ for simplicity), where

$$\lim_{n \to \infty} \text{var}\left(\sum_{j=1}^{n} \delta_j r(x_j)\right) = 0 \tag{9.17}$$

but

$$\lim_{n \to \infty} E\left(\sum_{j=1}^{n} \delta_j r(x_j)\right) > r(x_\Omega)$$

We need to transform expression (9.17) from dollar returns to returns measured in units of the consumption good. Key in this transformation is the identity

$$r(x_j) = \frac{\rho_1}{\rho_0} R(x_j) + \left(\frac{\rho_1}{\rho_0} - 1\right) \tag{9.18}$$

With this identity (9.17) becomes

$$\lim_{n \to \infty} \text{var}\left(\sum_{j=0}^{n} \delta_j R(x_j)\right) = 0$$

$$\lim_{n \to \infty} E\left(\sum_{j=0}^{n} \delta_j R(x_j)\right) > R(x_0)$$

(9.19)

where $R(x_0)$ is the riskless return in units of the consumption good.

Consider the portfolio $(\psi_0, \psi_1, \psi_2, \ldots)$ defined by

$$\psi_0 = \delta_0 - 1 + w_0$$

$$\psi_j = \delta_j + w_j \quad \text{for} \quad j = 1, \ldots, n$$

$$\psi_j = w_j \quad\quad \text{for} \quad j = n + 1, \ldots, \infty$$

The portfolio is feasible since $\sum_{j=0}^{\infty} \psi_j = 1$, and we claim it also increases the investor's utility as $n \to \infty$. To prove this, consider the following equations:

$$\lim_{n \to \infty} E\left(V\left(C_0, \overline{C}_1 + W_0 + W_0\left(\sum_{j=0}^{\infty} \psi_j R(x_j)\right)\right)\right)$$

$$= \lim_{n \to \infty} E\left(V\left(C_0, \overline{C}_1 + W_0 + W_0\left(\sum_{j=0}^{\infty} w_j R(x_j) + \sum_{j=0}^{n} \delta_j R(x_j) - R(x_0)\right)\right)\right)$$

$$= E\left(V\left(C_0, \overline{C}_1 + W_0 + W_0\left(\sum_{j=0}^{\infty} w_j R(x_j) + \lim_{n \to \infty} E\left(\sum_{j=0}^{n} \delta_j R(x_j)\right) - R(x_0)\right)\right)\right)$$

$$> E\left(V\left(C_0, \overline{C}_1 + W_0 + W_0\left(\sum_{j=0}^{\infty} w_j R(x_j)\right)\right)\right)$$

since

$$\lim_{n \to \infty} E\left(\sum_{j=0}^{n} \delta_j R(x_j) - R(x_0)\right) > 0$$

by expression (9.19) and monotonicity of the utility function (assumption 7.1). The second equal sign (the interchange of limits) follows because

$$\text{(i)} \quad \lim_{n \to \infty} \text{var}\left(\sum_{j=0}^{n} \delta_j R(x_j)\right) = 0$$

implies

$$\left[\sum_{j=0}^{n} \delta_j R(x_j) - \sum_{j=0}^{n} \delta_j ER(x_j)\right]$$

converges in probability to zero (by Bartle [2, p. 69]). This implies

$$\text{(ii)} \quad \left(\sum_{j=0}^{n} \delta_j R(x_j) - \sum_{j=0}^{n} \delta_j ER(x_j) + \sum_{j=0}^{\infty} w_j R(x_j)\right)$$

converges in probability to $\Sigma_{j=0}^{\infty} w_j R(x_j)$. This implies

$$\text{(iii)} \quad \left(\sum_{j=0}^{n} \delta_j R(x_j) - \sum_{j=0}^{n} \delta_j ER(x_j) + \sum_{j=0}^{\infty} w_j R(x_j) \right)$$

converges in distribution to $\Sigma_{j=0}^{\infty} w_j R(x_j)$ (by Billingsley [3, p. 284]). Finally by axiom 7.8 (continuity), this implies the limit operator can go under $E(V(\cdot))$. This completes the proof. $\square$

Hence, we have shown that under the preference axioms 7.1–7.8 and assumption 7.1 of monotonicity, an infinite asset arbitrage opportunity would imply that a utility-increasing trading strategy exists. This implication also follows with a drastic reduction in the rationality axioms required. In fact, it can be shown that only the axioms of reflexivity 7.1, comparability 7.2, transitivity 7.3, and continuity 7.8 and the monotonicity assumption 7.1 are required (see Jarrow [8]). This set excludes the strong independence axiom, among others. This structure is significantly weaker than the preference structure required to obtain the equilibrium pricing models of subsequent chapters.

9.5. PROOF OF THEOREM 9.1

The proof of this theorem is by contradiction. Suppose

$$\sum_{j=1}^{\infty} \lambda_{j,K+j}^2 (E_s(u_j) - r(x_\Omega))^2 = +\infty \quad \text{for some investor } s$$

For convenience, let the returns on x_j equal f_j for $j = 1, \ldots, K$. This is without loss of generality since we could always increase the set of primary assets and then renumber them.

For simplicity of notation, let us also agree to write $\lambda_{j,K+j} \equiv \eta_j, r(x_j) \equiv r_j$, for $j = K+1, \ldots, \infty$, and $r(x_\Omega) = r$. Choose $n > K$ and form the portfolio sequence

$$w_i^n = \eta_i (E_s(u_i) - r) / \sum_{j=K+1}^{n} (E_s(u_j) - r)^2 \eta_j^2 \quad \text{for } i = K+1, \ldots, +\infty$$

$$w_j^n = - \sum_{i=K+1}^{n} \lambda_{ij} w_i^n \quad \text{for } j = 1, \ldots, K$$

$$w_0^n = - \sum_{j=1}^{n} w_j^n + 1$$

Then, by the definition of w_0^n, $\Sigma_{i=0}^{n} w_i^n = w_0^n + \Sigma_{i=1}^{n} w_i^n = 1$ for all n. Also

$$\sum_{j=0}^{n} w_j^n r_j = w_0^n r + \sum_{j=1}^{K} w_j^n r_j + \sum_{j=K+1}^{n} w_j^n r_j$$

Use of $r_j = f_j$ for $j = 1, \ldots, K$ and the definition of w_0^n gives

$$\sum_{j=0}^{n} w_j^n r_j = -\sum_{j=1}^{n} w_j^n r + r + \sum_{j=1}^{K} w_j^n f_j + \sum_{j=K+1}^{n} w_j^n r_j$$

$$= r + \sum_{j=1}^{K} w_j^n (f_j - r) + \sum_{j=K+1}^{n} w_j^n (r_j - r)$$

Use of the definition of w_j^n for $j = 1, \ldots, K$ gives

$$\sum_{j=0}^{n} w_j^n r_j = r - \sum_{i=K+1}^{n} w_i^n \sum_{j=1}^{K} \lambda_{ij}(f_j - r) + \sum_{j=K+1}^{n} w_j^n (r_j - r)$$

Use of expression (9.4a) gives

$$\sum_{j=0}^{n} w_j^n r_j = r + \sum_{i=K+1}^{n} w_i^n(\eta_i(u_i - r)) \quad \text{for all } n$$

So

$$\sum_{j=0}^{n} w_j^n E_s(r_j) = r + \sum_{i=K+1}^{n} w_i^n[E_s(u_i) - r]\eta_i$$

But, by the definition of w_j^n for $j = K + 1, \ldots, \infty$

$$\sum_{j=0}^{n} w_j^n E_s(r_j) = r + 1 \quad \text{for all } n$$

Also

$$\text{var}_s\left(\sum_{j=0}^{n} w_j^n r_j\right) = \sum_{i=K+1}^{n} (w_i^n)^2 \text{var}_s(\eta_i(u_i - r))$$

This variance is uniformly bounded by the linear factor hypothesis, assumption 9.9, so

$$\text{var}_s\left(\sum_{j=0}^{n} w_j^n r_j\right) \leq \bar{\sigma}^2 \sum_{i=K+1}^{n} (w_i^n)^2 = \bar{\sigma}^2 \frac{1}{\sum_{i=K+1}^{n} (E_s(u_i) - r))^2 \eta_i^2} \longrightarrow 0$$

by hypothesis, but $E_s(\sum_{j=0}^{n} w_j^n r_j) \to 1 + r > r$. This contradicts the no infinite asset arbitrage opportunity assumption 9.10. $\square$

9.6. SUMMARY

This chapter presents Ross's APT as a special case of the generalized arbitrage pricing theory developed in Chap. 8. The arbitrage pricing theory of Chap. 8 is restricted by the introduction of four additional assumptions. The first is technical in nature, restricting attention to assets having finite variances. The second restricts the economy to having a basis set of assets consisting of at most a countably infinite number of elements. The third imposes a linear factor structure on asset returns, while the fourth excludes limiting arbitrage opportunities.

Given this structure, it is proven that the excess expected return on the residual component is "approximately zero." The phrase approximately zero manifests a weakness of the APT. The approximate pricing model only holds on average and not uniformly across all assets. An equilibrium version of the APT is given in Chap. 18.

9.7. REFERENCES

1. Admati, Anat, and Paul Pfleiderer, "Interpreting the Factor Risk Premia in the Arbitrage Pricing Theory," *Journal of Economic Theory*, 35 (1985), 191–195.
2. Bartle, Robert, *The Elements of Integration*. New York: John Wiley, 1966.
3. Billingsley, Patrick, *Probability and Measure*. New York: John Wiley, 1979.
4. Chamberlain, Gary, and Michael Rothschild, "Arbitrage, Factor Structure, and Mean-Variance Analysis on Large Asset Markets," *Econometrica*, 51 (September 1983), 1281–1304.
5. Dyvbig, Philip, and Stephen Ross, "Yes. The APT Is Testable," *Journal of Finance* (September 1985), 1173–1188.
6. Huberman, Gus, "A Simple Approach to Arbitrage Pricing Theory," *Journal of Economic Theory*, 28 (1982), 183–191.
7. Ingersoll, Jonathan, "Some Results in the Theory of Arbitrage Pricing," *Journal of Finance* (September 1984), 1021–1039.
8. Jarrow, Robert, "Preferences, Continuity, and the Arbitrage Pricing Theory," unpublished manuscript, Ithaca, N.Y.: Cornell University, 1986.
9. Ross, Stephen A., "The Arbitrage Theory of Capital Asset Pricing," *Journal of Economic Theory*, 13 (1976), 341–360.
10. Rudin, Walter, *Principles of Mathematical Analysis*, 3rd ed. New York: McGraw-Hill, 1976.
11. Shanken, Jay, "The Arbitrage Pricing Theory: Is It Testable?" *Journal of Finance* (December 1982), 1129–1140.
12. _____, "Multi-beta CAPM or Equilibrium APT?: A Reply," *Journal of Finance* (September 1985), 1189–1196.

10

DIVIDEND POLICY

This chapter applies the arbitrage pricing methodology introduced in Chap. 8 to study an important issue in corporate finance, the dividend policy issue: Is there an optimal dividend per share? The analysis is divided into two sections. Section 10.1 studies this issue in a frictionless market with no personal income taxes. Section 10.2 studies this same issue after the introduction of personal taxes. Personal taxes are shown to make a difference.

   The analysis in this chapter generalizes the similar analysis in Chap. 4. The arguments and motivations are identical. Contrary to that in Chap. 4, however, this chapter's model is meant to be applied to the actual security markets.

10.1. NO PERSONAL TAXES

Consider the single period model introduced in Sec. 8.1 of Chap. 8. We will study the dividend policy question in the context of that asset model. Recall the structure of the model. There are two time periods: today (0) and tomorrow (1). The uncertainty in the economy at time 1 is characterized by the state space Ω. An asset is specified by a function $x(\omega)$ giving the cash flow to asset x at time 1 under state $\omega \in \Omega$. The set of assets that trade in an organized market at time 0 is denoted by M. If asset $x \in M$, then its price at time 0 is denoted $p(x)$. The economy satisfies assumptions 8.1–8.6. Assumption 8.1 states that if two assets trade, then all portfolios composed of asset x and asset y trade as a package.

Assumptions 8.2–8.3 concern investor beliefs. They state that investors agree on the state contingent cash flows to each asset $x \in M$ (assumption 8.2) and that investors agree on zero probability events (assumption 8.3). The market is frictionless (assumption 8.4) and competitive (assumption 8.5) and contains no arbitrage opportunities (assumption 8.6). Given this economy, we can proceed.

As in Chap. 4, all of the effort involved in studying the dividend policy issue is expended in the construction of a controlled experiment. The idea is to construct a model consisting of two identical firms, with one exception. The firms' dividends paid per share of common equity differ. By comparing their common equity values, we can isolate the influence of dividends per share. Everything else will be held constant. We now turn to this task.

Let two of the assets that trade represent the common equity of two different firms, firm A and firm B. These are the candidates for the controlled experiment. Let

$x_A(\omega)$ = the cash flows to firm A at time 1 under state $\omega \in \Omega$ after
      (i) all refinancing of liabilities is completed except with respect to common equity, and
      (ii) all investments (new and continuing) are made;

$d_A(\omega)$ = dividends paid per share on firm A's common equity at time 1 under state $\omega \in \Omega$;

n = the number of common equity shares of firm A outstanding at time 0;

$\Delta n_A(\omega)$ = the change in the number of firm A's common equity shares outstanding at time 1 under state $\omega \in \Omega$; and

$s_A(\omega)$ = the common equity value in dollars of firm A at time 1 under state $\omega \in \Omega$ (after the payment of the dividends and after refinancing of the equity shares).

Similarly, the terms $x_B(\omega)$, $d_B(\omega)$, n, $\Delta n_B(\omega)$, and $s_B(\omega)$ are defined for firm B. By construction, both firms have n shares of common equity outstanding at time 0. This is a trivial part of the identical firm hypothesis.

At time 1 under any state $\omega \in \Omega$, the firm's cash flows must satisfy the following accounting identity:

$$x_A(\omega) = nd_A(\omega) - \Delta n_A(\omega)s_A(\omega)$$
$$x_B(\omega) = nd_B(\omega) - \Delta n_B(\omega)s_B(\omega)$$
(10.1)

For firm A this identity states that the remaining cash flows at time 1 under state $\omega \in \Omega$ after investments and refinancing (except with respect to equity) is either paid out as dividends ($nd_A(\omega)$) or used to refinance equity ($\Delta n_A(\omega)s_A(\omega)$). There are no other possibilities. The negative sign appears prior to the refinancing equity term since if equity is repurchased, Δn_A is negative. Yet this represents a positive cash outflow. The negative sign preceding Δn_A corrects for this; i.e., $-\Delta n_A > 0$ in this case. A similar interpretation of this identity holds for firm B. This accounting identity is really just a precise restatement of the definitions of x_A and x_B in terms of the other quantities.

To finish constructing the controlled experiment, we need to make firms A and B identical with the exception of their dividend policies at time 1. The next two assumptions fulfill this task.[1]

Assumption 10.1: Identical Cash Flows at Time 1

$$x_A(\omega) = x_B(\omega) \quad \text{for all } \omega \in \Omega$$

Assumption 10.2: Identical Cash Flows to Equity in the Future

$$(n + \Delta n_A(\omega))s_A(\omega) = (n + \Delta n_B(\omega))s_B(\omega) \quad \text{for all } \omega \in \Omega$$

Assumption 10.1 guarantees that the cash flows to both firms, prior to dividend payments or equity refinancing, are identical.[2] This is the first control in our analytic experiment. Without this assumption we would never be sure whether differing dividend policies or differing cash flows cause the observed results. The second control is assumption 10.2, which states that the time 1 value of the total equity in firm A and firm B is identical. This is necessitated by the single period aspect of the model. This would be true if the cash flows to all equity holders after time 2 are identical. That is, there are identical dividend policies and identical investment opportunities from time 2 onward. In a more general model, this assumption would be a derived implication. Hence, through assumptions 10.1 and 10.2 the firms are identical with the exception that we allow only a change in the dividend policy at time 1. The equity refinancing is the residual decision.

Finally, we specify how the dividend policies for the two firms differ at time 1 under all states $\omega \in \Omega$, i.e.

$$d_A(\omega) > d_B(\omega) \quad \text{for all } \omega \in \Omega$$

We let firm A pay more dividends per share than firm B.

The relevance of a firm's dividend policy can now be addressed by comparing the time 0 value of firm A's equity to the time 0 value of firm B's equity. If they are equal, dividend policy is irrelevant. If they differ, dividend policy matters. The following proposition gives the result. We note that $p(d_A + s_A)$ represents the time 0 per share price (in dollars) in firm A's common equity. Each share of common equity gets a dividend, d_A, and a liquidating value, s_A.

---

[1] These assumptions could be weakened to "with probability one" versus "for all $\omega \in \Omega$."

[2] In particular, it implicitly assumes that investment policy is independent of the dividend policy decision.

The price functional $p(\cdot)$ is applied to the time 1 dollar cash flow per share of common equity. Similarly, $p(d_B + s_B)$ represents the time 0 per share price of firm B's common equity.

Theorem 10.1: Dividend Irrelevance

Given the identical firm assumptions 10.1 and 10.2

$$p(d_A + s_A) = p(d_B + s_B)$$

Proof

By assumption 10.1, expression (10.1) becomes

$$nd_A(\omega) - \Delta n_A(\omega)s_A(\omega) = nd_B(\omega) - \Delta n_B(\omega)s_B(\omega)$$

for all $\omega \in \Omega$.

Assumption 10.2 implies that $ns_A(\omega) - ns_B(\omega) = \Delta n_B(\omega)s_B(\omega) - \Delta n_A(\omega)s_A(\omega)$. Substitution of this result into the previous expression gives

$$d_A(\omega) + s_A(\omega) = d_B(\omega) + s_B(\omega) \quad \text{for all } \omega \in \Omega$$

Hence

$$p(d_A + s_A) = p(d_B + s_B) \quad \square$$

This proposition shows that dividend policy is irrelevant since the price of firm A's common equity, $p(d_A + s_A)$, equals the price of firm B's common equity, $p(d_B + s_B)$. This proposition generalizes the result obtained in Chap. 4 under certainty. The proof is almost identical.

To understand the economics of this result, let us compare the capital gains components of firms A and B. Firm A's capital gain is $(s_A(\omega) - p(s_A + d_A))$, while firm B's capital gain is $(s_B(\omega) - p(s_B + d_B))$. The total returns, by theorem 10.1, are identical:

$$[s_A(\omega) - p(s_A + d_A)] + d_A(\omega)$$
$$= [s_B(\omega) - p(s_B + d_B)] + d_B(\omega) \quad \text{for all } \omega \in \Omega$$

Hence, although firm A's shareholders earn more in dividends, firm B's shareholders earn more in capital gains. In fact, they exactly offset each other.

Inspection of the above theorem and its proof reveals that there are only two crucial requirements. The first is the exclusion of arbitrage opportunities under frictionless markets. The second is the identical firm hypothesis, assumptions 10.1 and 10.2. If any of these assumptions are false, the irrelevance proposition does not hold. If they are a reasonable approximation to the actual economy, we would expect dividend policy to be irrelevant.

If dividend policy were irrelevant, i.e., a matter of indifference, we might expect to find dividend policies randomly distributed across firms in the economy. However, this does not appear to be the case (see Lintner [5] or Brealey and Myers [3]). Most firms pay dividends, and there appears to be systematic dividend policies. One common policy is for dividends to be stable and to increase only when the change is expected to continue for the indefinite future. This evidence appears to be inconsistent with theorem 10.1.

Although this theorem does not appear consistent with actual dividend policy, the model developed is still extremely useful. It focuses our attention on the proper issues to pursue. If dividend policy matters, then it is because one (or more) of our assumptions has been violated: perhaps the frictionless market assumption (this is pursued in Sec. 10.2); perhaps the identical firm hypothesis, assumption 10.2 (this is pursued in Sec. 10.3).

10.2. DIFFERENTIAL PERSONAL TAXES

This section generalizes the above model by allowing differential personal income taxes on dividends versus capital gains. The idea is that if dividends are taxed at a higher rate than capital gains, people will prefer obtaining capital gains. Hence they will dislike dividends, and share prices will reflect this. Dividend policy will be relevant.

To generalize the model, we keep all the previous assumptions but revise them in the following way. The price functional $p(\cdot)$ is applied to the cash flow of an asset $x(\omega)$ *after personal income taxes* at time 1 under state $\omega \in \Omega$. Hence $p(x)$ now gives the time 0 price of the asset x, which is identified by its after-tax cash flows.

We need to add the following assumption:

Assumption 10.3: Marginal Tax Rates

All investors face the same tax rates. These are τ_d for dividends and τ_c for capital gains, with $1 > \tau_d > \tau_c \geq 0$.

This assumption states that all investors face the same marginal tax rates on dividend income (τ_d) and capital gains income (τ_c). Furthermore, it is assumed that the tax rate on dividend income exceeds the tax rate on capital gains income ($\tau_d > \tau_c$). This is a first approximation to the U.S. personal income tax code.

We also need the following assumption:

Assumption 10.4: Nontaxable Riskless Bond Price

The riskless asset x_Ω trades and has a price of $p(x_\Omega) \leq 1$.

We assume that the riskless asset x_Ω trades. The asset x_Ω represents an after-tax cash flow of 1 dollar under all states $\omega \in \Omega$. Hence one can view x_Ω as a nontaxable riskless bond (e.g., a high-grade municipal bond). We require that its price, $p(x_\Omega)$, be less than 1 dollar. This assumption is not very restrictive.

We retain the same notation as in Sec. 10.1. The major difference in the analysis occurs when calculating time 1 after-tax cash flows to the firms' equity shares. Let us investigate this issue.

The time 1 cash flow to firm A, before personal taxes, is $d_A(\omega) + s_A(\omega)$. Let us denote the after-tax cash flow as $y_A(\omega)$. The after-tax cash flow is

$$y_A(\omega) = d_A(\omega)(1 - \tau_d) + [s_A(\omega) - p(y_A)](1 - \tau_c) + p(y_A) \qquad (10.2)$$

The first term on the right-hand side of (10.2) represents the after-tax cash flow due to dividends. A tax of $d_A(\omega)\tau_d$ is paid, leaving $d_A(\omega)(1 - \tau_d)$. The second and third terms represent the after-tax cash flows due to capital gains income. The purchase price of the asset, $p(y_A)$, is not taxed. The capital gain, $[s_A(\omega) - p(y_A)]$, is taxed at the rate τ_c, leaving $[s_A(\omega) - p(y_A)](1 - \tau_c)$ as the after-tax income. With this expression, we can now state theorem 10.2. Recall that firm A, by construction, pays more dividends than firm B; i.e., $d_A(\omega) > d_B(\omega)$ for all $\omega \in \Omega$.

Theorem 10.2: Dividend Relevance

Given assumptions 10.1–10.4

$$p(y_A) < p(y_B)$$

where $\quad p(y_A)$ equals the time 0 price of one share of firm A's common equity, and

$\quad\quad\quad p(y_B)$ equals the time 0 price of one share of firm B's common equity.

Proof

The price of this asset, $p(y_A)$, is

$$p(y_A) = p(d_A(1 - \tau_d) + [s_A - p(y_A)](1 - \tau_c) + p(y_A))$$
$$= p[(1 - \tau_c)(d_A + s_A) - (\tau_d - \tau_c)d_A] + \tau_c p(y_A)p(x_\Omega)$$

The last step uses the fact that $p(p(y_A)) = p(y_A)p(x_\Omega)$, and the fact that both x_Ω, y_A trading implies that $(1 - \tau_c)(d_A + s_A) - (\tau_d - \tau_c)d_A$ trades by assumption 8.1 and expression (10.2). Solving for $p(y_A)$ yields

$$p(y_A) = p[(1 - \tau_c)(d_A + s_A) - (\tau_d - \tau_c)d_A]/(1 - \tau_c p(x_\Omega))$$

By the accounting identity (10.1) and assumptions 10.1 and 10.2 as in the proof of theorem 10.1, it is true that

$$d_A(\omega) + s_A(\omega) = d_B(\omega) + s_B(\omega) \quad \text{for all } \omega \in \Omega$$

Now

$$p(y_A) = p[(1 - \tau_c)(d_A + s_A) - (\tau_d - \tau_c)d_A]/(1 - \tau_c p(x_\Omega))$$

and

$$p(y_B) = p[(1 - \tau_c)(d_B + s_B) - (\tau_d - \tau_c)d_B]/(1 - \tau_c p(x_\Omega))$$

So $p(y_B) - p(y_A) = [p(d_A - d_B)(\tau_d - \tau_c)]/(1 - \tau_c p(x_\Omega))$. Assumption 8.1 is used again in this last step. This last term is positive because, by assumption 8.6, $p((d_A - d_B)(\tau_d - \tau_c)) > 0$ since $(d_A - d_B)(\tau_d - \tau_c) > 0$, and $1 > \tau_c p(x_\Omega)$ because $p(x_\Omega) \leq 1$. $\square$

In an economy where dividends are taxed at a higher rate than capital gains income, the higher the dividend paid per share (everything else constant), the lower the share price. Dividends matter in this economy! The implication of this model for dividend policy is that the firm should pay no dividends.

This is contrary to actual dividend policy practice (see Sec. 10.1) and suggests that our model is still not complete.[3] Perhaps our assumption concerning uniform marginal tax rates across investors is a poor approximation. Relaxing this uniformity would lead to clienteles across investors, where different investors prefer different dividend policies. This is consistent with the evidence. Perhaps in reality there are trading strategies available to avoid paying taxes on dividends, and $\tau_d \cong \tau_c$ (see Miller and Scholes [6]). This would again lead to an irrelevance proposition, as in theorem 10.1. In this case, as argued previously, the theory is probably still not complete. Or perhaps the identical firm hypothesis can never be satisfied. This is discussed in the next section.

10.3. INFORMATIONAL CONTENT OF DIVIDENDS

This section will only briefly discuss dividends' informational effects on share value. The section is meant to introduce information and discuss its influence on the previous models. This corresponds to the relaxation of assumption 10.2. Recall that assumption 10.2 stated that *independent of dividends per share*

$$(n + \Delta n_A(\omega))s_A(\omega) = (n + \Delta n_B(\omega))s_B(\omega)$$

That is, total equity value at time 1 is equal across firms A and B. This assumption was justified by arguing that if both the dividend policies and all future cash flows are the same from time 1 onward, then the equity values will be the same. This, of course, will be true if there exist no information asymmetries in the market either across investors or across firms.

But suppose that the information available about future investment projects for firms A and B is not freely available. Furthermore, suppose it is believed that higher dividends per share indicate better future prospects. In this case, dividends provide information. They are used by investors as a signal about future cash flows, and hence if firm A has more dividends than firm B, $(n + \Delta n_A(\omega))s_A(\omega) > (n + \Delta n_B(\omega))s_B(\omega)$ is possible as an "equilibrium" at time 1. This would imply that dividends increase share value, i.e., $p(s_A + d_A) > p(s_B + d_B)$ if $d_A > d_B$.

---

[3] The other alternative is that the firms in our economy are systematically in error. This possibility is recognized but rejected as being unlikely.

This is only one scenario. There are many others. For example, higher dividends per share might signal the absence of good future projects within the firm. In this case, $(n + \Delta n_A(\omega))s_A(\omega) < (n + \Delta n_B(\omega))s_B(\omega)$ is possible as a time 1 "equilibrium." In either case, the informational content of dividends is an important area for future research. The existing literature is still in its infancy. A partial list of references includes Bhattacharya [1, 2] and Kose and Williams [4].

10.4. SUMMARY

This chapter applied the arbitrage pricing theory developed in Chap. 8 to study corporate dividend policy. In a frictionless economy, with no arbitrage opportunities and no differential taxes on dividend income versus capital gains income, it was shown that dividend policy is irrelevant. To prove this proposition, a carefully constructed controlled experiment was performed. Two identical firms were constructed, differing only in dividends paid per share. It was shown that the common equity price per share of both firms is identical.

The model was generalized to include differing taxes on dividends versus capital gains. It was shown that if dividends are taxed at a higher rate than capital gains, dividend policy matters. The higher the dividend per share, everything else constant, the lower the common equity price per share.

Possible omissions in the analyses were discussed. Attention was focused on asymmetric information in the economy and the possible signaling role of dividends. This direction of research is still in its infancy.

10.5. REFERENCES

1. Bhattacharya, Sudipto, "Imperfect Information, Dividend Policy, and 'The Bird in the Hand Fallacy,'" *Bell Journal of Economics*, 10 (1979), 259–270.
2. _____, "Nondissipative Signalling Structures and Dividend Policy," *Quarterly Journal of Economics*, 95 (1980), 1–24.
3. Brealey, Richard, and Stewart Myers, *Principles of Corporate Finance*. New York: McGraw-Hill, 1981.
4. Kose, John, and Joseph Williams, "Dividends, Dilution, and Taxes: A Signalling Equilibrium," *Journal of Finance* (September 1985), 1053–1070.
5. Lintner, John, "Distribution of Incomes of Corporations Among Dividends, Retained Earnings, and Taxes," *American Economic Review*, 46 (May 1956), 97–113.
6. Miller, Merton, and Myron Scholes, "Dividends and Taxes," *Journal of Financial Economics*, 6 (1978), 333–364.

11

DEBT/EQUITY POLICY

This chapter studies the corporate finance issue of whether debt/equity policy influences firm value. The methodology employed is the arbitrage pricing theory developed in Chap. 8. There is a large literature studying the corporate debt/equity decision. Consequently, this chapter serves only as a brief introduction; suggested references are Chen and Kim [1] and Myers [5].

The first model discussed in this chapter excludes both personal and corporate income taxes. A debt/equity irrelevance proposition results that states that firm value is independent of the firm's liability structure. This model is then generalized to include corporate income taxes. In this generalization, debt/equity policy matters. The more debt in the firm, the larger the firm's value. Personal income taxes and/or bankruptcy costs change this assertion. Both of these frictions are studied here. The chapter ends with a discussion of the limitations of the arbitrage pricing theory approach.

11.1. NO TAXES

This section employs the asset pricing model introduced in Sec. 8.1 of Chap. 8. There are two dates, given by today (0) and tomorrow (1). The state space Ω characterizes the uncertainty in the economy at time 1. Assets are represented by dollar cash flows at time 1 under each state $\omega \in \Omega$, so an asset x is a mapping from Ω into the real line, with a cash flow denoted $x(\omega)$ under state ω. The price of asset x at time 0 is denoted $p(x)$. The economy is populated with a finite number of investors whose beliefs satisfy assumptions 8.2 and 8.3. That is, investors agree about the state contingent payoffs to the traded assets and they agree on zero probability events. The time 0 asset markets are frictionless (assumption 8.4) and competitive (assumption 8.5) and contain no arbitrage opportunities (assumption 8.6). Furthermore, if two assets trade, then all portfolios composed of these two assets also trade (assumption 8.1).

As in Chap. 4, all of the work involved in modeling the debt/equity decision goes into setting up the proper controlled experiment. The idea is to construct a model with two identical firms with the exception of their debt/equity policy. Firm values are then compared. If their firm values differ, debt/equity policy matters. If their firm values are identical, debt/equity policy does not matter. This is the task to which we now turn.

Suppose four of the assets that trade are related to two distinct firms, firm A and firm B. Firm A's liabilities (right side of the balance sheet) are composed of debt and common equity. Both of these liabilities trade in the market at time 0.

The debt consists of m_A bonds each with a *contracted* interest rate of i percent on a face value of D dollars. The *promised* cash flow at time 1 is therefore $D(1 + i)$. The actual cash flow per bond at time 1 under state $\omega \epsilon \Omega$ is denoted $x_A^b(\omega)$. This cash flow can differ from the promised payment. This cash flow is, therefore, constrained by

$$0 \leq x_A^b(\omega) \leq (1 + i)D \quad \text{for all } \omega \epsilon \Omega \tag{11.1}$$

These bonds are risky, and bankruptcy is possible since $x_A^b(\omega) < (1 + i)D$ can occur with positive probability. The price per bond at time 0 is $p(x_A^b)$. We have that $D = p(x_A^b)$ since this represents the price of the cash flow from the firm at time 1.

Let a riskless bond, $x_\Omega(\omega) = 1$ for all $\omega \epsilon \Omega$, trade. The riskless interest rate $r(x_\Omega)$ is $[1 - p(x_\Omega)]/p(x_\Omega)$. The possibility of bankruptcy of firm A suggests that the contracted interest rate i on the bonds exceeds the riskless rate $r(x_\Omega)$.

The common equity consists of n_A shares each with a cash flow of $x_A^e(\omega)$ at time 1 under state $\omega \epsilon \Omega$. Its price per share at time 0 is, therefore, $p(x_A^e)$.

The total value of firm A's liabilities at time 0, called the *firm value*, is

$$V_A \equiv m_A p(x_A^b) + n_A p(x_A^e) \tag{11.2}$$

The quantity $m_A p(x_A^b)$ equals the market value of firm A's debt at time 0, while $n_A p(x_A^e)$ equals the time 0 market value of firm A's equity. The debt/equity ratio is $m_A p(x_A^b)/n_A p(x_A^e)$. Note that $m_A D = m_A p(x_A^b)$.

The total cash flow to firm A at time 1 is defined by

$$x_A(\omega) \equiv m_A x_A^b(\omega) + n_A x_A^e(\omega) \tag{11.3}$$

This cash flow is generated from firm A's assets.

To clarify the distribution to the liability holders of firm A's cash flows at time 1, consider Table 11.1. Bankruptcy occurs if the cash flows to the firm,

TABLE 11.1: Cash flow distribution to liability holders at time 1

	bankruptcy	**no bankruptcy**
	$x_A(\omega) < (1 + i)Dm_A$	$x_A(\omega) \geq (1 + i)Dm_A$
bonds $m_A x_A^b(\omega)$	$x_A(\omega)$	$(1 + i)Dm_A$
equity $n_A x_A^e(\omega)$	0	$x_A(\omega) - (1 + i)Dm_A$

$x_A(\omega)$, are less than the obligated payment, $(1 + i)Dm_A$. If this is true, the equity holders get nothing, while the bondholders split $x_A(\omega)$. If bankruptcy does not occur, then $x_A(\omega) \geq (1 + i)Dm_A$. The bondholders get their promised payment $(1 + i)Dm_A$, and the equity holders split the remaining cash flow.

We will contrast firm A with an "identical" firm (to be made precise), firm B, except that firm B will have no debt. The corresponding notation is as follows:

n_B = the number of common equity shares outstanding on firm B at time 0;

$x_B^e(\omega)$ = the time 1 cash flow to firm B's common equity under state $\omega \in \Omega$;

$x_B(\omega) = n_B x_B^e(\omega)$ = the total firm B cash flow at time 1 under state $\omega \in \Omega$;

$p(x_B^e)$ = the price per share of firm B's common equity at time 0; and

$V_B = n_B p(x_B^e)$ = the value of firm B at time 0.

Since firm B has no debt, its equity holders get all of firm B's cash flows at time 1.

These firms are identical, with this exception of their debt positions, as ensured by the following assumption:

Assumption 11.1: Identical Cash Flows at Time 1

$$x_A(\omega) = x_B(\omega) \quad \text{for all } \omega \in \Omega$$

The firms' cash flows at time 1 under all states are identical. This implies that they have the same assets, sales force, and so on.[1] The firms differ only in their liability structure. The controlled experiment is now constructed. To determine the relevance of the debt/equity ratio we need to relate firm A's value to firm B's value. This is done in theorem 11.1.

---

[1] This assumption implies that the investment projects undertaken by either firm are independent of the debt/equity policy.

Theorem 11.1: Debt/Equity Irrelevance

Given the identical firm assumption 11.1

$$V_A = V_B$$

Proof

$$
\begin{aligned}
V_A &= m_A p(x_A^b) + n_A p(x_A^e) \\
&= p(m_A x_A^b + n_A x_A^e) \text{ by assumption 8.6} \\
&= p(x_A) \\
&= p(x_B) \text{ by assumption 11.1, so} \\
&= p(n_B x_B^e) \\
&= n_B p(x_B^e) \text{ by assumption 8.6} \\
&= V_B \quad \square
\end{aligned}
$$

Theorem 11.1 shows that debt/equity policy does not change firm value. Although firm A has debt and firm B does not, both firms have identical value. The logic of this theorem is straightfoward. Both firms generate equal total cash flows, but they distribute these cash flows differently across liability holders. If the two firms had different values, an arbitrage opportunity would present itself. Investors could construct a portfolio duplicating the value of the cheaper firm and simultaneously sell a portfolio duplicating the value of the more expensive firm. This position would have zero cash flows at time 1, therefore representing an arbitrage opportunity.

There is an alternative proof of this proposition, which was first provided by Modigliani and Miller [3, 4]. For completeness, we present this alternate proof.

Alternate Proof

Suppose $V_A \neq V_B$, say, $V_A < V_B$. To construct an arbitrage opportunity, buy α percent of firm A's bonds and equity while simultaneously short selling α percent of firm B's equity. The price of the long position is $\alpha m_A p(x_A^b) + \alpha n_A p(x_A^e) = \alpha V_A$. The price of the short position is $\alpha n_B p(x_B^e) = \alpha V_B$. This generates a time 0 cash flow of $\alpha V_B - \alpha V_A = \alpha(V_B - V_A) > 0$. At time 1, the cash flow to the long position is $\alpha[x_A(\omega) + 0]$ if bankruptcy occurs and $\alpha[(1 + i)Dm_A + x_A(\omega) - (1 + i)Dm_A] = \alpha x_A(\omega)$ if there is no bankruptcy. This is always equal to $\alpha x_A(\omega)$. The cash outflow from the short position is $\alpha x_B(\omega)$. By assumption 11.1 these are equal. Hence this strategy represents an arbitrage opportunity. This contradicts assumption 8.6; therefore $V_A \geq V_B$ is the only possibility. If $V_A > V_B$, reversing the above strategy also generates a contradiction. Hence $V_A = V_B$ is the only possibility. $\square$

The implication of theorem 11.1 for corporate managements is that they should be indifferent to different debt/equity ratios. If this model were a good approximation, one would expect to see debt/equity ratios randomly distributed across firms in the economy. This is not the case, as there appear to be systematic patterns in debt/equity ratios (see Myers [5]). Consequently, the above model appears not to fit the observed economy. This motivates us to generalize the model in two steps. The first step is to include corporate income taxes.

11.2. CORPORATE INCOME TAXES

We now introduce corporate income taxes into the analysis. In the U.S. tax code, the interest paid on corporate debt is tax deductible by the corporation. Hence, in comparison to common equity, corporate debt can be used to reduce tax payments on corporate earnings. This benefit should make debt a preferred means of financing to equity, everything else constant. This is in fact the case, which we now show.

Let τ_c denote the corporate marginal tax rate, where $1 > \tau_c > 0$. By construction, we assume that the corporation pays less than 100 percent of its earnings in taxes and more than 0 percent.

Important in the subsequent analysis is the procedure for handling the tax deductibility of interest payments in the case of bankrupty. Numerous approximations to the U.S. tax code are possible. For simplicity, we assume that the entire promised interest payment (iDm_A) is *always* tax deductible, even if the taxable income is less than iDm_A. The idea is that the firm can sell its tax shield. Although this may not occur as a direct transaction, it could alternatively be accomplished perhaps through a merger with another firm or through tax loss carrybacks.

Assumption 11.2: Tax Deductibility of Interest

$(iDm_A)\tau_c$ is always the tax shield, even in the case of bankruptcy.

Any other well-specified procedure could be incorporated into the following analysis. The general results would still hold.

The model employed is the same model as that used in Sec. 11.1, with one exception. The exception is that both $x_A(\omega)$ and $x_B(\omega)$ represent *before corporate income tax* cash flows. The identical cash flow hypothesis, assumption 11.1, now states that the taxable cash flows, before corporate income taxes, are equal.

The after-tax cash flows to the two firms are as follows:

$$x_A(\omega)(1 - \tau_c) + i\tau_c Dm_A \tag{11.4a}$$

$$x_B(\omega)(1 - \tau_c) \tag{11.4b}$$

Expression (11.4a) gives the after-tax cash flow to firm A. To understand this expression, we break down the cash flow into two cases (see Table 11.2). The two cases are bankruptcy and no bankruptcy. Bankruptcy occurs when $x_A(\omega) <$

TABLE 11.2: After corporate tax cash flow distribution to liability
holders at time 1

	no bankruptcy	bankruptcy
	$x_A(\omega) \geq im_A D + \dfrac{m_A D}{(1 - \tau_c)}$	$x_A(\omega) < im_A D + \dfrac{m_A D}{(1 - \tau_c)}$
bond-holders	$(1 + i)m_A D$	$(x_A(\omega) - iDm_A)(1 - \tau_c) + iDm_A$
equity holders	$(x_A(\omega) - iDm_A)(1 - \tau_c) - Dm_A$	0
total	$x_A(\omega)(1 - \tau_c) + i\tau_c Dm_A$	$x_A(\omega)(1 - \tau_c) + i\tau_c Dm_A$

$im_A D + m_A D/(1 - \tau_c)$. To understand this condition, rearrange this inequality
to obtain

$$(x_A(\omega) - im_A D)(1 - \tau_c) < m_A D$$

This states that the corporate after-tax earnings are not sufficient to pay back the
debt's face value.

Table 11.2 shows the distribution of the cash flows to both the debt and
equity holders in case of bankruptcy and otherwise. The only difficult case is
when $x_A(\omega) < iDm_A$; i.e., corporate before-tax earnings are less than the interest
promised on debt. Here the firm is bankrupt. Since $[x_A(\omega) - iDm_A] < 0$, corporate income is not taxed. Hence the bondholders get all of $x_A(\omega)$. There is also
a tax loss $[x_A(\omega) - iDm_A](1 - \tau_c) < 0$. The firm gets the tax shield of
$-[x_A(\omega) - iDm_A]\tau_c > 0$, which goes to the bondholders. This is by assumption
11.2. The sum of these two cash flows to the bondholders is $x_A(\omega)(1 - \tau_c) +$
$i\tau_c m_A D$—exactly as given in Table 11.2.

The other cases in Table 11.2 are straightforward and left to the reader to
decipher. The after-tax cash flow to firm B is also straightforward since it is
always taxable.

Theorem 11.2: Debt/Equity Relevance

Given assumptions 11.1 and 11.2

$$V_A = V_B + i\tau_c(m_A D)p(x_\Omega) \tag{11.5}$$

Proof

$$V_A = p(x_A(\omega)(1 - \tau_c) + i\tau_c Dm_A)$$
$$= p(x_A(\omega))(1 - \tau_c) + i\tau_c Dm_A p(x_\Omega)$$

by assumption 8.6 and the fact that x_Ω, $[x_A(1 - \tau_c) + i\tau_c Dm_A x_\Omega]$ trading implies $x_A(1 - \tau_c)$ trades by assumption 8.1.

$$= p(x_B(\omega))(1 - \tau_c) + i\tau_c Dm_A \, p(x_\Omega) \quad \text{by assumption 11.1}$$

$$= p(x_B(\omega)(1 - \tau_c)) + i\tau_c Dm_A \, p(x_\Omega)$$

$$= V_B + i\tau_c Dm_A \, p(x_\Omega) \quad \square$$

This theorem states that the value of firm A, V_A, is equal to the value of firm B, V_B, plus the present value of the tax shield due to debt, $i\tau_c(m_A D)p(x_\Omega)$. We see that the tax shield benefit of debt increases the value of the firm.

An alternate proof of this theorem could be given along the lines of the alternate proof provided for theorem 11.1. Since the steps of the proof are analogous to those given earlier, we leave this proof as an exercise to the interested reader.

From the managerial perspective, the optimal debt/equity ratio would be to have *all* debt. As D increases, V_A increases. This relationship is graphed in Fig. 11.1. By itself, this implication is unsatisfactory. Firms do not have 100 percent debt. In fact, the Internal Revenue Service would probably consider 100 percent debt as 100 percent equity! We can modify the above theorem by including a specific market friction, i.e., bankruptcy costs.

11.2.1. Bankruptcy Costs

If the firm enters bankruptcy, i.e., those states where $x_A(\omega) < im_A D + m_A D/(1 - \tau_c)$, there are normally additional associated costs. There are the legal costs as well as the more subtle agency costs, e.g., management's making suboptimal investment decisions as bankruptcy nears in order to retain their jobs. These costs often increase with the size of the debt issue. We formalize this belief with an exogenous assumption.

FIGURE 11.1: Graph of expression (11.5): $V_A = V_B + i\tau_c m_A Dp(x_\Omega)$.

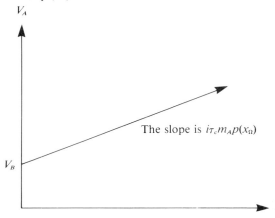

The slope is $i\tau_c m_A p(x_\Omega)$

Assumption 11.3a: Bankruptcy Costs

The bankruptcy costs are

$$c(\omega) \equiv \begin{cases} 0 & \text{if } x_A(\omega) \geq im_A D + m_A D/(1 - \tau_c) \\ c(\omega, D) & \text{if } x_A(\omega) < im_A D + m_A D/(1 - \tau_c) \end{cases}$$

where $c(\omega, D) > 0$ for all ω, D and $c(\omega, D)$ increases in D for all $\omega \in \Omega$.

Given this assumption, the after-tax flows to firm A (i.e., its liability holders) change to $x_A(\omega)(1 - \tau_c) + r\tau_c Dm_A - c(\omega)$. The bankruptcy costs are subtracted since they belong to third parties. With this change, theorem 11.2 changes to

Theorem 11.3: Debt/Equity Relevance with Bankruptcy

Given assumptions 11.1–11.3a

$$V_A = V_B + i\tau_c(m_A D)p(x_\Omega) - p(c) \tag{11.6}$$

where $p(c)$ increases with D.

Proof

$$V_A = p(x_A(\omega)(1 - \tau_c) + i\tau_c Dm_A - c(\omega))$$

$$= p(x_A)(1 - \tau_c) + i\tau_c Dm_A p(x_\Omega) - p(c)$$

by assumption 8.6 and the fact that $x_A(1 - \tau_c) = x_B(1 - \tau_c)$, x_Ω, and $[x_A(1 - \tau_c) + i\tau_c Dm_A x_\Omega - c]$ trading implies that c trades by assumption 8.1.

$$= p(x_B)(1 - \tau_c) + i\tau_c Dm_A p(x_\Omega) - p(c) \quad \text{by assumption 11.1}$$

$$= V_B + i\tau_c Dm_A p(x_\Omega) - p(c)$$

By assumption 11.3, if $D_1 > D_2$, then $c(\omega, D_1) > c(\omega, D_2)$ for all $\omega \in \Omega$. By assumption 8.6, $p(c(D_1)) > p(c(D_2))$ as long as the states over which $c(\omega, D_1) > c(\omega, D_2)$ have positive probability. $\square$

This theorem shows that the firm with debt, firm A, has its value reduced by the present value of the bankruptcy costs, $p(c)$. Furthermore, these bankruptcy costs increase with D.

A trade-off now exists between the tax savings of debt and the cost of bankruptcy. Depending on the specific firm under consideration and its bankruptcy costs, an optimal debt/equity ratio could exist, as graphed in Fig. 11.2. Depending on the cost curves, other possibilities also exist. The firm may have

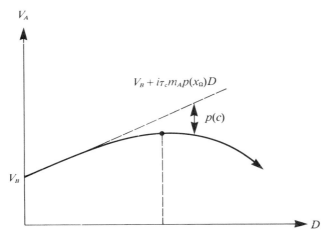

FIGURE 11.2: Graph of expression (11.6): $V_A = V_B +$
$i\tau_c m_A Dp(x_\Omega) - p(c)$.

either no debt or all debt as possible optimums as well. This last generalization
of the theory is consistent with the empirical evidence. It allows an array of
possible optimal debt/equity ratios that are firm specific. There is an alternative
generalization also worthy of study.

11.2.2. Personal Taxes

We could also generalize theorem 11.2 by including differential personal
taxes on the income from corporate debt versus the income from common
equity. The idea is simple. Suppose the income from debt at the personal level
is taxed at a higher rate than the income from equity. Now, although firms get
a tax savings on corporate income from using debt, the debt holders pay taxes
on their interest income. If this interest income is taxed at a high enough rate,
it will offset the tax savings of debt on corporate income. In this situation, debt
will never be employed. We start out with an assumption.

Assumption 11.3b: Personal Income Taxes

All investors face the same marginal tax rates

$$1 > \tau_b > 0$$

$$1 > \tau_e > 0$$

where τ_b is the marginal personal tax rate on the corporate debt interest, and

τ_e is the marginal personal tax rate on common equity income.

The same model is employed as earlier with corporate taxes alone. However, the price functional is now applied to the after personal income tax cash flows at time 1 under state ω. Hence an asset is identified with its after personal income tax cash flow. To make the analysis simpler, we assume the following:

Assumption 11.4: Riskless Debt[2]

$$[x_A(\omega) - iDm_A](1 - \tau_c) \geq Dm_A \quad \text{for all } \omega \in \Omega$$

For a reference relaxing this assumption, see Turnball [8].

Let us now identify the after personal tax flows to firm A and firm B. Denote these flows by y_A and y_B, respectively.

$$y_A(\omega) = (x_A(\omega) - iDm_A)(1 - \tau_c)(1 - \tau_e) + iDm_A(1 - \tau_b) + \tau_e p(y_A) \tag{11.7a}$$

$$y_B(\omega) = x_B(\omega)(1 - \tau_c)(1 - \tau_e) + \tau_e p(y_B) \tag{11.7b}$$

These expressions were obtained as follows. Consider firm A first. The after personal income tax flow to the equity holders is

$$Z_A^e = [(x_A - iDm_A)(1 - \tau_c) - m_A D - n_A p(Z_A^e)](1 - \tau_e) + p(Z_A^e)n_A$$

The first expression is the capital gains income, taxed at a rate τ_e. The principal $p(Z_A^e)n_A$ is not taxed. The after personal income tax flow to the bondholders is $Z_A^b = m_A D + iDm_A(1 - \tau_b)$. The principal is not taxed, $m_A D$, but the interest is taxed at the rate τ_b. Now

$$y_A = Z_A^e + Z_A^b = [x_A - iDm_A](1 - \tau_c)(1 - \tau_e) + iDm_A(1 - \tau_b)$$
$$+ \tau_e(m_A D + n_A p(Z_A^e))$$

Recall that, by definition, the face value of the debt equals its market price, $D = p(Z_A^b)$, and $p(y_A) = m_A p(Z_A^b) + n_A p(Z_A^e)$. Substitution gives expression (11.7a).

For firm B, the cash flow is $y_B = [x_B(1 - \tau_c) - p(y_B)](1 - \tau_e) + p(y_B)$, which is expression (11.7b). With these expressions, our next theorem can be stated and proved.

---

[2] We could make this assumption with "probability one" instead of "for all $\omega \in \Omega$."

Theorem 11.4: Debt/Equity Relevance with Personal Taxes

Given assumptions 11.1–11.4

$$V_A = V_B + iDm_A p(x_\Omega)[(1 - \tau_b) - (1 - \tau_c)(1 - \tau_e)]/[1 - \tau_e p(x_\Omega)]$$

Proof

$$V_A = p(y_A) = p((x_A - iDm_A)(1 - \tau_c)(1 - \tau_e) + iDm_A(1 - \tau_b) + \tau_e p(y_A))$$

$$= p(x_A)(1 - \tau_c)(1 - \tau_e) + iDm_A[(1 - \tau_b) - (1 - \tau_c)(1 - \tau_e)] p(x_\Omega)$$

$$+ \tau_e p(y_A)p(x_\Omega)$$

by assumption 8.6 and the fact that y_A and x_Ω trading implies that $x_A(1 - \tau_c)(1 - \tau_e)$ trades by assumption 8.1. Solving for $p(y_A)$ gives

$$p(y_A) = [p(x_A)(1 - \tau_c)(1 - \tau_e) + iDm_A[(1 - \tau_b)$$

$$- (1 - \tau_c)(1 - \tau_e)]p(x_\Omega)]/(1 - \tau_e p(x_\Omega))$$

$$= [p(x_A(1 - \tau_c)(1 - \tau_c))$$

$$+ iDm_A p(x_\Omega)[(1 - \tau_b) - (1 - \tau_c)(1 - \tau_e)]]/(1 - \tau_e p(x_\Omega))$$

By assumption 11.1

$$= [p(x_B(1 - \tau_c)(1 - \tau_e)) + iDm_A p(x_\Omega)[(1 - \tau_b)$$

$$- (1 - \tau_c)(1 - \tau_e)]]/(1 - \tau_e p(x_\Omega))$$

$$= p(x_B(1 - \tau_c)(1 - \tau_e))/(1 - \tau_e p(x_\Omega)) + iDm_A p(x_\Omega)[(1 - \tau_b)$$

$$- (1 - \tau_c)(1 - \tau_e)]/[1 - \tau_e p(x_\Omega)]$$

$$= V_B + iDm_A p(x_\Omega)[(1 - \tau_b) - (1 - \tau_c)(1 - \tau_e)]/[1 - \tau_e p(x_\Omega)]$$

since

$$V_B = p(y_B) = p(x_B(1 - \tau_c)(1 - \tau_e))/(1 - \tau_e p(x_\Omega)) \quad \Box$$

This theorem shows that the debt/equity ratio influences firm value. If $(1 - \tau_b) > (1 - \tau_c)(1 - \tau_e)$, then more debt increases firm value. This is because the after personal tax retention rate $(1 - \tau_b)$ is greater than the after personal tax retention rate for equity (compounding by the corporate tax) $(1 - \tau_c)(1 - \tau_e)$. So on an after personal income tax basis, debt is cheaper. If $(1 - \tau_b) = (1 - \tau_c)(1 - \tau_e)$, debt is irrelevant. If $(1 - \tau_b) < (1 - \tau_c)(1 - \tau_e)$, debt should not be issued.

One could further complicate this analysis by using different tax rates (τ_b, τ_e) for different investors. This would create clienteles for the firm's securities.

Different taxable investors would prefer different securities. In simple equilibrium economies (see Miller [2], Taggart [7]), one can show that $\tau_b \approx \tau_c$ and $\tau_e \approx 0$, giving debt irrelevance (on the margin). These more complicated equilibrium analyses are also consistent with much of the empirical evidence. They imply that there is debt irrelevance on the firm level but optimal debt/equity ratios at the economy-wide level.

11.3. INFORMATIONAL CONTENT OF THE DEBT/EQUITY RATIO

A key aspect of an economy that the previous models ignore is asymmetric information and the informational content of the debt/equity ratio. If information is incomplete in an economy, then investors could potentially use the debt/equity ratio to infer information about the firm and its future investment projects. This informational aspect of debt/equity ratios would mean the violation of assumption 11.1; i.e., cash flow valuation is dependent on the debt/equity ratio. If this were the case, then an "equilibrium" analysis could easily generate an optimal debt/equity ratio, even in a world with corporate taxes. Suggested references are Ross [6] and Myers [5]. This is an exciting area for future research.

11.4. SUMMARY

This chapter applies the arbitrage pricing method of Chap. 8 to study a corporation's debt/equity decision. It was shown in a frictionless, no tax economy that no arbitrage opportunity implies debt/equity irrelevance. That is, the debt/equity ratio does not change firm value. This analysis was obtained by carefully constructing a controlled experiment involving two nearly identical firms, the only difference being the debt/equity ratio.

This simple model was extended to include corporate taxes and the tax deductibility of interest payments. The tax deductibility of debt payments made it optimal for firms to issue as much debt as possible. The introduction of bankruptcy costs, however, which increase in present value as debt increases, creates a trade-off against the tax savings. An optimal debt/equity ratio could result.

The final extension considered was personal income taxes with different marginal tax rates on interest income versus equity income. Depending on the relative weight of taxation at the corporate and personal levels, debt was shown to be either preferred to equity, indifferent to equity, or inferior to equity. The limitations of this analysis due to the exclusion of asymmetric information in an economy was mentioned. This is an exciting area for future research.

11.5. REFERENCES

1. Chen, Andrew, and E. Han Kim, "Theories of Corporate Debt Policy: A Synthesis," *Journal of Finance* (May 1979), 371–384.
2. Miller, Merton, "Debt and Taxes," *Journal of Finance* (May 1977), 261–275.
3. Modigliani, F., and M. Miller, "The Cost of Capital, Corporate Finance, and the Theory of Investment," *American Economic Review,* 48 (June 1958), 261–297.
4. _____ , "Reply to Heins and Sprenkle," *American Economic Review*, 59 (September 1969), 592–595.
5. Myers, Stewart C., "The Capital Structure Puzzle," *Journal of Finance* (July 1984), 575–592.
6. Ross, S. A., "The Determination of Financial Structure: The Incentive-Signalling Approach," *Bell Journal of Economics*, 8 (Spring 1977), 23–40.
7. Taggart, R., "A Model of Corporate Financing Decisions," *Journal of Finance*, 32 (December 1977), 1467–1484.
8. Turnball, Stuart, "Debt Capacity," *Journal of Finance* (September 1979), 931–940.

12

DEFAULT-FREE BONDS
AND THE TERM STRUCTURE
OF INTEREST RATES

The previous three chapters have provided detailed applications of the arbitrage pricing methodology introduced in Chap. 8 to study Ross's APT, dividend policy, and debt/equity policy. Each of these applications has been confined to a single period economy, with two dates. The purpose of this chapter and the next is to extend the arbitrage pricing methodology to multiperiod economies. A two-stage procedure is employed. This chapter will study the simplest multiperiod extension of the material in Chap. 8 to study the pricing of default-free bonds. Chapter 13 will complicate the economy even more to price call and put options on traded assets. The differing complexity of the two models revolves around the trading strategies required to price the differing financial securities. This chapter requires only simple buy and hold strategies, while the next chapter requires dynamic trading strategies that are adjusted over time.

The first two sections of this chapter study the term structure of interest rates. The second section utilizes the term structure of interest rates to price default-free coupon bonds in two economies: one with and one without differential personal income taxes on coupons versus capital gains income. Since there is a vast literature applying the arbitrage pricing methodology to the study of the term structure of interest rates, this chapter merely serves as a brief introduction. Suggested readings are the papers by Cox, Ingersoll, and Ross [1, 2].

12.1. PRELIMINARIES

The model employed to study the pricing of default-free coupon bonds is a modification of the asset model introduced in Chap. 8. The modification occurs because bond pricing is a multiperiod phenomenon, while the theory in Chap. 8 is developed only for a single period economy. Since the extended model is based on the model in Chap. 8, detailed discussions concerning the assumptions are needed only for the modifications.

In the extended model, there are T time periods from the date $t = 0$ to the date $t = T$. The uncertainty in the economy is again characterized by a state space, Ω, at time T, with an arbitrary state denoted by $\omega \in \Omega$. A state ω at time T supplies a complete description of the economy's condition over the entire time period 0 to T.

An asset is now identified by its dollar cash flows across all states and across *all times* $t = 1, \ldots, T$ after date 0. That is, an asset is a mapping x from $\Omega \times \{1, \ldots, T\}$ into the real line, where $x(t, \omega)$ represents the cash flow to asset x at time t under state ω. This differs from the definition of an asset in Chap. 8 to the extent that multiple period cash flows are included.

The set of assets that trade in an organized market at time 0 is denoted by the set M. We let the same set of assets trade at times $t = 1, \ldots, T - 1$ as well.

Assumption 12.1: Marketed Assets

If $x, y \in M$ and $\alpha, \beta \in \mathbb{R}$, then $\alpha x + \beta y \in M$.

If assets x and y trade at time t, then the package consisting of α units of asset x and β units of asset y also trades at time t. This is true for all trading dates $t = 0, \ldots, T - 1$.

The cash flows from the assets at time t and before generate an information set that we denote by $\sigma(M_t)$. The subscript on M indicates that only the cash flows at and preceding time t are utilized to determine which events are included in $\sigma(M_t)$. The events in $\sigma(M_t)$ are the subsets of Ω from which knowledge about the cash flows to the traded assets at and preceding time t can determine if the event occurred.

It is natural to expect that as time passes, investors learn more about the "true" state of nature by observing the cash flows to the traded assets. This idea is captured by the following assumption:

Assumption 12.2: Resolution of Uncertainty

(i) $\sigma(M_t) \subseteq \sigma(M_s)$ for $0 \leq t \leq s \leq T$ and

(ii) $\sigma(M_0) = \{\phi, \Omega\}$

Assumption 12.2 states that as time passes, more information becomes available. This is condition (i). Condition (ii) states that at time 0, no information is available. By construction, there are no cash flows at time 0. So the only events that the nonexistent cash flows at time 0 can determine are the empty set ϕ and the entire state space Ω. But we already knew these.

Assumption 12.3: Conditional Homogeneous Beliefs

Given an asset $x \in M$, every investor agrees that $x(t, \omega)$ is the cash flow in dollars to asset x at time $t \in \{1, \ldots, T\}$ given state $\omega \in \Omega$ occurs.

There are a finite number of investors in the economy each with subjective probability beliefs, $\text{Prob}_i[\cdot]$, defined over the largest information set $\sigma(M_T)$. The information set $\sigma(M_T)$ is the set containing the most events due to the resolution of uncertainty assumption 12.2. Beliefs across investors are restricted by the following assumption.

Assumption 12.4: Unconditional Beliefs

Given an event $H \in \sigma(M_T)$, $\text{Prob}_i(H) = 0$ if and only if $\text{Prob}_j(H) = 0$ for all investors i, j.

This assumption is analogous to the unconditional beliefs assumption of the preceding chapters.

Assumption 12.5: Frictionless Markets

The asset markets from times 0 to $T - 1$ have no transaction costs, no taxes, and no restrictions on short sales, and asset shares are divisible.

Assumption 12.6: Competitive Markets

Every investor acts as a price taker.

These are the standard, ideal market assumptions previously employed. (Personal income taxes are introduced in a later section.)

We define a price functional at time 0 over the assets traded in M, $p:M \to \mathbb{R}$, where $p(x)$ gives the time 0 price in dollars of asset $x \in M$. This price functional satisfies the following assumption:

Assumption 12.7: No Buy and Hold Strategy Arbitrage Opportunities

(i) Value additivity

If for some investor i, some assets x, y, $z \in M$, and some shares α, $\beta \in \mathbb{R}$ we have

$$\text{Prob}_i[\omega \in \Omega: \alpha x(t, \omega) + \beta y(t, \omega) = z(t, \omega)] = 1 \text{ for all } t$$

then $\alpha p(x) + \beta p(y) = p(z)$.

(ii) Dominance

If for some investor i and some asset $x \in M$ we have

$$\text{Prob}_i[\omega \in \Omega: x(t, \omega) \geq 0] = 1 \text{ for all } t = 1, \ldots, T$$

and

$$\text{Prob}_i[\omega \in \Omega: x(t, \omega) > 0] > 0 \text{ for some } t \in \{1, \ldots, T\}$$

then $p(x) > 0$.

This assumption generalizes the single period notion of an arbitrage opportunity to the multiperiod economy. An arbitrage opportunity is a traded asset that violates either condition (i) or (ii) in assumption 12.7. These arbitrage opportunities involve positions entered into at time 0 and held until time T—hence the terminology *buy and hold* strategies.

For example, if asset z violated condition (i), value additivity, then for some investor i, $\text{Prob}_i[\alpha x + \beta y = z] = 1$, but, say, $\alpha p(x) + \beta p(y) < p(z)$. That is, with probability one, the investor sees the cash flows (under all states and times) to the portfolio (formed at time 0 and held until time T) consisting of α shares of asset x and β shares of y as equal to asset z. Yet the portfolio sells for less than does asset z. To obtain a utility-increasing trading strategy (at no risk) the investor should sell asset z and buy and hold the indicated portfolio until time T. This strategy is analogous to the arbitrage opportunity in Chap. 8 involving value additivity.

Next consider condition (ii), dominance. The traded asset x included in this condition is a *limited liability* asset because its cash flows (across states and times) are always nonnegative and sometimes strictly positive with positive probability. If condition (ii) is violated, then it states that a limited liability asset has a zero or negative price. To take advantage of this situation, the investor should simply buy the asset x at time 0 and hold it until time T. This generates positive or zero cash inflows at time 0 and positive or zero cash flows across all times and states. In addition, under some states, there are strictly positive cash flows. This strategy represents a multiperiod probabilistic money pump.

Although conditions (i) and (ii) of this assumption are stated for some investor i, by the unconditional beliefs assumption 12.4, we could replace "for some investor *i*" by "for all investors." This follows because if one investor believes that condition (i) or (ii) is satisfied, then all investors do. Indeed, investors agree on zero probability events (or, equivalently, probability one events by taking complements).

Finally, assumption 12.7 restricts consideration to buy and hold strategies. Although other portfolio strategies are possible, we do not need these strategies for the analysis in this chapter. More complicated strategies, however, will be needed in Chap. 13 when pricing call and put options.

12.2. THE TERM STRUCTURE OF INTEREST RATES

This section studies the term structure of interest rates. As a start, we assume that default-free discount bonds of all maturities trade in the market at time 0. A discount bond is a bond that has no cash flow associated with it, except when the bond matures. These bonds will form the set of assets against which other assets, in particular, coupon bonds, will be priced.

Assumption 12.8: Marketed Default-Free Discount Bonds

The assets $\chi_s \in M$ for $s = 1, \ldots, T$, where

$$\chi_s(t, \omega) = \begin{cases} 1 & \text{for all } \omega \in \Omega \text{ if } t = s \\ 0 & \text{otherwise} \end{cases}$$

A default-free discount bond of maturity s, denoted by χ_s, pays one dollar at time s no matter which state occurs. It has zero cash flows otherwise. Exogenously given in this economy are the prices of the default-free discount bonds of all maturities, $p(\chi_s)$.

The market yield on the discount bond χ_s is defined to be the internal rate of return on the bond, i.e.

Definition: Market Yield on χ_s

The *market yield*, $y(s)$, on the bond χ_s is defined by

$$p(\chi_s) = \frac{1}{[1 + y(s)]^s} \tag{12.1}$$

that is

$$y(s) = [p(\chi_s)^{-1/s} - 1]$$

The market yield is that rate, per unit time, that the bond earns *if* the bond is held until maturity. It does not correspond to the rate earned on the bond over any intermediate period, in particular, over the time period $[0, 1]$, unless the bond matures at time 1, i.e., $s = 1$. Indeed, for longer maturity bonds ($s > 1$), the price of the same bond at time 1 is stochastic and the expected return earned over the time period $[0, 1]$ is not necessarily the market yield. The shortest maturity bond, $s = 1$, is the only case where the yield equals the *known* return on the bond over the time period $[0, 1]$. This bond is special, and for this reason its market yield has special names. It is sometimes called the *spot rate* at time 0 or the *riskless rate*.

By construction, there is a one-to-one correspondence between the bond's price, $p(\chi_s)$, and the bond's yield, $y(s)$. Both provide identical information about the bond and the future path of interest rates. This statement, although straightforward, will have profound implications later on. We mention it now for future reference.

The graph of the bond's yield $y(s)$ versus the bond's maturity $s = 1, \ldots, T$ is called the *yield* curve (see Fig. 12.1). The shape of the graph of $y(s)$ is known as the *term structure of interest rates*. Historically, professional bond traders have attempted to utilize the shape of the yield curve to forecast the future path of interest rates, i.e., future spot rates. Although the shape of the yield curve has information embedded within it about the future path of spot rates, the information is convoluted and not easily interpreted. Some insights into the validity of this assertion can be obtained by realizing that the yield curve contains no more information than the bond prices $p(\chi_s)$ for $s = 1, \ldots, T$. Information about the future path of prices is embedded in $p(\chi_s)$, but it is convoluted by the market mechanism, in particular, the equilibrium process.

Perhaps the idea that the shape of the yield curve reveals information about the future path of interest rates comes from the concept of a forward rate.

FIGURE 12.1: The yield curve: graph of $y(s)$ versus s.

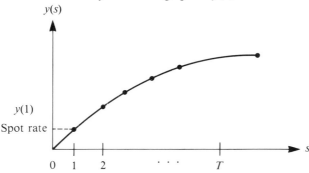

Definition: The Forward Rate

The *forward rate* over $[t, t + 1]$ is defined by

$$[1 + f(t)] = \frac{[1 + y(t + 1)]^{t+1}}{[1 + y(t)]^t} \qquad (12.2)$$

The forward rate is the ratio of the market yield for a $t + 1$ maturity bond, $y(t + 1)$, compounded $t + 1$ times, divided by the market yield on a t maturity bond, $y(t)$, compounded t times. It is a measure that attempts to capture the difference in rates over the future time period $[t, t + 1]$.

The forward rate is equivalent to the rate one can contract today, at time 0, on a riskless loan over the time period $[t, t + 1]$. To see why this is true, consider the following traded asset:

$$z = \chi_{t+1} - N\chi_t \quad \text{where } N = p(\chi_{t+1})/p(\chi_t)$$

The cash flows from asset z are

$$z(s, w) = \begin{cases} 1 & \text{for all } \omega \in \Omega \text{ if } s = t + 1 \\ -N & \text{for all } \omega \in \Omega \text{ if } s = t \\ 0 & \text{otherwise} \end{cases}$$

So z is entered into at time 0 with a price of $p(z) = p(\chi_{t+1}) - Np(\chi_t) = 0$ by the definition of N. No cash inflows or outflows occur until date t, at which time a cash outflow of $-N$ dollars occurs. At time $t + 1$ a cash inflow of one dollar occurs. This is a riskless investment (contracted at time 0) costing N dollars at time t for a certain inflow of one dollar at time $t + 1$. The rate of return on this contract over $[t, t + 1]$ is

$$\frac{1 - N}{N} = \frac{1 - p(\chi_{t+1})/p(\chi_t)}{p(\chi_{t+1})/p(\chi_t)} = \frac{p(\chi_t)}{p(\chi_{t+1})} - 1 = \frac{\dfrac{1}{[1 + y(t)]^t}}{\dfrac{1}{[1 + y(t + 1)]^{t+1}}} - 1$$

$$= \frac{[1 + y(t + 1)]^{t+1}}{[1 + y(t)]^t} - 1 = 1 + f(t) - 1 = f(t)$$

This is the forward rate.

In summary, the argument shows that the forward rate is the interest rate one can contract for today (time 0) on a riskless investment over the future time period $[t, t + 1]$.

An alternative strategy to attain a riskless investment over the time period $[t, t + 1]$ is to wait until time t and then to invest in the bond that matures at time $t + 1$, i.e., χ_{t+1}. If spot rates are stochastic, which is indeed the case, the rate attainable by waiting may be different from the forward rate attainable at time 0. The difference between these two strategies is represented by the investment risks present. The forward rate strategy locks in the certain rate at time 0. The waiting strategy does not. One would expect that expectations regarding the future spot rate over the time period $[t, t + 1]$ greatly influence the relative attractiveness of these two strategies and therefore the size of the forward rate $f(t)$. Supply and demand considerations also enter the picture, since if more people want to avoid this risk than to bear it, the forward rate $f(t)$ will exceed the expected spot rate over $[t, t + 1]$ by a *liquidity premium*. The liquidity premium provides the incentive for investors to enter the market and bear this risk. The determinates of this liquidity premium are the subject of much research; some initial references include Cox, Ingersoll, and Ross [1, 2], Jarrow [3], and McCulloch [4].

12.3. THE PRICING OF DEFAULT-FREE COUPON BONDS

Given the prices of the discount bonds, this section prices coupon bonds. The pricing of coupon bonds differs according to the relative taxing of coupon income versus capital gains income. We study both cases. The first case studied is the easiest, an economy with no personal income taxes.

12.3.1. No Personal Income Taxes

Given the exogenous specification of the discount bond prices $p(\chi_s)$ for $s = 1, \ldots, T$, we can now price a default-free coupon bond. The default-free coupon bond is defined by its cash flows, i.e.

$$b(t, \omega; C, T, F) = \begin{cases} C & \text{for all } \omega \in \Omega \text{ if } t = 1, 2, \ldots, T - 1 \\ C + F & \text{for all } \omega \in \Omega \text{ if } t = T \\ 0 & \text{otherwise} \end{cases} \quad (12.3)$$

where $b(C\ T, F) \in M$.

The bond's cash flow is diagrammed in Fig. 12.2. The bond's cash flows are certain—hence the term *default free*. The bond is indexed by three indices: C, T, and F. The symbol C refers to the dollar coupon paid each period; T refers to the maturity date of the bond; and F is the bond's face value, paid at maturity.

It is easily seen by the definition of the discount bonds χ_s that for all $\omega \in \Omega$

$$b(C, T, F) = \sum_{t=1}^{T-1} C\chi_t + [C + F]\chi_T \quad (12.4a)$$

That is, a coupon bond is equivalent to a portfolio of discount bonds where C shares of the bond maturities $1, \ldots, T - 1$ are combined with $C + F$ shares

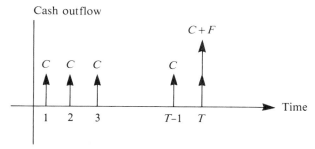

FIGURE 12.2: Cash outflows from a default-free coupon bond across all states $\omega \in \Omega$.

of the T maturity bond. Hence by the no arbitrage opportunity assumption 12.7

$$p(b(C, T, F)) = \sum_{t=1}^{T-1} Cp(\chi_t) + [C + F]p(\chi_T) \qquad (12.4b)$$

Expression (12.4b) gives the price of the coupon bond in terms of the prices of the discount bonds. The coupon bond's price is seen to be equivalent to the price of a portfolio of discount bonds. The number of discount bonds of each type included in the portfolio are represented by the coefficients preceding each discount bond's price in expression (12.4b). Expression (12.4b) is a typical example of how the arbitrage pricing methodology works. The price of some asset, the coupon bond, is determined as a function of the prices of another set of traded assets, the discount bonds.

12.3.2. Differential Taxes

We now consider the situation where the coupon payments, C, are taxed at a different personal income tax rate than the capital gains income. This difference is made explicit by the following assumption.

Assumption 12.9: Identical Marginal Tax Rates

All investors have the same constant marginal tax rates

$$\begin{aligned} 1 &> \tau_0 > 0 \\ 1 &> \tau_g > 0 \end{aligned} \quad \text{for all times } t = 1, \ldots, T$$

where τ_0 is the marginal tax rate on ordinary income, and

τ_g is the marginal tax rate on capital gains income.

As a first approximation to the U.S. tax code, we assume that $\tau_0 > \tau_g$.

We retain the assumption that discount bonds of all maturities trade (12.8); however, we now let the price functional apply to *after personal* income tax flows. To determine the after-tax flows of the discount bonds, we add the following assumption.

Assumption 12.10: Tax Status of Discount Bonds

The capital gains from discount bonds are taxed at the ordinary income tax rate.

We assume that the capital gains income from discount bonds is taxed at the ordinary income tax rate. This is to approximate the U.S. tax code. Any other well-specified tax structure could also be studied using the techniques introduced below.

The after personal income tax flow, z_t, to the discount bond of maturity t can now be determined:

$$z_t = ([1 - p(z_t)](1 - \tau_0) + p(z_t))\chi_t \tag{12.5}$$

The after-tax cash flow occurs at time t and is divided into two components: the capital gains component adjusted for taxes, $(1 - p(z_t))(1 - \tau_0)$, and the principal component, $p(z_t)$, which is not taxed. These after-tax cash flows are received at time t under all states ω. The asset χ_t has the interpretation of being a *tax-free* discount bond. It trades by the marketed assets assumption 12.1 because it is a portfolio of the traded asset z_t. The prices of the taxable discount bonds are given in the following theorem.

Theorem 12.1: Discount Bond Prices

Under assumptions 12.1–12.10

$$p(z_t) = \frac{(1 - \tau_0)p(\chi_t)}{(1 - \tau_0 p(\chi_t))} \tag{12.6}$$

Proof

From condition (12.5)

$$p(z_t) = p([1 - p(z_t)](1 - \tau_0) + p(z_t))\chi_t)$$
$$= [1 - p(z_t)](1 - \tau_0)p(\chi_t) + p(z_t)p(\chi_t)$$

This last expression uses the fact that $\chi_t \in M$ since $z_t \in M$ and assumption 12.1. So

$$p(z_t)[1 + (1 - \tau_0)p(\chi_t) - p(\chi_t)] = (1 - \tau_0)p(\chi_t)$$

or

$$p(z_t) = \frac{(1 - \tau_0)p(\chi_t)}{1 - \tau_0 p(\chi_t)} \quad \Box$$

Utilizing theorem 12.1, we can alternatively rewrite the tax-exempt coupon bond's price in terms of the taxable discount bond's price by manipulating expression (12.6):

$$p(\chi_t) = p(z_t)/(1 + \tau_0 p(z_t) - \tau_0) \tag{12.7}$$

This alternative pricing formula is more useful when taxable discount bonds trade and $p(z_t)$ is directly observable but the price of tax-exempt discount bonds, $p(\chi_t)$, is not.

To price a coupon bond, we need to determine its after personal income tax cash flow, $B(C, F, T)$. B distinguishes this bond from the similar bond studied in an economy with no personal income taxes.

$$B(s, \omega; C, F, T) = \begin{cases} C(1 - \tau_0) & \text{for all } \omega \in \Omega \text{ if } s = 1, 2, \ldots, T - 1 \\ C(1 - \tau_0) + [F - p(B(C, F, T))](1 - \tau_g) \\ \quad + p(B(C, F, T)) & \text{for all } \omega \in \Omega \text{ if } s = T \\ 0 & \text{otherwise} \end{cases} \tag{12.8}$$

In expression (12.8), coupon income is taxed at the rate τ_0. At time T, the capital gains income $(F - p(B(C, F, T)))$ is taxed at the rate τ_g, and the bond's purchase price, $p(B(C, F, T))$, is not taxed.

The next theorem gives the price of this bond.

Theorem 12.2: Coupon Bond Prices

Under assumptions 12.1–12.10

$$p(B(C, F, T)) = \left[\sum_{t=1}^{T} C(1 - \tau_0)p(\chi_t) + F(1 - \tau_g)p(\chi_T) \right] / [1 - \tau_g p(\chi_T)] \tag{12.9}$$

Proof

$$B(C, F, T) = \sum_{t=1}^{T} C(1 - \tau_0)\chi_t$$

$$+ [F - p(B(C, F, T))](1 - \tau_g)\chi_T + p(B(C, F, T))\chi_T$$

Taking prices of both sides yields

$$p(B(C, F, T)) = \sum_{t=1}^{T} C(1 - \tau_0)p(\chi_t)$$
$$+ F(1 - \tau_g)p(\chi_T) + p(B(C, F, T))(1 - (1 - \tau_g))p(\chi_T)$$

or

$$p(B(C, F, T))(1 - \tau_g p(\chi_T)) = \sum_{t=1}^{T} C(1 - \tau_0)p(\chi_t) + F(1 - \tau_g)p(\chi_T)$$

Division by $(1 - \tau_g p(\chi_T)) \neq 0$ gives the result. ☐

Theorem 12.1 gives an explicit pricing formula for a coupon bond in terms of the marginal tax rates on ordinary income, capital gains income, and the prices of tax-exempt discount bonds. If these tax-exempt discount bond prices are not directly observable, expression (12.7) can be used to transform the prices of the tax-exempt discount bonds into the observable prices of the taxable discount bonds.

12.4. SUMMARY

This chapter utilizes the arbitrage pricing theory developed in Chap. 8 to study the pricing of default-free coupon bonds. Since the pricing of bonds is inherently a multiperiod problem, the asset model of Chap. 8 was extended to handle this generalization. Given the existence of default-free discount bonds of all maturities, it is an easy exercise to price coupon bonds. This was done both with and without differential taxes on coupon income versus capital gains income. The only concept needed was the absence of arbitrage opportunities for buy and hold strategies, i.e., strategies entered into at time 0 and held until time T. These strategies need to be expanded, as in Chap. 13, when considering call and put options.

12.5. REFERENCES

1. Cox, J., J. Ingersoll, and S. Ross, "A Re-examination of Traditional Hypotheses about the Term Structure of Interest Rates," *Journal of Finance*, 36 (1981), 769–799.
2. ———, "A Theory of the Term Structure of Interest Rates," *Econometrica*, 53 (1985) 385–408.
3. Jarrow, R., "Liquidity Premiums and the Expectations Hypothesis," *Journal of Banking and Finance*, 5 (1981), 539–546.
4. McCulloch, J. Huston, "An Estimate of the Liquidity Premium," *Journal of Political Economy*, 83 (1975), 95–119.

13

OPTION PRICING

Chapter 12, on default-free bonds and the term structure of interest rates, extended the single period arbitrage pricing methodology of Chap. 8 to a multiperiod economy. The simplest extension of the single period economy was examined where only buy and hold strategies were needed to price (default-free) coupon bonds with the prices of (default-free) discount bonds. This chapter extends the multiperiod arbitrage pricing techniques even more by introducing dynamic trading strategies. These strategies are sufficient to study the fundamental concepts involved with pricing call and put options on traded assets. There is a vast literature investigating this topic, and numerous theorems and facts are known; thus this chapter only serves as a brief introduction. Complete references are Cox and Rubinstein [2] and Jarrow and Rudd [4].

The study of call and put options has become central to financial economics. This is not because calls and puts trade on organized exchanges but rather because calls and puts are fundamental securities. By fundamental, we mean that the pricing of calls and puts underlies the pricing of *all* financial securities. This is because all financial securities can be veiwed as (limiting) combinations of various types of options (see Arditti and John [1], Green and Jarrow [3], John [5], and Ross [6]). For this reason, the pricing of calls and puts leads to an increased understanding of the pricing of all financial assets.

13.1. PRELIMINARIES

This section utilizes the economy presented in Sec. 12.1 of Chap. 12 on default-free discount bonds and the term structure of interest rates. For convenience, we briefly review the relevant notation and assumptions. For a more detailed discussion of the model and its assumptions, the reader is referred to Chap. 12. One major extension of the previous model is introduced, dynamic trading strategies, and discussed in some detail. We now present the model.

The economy consists of T time periods from $t = 0$ to $t = T$. At time T the uncertainty in the economy is characterized by the state space, Ω, with a state denoted by ω. An asset is identified by its dollar cash flows across all states and across all the times $t = 1, \ldots, T$; i.e., an asset is a function x from $\Omega \times \{1, \ldots, T\} \to \mathbb{R}$, where $x(t, \omega)$ represents the cash flow to asset x at time t under state ω. The set of assets that trade at time 0 is denoted by M. The same set of assets is assumed to trade at times $t = 1, \ldots, T - 1$. The marketed assets are assumed to be closed under the construction of portfolios.

Assumption 13.1: Marketed Assets

If assets $x, y \in M$ and $\alpha, \beta \in \mathbb{R}$, then $\alpha x + \beta y \in M$.

The cash flows from the assets at and preceding time t generate an information set denoted by $\sigma(M_t)$. This represents those events, subsets of Ω, which can be inferred at time t using only the knowledge of the traded assets' cash flows at and preceding time t. As time progresses, it is expected that more information about the true state of the economy is revealed by the assets' cash flows. This idea is formalized as the following assumption.

Assumption 13.2: Resolution of Uncertainty

(i) $\sigma(M_t) \subseteq \sigma(M_s)$ for $0 \leq t \leq s \leq T$

(ii) $\sigma(M_0) = \{\phi, \Omega\}$

Investors' beliefs are restricted by the following two assumptions.

Assumption 13.3: Conditional Homogeneous Beliefs

Given $x \in M$, every investor agrees that $x(t, \omega)$ is the cash flow in dollars to asset x at time $t \in \{1, \ldots, T\}$ given state $\omega \in \Omega$ occurs.

Assumption 13.4: Unconditional Beliefs

Given an event $H \in \sigma(M_T)$, $\text{Prob}_i(H) = 0$ if and only if $\text{Prob}_j(H) = 0$ for all investors i, j where $\text{Prob}_i(\cdot)$ is the ith investor's probability belief.

The markets at times $t = 0, \ldots, T - 1$ are approximated by a frictionless and competitive economy.

Assumption 13.5: Frictionless Markets

The asset markets at times 0 to $T - 1$ have no transaction costs, no taxes, and no restrictions on short sales, and asset shares are divisible.

Assumption 13.6: Competitive Markets

Every investor acts as a price taker.

We now introduce the first extension of the multiperiod model utilized in Chap. 12. To discuss dynamic trading strategies, we need to know prices for the traded assets not only at time 0 but at times $1, \ldots, T - 1$ as well. This requirement necessitates a generalization of the time 0 price functional used in previous chapters. What we need is a pricing functional that prices a traded asset at times $t = 0$ to time $t = T - 1$. In addition, since prices subsequent to time 0 are unknown (random) at time 0, future prices also need to depend on the unknown (random) state of the economy. With this motivation in mind, we define a *random* price functional $p_t(x, \omega)$ at time t for $t = 1, \ldots, T - 1$ over the assets traded in M where $p_t(x, \omega)$ gives the time t price in dollars of asset $x \in M$ under state $\omega \in \Omega$; i.e., $p_t : M \times \Omega \to \mathbb{R}$. This price represents the price *after* the cash flows to asset $x \in M$ are distributed at time t under state $\omega \in \Omega$. We assume that the asset's price is known at time t.[1] When there is no ambiguity, we will sometimes write $p_t(x)$ for $p_t(x, \omega)$. The price of an asset is random for times $t > 0$ since more information becomes available as time passes (by assumption 13.2). This information can change an investor's demand for an asset and hence its price.

Given prices at all dates under all states, we can now introduce dynamic trading strategies. A *dynamic self-financing trading* strategy is a portfolio involving n assets, $\{x_1, \ldots, x_n\} \in M$. It is initiated at time 0 and terminated at

[1] We assume that $p_t(x, \omega)$ is $\sigma(M_t)$ measurable for all t and all $x \in M$. This assumption could be relaxed in the subsequent analysis. The information set $\sigma(M_t)$ could be expanded to include the information set generated by $p_t(x, \omega)$ for all $x \in M$ at time t. The subsequent analysis applies unchanged given we interpret $\sigma(M_t)$ as this larger information set. This approach has the interpretation that investors are sophisticated in the sense of assumption 19.7 (see Chap. 19) and that investors use the additional information revealed by prices in their trading strategies.

time T. The portfolio is constructed to have no net cash inflows or outflows at times $t = 1, \ldots, T - 1$, and therefore it is called *self-financing*. It is called *dynamic* because the portfolio's composition is allowed to change over time, subject to the self-financing condition. Formally, a *dynamic self-financing trading strategy* is an n vector $\{\theta_1(t, \omega), \ldots, \theta_n(t, \omega)\}_{t=0}^{T-1}$, where $\theta_j(t, \omega)$ represents the number of shares of asset x_j held in the portfolio at time t under state ω, such that

(i) $\theta_i(t, \omega)$ depends only on the information available at time t, i.e., $\sigma(M_t)$,[2] and $\hfill$ (13.1)

(ii) $\displaystyle\sum_{j=1}^{n} \theta_j(t, \omega)p_t(x_j, \omega) = \sum_{j=1}^{n} \theta_j(t - 1, \omega)[p_t(x_j, \omega) + x_j(t, \omega)]$

for all $\omega \,\epsilon\, \Omega$ and $t = 1, \ldots, T - 1$. $\hfill$ (13.2)

A dynamic self-financing trading strategy is a portfolio involving n assets, $\{x_1, \ldots, x_n\}$, that change across time. The changes in the asset shares across time are subject to two constraints: Condition (i) regulates the information utilized in forming the trading rules about asset shares. It restricts the trading rule to depend on only information available in the market at the time the shares are purchased. For example, the number of shares of asset x_1 held at time t, $\theta_1(t, \omega)$, can only depend on the information available in the market at time t, denoted $\sigma(M_t)$. This information is sometimes called "public" information. It excludes use of knowledge about future events not already reflected in prices or the assets' cash flows. The reason for this restriction is that these trading strategies are introduced to discuss particular types of "arbitrage opportunities." An arbitrage opportunity should be a trading strategy that *all* investors agree is an arbitrage opportunity. For this to be the case, the same information needs to be available to everyone in the market for use in forming the trading rule. Although "insiders" could actually possess information beyond that contained in $\sigma(M_t)$ and trade successfully, we do not consider this type of information trading in this chapter and defer its discussion to Chap. 19.

Condition (ii) is the self-financing condition. The left-hand side of expression (13.2) represents the time t value of the *new* position in the portfolio taken at time t, $\sum_{j=1}^{n} \theta_j(t, \omega)p_t(x_j, \omega)$. The right-hand side of expression (13.2) represents the time t value of the *old* position in the portfolio taken at time $t - 1$, $\sum_{j=1}^{n} \theta_j(t - 1, \omega)p_t(x_j, \omega)$, plus the time t cash flows to the *old* position in the portfolio, $\sum_{j=1}^{n} \theta_j(t - 1, \omega)x_j(t, \omega)$. Note that the time subscripts on the right-hand side of expression (13.2) differ for the number of shares, $\theta_j(t - 1, \omega)$, and the price plus cash flow, $[p_t(x_j, \omega) + x_j(t, \omega)]$. Since trades can only take place at the discrete times $t = 0, 1, \ldots, T - 1$, expression (13.2) states that the value of the *new* position at time t (left-hand side) must equal the time t value plus cash flows of the *old* position taken at time $t - 1$. All cash flows are

---

[2] We assume that $\theta_i(t, \omega)$ is $\sigma(M_t)$ measurable for all t and all $x_i \,\epsilon\, M$.

reinvested within the portfolio, and changes in the asset shares are financed internally.

For example, the buy and hold strategy studied in Chap. 12 with reinvestment of cash flows is a trivial example of a dynamic self-financing trading strategy. For this example, the number of the shares in assets $\{x_1, \ldots, x_n\}$ are adjusted from time 0 to time $T - 1$ only to reinvest the cash flows, i.e.

$$\theta_i(t, \omega) = \theta_i(t - 1, \omega) \left[1 + x_i(t, \omega)/p_t(x_i, \omega) \right]$$

$$\text{for all } \omega \, \epsilon \, \Omega \text{ and } t = 0, \ldots, T - 1$$

This buy and hold strategy satisfies both conditions (i) and (ii). Indeed, condition (i) is satisfied since the shares held at any time t depend only on information available at time t (prices and cash flows). The second condition (ii) is also satisfied since the number of new shares purchased at time t is just sufficient to reinvest the cash flows received at time t.

We want to exclude arbitrage opportunities involving these dynamic self-financing trading strategies.

Assumption 13.7: No Dynamic Self-Financing Trading Strategy Arbitrage Opportunities Exist

(i) Value additivity
If for some investor i, some dynamic self-financing portfolio strategy $\{\theta_1(t), \ldots, \theta_n(t)\}_{t=0}^{T-1}$, and some asset $z \, \epsilon \, M$ we have

$$\text{Prob}_i \left[\omega \, \epsilon \, \Omega : \sum_{i=1}^{n} \theta_i(T, \omega) x_i(T, \omega) = z(T, \omega) \right] = 1$$

and
$$\text{Prob}_i[\omega \, \epsilon \, \Omega : z(t, \omega) = 0] = 1 \quad \text{for all } T > t \geq s$$
then

$$p_s(z, \omega) = \sum_{i=1}^{n} \theta_i(s, \omega) p_s(x_i, \omega)$$

This is true for all $s = 0, \ldots, T - 1$ and all $\omega \, \epsilon \, \Omega$.

(ii) Dominance
If for some investor i and some dynamic self-financing portfolio strategy $\{\theta_1(t), \ldots, \theta_n(t)\}_{t=0}^{T-1}$ we have

$$\text{Prob}_i \left[\omega \, \epsilon \, \Omega : \sum_{i=1}^{n} \theta_i(T, \omega) x_i(T, \omega) \geq 0 \right] = 1$$

and

$$\text{Prob}_i\left[\omega \in \Omega: \sum_{i=1}^{n} \theta_i(T, \omega)x_i(T, \omega) > 0\right] > 0$$

then

$$\sum_{i=1}^{n} \theta_i(s, \omega)p_s(x_i, \omega) > 0 \quad \text{for all } s = 0, \ldots, T - 1 \text{ and all } \omega \in \Omega$$

This generalizes the no buy and hold type arbitrage opportunity strategies of assumption 12.7 in Chap. 12. Condition (i) is called value additivity. If for some investor there exists an asset $z \in M$ with zero cash flows over times s, $\ldots, T - 1$, that can be duplicated with the self-financing portfolio $\{\theta_1(t), \ldots, \theta_n(t)\}$ $t = 0, \ldots, T - 1$, then the asset z and the portfolio must have the same value at time s. If this were not true, an "arbitrage opportunity" would present itself.

Condition (ii) is labeled dominance. It states that if a portfolio can be constructed that has zero cash flows over times $\{s, \ldots, T - 1\}$, and at time T is always nonnegative with a positive probability of a positive value, then its value at time s is strictly positive. Again, a violation of this condition would imply the existence of a probabilistic money pump, i.e., an "arbitrage opportunity."

Finally, we require that discount bonds of all maturities trade as in Chap. 12.

Assumption 13.8: Marketed Default-Free Discount Bonds

The bonds $\chi_s \in M$ for maturities $s = 1, \ldots, T$, where

$$\chi_s(t, \omega) = \begin{cases} 1 & \text{for all } \omega \in \Omega \text{ if } s = t \\ 0 & \text{otherwise} \end{cases}$$

For the subsequent analysis, we also impose the assumption of positive interest rates.

Assumption 13.9: Positive Interest Rates

$$0 < p_t(\chi_s, \omega) < 1 \text{ for } T \geq s \geq t \text{ and } t = 0, \ldots, T - 1$$

This last assumption requires that the price of a dollar received in the future for sure to be less than the price of a dollar today.

13.2. CALL AND PUT OPTIONS

This section defines the types of call and put options considered in this chapter, and presents some simple pricing relationships that exist among the various options. The pricing relationships will depend on excluding the arbitrage opportunities of the type in assumption 13.7. The arguments are very straightforward. Any difficulty inherent in the subsequent analysis is due to the complicated notation. Consequently, care should be taken in understanding the cash flow descriptions of the following call and put options.

Four types of call options will be considered: European calls, European puts, American calls, and American puts. These options will be issued against a *limited liability* asset $x \in M$. Recall that x is a limited liability asset if for some investor i, $\text{Prob}_i[x(t, \omega) \geq 0] = 1$ for all t and $\text{Prob}_i[x(t, \omega) > 0] > 0$ for some t. By the unconditional probability beliefs assumption 13.4, if one investor sees a limited liability asset, then all investors agree it is a limited liability asset. We define each type of option in turn.

Definition: European Call Option

A *European call option* on an asset $x \in M$ with an exercise price of K and a maturity date of τ gives its owner the right to purchase the asset x at time τ for a price of K dollars. The owner of the European call option decides whether or not to exercise (buy) the asset at time τ. Hence the call provides an option to exercise, not an obligation. The cash flow to the European call on asset $x \in M$, $c(x, K, \tau)$, is defined by

$$c(t, \omega; x, K, \tau) = \begin{cases} x(\tau, \omega) - K & \text{if } \omega \in \{\omega \in \Omega: x(\tau, \omega) > K\} \text{ and } t = \tau \\ 0 & \text{otherwise} \end{cases}$$

A European call option can only be exercised at time τ. Hence there are zero cash flows to the call for times $t < \tau$. At the maturity date, the call only has value if the asset's cash flow $x(\tau, \omega)$ exceeds the exercise price K. In this case, when $\omega \in \{\omega \in \Omega: x(\tau, \omega) > K\}$, by exercising the call's holder gets $x(\tau, \omega) - K$. Otherwise, the call expires unexercised and worthless. Analogously, we can define a European put option.

Definition: European Put Option

A *European put option* on an asset $x \in M$ with an exercise price of K and a maturity date of τ gives its owner the right to sell asset x at time τ for a price of K dollars. The put option is a right, not an obligation, to sell the asset for K dollars at time τ. The put owner will only exercise the option to sell when this process generates a positive cash flow. Hence the defining cash flows to a European put option, $d(x, K, \tau)$ are

$$d(t, \omega; x, K, \tau) = \begin{cases} K - x(\tau, \omega) & \text{if } \omega \in \{\omega \in \Omega : x(\tau, \omega) < K \text{ and } t = \tau \\ 0 & \text{otherwise} \end{cases}$$

The European put option is similar to the European call with the exception that the put is the right to *sell* the asset, while the call is the right to *buy*. Hence the put only has a value at the maturity date τ if the asset's cash flows, $x(\tau, \omega)$, are below the exercise price, K. In this case the put's value is $K - x(\tau, \omega)$. Otherwise, it has a zero cash flow. Since the put can only be exercised at maturity, it has zero cash flows for times $t \leq T - 1$ as well.

Definition: American Call Option

An *American call option* on an asset $x \in M$ with an exercise price of K and a maturity date of τ gives its owner the right to purchase asset x at *any* time $t = 0 \ldots , \tau$ for a price of K dollars. The American call option differs from the European call in that the American call can be exercised at any time t prior to the maturity date τ. Recall that the European call can be exercised only at maturity. The defining cash flows to an American call option, $C(x, K, \tau)$, are

$$C(t, \omega; x, K, \tau) = \begin{cases} p_t(x, \omega) - K & \text{if exercised at time } t < \tau \\ x(\tau, \omega) - K & \text{if } \omega \in \{\omega \in \Omega : x(\tau, \omega) > K\} \text{ at } t = \tau \\ & \text{and no exercise prior to } \tau \\ 0 & \text{otherwise} \end{cases}$$

(A capital letter distinguishes American type options' cash flows from European type options, which have a lowercase letter for their cash flows.)

The cash flow for an American call is more complicated than the European call's cash flow, due to the possibility of early exercise. The American call can be exercised any time during its life; hence if it is exercised at time $t < \tau$, the cash flow is $p_t(x, \omega) - K$. This represents the difference between the price of the asset at time t and the exercise price. If the call is not exercised prior to maturity, its cash flow is zero until the maturity date τ. At the maturity date, the cash flow is positive if and only if the call ends up in the money; i.e., the cash flow at time τ exceeds the exercise price, $x(\tau, \omega) > K$. We see that early exercise can significantly influence the cash flow pattern for an American call. A similar difference occurs for an American put option.

Definition: American Put Option

An *American put option* on an asset $x \in M$ with an exercise price of K and a maturity date of τ gives its owner the right to sell asset x at any time

$t = 0, \ldots, \tau$ for a price of K dollars. The defining cash flows to an American put option, $D(x, K, \tau)$, are

$$D(t, \omega; x, K, \tau) = \begin{cases} K - p_t(x, \omega) & \text{if exercised at time } t < \tau \\ K - x(\tau, \omega) & \text{if } \omega \in \{\omega \in \Omega: x(\tau, \omega) < K\} \text{ at } t = \tau \\ & \text{and no exercise prior to } \tau \\ 0 & \text{otherwise} \end{cases}$$

The description of the American put's cash flow is analogous to the American call's cash flow with the exception that the put gives the right to sell.

The American type options' cash flows are more difficult to quantify since the cash flows are determined by the *actions* of their holders with respect to early exercise. Using the arbitrage pricing methodology, we can state a sufficient condition for no early exercise. This is given in theorem 13.2. However, before we present that theorem, some preliminary results are needed. Theorem 13.1 derives some simple pricing relationships that must hold among these four types of options.

Theorem 13.1: Pricing Relationships

Given assumptions 13.1–13.8, if $C(x, K, \tau)$, $c(x, K, \tau)$, $d(x, K, \tau)$, $D(x, K, \tau)$, $x \in M$, then

(i) $p_t(C(x, K, \tau)) \geq p_t(c(x, K, \tau))$ for $t = 0, \ldots, \tau - 1$

(ii) $p_t(D(x, K, \tau)) \geq p_t(d(x, K, \tau))$ for $t = 0, \ldots, \tau - 1$

Proof

(i) An American call's exercise strategy can be set up in a manner to duplicate exactly a European call option. Indeed, simply do not exercise the American call option under any circumstances until maturity. At maturity, only exercise the call if $x(\tau, \omega)$ exceeds K. Hence $C(t, \omega; x, K, \tau) \geq c(t, \omega; x, K, \tau)$ for all $t = 0 \ldots, \tau$ and $\omega \in \Omega$. By the no arbitrage opportunity assumption 13.7, $p_t(C(x, K, \tau)) \geq p_t(c(x, K, \tau))$ for all t.

(ii) The same argument works for put options. □

This theorem states that the American type call and put options are always at least as valuable as a European type call and put options. The reasoning is straightforward. The American type option allows the investor to duplicate the European type option. In some circumstances, it may allow one to do better. Hence it should be worth at least as much to any investor. There are circumstances, however, where the additional flexibility of the American call is never of any use. One such set of circumstances is described in the following theorem.

Theorem 13.2:   Equivalence of American Calls and European Calls

Under assumptions 13.1–13.9, where $C(x, K, \tau)$, $c(x, K, \tau)$, $x \in M$, if the asset has no cash flows prior to maturity, i.e., $x(t, \omega) = 0$ for all $t < \tau$ and all $\omega \in \Omega$, then

$$p_t(C(x, K, \tau)) = p_t(c(x, K, \tau))$$

Proof

We will show that the American call is never exercised early and therefore

$$C(t, \omega; x, K, \tau) = c(t, \omega; x, K, \tau) \quad \text{for all } t \text{ and all } \omega \in \Omega$$

By the no arbitrage opportunity assumption 13.7, this will complete the proof.

To show that the American call is never exercised early, we will show its value *not* exercised is always strictly greater than its value exercised. Now, $c(t, \omega; x, K, \tau) \geq x(t, \omega) - K\chi_\tau$ for all t, $\omega \in \Omega$. This is true because $x(t, \omega) = 0$ and $c(t, \omega; x, K, \tau) = 0$ for $t < \tau$, and

$$c(\tau, \omega; x, K, \tau) = x(\tau, \omega) - K \quad \text{if } x(\tau, \omega) - K \geq 0$$

$$c(\tau, \omega; x, K, \tau) = 0 > x(\tau, \omega) - K \quad \text{if } x(\tau, \omega) - K < 0$$

So, by assumption 13.7, $p_t(c(x, K, \tau)) \geq p_t(x) - Kp_t(\chi_\tau) > p_t(x) - K$ because $p_t(\chi_\tau) < 1$ by assumption 13.9. Hence $p_t(C(x, K, \tau)) > p_t(x) - K$ for all $t \in \{0, \ldots, \tau - 1\}$ and $\omega \in \Omega$ by theorem 13.1. This completes the proof. ☐

This theorem states that if the underlying asset has no cash flows until the maturity date τ, then the American call's value equals the European call's value. In other words, it never pays to exercise an American call option early. Hence the early exercise privilege has zero value. If the underlying asset were a common stock, then the interpretation is that if the common stock pays no dividends, never exercise the American call early. The economic reasoning underlying this theorem is based on the observation that if you exercise the American call early, you give up K dollars today instead of at time τ. Early exercise costs in terms of interest lost. The benefits of exercising early are zero, since no cash flows are obtained from holding the underlying asset. If cash flows occur on the underlying asset, then early exercise is usually a distinct possibility. An example would be where the asset's cash flow at time $\tau - 1$, $x(\tau - 1) > K$ with probability one, but zero otherwise, i.e., $x(t) = 0$ with probability one for $t = 0, \ldots, \tau - 2$ and $t = \tau$. Here the European call has zero value, but the American call has positive value. The American call will surely be exercised at time $\tau - 2$, and its current value $p_t(C(x, \tau, K)) = p_t(x) - Kp_t(\chi_{\tau-2}) > 0$.

The same type of result given by theorem 13.2 does not hold for put options. For example, suppose the hypotheses of theorem 13.2 are satisfied, and suppose that $\text{Prob}_i[p_t(x, \omega) = 0] > 0$ for some $t < \tau$. For the set of states where $p_t(x, \omega) = 0$, it is optimal to exercise the put. If exercised, one gets K immediately. If one waits to exercise, even until the next time period, then one only gets K in the future, at a present value of $Kp_t(\chi_{t+1}) < K$. This distinction between puts and calls occurs because puts have a maximum possible gain of K dollars, while calls have unlimited possible gains. For this reason, pricing American puts is usually a more difficult exercise than pricing American calls.

We now provide a relationship between European type calls and puts.

Theorem 13.3: European Put-Call Parity

Under assumptions 13.1–13.9, given $c(x, \tau, K)$, $d(x, \tau, K)$, $x \in M$, if there are no cash flows on asset x prior to maturity, i.e., $x(t, \omega) = 0$ for $t < \tau$, then $p_t(c(x, \tau, K)) = p_t(d(x, \tau, K)) + p_t(x) - Kp_t(\chi_\tau)$.

Proof

We see that $c(t, \omega; x, \tau, K) = d(t, \omega; x, \tau, K) + x(t, \omega) - K\chi_\tau(t, \omega)$ for all $t < \tau$ and all $\omega \in \Omega$, since all the terms in this expression are zero when $t < \tau$. Note that $c(\tau, \omega; x, \tau, K) = d(\tau, \omega; x, \tau, K) + x(\tau, \omega) - K$ for all $\omega \in \Omega$, since if $x(\tau, \omega) - K > 0$, $d(\tau, \omega; x, \tau, K) = 0$ and $c(\tau, \omega; x, \tau, K) = x(\tau, \omega) - K$, while if $x(\tau, \omega) - K \le 0$, $c(\tau, \omega; x, \tau, K) = 0$ and $d(\tau, \omega; x, \tau, K) = K - x(\tau, \omega)$. Hence, by assumption 13.7, we get the result. $\square$

This put-call parity theorem is very good for developing intuition about the relationship between call and put options on an asset. It states that if there are no cash flows on the underlying asset, a call is equivalent to a portfolio consisting of a put, the asset, and selling K bonds with maturity date τ. Hence we see that a call is like buying the asset on margin $(x - K\chi_\tau)$, and also purchasing an insurance policy on the asset's price $(d(x, \tau, K))$. The insurance policy (the put) ensures the stock for K dollars at time τ.

Analogous put-call parity theorems exist for American type call and put options under varying hypotheses. The theorems in this section are just a sampling of the diverse theorems possible. The interested reader is referred to Jarrow and Rudd [4] or Cox and Rubinstein [2] for a more complete survey.

13.3. BINOMIAL OPTION PRICING

This section restricts the economy given in Secs. 13.1 and 13.2 to obtain an explicit pricing formula for a European call option. A European call option is chosen to avoid the issues of early exercise. However, given theorem 13.2, it will be seen that the following model prices American calls as well.

We use the simplest economy possible to demonstrate the procedure. Let $T = 2$, so the economy consists of only three periods: $t = 0, 1, 2$.

Assumption 13.10: Constant Interest Rates[3]

$$p_0(\chi_2, \omega) = e^{-2r} \quad \text{for all } \omega \in \Omega$$

$$p_1(\chi_2, \omega) = e^{-r} \quad \text{for all } \omega \in \Omega$$

$$\chi_2(2, \omega) = 1 \quad \text{for all } \omega \in \Omega$$

This assumption asserts that interest rates are constant over time and equal to r percent per unit time (compounded continuously).

Assumption 13.11: No Cash Flows Prior to Maturity

$$x(t, \omega) = 0 \quad \text{for } t = 1 \text{ and for all } \omega \in \Omega$$

This assumption states that underlying asset x has no cash flows until time 2, which will be the maturity date of the European call option. Hence, by theorem 13.2, this section also prices the corresponding American call option with the subsequent formula.

Let the state space be partitioned into four mutually exclusive events $\Omega = \phi_1 \cup \phi_2 \cup \phi_3 \cup \phi_4$, where $\phi_1, \phi_2, \phi_3, \phi_4$ are disjoint. We assume that each of these events occurs with strictly positive probability, i.e., $\text{Prob}_i(\phi_j) > 0$ for $j = 1, 2, 3, 4$. Finally, we need to specify the information sets $\sigma(M_1)$ and $\sigma(M_2)$. Let $\sigma(M_1) = \{\phi, \Omega, \phi_1 \cup \phi_2, \phi_3 \cup \phi_4\}$; i.e., at time 1, either $\{\phi_1 \cup \phi_2\}$ occurs or $\{\phi_3 \cup \phi_4\}$ occurs. Let $\sigma(M_2) = \{\text{all subsets of } \Omega\}$; i.e., either $\{\phi_1\}$ or $\{\phi_2\}$ or $\{\phi_3\}$ or $\{\phi_4\}$ occurs at time 2. On a tree diagram, these states would have the representation as given in Fig. 13.1. In essence, the state space consists of only four "states," each with positive probability of occurring.

We next give the asset's price an explicit stochastic process.

[3]The symbol $e^b = \sum_{j=0}^{\infty} (b)^j/j!$, the exponential function.

FIGURE 13.1: Tree diagram representation for the events and their probabilities.

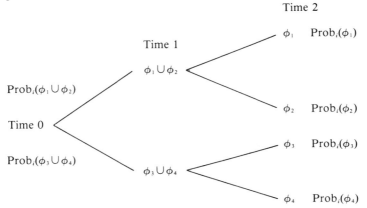

Assumption 13.12: Stochastic Process for Asset Price Movements

Define $p_0(x) \equiv S$.

$$p_1(x, \omega) = \begin{cases} Se^u & \text{if } \omega \in \phi_1 \cup \phi_2 \\ Se^v & \text{if } \omega \in \phi_3 \cup \phi_4 \quad \text{and} \end{cases} \tag{13.1}$$

$$x(2, \omega) = \begin{cases} Se^{2u} & \text{if } \omega \in \phi_1 \\ Se^{u+v} & \text{if } \omega \in \phi_2 \\ Se^{u+v} & \text{if } \omega \in \phi_3 \\ Se^{2v} & \text{if } \omega \in \phi_4 \end{cases} \tag{13.2}$$

where $u > r > v$.

This is a branching process (see Figure 13.2). The price of the asset x at time 0 is denoted by S. At time 1, the asset price can jump "up" to Se^u with probability $\text{Prob}_i(\phi_1 \cup \phi_2)$ and it can jump "down" to Se^v with probability $\text{Prob}_i(\phi_3 \cup \phi_4)$. If an upward jump occurs, the asset earns a return of u percent. Conversely, if the stock jumps down, it earns a return of only v percent. By construction $u > r > v$.

At time 2, the stock jumps again. Starting at Se^u it earns a return of u percent with probability $\text{Prob}_i(\phi_1)/\text{Prob}_i(\phi_1 \cup \phi_2)$ and a return of v percent with probability $\text{Prob}_i(\phi_2)/\text{Prob}_i(\phi_1 \cup \phi_2)$. Similarly, starting from Se^v it earns a return of u percent with probability $\text{Prob}_i(\phi_3)/\text{Prob}_i(\phi_3 \cup \phi_4)$ and a return of v percent with probability $\text{Prob}_i(\phi_4)/\text{Prob}_i(\phi_3 \cup \phi_4)$. If

$$\text{Prob}_i(\phi_1)/\text{Prob}_i(\phi_1 \cup \phi_2) = \text{Prob}_i(\phi_1 \cup \phi_2)$$

FIGURE 13.2: Tree diagram representation of the asset process.

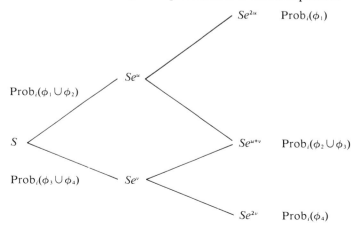

and

$$\text{Prob}_i(\phi_3)/\text{Prob}_i(\phi_3 \cup \phi_4) = \text{Prob}_i(\phi_1 \cup \phi_2)$$

then this stochastic process is a *random* walk. This restriction is not imposed below.

Note that expression (13.2) can also be written as

$$x(2, \omega) = \begin{matrix} p_1(x, \omega)e^u & \text{if } \omega \in \phi_1 \cup \phi_3 \\ p_1(x, \omega)e^v & \text{if } \omega \in \phi_2 \cup \phi_4 \end{matrix} \qquad (13.3)$$

This expression is useful in the derivation given below. The above stochastic model is called a *multiplicative binomial process*. It is perhaps the simplest model available for asset price movements. Fortunately, limiting forms of this model correspond to more realistic (continuous time) stochastic processes. Given the above process, the price of a European call option is determined by our previous assumptions.

Theorem 13.4: Binomial Option Pricing

Under assumptions 13.1–13.12, given x, $c(x, K, 2) \in M$

$$p_0(c(x, K, 2)) = e^{-2r} \sum_{j=0}^{2} \binom{2}{j} q^j (1 - q)^{2-j} \max(0, Se^{ju + (2-j)v} - K) \qquad (13.4)$$

where $q = (e^r - e^v)/(e^u - e^v)$.

Proof

The idea is first to construct a dynamic self-financing portfolio of the bond χ_2 and the asset x to duplicate the call's payoffs across all t and ω and then use assumption 13.7(i).

We start at time 1.

Let $n(1, \omega)$ be the number of assets held at time 1 under state ω, and $m(1, \omega)$ be the number of bonds held at time 1 under state ω. Choose $n(1), m(1)$ such that

$$n(1)x(2, \omega) + m(1)\chi_2(2, \omega) = \max[0, x(2, \omega) - K] \quad \text{for all } \omega \in \Omega$$

The right-hand side of this expression equals the call's value at time 2. This equation can be written as

$$n(1)p_1(x)e^u + m(1) = \max[0, p_1(x)e^u - K] \quad \text{if } \omega \in \phi_1 \cup \phi_3$$

$$n(1)p_1(x)e^v + m(1) = \max[0, p_1(x)e^v - K] \quad \text{if } \omega \in \phi_2 \cup \phi_4$$

This last set of expressions uses condition (13.3). The solution to this system is

$$n(1) = [\max[0, p_1(x)e^v - K] - \max[0, p_1(x)e^u - K]]/p_1(x)(e^v - e^u)$$

and

$$m(1) = [\max[0, p_1(x)e^u - K]e^v - \max[0, p_1(x)e^v - K]e^u]/(e^v - e^u)$$

Note that $n(1)$ and $m(1)$ only depend on information contained in $p_1(x)$, which is in $\sigma(M_1)$. So $n(1)$ and $m(1)$ are valid self-financing trading strategies. By construction, this strategy initiated at time $t = 1$ ensures that

$$n(1)x(2, \omega) + m(1)\chi_2(2, \omega) = c(2, \omega; x, K, 2) \quad \text{for all } \omega \in \Omega$$

Hence, by assumption 13.7

$$n(1)p_1(x) + m(1)p_1(\chi_2) = p_1(c(x, K, 2))$$

i.e.

$$n(1)p_1(x) + m(1)e^{-r} = p_1(c(x, K, 2))$$

Substitution for $n(1)$ and $m(1)$ along with algebra yields

$$p_1(c(x, K, 2)) = e^{-r}\{q \max(0, p_1(x)e^v - K)$$
$$+ (1 - q)\max(0, p_1(x)e^u - K)\}$$

where $q = (e^r - e^u)/(e^v - e^u)$.

Next, we go back to time 0.

At time 0, we want to choose $n(0), m(0)$ such that the portfolio is self-financing; i.e.

$$n(0)x(1, \omega) + m(0)\chi_2(1, \omega) = n(1)x(1, \omega) + m(1)\chi_2(1, \omega)$$

$$\text{for all } \omega \in \Omega$$

This is satisfied at time 1 if

$$n(0)Se^u + m(0)e^{-r} = n(1)Se^u + m(1)e^{-r} \quad \text{if } \omega \in \phi_1 \cup \phi_2$$

and

$$n(0)Se^v + m(0)e^{-r} = n(1)Se^v + m(1)e^{-r} \quad \text{if } \omega \in \phi_3 \cup \phi_4$$

Define

$$N_u \equiv n(1)Se^u + m(1)e^{-r} \quad \text{if } \omega \in \phi_1 \cup \phi_2$$
$$N_v \equiv n(1)Se^v + m(1)e^{-r} \quad \text{if } \omega \in \phi_3 \cup \phi_4$$

Note that $n(1)$ and $m(1)$ depend on ω through $p_1(x, \omega)$. The solution is

$$n(0) = \frac{N_v - N_u}{S(e^v - e^u)}$$

and

$$m(0) = \left[\frac{N_u e^v - N_v e^u}{e^v - e^u}\right]e^r$$

Substitution of N_u and N_v into these solutions verifies that these only depend on $\sigma(M_0)$. Hence they are valid trading strategies.

We have shown that the strategy $\{n(0), m(0); n(1), m(1)\}$ is a self-financing trading strategy that duplicates $c(x, K, 2)$ at time 2.

By assumption 13.7, we know that

$$n(0)p_0(x) + m(0)e^{-2r} = p_0(c(x, K, 2))$$

or

$$n(0)S + m(0)e^{-2r} = p_0(c(x, K, 2))$$

Substitution of $n(0)$ and $m(0)$ into the above expressions and algebra gives the theorem. $\square$

An interesting property of this pricing model, expression (13.4), is that it does not depend on the probabilities of upward movements. Alternatively stated, given the asset's price, two investors disagreeing about the probability of an upward jump will still agree about the call's value. This result occurs because by the stochastic process assumption 13.11 a call option can be constructed using the asset x and bond χ_τ with a dynamic trading strategy across all states, independent of the probabilities.

This theorem can easily be generalized from the three-period model with $T = 2$ to arbitrary time periods T. The corresponding formula is

$$p_0(c(x, K, T)) = e^{-rT} \sum_{j=0}^{T} \binom{T}{j} q^j (1 - q)^{T-j} \max (0, S\, e^{ju+(T-j)v} - K)$$

where $q = (e^r - e^u)/(e^v - e^u)$. This is called the *binomial option pricing* model.

This pricing model is of great practical importance. If we fix T and subdivide T into subintervals (approaching continuous trading), we can get the Black-Scholes formula from the above model. The Black-Scholes model is used by academics and professional traders alike. A detailed derivation of the Black-Scholes model and supporting comments are contained in Jarrow and Rudd [4].

13.4. SUMMARY

This chapter modifies the multiperiod arbitrage pricing theory of Chap. 12 to study the pricing of call and put options. The modification of the model in Chap. 12 involves including dynamic trading strategies into the analysis and excluding arbitrage opportunities based on these strategies (assumption 13.7).

Four different types of call and put options are defined: European calls, American calls, European puts, and American puts. Using the cash flow descriptions of these various financial securities, simple pricing relationships across the securities were derived. Theorem 13.3 derives the important put-call parity theorem and theorem 13.4 is the binomial option pricing model. Serving as an introduction to a vast literature, this chapter is a stepping stone to more study by providing the theoretical foundations. In doing so, this chapter completes the study of arbitrage pricing theory under uncertainty.

13.5. REFERENCES

1. Arditti, Fred D., and Kose John, "Spanning the State Space with Options," *Journal of Financial and Quantitative Analysis*, 15 (1980), 1–9.
2. Cox, John, and Mark Rubinstein, *Options Markets*. Englewood Cliffs, N.J.: Prentice-Hall, 1985.

3. Green, R., and R. Jarrow, "Spanning and Completeness in Markets with Contingent Claims," *Journal of Economic Theory*, 40 (1987).

4. Jarrow, R., and A. Rudd, *Option Pricing*. Homewood, Ill.: Richard D. Irwin, 1983.

5. John, K., "Efficient Funds in a Financial Market with Options: A New Irrelevance Proposition," *Journal of Finance*, 35 (1981), 685–695.

6. Ross, S., "Options and Efficiency," *Quarterly Journal of Economics* (February 1976), 75–89.

14

CARDINAL
UTILITY THEORY
The Optimal Consumption
and Portfolio Decision

The last seven chapters analyzed arbitrage pricing models in an uncertain economy. This chapter begins the study of equilibrium pricing theory in the same context. Analogous to the situation under certainty, more structure is necessary to develop equilibrium pricing theory. Additional assumptions concerning preferences and the meaning of an "equilibrium" price are required. This additional structure will both enrich the theory and limit its applicability. The benefits and costs of this trade-off are the subject of Sec. 15.6 in Chap. 15.

This chapter introduces the additional structure on preferences needed to pursue equilibrium pricing theory. To simplify the presentation, the discussion will focus on the asset model embedded within the consumption-saving model as presented in Sec. 8.3 of Chap. 8. We add one additional assumption, however, on the structure of the asset markets that will be employed throughout the remainder of the text. This assumption ensures that the marketed assets have a basis that consists of only a finite number of assets. It is invoked to simplify the analysis.

Two new utility concepts are also introduced: the notion of a certainty equivalent and the meaning of risk aversion. These concepts are crucial to the subsequent models, especially the capital asset pricing model (Chaps. 15 and 16) and the equilibrium version of Ross's APT (Chap. 18).

The last section of this chapter relates the exclusion of arbitrage opportunities to assumptions on preferences and the economy. This is accomplished through the derivation and proof of theorem 14.3. This theorem fulfills a promise repeatedly made in prior chapters that the exogenously imposed assumption of no arbitrage opportunities could be founded on the fundamentals of an economy (preferences, endowments, and market structures). As such, this theorem shows that the arbitrage pricing theories of earlier chapters are embedded within the equilibrium pricing theories developed here.

14.1. PRELIMINARIES

We consider a two-period economy with times 0 and 1. The consumer consumes a single consumption good in both periods. An individual is assumed to have preferences π defined over the choice set $\tilde{B}$ consisting of all probability distributions over consumption at times 0 and 1. Formally

$$\tilde{B} = \{\text{all joint probability distributions over } (C_0, C_1), \text{ where } C_0 \in \mathbb{R} \text{ and } C_1 \in \mathbb{R}\}$$

These preferences are assumed to satisfy the rationality axioms 7.1–7.8 of Chap. 7, and therefore by theorem 7.2, which guarantees the existence of a cardinal utility function, they are characterized by

$$E_b(V(C_0, C_1)) \quad \text{for all } b \in \tilde{B} \tag{14.1}$$

where $\quad V(C_0, C_1)$ is the cardinal utility function defined over the certain outcomes $C_0 \in \mathbb{R}$ and $C_1 \in \mathbb{R}$, and

$E_b(\cdot)$ is the expectation operator based on an objective probability distribution $\text{Prob}[C_0 \leq z_0, C_1 \leq z_1; b]$ for $z_0, z_1 \in \mathbb{R}$.

In addition, investors are assumed to prefer more consumption in any time period to less consumption:

Assumption 14.1: Monotonicity

Given $\delta > 0$, C_0 and C_1

then

$$V(C_0 + \delta, C_1) > V(C_0, C_1)$$

and

$$V(C_0, C_1 + \delta) > V(C_0, C_1)$$

The investor's consumption decision is made in the context of the asset model introduced in Chap. 8. The uncertainty in the economy at date 1 is characterized by a state space Ω, where a particular state is denoted by $\omega \in \Omega$. An asset is a mapping from the state space Ω into the real line, i.e., $x: \Omega \to \mathbb{R}$. So $x(\omega)$ represents the dollar cash flows to asset x at time 1 under state ω. The traded assets at time 0 are denoted by the set M called the *marketed* assets. The marketed assets satisfy assumption 8.1.[†] (This assumption has a dagger since it is an additional assumption not utilized before.)

Assumption 8.1: Marketed Assets—The Finite Dimensional Case[†]

The marketed assets M consist of $K + 1$ assets and all their portfolios:

$$M = \text{span}\{x_0, \ldots, x_K\} \quad \text{where}$$

$$x_j : \Omega \to \mathbb{R} \quad \text{for } j = 0, 1, \ldots, K$$

This assumption is stronger than assumption 8.1. The above assumption requires that the basis set of assets is finite and consists of at most $K + 1$ assets. This assumption is included to simplify the optimization theory presented below. Otherwise, the more complex infinite dimensional optimization theory would need to be employed. This added level of sophistication is not necessary for the models developed below.

The prices of the traded assets at time 0 are represented by a price functional, p, mapping M into the real line. The jth asset x_j has a price in dollars of $p(x_j)$ at time 0. To translate dollars into consumption goods, there are exogenously specified price levels of $\rho_0 > 0$ at time 0 and $\rho_1(\omega) > 0$ at time 1 under state $\omega \in \Omega$.

The asset markets are populated by a finite number of investors whose beliefs satisfy assumptions 8.2 and 8.3. Assumption 8.2 requires investors to agree upon the asset's state contingent payouts, while assumption 8.3 requires that investors agree upon zero probability events. The asset markets are frictionless (assumption 8.4) and competitive (assumption 8.5), and there are no arbitrage opportunities present in the economy (asumption 8.6).

The investor enters time 0 with an endowment of consumption goods and asset shares. The endowed consumption is $(\overline{C}_0, \overline{C}_1(\omega))$ for all $\omega \in \Omega$, and the endowed portfolio at time 0 is $\{\overline{N}_0, \ldots, \overline{N}_K\}$. Under this structure, the investor's portfolio decision is to maximize

$$E_b(V(C_0, C_1(\omega))) \quad \text{for } b \in \tilde{A} \tag{14.2}$$

where

$$\tilde{A} = \{(C_0, \text{Prob}_i[C_1 \leq z; C_0, N_0, \ldots, N_K]):$$

$$\overline{C}_0 + \sum_{j=0}^{K} \overline{N}_j p(x_j)/\rho_0 = C_0 + \sum_{j=0}^{K} N_j p(x_j)/\rho_0,$$

$$\overline{C}_1(\omega) + \sum_{j=0}^{K} N_j x_j(\omega)/\rho_1(\omega) = C_1(\omega) \quad \text{for all } \omega \in \Omega\}$$

The investor chooses consumption and buys and sells assets at time 0 to maximize his expected utility. His final consumption at time 0 is C_0 and his final portfolio is $\{N_0, \ldots, N_K\}$. These determine his consumption at time 1 under state ω, $C_1(\omega)$. Hence his constrained choice set, $\tilde{A}$, is partially specified by his choices $C_0, N_0, \ldots, N_K$. The partial specification of the choice set is completed by his subjective probability beliefs, $\text{Prob}_i[\cdot]$, since these determine the likelihood of getting $C_1(\omega)$ through $\text{Prob}_i[C_1 \leq z; C_0, N_0, \ldots, N_K]$ for all

$z \in \mathbb{R}$. This constrained choice set $\tilde{A}$ is a subset of $\tilde{B}$, the investor's choice set.[1] It is restricted in two ways: first, by the investor's subjective probability beliefs, and second, by the investor's budget constraints. An expanded discussion of condition (14.2) is in Sec. 8.3 of Chap. 8.

14.2. OPTIMALITY

Equilibrium theory is concerned with determining an investor's optimal consumption and portfolio decision. In the consumption-saving model of expression (14.2), the optimal decision is to choose a probability distribution b^* from the constrained choice set $\tilde{A}$, a subset of the choice set $\tilde{B}$, such that expected utility, $E_b(V(C_0, C_1))$, is maximized. The subset $\tilde{A}$ is specified by the individual's budget constraints and his subjective probability beliefs. Unless additional assumptions are imposed, the individual's optimal choice b^* may not exist. We will assume the existence of an optimal probability distribution directly.

Assumption 14.2: Existence of an Optimal Distribution for Consumption

There exists a probability distribution $b^* \in \tilde{A}$ such that $E_{b^*}(V(C_0, C_1)) \geq E_b(V(C_1, C_1))$ for all $b \in \tilde{A}$.

An analysis of the assumptions that can alternatively be imposed on the restricted choice set $\tilde{A}$, preferences $V(C_0, C_1)$, and subjective beliefs, $\text{Prob}_i[C_0 \leq z_0, C_1 \leq z_1]$, such that assumption 14.2 is a theorem can be found in Bertsekas [2]. For the purpose of this text, however, these issues are secondary and assumption 14.2 will suffice.

Given the existence of an optimal element of the constrained choice set $\tilde{A}$, the second issue we must address is its characterization. To characterize this optimal element, we want to utilize calculus. Consequently, additional structure on both the utility function $V(C_0, C_1)$ and the subjective probability distribution $\text{Prob}_i[C_0 \leq z_0, C_1 \leq z_1]$ is needed. Before giving this structure, we rewrite expression (14.2) in an equivalent but more convenient form. The investor's choice problem is equivalent to choosing $\{C_0, N_0, \ldots, N_K\}$ to maximize $E_i(V(C_0, C_1))$ subject to

$$\overline{C}_0 + \sum_{j=0}^{K} \overline{N}_j p(x_j)/\rho_0 = C_0 + \sum_{j=0}^{K} N_j p(x_j)/\rho_0, \quad \text{and}$$

$$\overline{C}_1(\omega) + \sum_{j=0}^{K} N_j x_j(\omega)/\rho_1(\omega) = C_1(\omega) \quad \text{for all } \omega \in \Omega$$

(14.3)

[1]As a technical aside, we must expand probability beliefs over the information set generated by M, $\overline{C}_1$, and ρ_1 as well; i.e., the smallest σ-algebra generated by these random variables.

where $E_i(\cdot)$ is expectation with respect to the investor's subjective probability beliefs $\text{Prob}_i[\cdot]$.[2]

We point out in passing that to be precise, the cardinal utility function $V(C_0, C_1)$ should also be subscripted by an i to make it investor dependent. Although not necessary here, this additional subscript will be needed in subsequent chapters.

Assumption 14.3: Regularity of $E_i(V(C_0, C_1))$

We assume there exists a cardinal utility function such that

(a) $V(C_0, C_1)$ has continuous second-order partial derivatives, and
(b) differentiation (up to the second order)[3] under the expectation operator $E_i(\cdot)$ is a valid operation.

This assumption will allow us to use differentiation in identifying an optimal consumption and portfolio choice.

Although our use of theorem 7.2 has guaranteed that there exists a cardinal utility function, unique up to a positive affine transformation, it does not guarantee that a function as identified by the regularity assumption 14.3 exists. Consequently, assumption 14.3 implicitly imposes additional structure on investor preferences. From now on, given this assumption, the cardinal utility function chosen will always be one that has these regularity properties.

14.3. RISK AVERSION

The previous two sections introduced enough additional structure on preferences to guarantee the existence of an optimal probability distribution b^* from the constrained choice set $\tilde{A}$ and to enable calculus to be employed. Yet, in this application of calculus, to identify uniquely the optimal element using the Lagrangian multiplier techniques, additional structure is still needed. We need an assumption analogous to that given by the strict convexity of preferences assumption 5.4 of Chap. 5 in the certainty case. One approach would be to apply the strict convexity of preferences assumption 5.4 to the choice set $\tilde{B}$ (instead of B) and proceed exactly as in Sec. 5.2 (see Debreu [3, p. 101]). Strict convexity could then be related to risk aversion. This is not the approach we will employ. Instead, we will assume that the cardinal utility function defined over certain outcomes, $V(C_0, C_1)$, is concave. This is consistent with cardinal utility theory

---

[2]The time 1 budget constraint need only hold with probability one. This qualification will be omitted throughout the remainder of the text. No loss in generality occurs due to this omission since we could always redefine C_1 on the set of probability zero to make it hold everywhere.

[3]The underlying assumptions on both $V(C_0, C_1)$ and $\text{Prob}_i[C_0 \le z_0, C_1 \le z_1]$ which generate condition (b) are explored in Bartle [1, corollary 5.9; p. 46].

because any positive affine transformation of the utility function V preserves concavity.[4] This was not the case with ordinal utility functions. To motivate the economic interpretation of the concavity assumption, we first analyze the concept of a certainty equivalent.

14.3.1. Certainty Equivalents

In the context of the consumption-saving model, the investor's objective function is

$$E_i(V(C_0, C_1))$$

Let us fix consumption at time 0, $C_0 = c$, at the optimal level c. The objective function with this constraint can now be written as

$$E_i(V(c, C_1)) \tag{14.4}$$

For convenience, we define $V(c, C_1) = v(C_1)$ and obtain the simplified objective function

$$E_i(v(C_1)) \tag{14.5}$$

In the investor's choice problem, only the time 1 consumption has any uncertainty associated with it. Expression (14.5) focuses on this aspect of the model by considering consumption at time 0 as fixed (at c).

Next consider a risky asset or gamble, b_0, where $b_0(\omega)$ is the payoff in units of the consumption good to asset b_0 under state ω at time 1, i.e., $b_0: \Omega \rightarrow \mathbb{R}$ where $\text{var}_i(b_0) > 0$.[5] This asset has a utility level to the investor that can be quantified using expression (14.5) as $E_i(v(b_0))$. What riskless amount y will make the investor indifferent, in terms of utility, to the asset b_0? By riskless, we mean $\text{var}_i(y) = 0$ so that $E_i(v(y)) = v(y)$. Algebraically, what certain amount y satisfies the following?

$$v(y) = E_i(v(b_0)) \tag{14.6}$$

The amount y that satisfies expression (14.6) is called the *certainty equivalent to the asset* b_0. An example will help to clarify this concept.

[4]To see this, suppose $V(C_0, C_1)$ is concave. A function $V(C_0, C_1)$ is *concave* if $V(\beta C_0 + (1 - \beta)C_0^*, \beta C_1 + (1 - \beta)C_1^*) \geq \beta V(C_0, C_1) + (1 - \beta)V(C_0^*, C_1^*)$ for all $\beta \epsilon (0, 1)$ and $C_0, C_1, C_0^*, C_1^* \epsilon \mathbb{R}$. Consider a positive affine transformation $G(x) = \delta x + \alpha$ for $\delta > 0$. Now we claim that $G(V(C_0, C_1))$ is concave. Note that

$$G(V(\beta C_0 + (1 - \beta)C_0^*, \beta C_1 + (1 - \beta)C_1^*)) =$$

$$\delta V(\beta C_0 + (1 - \beta)C_0^*, \beta C_1 + (1 - \beta)C_1^*) + \alpha \geq$$

$$\delta[\beta V(C_0, C_1) + (1 - \beta)V(C_0^*, C_1^*)] + \alpha, \quad \text{by the concavity of } V.$$

This equals $\beta G(V(C_0, C_1)) + (1 - \beta)G(V(C_0^*, C_1^*))$ by the definition of G. This completes the proof.

[5]All operators like $E_i(\cdot)$ and $\text{var}_i(\cdot)$ are based on $\text{Prob}_i[C_1 \leq z]$.

Example 1   Certainty Equivalent

Let the state space consist of two states, i.e., $\Omega = \{1, 2\}$, and define the asset b_0 as follows:

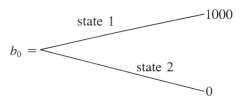

The asset pays off 1000 units of consumption under state 1 and 0 units of consumption under state 2. Let the investor believe the two states are equally likely, i.e., $\text{Prob}_i(\omega = 1) = \text{Prob}_i(\omega = 2) = 1/2$ and let the certainty equivalent y be 300. In this case, y satisfies

$$v(300) = E_i(v(b_0))$$

Suppose the individual owned the asset represented by b_0. If you offered him more than 300 for b_0, he would sell the asset. If you offered him less than 300, he would not sell it. If you offered him 300, he would be indifferent. So 300 is the correct value of the asset to this individual. Although the expected payoff of the asset b_0 is 500, the investor will sell it for as little as 300 units of consumption. This indicates that the investor is "averse" to risk. We will generalize this observation in Sec. 14.3.2.   □

14.3.2. Concavity

Given the concept of a certainty equivalent, we now generalize the above example to define an investor's aversion to risk. Given a risky asset b_0 with $\text{var}_i(b_0) > 0$ and its certainty equivalent y, an investor is said to be

$$\text{risk averse if } \quad y < E_i(b_0)$$
$$\text{risk neutral if } \quad y = E_i(b_0) \qquad (14.7)$$
$$\text{risk loving if } \quad y > E_i(b_0)$$

By the definition, an individual is risk averse if she would sell the risky asset b_0 for less than its expected payoff. The idea is that the investor is willing to give up some of the expected payoff to avoid the risk associated with asset b_0. So she is risk averse. If the individual would sell the asset for no less than its expected payoff, then she is risk neutral. Here she is not willing to give up any expected payoff to shed risk. Finally, an analogous interpretation applies to a risk-loving individual. This interpretation is left to the reader as an exercise.

We can find an equivalent characterization for risk aversion in terms of the utility function v defined in expression (14.5). Using the monotonicity of v, assumption 14.1, an individual is risk averse if and only if

$$v(y) < v(E_i(b_0))$$

By the definition of the certainty equivalent, 14.6, $v(y) = E_i(v(b_0))$, so an individual is risk averse if and only if

$$E_i(v(b_0)) < v(E_i(b_0)) \qquad (14.8)$$

Expression 14.8 says that the investor is risk averse if the utility of a riskless asset paying off $E_i(b_0)$ for sure, the right-hand side, exceeds the utility of the asset b_0, the left-hand side. Restated, receiving the expected value of the asset for certain is more valuable than receiving the asset. Expression (14.8) is related to the concavity of the utility function $v(\cdot)$. This relationship motivates the following assumption.

Assumption 14.4: Concavity of V

$V(C_0, C_1)$ is strictly concave, i.e., $V(\alpha C_0 + (1 - \alpha)C_0^*, (1 - \alpha)C_1 + (1 - \alpha)C_1^*) > \alpha V(C_0, C_1) + (1 - \alpha)V(C_0^*, C_1^*)$ for all $\alpha \in (0, 1)$.

An economic interpretation of assumption 14.4 follows from the previous analysis. First, the concavity of the utility function V implies that the individual is risk averse. To see this, note that for fixed time 0 consumption C_0, by Jensen's inequality (see Mood, Graybill, and Boes [4, p. 72])

$$E_i(V(C_0, C_1)) < V(C_0, E_i(C_1))$$

But this is condition (14.8), which characterizes risk aversion.

Second, the concavity of the utility function V also implies (under assumption 14.3) that

$$\frac{\partial^2 V(C_0, C_1)}{\partial C_0^2} < 0$$

which means there is diminishing marginal utility for time 0 consumption, C_0. That is, as C_0 increases, utility of time 0 consumption increases but at a decreasing rate. The concavity assumption 14.4 is central to the subsequent equilibrium pricing theories.

14.3.3. Measures of Risk Aversion

For interpreting subsequent assumptions required in the equilibrium pricing theories, we briefly pause to discuss measures of an investor's aversion to risk. A global measure of risk aversion is obtained by defining the *risk premium of the asset* b_0, $\theta(b_0)$, to be the difference between the asset's expected payoff and its certainty equivalent y:

$$\theta(b_0) \equiv E_i(b_0) - y \qquad (14.9)$$

This measure $\theta(b_0)$ can be compared across individuals. Consider the example discussed earlier.

Example 2   Risk Premium

Consider the asset b_0 of example 1. The economy has two states $\Omega = \{1, 2\}$ and the asset's payoffs are

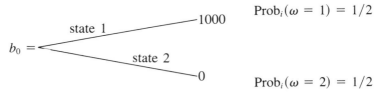

The expected payoff to asset b_0 is $E_i(b_0) = 500$. For person 1, let the certainty equivalent be 300 units of consumption. For person 2, let the certainty equivalent be 400. Person 1's risk premium is then $500 - 300 = 200$ and person 2's risk premium is $500 - 400 = 100$. Person 1 is more risk averse than person 2. He would sell the asset for fewer units of consumption.   □

Local measures of risk aversion are obtained by examining the preference function $V(C_0, C_1)$ for small changes in time 1 consumption across states. For C_0 fixed at c, consider the restricted utility function $V(c, C_1) \equiv v(C_1)$ again. The first local measure of risk aversion considered is given in the following theorem.

Theorem 14.1: Local Risk Aversion Measure

Consider two assets $a:\Omega \to \mathbb{R}$ and $b:\Omega \to \mathbb{R}$ such that a and b are statistically independent with respect to $\text{Prob}_i[\cdot]$. Then

$$\theta(a + b) \approx -\frac{E_i\left(\dfrac{d^2 v(b)}{dC_1^2}\right)}{E_i\left(\dfrac{dv(b)}{dC_1}\right)} \frac{E_i(a^2)}{2} \qquad (14.10)$$

if

$$\text{var}_i(a) \approx 0, \quad \text{var}_i(b) \approx 0, \quad \text{and} \quad \frac{\text{var}_i(b)}{E_i(a^2)} \approx 0$$

where the symbol $\approx$ means approximately.

*Proof

(The proof of this theorem is more complex than the previous material in this chapter.) By a Taylor series approximation around b (Rudin [6, p. 111]), $v(a + b)$ evaluated at a fixed $\omega \epsilon \Omega$ gives

$$v(a + b) = v(b) + \frac{dv(b)}{dC_1} a + \frac{d^2v(b)}{dC_1^2} (a^2/2) + o[a^2] \quad \text{and}$$

$$v(y) = v(b) + \frac{dv(b)}{dC_1} (y - b) + o(y - b)$$

where y is defined to be the certainty equivalent for $a + b$, and $o(x)$ means $\lim_{x \to 0} o(x)/x = 0$. Taking expectations of both sides gives

$$E_i(v(a + b)) = E_i(v(b)) + E_i\left(\frac{dv(b)}{dC_1}\right)E_i(a) + E_i\left(\frac{d^2v(b)}{dC_1^2}\right)\frac{E_i(a^2)}{2} + o[a^2]$$

$$v(y) = E_i(v(b)) + E_i\left(\frac{dv(b)}{dC_1}\right)E_i(y - b) - \text{cov}_i\left(\frac{dv(b)}{dC_1}, b\right) + o(y - b)$$

In the above two expressions we write $E_i(o(a^2))$ and $E_i(o(y - b))$ as $o(a^2)$ and $o(y - b)$, respectively, and we use the fact that

$$E_i\left(\frac{dv(b)}{dC_1} a\right) = E_i\left(\frac{dv(b)}{dC_1}\right)E_i(a)$$

which follows because a and b are statistically independent, and

$$E_i\left(\frac{dv(b)}{dC_1}(y - b)\right) = E\left(\frac{dv(b)}{dC_1}\right)E(y - b) + \text{cov}_i\left(\frac{dv(b)}{dC_1}, y - b\right)$$

$$= E\left(\frac{dv(b)}{dC_1}\right)E(y - b) + \text{cov}_i\left(\frac{dv(b)}{dC_1}, -b\right)$$

since y is a constant. By construction, y is the certainty equivalent of $a + b$, i.e., $v(y) = E_i(v(a + b))$, so equating the above two expressions gives

$$E_i\left(\frac{dv(b)}{dC_1}\right)E_i(a + b - y)$$

$$= -E_i\left(\frac{d^2v(b)}{dC_1^2}\right)\frac{E_i(a^2)}{2} - \text{cov}_i\left(\frac{dv(b)}{dC_1}, b\right) + o(y - b) + o(a^2)$$

By Taylor's theorem again

$$\frac{dv(b)}{dC_1} = \frac{dv(y)}{dC_1} + \frac{d^2v(y)}{dC_1^2}(b - y) + o(b - y)$$

Taking expectations and substituting into the above expression give

$$E_i\left(\frac{dv(b)}{dC_1}\right)E_i(a + b - y)$$

$$= -E_i\left(\frac{d^2v(b)}{dC_1^2}\right)\frac{E_i(a^2)}{2} - \frac{d^2v(y)}{dC_1^2}\,\text{var}_i(b) + o(y - b) + o(a^2)$$

Noting that $E_i(a + b - y) = \theta(a + b)$ and ignoring the $o(\cdot)$ terms give the result. $\square$

This theorem says that

$$-E_i\left(\frac{d^2v(b)}{dC_1^2}\right)/E_i\left(\frac{dv(b)}{dC_1}\right) \approx \theta(a + b)2/E_i(a^2) \tag{14.11}$$

when $\text{var}_i(a) \approx 0$ and $\text{var}_i(b) \approx 0$.

The left side of condition (14.11) is a risk aversion measure. We see that it is proportional to the risk premium. The larger the risk premium $\theta(a + b)$, the more risk averse the individual is and the larger is expression (14.11). Hence (14.11) is a local risk aversion measure. The word "local" is needed because it is valid only when $\text{var}_i(a)$ and $\text{var}_i(b)$ are "small." This theorem will be used in Chap. 18 to motivate a key assumption underlying the equilibrium version of Ross's APT.

A more familiar measure of risk aversion is obtained as a corollary to theorem 14.1:

Corollary: Absolute Risk Aversion Measure

If the asset b is riskless with zero payoff, then

$$\theta(a) \approx -\frac{\dfrac{d^2v(0)}{dC_1^2}}{\dfrac{dv(0)}{dC_1}}\frac{E_i(a^2)}{2}$$

Proof

Immediate from theorem 14.1, since $b = 0$ is not random. $\square$

The measure in this corollary was developed by Pratt [5] and it is the quantity $A_h(0)$ introduced in Sec. 7.3 of Chap. 7. Other risk aversion measures are also available (see Pratt [5]).

14.4. THE OPTIMAL PORTFOLIO DECISION

This section incorporates the previous assumptions to study an investor's optimal portfolio. There are two key results. The first is that the existence of an optimal investment portfolio precludes the existence of arbitrage opportunities (theorem 14.3). The second is that the optimal portfolio is unique if and only if none of the $K + 1$ assets can be constructed from a portfolio of the remaining K (theorem 14.4).

The consumption-saving decision as stated in condition (14.3) is repeated here for convenience: Choose $C_0, N_0, \ldots, N_K$ to maximize $E_i(V(C_0, C_1))$, subject to

$$\overline{C}_0 + \sum_{j=0}^{K} \overline{N}_j p(x_j)/\rho_0 = C_0 + \sum_{j=0}^{K} N_j p(x_j)/\rho_0 \quad \text{and} \quad (14.12)$$

$$\overline{C}_1(\omega) + \sum_{j=0}^{K} N_j x_j(\omega)/\rho_1(\omega) = C_1(\omega) \quad \text{for all } \omega \in \Omega$$

That this form is equivalent to expression (14.2) in terms of the constrained choice set $\tilde{A}$ can be seen by recognizing that $C_0, N_0, \ldots, N_K$ uniquely determines the probability distribution C_0, $\text{Prob}_i[C_1 \le z; C_0, N_0, \ldots, N_K]$, given that the investor's subjective beliefs $\text{Prob}_i[\cdot]$ are fixed.

By the existence of an optimal distribution for consumption assumption 14.2, we know an optimal probability distribution $b^* \in \tilde{A}$ exists, and hence an optimal $(C_0^*, \{N_0^*, \ldots, N_K^*\})$ exists.

Theorem 14.2: Existence of an Optimal Investment Portfolio

There exists an optimal investment portfolio $\{N_0^*, \ldots, N_K^*\}$.

The existence of an optimal investment portfolio is just assumption 14.2 restated. We next show that the existence of this optimal portfolio implies that no arbitrage opportunities exist. In other words, assumption 8.6 is redundant in the above model.

Theorem 14.3: Optimality Implies No Arbitrage Opportunities

In the above model, the preference assumptions 14.1–14.4 and the market assumptions 8.1–8.5 imply the no arbitrage opportunity assumption 8.6; i.e., the existence of an optimal investment portfolio implies that no arbitrage opportunities exist.

Proof

The proof is by contradiction. Let $(N_0^*, \ldots, N_K^*)$ represent the optimal investment portfolio. Suppose there exists an arbitrage opportunity. By condition (8.16), we see that $(N_0^*, \ldots, N_K^*)$ plus the arbitrage opportunity lies in the feasible set and also increases the investor's expected utility. This contradicts $(N_0^*, \ldots, N_K^*)$ being the optimal investment portfolio. $\quad\square$

This theorem gives a sufficient set of conditions on preferences and the economy to guarantee the satisfaction of the no arbitrage opportunity assumption 8.6. The sufficient conditions given in theorem 14.3 will form the nucleus of the subsequent equilibrium pricing models, in particular, the capital asset pricing model and the equilibrium version of Ross's APT. Hence the arbitrage pricing theory of Chap. 8 will be embedded within, and therefore implied by, the equilibrium pricing theories studied.

Let us now consider the optimal investment portfolio in more detail. By construction of the constrained choice set $\bar{A}$, the existence of this optimal portfolio implies that the optimal consumption at time 1 under state ω, $C_1^*(\omega)$, exists. This is due to the time 1 budget constraint. Applying the concavity assumption 14.4, we can also show that $(C_0^*, C_1^*(\omega)$ for all $\omega \in \Omega)$ is *unique*.[6] The next issue we address is the uniqueness of the optimal portfolio.

Theorem 14.4: Uniqueness of the Optimal Portfolio

Let $\{x_0, \ldots, x_n\}$ for $n \le K$ be a maximal set of linearly independent assets in M.

(a) There exists a unique investment portfolio if and only if $n = K$.
(b) There exists an optimal investment portfolio of assets $\{0, \ldots, n\}$.

Proof

Statement (b) proves statement (a). To see this, one must use the fact that if $n < K$, then there is no unique set of n basis assets from among the $K + 1$ assets.

[6]Let $(C_0^*, C_1^*(\omega))$ and $(C_0^\#, C_1^\#(\omega))$ be two distinct optimal consumption pairs. Now consider $(\alpha C_0^* + (1 - \alpha)C_0^\#, \alpha C_1^*(\omega) + (1 - \alpha)C_1^\#(\omega))$ for $\alpha \in (0, 1)$. By definition of strict concavity,

$$V(\alpha C_0^* + (1 - \alpha)C_0^\#, \alpha C_1^*(\omega) + (1 - \alpha)C_1^\#(\omega))$$
$$> \alpha V(C_0^*, C_1^*(\omega)) + (1 - \alpha)V(C_0^\#, C_1^\#(\omega))$$

But $V(C_0^*, C_1^*(\omega)) = V(C_0^\#, C_1^\#(\omega))$. Substitution and taking expectations give

$$E_i(V(\alpha C_0^* + (1 - \alpha)C_0^\#, \alpha(C_1^*(\omega) + (1 - \alpha)C_1^\#(\omega)))) > E_i(V(C_0^*, C_1^*(\omega)))$$

This is a contradiction of the optimality of $(C_0^*, C_1^*(\omega))$. $\quad\square$

To prove (b), let $\{N_0^*, \ldots, N_K^*\}$ be an optimal investment portfolio. It exists by theorem 14.2.

Now, by the definition of linear independence, there exist constants N_i^j for $j = n + 1, \ldots, K$ and $i = 0, \ldots, n$ such that

$$x_{n+1} = \sum_{i=0}^{n} N_i^{n+1} x_i$$

$$\cdot$$
$$\cdot$$
$$\cdot$$

$$x_K = \sum_{i=0}^{n} N_i^K x_i$$

Consider the new portfolio:

$$M_0 = N_0^* + \sum_{j=n+1}^{K} N_0^j N_j^*$$

$$\cdot$$
$$\cdot$$
$$\cdot$$

$$M_n = N_n^* + \sum_{j=n+1}^{K} N_n^j N_j^*$$

We claim this is an optimal portfolio. First

$$\sum_{i=0}^{n} M_i x_i = \sum_{i=0}^{n} N_i^* x_i + \sum_{i=0}^{n} \left(\sum_{j=n+1}^{K} N_i^j N_j^* \right) x_i$$

$$= \sum_{i=0}^{n} N_i^* x_i + \sum_{j=n+1}^{K} N_j^* \left(\sum_{i=0}^{n} N_i^j x_i \right)$$

$$= \sum_{i=0}^{K} N_i^* x_i$$

Hence the portfolio $\{M_0, \ldots, M_n\}$ duplicates $\{N_0^*, \ldots, N_K^*\}$. Second

$$p\left(\sum_{i=0}^{n} M_i x_i \right) = \sum_{i=0}^{n} M_i p(x_i) = p\left(\sum_{i=0}^{K} N_i^* x_i \right) = \sum_{i=0}^{K} N_i^* p(x_i)$$

so the portfolio is feasible. This completes the proof. $\square$

Theorem 14.4 generalizes the corresponding theorem 5.3 of Chap. 5. We see that a basis set of assets, $\{x_0, \ldots, x_n\}$, where $n \leq K$, is sufficient to determine an optimal portfolio. The remaining assets, $\{x_{n+1}, \ldots, x_K\}$ are redundant, in the sense that they can be obtained from portfolios of the other assets, $\{x_1, \ldots, x_n\}$. Given this theorem, we are justified in excluding assets $\{n + 1, \ldots, K\}$ from our economy. We can always price these assets using the GAPT theorem 8.2 given the equilibrium prices of assets $\{x_1, \ldots, x_n\}$. Without loss of generality, we will let $n = K$ in the subsequent model. By theorem 14.4, this will imply that $\{N_0^*, \ldots, N_K^*\}$ is *unique*.

14.5. SUMMARY

This chapter uses the utility theory developed in Chap. 8 to study an investor's optimal consumption and portfolio decision. The asset model of Chap. 8 is embedded into the consumption-saving model. Three additional assumptions on preferences are added in order to characterize the investor's optimal decision. First, assumption 14.2 guarantees the existence of an optimal distribution for consumption. Second, assumption 14.3 guarantees that preferences are regular enough so that standard calculus techniques can be employed. Third, assumption 14.4 asserts that preferences are strictly concave. This guarantees the uniqueness of the optimal decision.

Section 14.3 develops an economic interpretation of the strict concavity assumption 14.4 and relates strict concavity to an investor's risk aversion. Risk aversion is defined by considering a gamble and its "certainty equivalent." An investor is risk averse if he would sell a gamble for less than its expected payoff. The least price he would sell the gamble for is the gamble's certainty equivalent.

The last section of the chapter gives necessary and sufficient conditions for the uniqueness of the optimal portfolio. The optimal portfolio is unique if and only if the $K + 1$ traded assets are linearly independent. This section also provides a theorem that derives the no arbitrage assumption 8.6 from restrictions placed on preferences and the economy.

14.6. REFERENCES

1. Bartle, Robert G., *The Elements of Integration*. New York: John Wiley, 1966.
2. Bertsekas, Dimitri, "Necessary and Sufficient Conditions for Existence of an Optimal Portfolio," *Journal of Economic Theory*, 8 (1974), 235–247.
3. Debreu, G., *Theory of Value*. New York: John Wiley, 1959.
4. Mood, Alexander, Franklin Graybill, and Duane Boes, *Introduction to the Theory of Statistics*, 3rd ed. New York: McGraw-Hill, 1974.
5. Pratt, John W., "Risk Aversion in the Small and in the Large," *Econometrica*, (January–April 1964), 122–136.
6. Rudin, Walter, *Principles of Mathematical Analysis*, 3rd ed. New York: McGraw-Hill, 1976.

15

THE CAPITAL ASSET
PRICING MODEL (CAPM)

This chapter presents the capital asset pricing model (CAPM). The CAPM is an equilibrium pricing model within a pure exchange economy; hence this chapter generalizes the pure exchange economy contained in Chap. 6. The CAPM, originally developed by Lintner [3], Sharpe [6], and Mossin [4], has become a cornerstone of finance theory. Generalizations of this model to a multiperiod economy are presented in Chap. 17.

The central idea utilized in the CAPM to price securities is a competitive equilibrium. In a competitive equilibrium, a set of trades and prices is determined such that aggregate supply equals aggregate demand and such that all investors are at their optimal consumption and portfolio positions. This is a static concept. Nonetheless, if a competitive equilibrium is achieved in an economy, it is a stable situation. All investors are satisfied and there are no forces in the economy for change. The concept of a competitive equilibrium is discussed at length in Chap. 6.

The derivation of the CAPM presented here is new to the extent that it deemphasizes the construction of the mean-variance frontier and emphasizes the equilibrium aspects of the model as well as the consumption beta. This emphasis is consistent with current research trends, and it facilitates the model's generalization to incorporate multiperiods (Chap. 17) and differential beliefs or information (Chap. 19). The more traditional terminology and uses of the CAPM are briefly discussed in Chap. 16.

15.1. PRELIMINARIES

The pure exchange economy studied here is presented in Sec. 14.1 of Chap. 14. For convenience, we summarize the major assumptions of that model. Modifications in the assumptions are noted with a dagger and discussed in greater detail.

The model has two dates, times 0 and 1. At time 1 the uncertainty in the economy is characterized by a state space Ω. An asset x is identified by its dollar cash flows across all states $\omega \in \Omega$ at time 1, $x(\omega)$, where x: $\Omega \to \mathbb{R}$. The set of assets that trade at time 0 is denoted by M. The marketed assets are closed under the construction of portfolios, i.e.

Assumption 15.1: Marketed Assets

If assets x, $y \in M$, then $\alpha x + \beta y \in M$ for all α, $\beta \in \mathbb{R}$.

The marketed assets generate an event set denoted by $\sigma(M)$. This represents those events, subsets of the state space Ω, that can be discerned using knowledge of the assets' time 1 cash flows. The economy is populated by a finite number of investors whose probability beliefs satisfy the following assumption:

Assumption 15.2: Conditional Homogeneous Beliefs

Given an asset $x \in M$, every investor agrees that $x(\omega)$ is the cash flow in dollars to asset x at time 1 given state ω occurs.

Assumption 15.3: Homogeneous Beliefs[†]

Given an event $H \in \sigma(M)$, $\text{Prob}_i(H) = \text{Prob}_j(H)$ for all investors i, j, where $\text{Prob}_i(\cdot)$ represents investor i's subjective probability belief.

This assumption restricts investors' beliefs beyond the earlier unconditional probability beliefs assumption 8.3. Assumption 8.3 only requires investors to agree on zero probability events. In contrast, the homogenous beliefs assumption 15.3 requires investors to agree on the probabilities of all events, zero or nonzero. This implies that investors will agree about an asset's expected cash flows, variance of cash flows, and covariance of cash flows with other assets. It is a very strong assumption.

It can be partially justified by the following argument. Institutional trading is a major factor in the determination of security prices. If professional investment managers have similar beliefs, then assumption 15.3 may hold as a first approximation. Professional managers are likely to have similar beliefs because they have access to similar information sources. This uniformity of information over time would tend to generate similar beliefs. Unfortunately, this assumption is intimately linked with the traditional CAPM, and therefore we will analyze its consequences. The relaxation of this assumption is studied in Chap. 19, on market efficiency.

Given investors' beliefs are identical, for convenience we drop the subscript i on the probability beliefs.

Assumption 15.4: Finite Second Moments

For any traded asset $x \in M$, $E(x^2) < +\infty$.

Assumption 15.4 is a technical assumption, included to ensure that the expected values, variances, and covariances exist of the asset's time 1 cash flows.[1] It does not really limit the applicability of the model.

Markets are assumed to be frictionless and competitive.

Assumption 15.5: Frictionless Markets

The asset market has no transaction costs, no taxes, and no restrictions on short sales, and asset shares are divisible.

Assumption 15.6: Competitive Markets

Every investor acts as a price taker.

A price functional is defined over the traded assets in M, $p : M \to \mathbb{R}$, where $p(x)$ gives the time 0 price in dollars of asset $x \in M$. The price functional satisfies the following assumption:

Assumption 15.7: No Finite Asset Arbitrage Opportunities

The asset market contains no arbitrage opportunities as defined in Chap. 8; i.e., the price functional p satisfies value additivity, and all limited liability assets have strictly positive prices.

This assumption could actually be omitted, since it is a consequence of additional assumptions to be made on preferences (see theorem 14.3). However, for comparison with the arbitrage pricing theories, we include it.

---

[1]See Chap. 9, footnote 1, for a proof of this statement.

Assumption 15.8: Finite Dimensional Economy with a Riskless Asset[†]

The marketed assets M consist of $K + 1$ *limited liability* assets, one of which is the riskless asset, and all their portfolios—i.e., $M = $ span $\{x_0, \ldots, x_K\}$, where $x_j{:}\Omega \rightarrow \mathbb{R}$ for $j = 0, \ldots, K$, x_j—are linearly independent, and $x_0(\omega) = 1$ for all $\omega \in \Omega$.

This additional assumption assumes that the basis set of assets consists of exactly $K + 1$ *limited liability* assets, x_j, for $j = 0, \ldots, K$. The zeroth asset is assumed to be risk free (in dollar payoffs). The basis assets, of course, are linearly independent. This linear independence is without loss of generality due to the optimal portfolio theorem 14.4 of Chap. 14. The linear independence merely removes redundancy from the economy. Any redundancy can be subsequently handled with the arbitrage technology of Chap. 8. Hence the content of assumption 15.8 is that the economy contains at most a finite number of basis assets, one of which is riskless.

The return on any asset $x \in M$ with $p(x) \neq 0$ is defined by $r(x) = [x - p(x)]/p(x)$. This is a random variable. By assumption 15.8, since x_j are of limited liability, the basis asset returns $r(x_j)$ for $j = 0, \ldots, K$ are all well defined.

We now embed this model into the consumption-saving framework. The detailed construction is contained in Sec. 14.1, Chap. 14. Recall that there is a single consumption good available in both dates 0 and 1. The ith consumer enters the economy with an endowment consisting of units of the consumption good in time 0 and time 1, $(\overline{C}_0^i, \overline{C}_1^i(\omega))$ for all $\omega \in \Omega$, where $\overline{C}_0^i > 0$, and an endowed portfolio consisting of the shares $\{\overline{N}_0^i, \ldots, \overline{N}_K^i\}$, where $\overline{N}_j^i$ is the number of shares of asset j held by investor i. We assume that the endowed consumption goods at time 1 are constant, i.e., $\overline{C}_1^i(\omega) = \overline{C}_1^i$ for all $\omega \in \Omega$. This simplification implies later, through theorem 15.8, that aggregate consumption trades. Also, we assume that the aggregate supply of asset j's shares is positive, $\Sigma_i \overline{N}_j^i > 0$ for all $j = 0, \ldots, K$ and that the aggregate supply of consumption goods available at time 1 is positive, $\Sigma_i \overline{C}_1^i > 0$.

To convert dollars into units of the consumption good there is an exogenous price level of $\rho_0 > 0$ at time 0 and $\rho_1(\omega) > 0$ for all $\omega \in \Omega$ at time 1.[2]

Given this structure, under the rationality axioms 7.1–7.8 and as developed in Chap. 14, the ith consumer's decision is to choose

$$\{C_0, N_0, \ldots, N_K\} \quad \text{to maximize } E[V^i(C_0, C_1)] \qquad (15.1a)$$

---

[2]We assume that $\rho_1(\omega)$ is $\sigma(M)$ measurable, or alternatively that investors' beliefs are defined over $\sigma(M, \rho_1)$ and satisfy assumption 15.3 over this new information set $\sigma(M, \rho_1)$.

subject to

$$\overline{C}_0^i + \sum_{j=0}^{K} \overline{N}_j^i p(x_j)/\rho_0 = C_0 + \sum_{j=0}^{K} N_j p(x_j)/\rho_0 \qquad (15.1b)$$

$$\overline{C}_1^i + \sum_{j=0}^{K} N_j x_j(\omega)/\rho_1(\omega) = C_1(\omega) \quad \text{for all } \omega \in \Omega \qquad (15.1c)$$

where $V^i(C_0, C_1)$ is the ith individual's cardinal utility function defined over known consumption at times 0 and 1, and $E(\cdot)$ is the expectation operator based on the homogenous probability beliefs of assumption 15.3. The utility function $V^i(C_0, C_1)$ is assumed to satisfy the following four assumptions:

Assumption 15.9: Monotonicity

Given $\delta > 0$, C_0, and C_1, then $V^i(C_0 + \delta, C_1) > V^i(C_0, C_1)$ and $V^i(C_0, C_1 + \delta) > V^i(C_0, C_1)$. This is true for all investors i.

Assumption 15.10: Existence of an Optimal Distribution over Consumption

For all investors, there exists an optimal solution to the decision problem stated in expression (15.1).

Assumption 15.11: Regularity of $E(V^i(C_0, C_1))$

For all investors

(a) $V^i(C_0, C_1)$ has continuous second-order partial derivatives, and
(b) differentiation (up to the second order) under the expectation operator is a valid operation.

Assumption 15.12: Concavity of V

For all investors, $V^i(C_0, C_1)$ is strictly concave in both C_0 and C_1.

Assumptions 15.9–15.12 combined with theorems 14.2 and 14.4 give the existence of a *unique* solution to the consumer's decision problem 15.1. These assumptions are discussed in detail in Chap. 14. Before characterizing the solution, we add one additional assumption. This crucial assumption gives the CAPM its alternate name, the *mean-variance model*.

Assumption 15.13: Mean-Variance Preference Functions[†]

For all investors, $E(V^i(C_0, C_1)) = v^i(C_o, EC_1, \text{var}(C_1))$, where

$$\frac{\partial v^i(C_0, EC_1, \text{var}(C_1))}{\partial(EC_1)} > 0$$

$$\frac{\partial v^i(C_0, EC_1, \text{var}(C_1))}{\partial(\text{var}(C_1))} < 0$$

This assumption states that the preference function $V^i(C_0, C_1)$ can be written as some other function v of only consumption at time 0, C_0, expected consumption at time 1, EC_1, and the variance of consumption at time 1, $\text{var}(C_1)$. No other parameters of the distribution of time 1 consumption C_1 enter the preference function. In addition, as EC_1 increases utility increases, and as $\text{var}(C_1)$ increases utility declines. That is, the more expected time 1 consumption, the better off the investor is. Conversely, the more variance of the time 1 consumption, the worse off the investor is. This assumption is crucial to the CAPM. For this reason, we need to explore its meaning in greater detail.

Suppose the investor's utility function $V^i(C_0, C_1)$ is an *entire analytic function*; i.e., $V^i(C_0, C_1)$ has a power series expansion over all $C_0 \in \mathbb{R}$ and $C_1 \in \mathbb{R}$. By standard results (see Rudin [5, p. 173]) we can write $V^i(C_0, C_1)$ as

$$V^i(C_0, C_1) = V^i(C_0, EC_1) + \frac{\partial V^i(C_0, EC_1)}{\partial C_1}(C_1 - EC_1)$$

$$+ \frac{\partial^2 V^i(C_0, EC_1)}{\partial C_1^2} \frac{(C_1 - EC_1)^2}{2} + \sum_{j=3}^{\infty} \frac{\partial^j V^i(C_0, EC_1)}{\partial C_1^j} \frac{(C_1 - EC_1)^j}{j!}$$

(15.2)

Taking expectations of both sides of expression (15.2) gives

$$EV^i(C_0, C_1) = V^i(C_0, EC_1) + \frac{\partial^2 V^i(C_0, EC_1)}{\partial C_1^2} \frac{\text{var}(C_1)}{2}$$

$$+ \sum_{j=3}^{\infty} \frac{\partial^j V^i(C_0, EC_1)}{\partial C_1^j} \frac{E[(C_1 - EC_1)^j]}{j!}$$

(15.3)

In general, expression (15.3) shows that the ith investor's objective function $EV^i(C_0, C_1)$, depends on all the central moments of time 1 consumption, i.e., EC_1, $\text{var}(C_1)$, $E(C_1 - EC_1)^3$, . . . , and so on. So the mean-variance assumption 15.13 is a restriction. For the objective function $EV^i(C_0, C_1)$ to depend on only the first two moments, EC_1 and $\text{var}(C_1)$, as in assumption 15.13, one of two things must happen. Either all the terms in expression (15.3) for

$j = 3, \ldots, \infty$ are zero, or all the terms involving the higher order moments, $E[(C_1 - EC_1)^j]$ for $j \geq 3$, must be functions of the first two moments, EC_1 and $\mathrm{var}(C_1)$ alone.

The following theorem gives two different sets of sufficient conditions to obtain the mean-variance assumption 15.13.

Theorem 15.1: Sufficient Conditions for the Mean-Variance Assumption 15.13

If $V^i(C_0, C_1)$ is an entire analytic function, then

(a) Quadratic Utility Functions
For arbitrary beliefs Prob $[\cdot]$, $E(V^i(C_0, C_1)) = v_i(C_0, EC_1, \mathrm{var}(C_1))$ if and only if

$$V^i(C_0, C_1) = f_1(C_0) + f_2(C_0)C_1 + \frac{f_3(C_0)}{2}C_1^2$$

where f_1, f_2, f_3 are arbitrary functions of C_0, independent of C_1.

(b) Normally Distributed Returns
For arbitrary preferences $V^i(C_0, C_1)$, if the distribution over returns

$$\mathrm{Prob}\left[\frac{x_1}{\rho_1} \leq \alpha_1, \ldots, \frac{x_K}{\rho_1} \leq \alpha_K\right] \quad \text{for } \alpha_1, \ldots, \alpha_K \in \mathbb{R}$$

has a multivariate normal distribution, then $E(V^i(C_0, C_1)) = v^i(C_0, EC_1, \mathrm{var}(C_1))$.

Proof of Part (a)

Step 1. Suppose $V^i(C_0, C_1) = f_1(C_0) + f_2(C_0)C_1 + (f_3(C_0)/2)C_1^2$, where f_1, f_2, f_3 are functions satisfying the hypothesis of the theorem. Taking the expectation gives $EV^i(C_0, C_1) = f_1(C_0) + f_2(C_0)EC_1 + (f_3(C_0)/2)[\mathrm{var}(C_1) + (E(C_1))^2]$. This uses the well-known fact that $\mathrm{var}(x) = E(x^2) - (E(x))^2$. Hence $EV^i(C_0, C_1)$ is a function of C_0, $E(C_1)$, and $\mathrm{var}(C_1)$ alone.

Step 2. Suppose $E(V^i(C_0, C_1))$ can be written as some function $v^i(C_0, EC_1, \mathrm{var}(C_1))$. Then, from condition (15.3)

$$\frac{\partial^3 V^i(C_0, EC_1)}{\partial C_1^3} = 0$$

Solving this as a differential equation in C_1 gives the following series of equalities:

$$\frac{\partial^2 V^i(C_0, EC_1)}{\partial C_1^2} = f_3(C_0)$$

$$\frac{\partial V^i(C_0, EC_1)}{\partial C_1} = f_2(C_0) + f_3(C_0)C_1, \quad \text{and}$$

$$V^i(C_0, C_1) = f_1(C_0) + f_2(C_0)C_1 + \frac{f_3(C_0)}{2}C_1^2$$

This completes the proof of part (a).

Proof of Part (b)

If $\text{Prob}\left[\frac{x_1}{\rho_1} \le \alpha_1, \ldots, \frac{x_K}{\rho_1} \le \alpha_K\right]$ has a multivariate normal distribution, then

$$C_1(\omega) = \sum_{j=0}^{k} N_j x_j(\omega)/\rho_1 + \overline{C}_1^i$$

is normally distributed. Hence $E(C_1 - EC_1)^j = 0$ if j is odd and $E(C_1 - EC_1)^j = (j!/(j/2)!)(\text{var}(C_1)^{j/2})/2^{j/2}$ if j is even, and substitution into condition (15.3) gives $EV^i(C_0, C_1)$ equal to some function $v^i(C_0, EC_1, \text{var}(C_1))$. $\square$

This theorem states that there are essentially two justifications for the mean-variance assumption 15.13. Either preferences are quadratic in consumption at time 1, C_1, or asset prices are jointly normally distributed. For a generalization of part (b) of theorem 15.1, see Chamberlain [1]. Chamberlain gives necessary and sufficient conditions for the mean-variance assumption under a slightly different class of preferences.

Both of these sufficient conditions have theoretical problems. If the utility function $V^i(C_0, C_1)$ is quadratic in C_1, then monotonicity implies that $(\partial V^i/\partial C_1)(C_0, C_1) > 0$, but risk aversion implies that $(\partial^2 V^i/\partial C_1^2)(C_0, C_1) < 0$ for all $C_1 \in \mathbb{R}$. However, these are inconsistent.[3] Hence, the monotonicity assumption (15.9), the concavity assumption (15.12), and quadratic preferences cannot all hold.

Next, consider normally distributed returns. If asset cash flows are normally distributed, then the basis asset x_j cannot be of limited liability since $\text{Prob}[x_j < 0] > 0$ for a normal distribution. This violates the finite basis set assumption 15.8.

These inconsistencies can be finessed. This last problem can be sidestepped if we remove the assumption that the basis asset x_j is of limited liability

---

[3]To prove this statement, note $(\partial V^1/\partial C_1)(C_0, C_1) = f_2(C_0) + f_3(C_0)C_1 > 0$, $(\partial^2 V^i/\partial C_1^2)(C_0, C_1) = f_3(C_0) < 0$. So for C_1 large enough $(\partial V^i(C_0, C_1)/\partial C_1) \le 0$ will occur.

Probability density

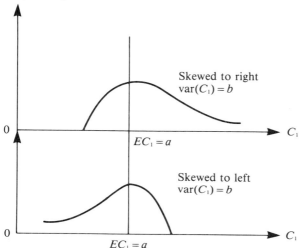

FIGURE 15.1: Two distributions for consumption at time 1 with the same variance and mean.

and impose the alternative condition that $p(x_j) \neq 0$ instead. For quadratic preferences, we could eliminate the inconsistency by restricting the range of values for C_1 such that both the monotonicity assumption 15.9 and the concavity assumption 15.12 hold.

Even with these inconsistencies removed, however, the mean-variance assumption 15.13 is rather restrictive. It says that given two distributions over consumption at time 1, as in Fig. 15.1, with the same variance and mean, all investors will be indifferent between the two distributions. This is true regardless of differences in skewness or higher order moments. A glance at Fig. 15.1 suggests that this need not be the case. Most readers will prefer the distribution skewed to the right, suggesting a limitation of the mean-variance assumption 15.13. This assumption will be relaxed in Chap. 17, on the multiperiod CAPM. For now, however, it is useful to retain this assumption. At the very least, the intuition developed by retaining this assumption will be useful in aiding our understanding of the material contained in the more difficult Chap. 17.

Finally, we add

Assumption 15.14: Certain Inflation

$$\rho_1(\omega) = \rho_1 \quad \text{for all } \omega \in \Omega$$

This assumption is included to simplify the analysis. It could be removed. Without the certain inflation assumption 15.14, the exact same analysis follows. However, the assumptions dealing with the marketed assets, 15.1, 15.2, and

15.8, need to be modified by requiring that each asset x is denominated in units of the *consumption good* and *not* dollars. This is equivalent to setting the price levels $\rho_1(\omega) \equiv 1$ and $\rho_0 \equiv 1$ in the preceding analysis. In this case all the results hold in real return form, and dollars do not enter the analysis.

15.2. CHARACTERIZING THE OPTIMAL CONSUMPTION AND INVESTMENT DEMANDS

This section utilizes Lagrangian multiplier techniques to characterize the optimal consumption and investment demands of an arbitrary investor. Utilizing assumptions 15.1–15.14, consumer i's decision problem is to choose

$$\{C_0, N_0, \ldots, N_K\} \quad \text{to maximize } v^i(C_0, EC_1, \text{var }(C_1)) \quad (15.4a)$$

subject to

$$\overline{C}_0^i + \sum_{j=0}^{K} \overline{N}_j^i p(x_j)/\rho_0 = C_0 + \sum_{j=0}^{K} N_j p(x_j)/\rho_0 \quad (15.4b)$$

$$\overline{C}_1^i + \sum_{j=0}^{K} N_j x_j(\omega)/\rho_1(\omega) = C_1(\omega) \quad \text{for all } \omega \in \Omega \quad (15.4c)$$

Now we rewrite this decision problem to remove the constraint (15.4c). To do this, note that

$$EC_1 = \overline{C}_1^i + \sum_{j=0}^{K} N_j E(x_j/\rho_1) \quad \text{and}$$

$$\text{var}(C_1) = \sum_{j=0}^{K} \sum_{k=0}^{K} N_j N_k \, \text{cov}(x_j/\rho_1, x_k/\rho_1)$$

Substitution of these identities into expression (15.4) yields

$$\text{choose} \quad \{C_0, N_0, \ldots, N_K\} \quad \text{to maximize}$$

$$v^i(C_0, \overline{C}_1^i + \sum_{j=0}^{K} N_j E(x_j/\rho_1), \sum_{j=0}^{K} \sum_{k=0}^{K} N_j N_k \, \text{cov}(x_j/\rho_1, x_k/\rho_1)) \quad (15.5a)$$

subject to

$$\overline{C}_0^i + \sum_{j=0}^{K} \overline{N}_j^i p(x_j)/\rho_0 = C_0 + \sum_{j=0}^{K} N_j p(x_j)/\rho_0 \quad (15.5b)$$

Expression (15.5a) is the condensed objective function. It incorporates the previous constraint (15.4c), leaving only the time 0 budget constraint (15.5b) remaining.

It will be convenient to have the following terminology. Define the *inflation rate* at time 1 for a state $\omega \in \Omega$ by $\Pi(\omega) = [\rho_1(\omega) - \rho_0]/\rho_0$. This is the rate of change in the price level. Next, define the *real return* on an asset $x \in M$ by $R(x) = [1 + r(x)]/[1 + \Pi] - 1$ as long as $r(x)$ is well defined. Note that $R(x)$ is a random variable. Using this notation, the next theorem characterizes the optimal consumption and investment demands of the ith investor.

Theorem 15.2: Optimal Consumption and Investment Demands

Given assumptions 15.1–15.14, $(C_0^i, C_1^i, N_0^i, \ldots, N_K^i)$ are optimal consumption and investment demands if and only if they are the solutions to

$$E(R(x_j)) - R(x_0) + 2 \left[\frac{\dfrac{\partial v^i(C_0^i, EC_1^i, \mathrm{var}(C_1^i))}{\partial \mathrm{var}(C_1)}}{\dfrac{\partial v^i(C_0^i, EC_1^i, \mathrm{var}(C_1^i))}{\partial EC_1}} \right]$$

$$\times \sum_{k=1}^{K} N_k^i(p(x_k)/\rho_0) \, \mathrm{cov}(R(x_k), R(x_j)) = 0 \quad \text{for } j = 1, \ldots, K \qquad (15.6a)$$

$$1 + R(x_0) = \left[\frac{\dfrac{\partial v^i(C_0^i, EC_1^i, \mathrm{var}(C_1^i))}{\partial C_0}}{\dfrac{\partial v^i(C_0^i, EC_1^i, \mathrm{var}(C_1^i))}{\partial EC_1}} \right] \qquad (15.6b)$$

$$\overline{C}_0^i + \sum_{j=0}^{K} \overline{N}_j^i p(x_j)/\rho_0 = C_0^i + \sum_{j=0}^{K} N_j^i p(x_j)/\rho_0 \qquad (15.6c)$$

$$C_1^i(\omega) = \overline{C}_1^i + \sum_{j=0}^{K} N_j^i x_j(\omega)/\rho_1 \quad \text{for all } \omega \in \Omega \qquad (15.6d)$$

Proof

See Sec. 15.7. □

The optimal consumption and investment demands are given as the implicit solutions to a messy system of $K + 3$ equations. Expression (15.6a) is a transformation of a condition that states that for asset x_j, the marginal change in the optimal utility from investing one more dollar in asset j and financing it with one additional dollar of borrowing at the riskless rate, $R(x_0)$, is zero.[4] If the

---

[4]This statement says that

$$\left. \frac{\partial v^i(C_0^i, EC_1^i(\epsilon), \mathrm{var}(C_1^i(\epsilon)))}{\partial \epsilon} \right|_{\epsilon=0} = 0 \qquad \text{where}$$

$$C_1^i(\epsilon) = \sum_{k=0}^{K} N_k^i x_k/\rho_1 + \frac{\epsilon x_j/\rho_1}{p(x_j)/\rho_0} - \frac{\epsilon x_0/\rho_1}{p(x_0)/\rho_0} + \overline{C}_1^i$$

This represents investing $N_0^i - \epsilon\rho_0/p(x_0)$ in asset 0 and $N_j^i + \epsilon\rho_0/p(x_j)$ in asset j at time 0, and N_k^i in asset k for $k \neq 0, j$.

marginal change were positive, utility could be increased by making the revision. If the marginal change were negative, reversing the strategy would create a utility-increasing revision. Either of these possibilities contradicts the optimality of C_0^i, EC_1^i, and var(C_1^i). Condition (15.6a) holds for all risky assets $j = 1, \ldots, K$.

Condition (15.6b) states that at the optimum, the marginal change in utility from increasing consumption at time 0 by one unit versus decreasing consumption at time 1 by borrowing at the riskless asset rate, $R(x_0)$, is zero.[5] If the marginal change were positive, utility could be increased by making the revision. If the marginal change were negative, reversing the strategy would create a utility-increasing revision. Either of these possibilities contradicts the optimality of C_0^i, EC_1^i, and var(C_1^i).

Condition (15.6c) is the time 0 budget constraint, and condition (15.6d) is the time 1 budget constraint. The algebraic manipulation of these conditions yields the standard form of the CAPM as given in theorem 15.5. Before this, however, we need to recall the notion of a competitive equilibrium.

15.3. COMPETITIVE EQUILIBRIUM

This section defines the concept of a competitive equilibrium for the economy of Secs. 15.1 and 15.2. A competitive equilibrium is a static concept. It is a set of prices and demands such that everyone is at his or her optimal utility level subject to budget constraints, taking the prices as given, and aggregate demand equals aggregate supply. This is a stable situation in the economy since there are no forces for change. Everyone is satisfied (at the constrained optimum) and everyone gets what he or she demands (aggregate supply equals aggregate demand). It is a static concept since it does not describe how the economy reaches such a position. The concept only defines what the desired position is. We characterize prices for such a competitive equilibrium in Sec. 15.4.

---

[5] This statement is equivalent to

$$\frac{\partial v^i(C_0^i(\epsilon), E(C_1^i(\epsilon)), \text{var}(C_1^i(\epsilon)))}{\partial \epsilon}\bigg|_{\epsilon=0} = 0$$

where $C_0^i(\epsilon) = C_0 + \epsilon$.

$$C_1^i(\epsilon) = \overline{C}_1^i + \sum_{j=0}^{K} N_j x_j / \rho_1 - \frac{\epsilon x_0 / \rho_1}{p(x_0)/\rho_0}$$

This represents the portfolio of

$$N_k^i(\epsilon) = \begin{cases} N_k^i & \text{for } k = 1, \ldots, K \\ N_0^i - \epsilon \rho_0 / p(x_0) & \text{for } k = 0 \end{cases}$$

Definition: Asset Market Equilibrium

An *asset market equilibrium* is a set of asset demands $\{N_0^i, \ldots, N_K^i\}$ for all investors and a set of prices $\{p(x_0), \ldots, p(x_K)\}$ such that

(i) N_j^i for $j = 0, \ldots, K$ satisfy conditions (15.6a) and (15.6c), and

(ii) $\Sigma_{i \in I} \overline{N}_j^i = \Sigma_{i \in I} N_j^i$ for $j = 0, \ldots, K$

An asset market equilibrium is defined to be a set of optimal asset demands, condition (i), and a set of prices such that the aggregate demand for shares ($\Sigma_{i \in I} N_j^i$) equals the aggregate supply ($\Sigma_{i \in I} \overline{N}_j^i$), condition (ii). The market clearing condition (ii) represents $K + 1$ equations in the $K + 1$ unknown prices $\{p(x_0), \ldots, p(x_K)\}$. The solution of this market clearing condition determines prices.

It is important to point out that if there is an asset market equilibrium, then the consumption good market is also in equilibrium. This is known as the *Walras law* (see Chap. 6). The following theorem generalizes the corresponding theorem 6.3.

Theorem 15.3: Consumption Goods Market Equilibrium

If $\{N_0^i, \ldots, N_K^i\}_{i \in I}$ and $\{p(x_0), \ldots, p(x_K)\}$ is an asset market equilibrium, then

(i) $$\sum_{i \in I} \overline{C}_0^i = \sum_{i \in I} C_0^i \quad \text{and}$$

(ii) $$\sum_{i \in I} \overline{C}_1^i + \sum_{i \in I} \left(\sum_{j=0}^{K} \overline{N}_j^i x_j / \rho_1 \right) = \sum_{i \in I} C_1^i$$

where C_0^i and C_1^i satisfy conditions (15.6b) and (15.6d).

Proof

By the time 0 budget constraint, (15.6c), we have

$$\overline{C}_0^i + \sum_{j=0}^{K} \overline{N}_j^i p(x_j) / \rho_0 = C_0^i + \sum_{j=0}^{K} N_j^i p(x_j) / \rho_0$$

Summing across all investors and rearranging terms gives

$$\sum_{i \in I} \overline{C}_0^i - \sum_{i \in I} C_0^i = \sum_{i \in I} \sum_{j=0}^{K} N_j^i p(x_j) / \rho_0 - \sum_{i \in I} \sum_{j=0}^{K} \overline{N}_j^i p(x_j) / \rho_0$$

$$= \sum_{j=0}^{K} (p(x_j) / \rho_0) \left[\sum_{i \in I} N_j^i - \sum_{i \in I} \overline{N}_j^i \right]$$

By the definition of an asset market equilibrium, the second term is zero and we get condition (i).

Condition (ii) follows in an analogous manner from expression (15.6d). □

Given the concept of an asset market equilibrium, the question of its existence needs to be discussed. Not all economies have asset market equilibriums. Necessary and sufficient conditions on the economy of Secs. 15.1 and 15.2 such that an equilibrium exists can be found in Hart [2]. Rather than imposing additional assumptions on the marketed assets and investors' beliefs, we assume this existence directly.

Assumption 15.15: Existence of an Asset Market Equilibrium†

An asset market equilibrium exists for the previous economy.

Given Hart's [2] results, we are assured that this assumption is not vacuous. A more detailed digression into the subtleties associated with the existence of competitive equilibriums are beyond the scope of this text. This completes our discussion of the meaning of a competitive equilibrium. The next two sections characterize competitive equilibrium prices in the context of the mean-variance model.

15.4. THE MARKET BETA

This section presents a set of theorems that characterize investor demands and asset prices in equilibrium. The goal of this section is to derive the market beta form of the CAPM. First, however, some primary theorems are needed. The first theorem states that, in equilibrium, everyone holds a portfolio containing assets $j = 1, \ldots, K$; i.e., investors hold *diversified* portfolios.

Theorem 15.4: Diversification

Under assumptions 15.1–15.15, given that $\{N_0^i, \ldots, N_K^i\}_{i \in I}$ and $\{p(x_o), \ldots, p(x_K)\}$ is an asset market equilibrium, $N_j^i > 0$ for all risky assets $j = 1, \ldots, K$ and for all investors i.

Proof

See Sec. 15.7. □

This theorem states that in equilibrium, every investor holds every risky asset ($j = 1, \ldots, K$) in a positive amount. It does not yet specify the relative composition of the holdings. Alternatively stated, theorem 15.4 says that no investor only holds the riskless asset. Since every investor holds every risky asset, the investor's portfolio is said to be *diversified*.

This theorem will subsequently be strengthened to generate a *mutual fund* theorem. The mutual fund theorem will state that every investor's optimal portfolio $\{N_0^i, \ldots, N_K^i\}$ can be broken down into two parts. The first part is an investment in the riskless asset of N_0^i shares and the second part is an investment of N^* shares in a fixed traded asset $m \in M$. The investment in the fixed asset $m \in M$ will duplicate the portfolio shares $\{N_1^i, \ldots, N_K^i\}$. The fixed portfolio $m \in M$ is called a *mutual fund*. This mutual fund will subsequently be identified as the *market portfolio*.

The *market portfolio* is defined to be any portfolio such that the percentage of the portfolio's value in risky asset j for $j = 1, \ldots, K$, denoted by mkt_j, satisfies

$$\mathrm{mkt}_j = \frac{[\sum_{i \in I} \overline{N}_j^i] p(x_j)}{\sum_{k=1}^{K} [\sum_{i \in I} \overline{N}_k^i] p(x_k)} \tag{15.7}$$

where

$$\sum_{j=1}^{K} \mathrm{mkt}_j = 1$$

The market portfolio weight mkt_j equals the total market value of asset j's shares to the total market value of all the risky asset shares. This definition depends only on prices and the aggregate supply of risky asset shares outstanding. It, therefore, has meaning independent of the equilibrium model under discussion. For that manner, it has meaning independent of any equilibrium model.

The mutual fund theorem follows easily after the development of one additional theorem. In fact, it will be shown to be a corollary of the next theorem, theorem 15.5. Theorem 15.5 is a revision of the optimal consumption and portfolio characterization theorem 15.3 based on the diversification theorem 15.4.

Theorem 15.5: Risk-Return Tradeoff

Given assumptions 15.1–15.5 and that $\{N_0^i, \ldots, N_K^i\}_{i \in I}$ and $\{p(x_0), \ldots, p(x_K)\}$ is an asset market equilibrium

$$E(R(x_j)) = R(x_0) + \frac{\mathrm{cov}(R(m), R(x_j))}{\mathrm{var}(R(m))} (E(R(m)) - R(x_0))$$

$$\text{for } j = 1, \ldots, K \tag{15.8}$$

where $m = \sum_{j=1}^{K} N_j^i x_j$ is the ith investor's optimal portfolio of risky assets.

Proof

See Sec. 15.7. $\square$

This theorem gives an equilibrium relationship between the expected return on asset x_j, the risk-free rate $R(x_0)$, the excess expected return on the *optimal portfolio of risky assets* $E(R(m)) - R(x_0))$, and the ratio $\operatorname{cov}(R(m), R(x_j))/\operatorname{var}(R(m))$. The remaining limitation of expression (15.8) is that the portfolio m is still investor specific. The next theorem removes this difficulty.

First, we note that the return on the optimal portfolio of risky assets can be written in simplified form:

$$R(m) = \frac{\sum\limits_{j=1}^{K} N_j^i x_j/\rho_1 - \sum\limits_{j=1}^{K} N_j^i p(x_j)/\rho_0}{\sum\limits_{j=1}^{K} N_j^i p(x_j)/\rho_0} = \sum\limits_{j=1}^{K} w_j^i R(x_j)$$

where

$$w_j^i = \frac{N_j^i p(x_j)/\rho_0}{\sum\limits_{j=1}^{K} N_j^i p(x_j)/\rho_0}, \qquad \sum\limits_{j=1}^{K} w_j^i = 1, \quad \text{and } w_j^i$$

represent the ith person's optimal portfolio weight in the jth risky asset. The mutual fund theorem now follows.

Theorem 15.6: Mutual Fund Theorem

Given assumptions 15.1–15.5 and that $\{N_0^i, \ldots, N_K^i\}_{i \in I}$ and $\{p(x_0), \ldots, p(x_K)\}$ is an asset market equilibrium

$$\sum_{j=1}^{K} N_j^i x_j/\rho_1 = \left(\bar{C}_0^i + \sum_{j=0}^{K} \bar{N}_j^i p(x_j)/\rho_0 - C_0^i \right)\left(1 + \sum_{j=1}^{K} \operatorname{mkt}_j R(x_j) \right) \qquad (15.9)$$

Proof

See Sec. 15.7. $\square$

To understand the mutual fund theorem 15.6, let us investigate condition (15.9). The left side of condition (15.9) corresponds to the time 1 cash flow in units of the consumption good to investor i's optimal portfolio of risky assets. The right side is a constant $(\bar{C}_0^i + \sum_{j=0}^{K} \bar{N}_j^i p(x_j)/\rho_0 - C_0^i)$ dependent on investor i multiplied by a unit investment in the market portfolio with a return of $(1 + \sum_{j=1}^{K} \operatorname{mkt}_j R(x_j))$. The constant isolated is the total units of the consumption good investor i must invest in the market portfolio to duplicate his optimal portfolio of risky assets. Hence condition (15.9) says that investor i's optimal portfolio of *risky* assets is equivalent to an investment in the market portfolio.

Next, given the investor invests optimally N_0^i shares in the riskless asset, we get a corollary to the mutual fund theorem. The corollary corresponds to an investor's entire portfolio, not just the risky assets. The corollary is that the investor's optimal portfolio can be obtained by investing N_0^i shares in the riskless asset and $(\bar{C}_0^i + \Sigma_{j=0}^K \bar{N}_j^i p(x_j)/\rho_0 - C_0^i)$ shares in the market portfolio. This is a two-fund theorem in that at most two funds are sufficient to duplicate an investor's entire portfolio, the riskless asset and the market portfolio.

As another corollary to the mutual fund theorem 15.6, we get the *market beta* form of the CAPM.

Corollary 15.7: Market Beta Form of the CAPM

Under the hypotheses of the mutual fund theorem 15.6

$$E(R(x_j)) = R(x_0) + \frac{\text{cov}(R(m^*), R(x_j))}{\text{var}(R(m^*))}(E(R(m^*)) - R(x_0))$$

$$\text{for } j = 1, \ldots, K \qquad (15.10a)$$

where $m^* = \Sigma_{j=1}^K \text{mkt}_j x_j$; i.e., $R(m^*)$ is defined to be the return on the market portfolio.

Proof

This follows from the proof of theorem 15.6 where it is shown that

$$R\left(\sum_{j=1}^K N_j^i x_j\right) = \sum_{j=1}^K w_j^i R(x_j) = \sum_{j=1}^K \text{mkt}_j R(x_j) = R(m^*) \quad \square$$

Expression (15.10a) is the standard form of the CAPM. It is called the market beta form since

$$\beta_j \equiv \text{cov}(R(m^*), R(x_j))/\text{var}(R(m^*))$$

is called the *market beta* of asset j. Using this simplified notation, expression (15.10a) reduces to

$$E(R(x_j)) = R(x_0) + \beta_j[E(R(m^*)) - R(x_0)] \text{ for } j = 1, \ldots, K \qquad (15.10b)$$

The excess expected return on asset j, $(E(R(x_j)) - R(x_0))$, equals the market beta, β_j, times the excess expected return on the market portfolio, $E(R(m^*)) - R(x_0)$. The β_j is a measure of asset j's *portfolio risk*. The higher the portfolio risk, the higher the expected excess return on asset j in equilibrium.

An alternative way of reading expression (15.10b) is that the expected return on asset j can be broken down into two components. The first component is the risk-free return, $R(x_0)$. The second component is an adjustment for the risk of the asset, $\beta_j(E(R(m^*)) - R(x_0))$. The standard of comparison is the market portfolio.

Although expression (15.10a) applies only to assets $j = 1, \ldots, K$ as written, it can be modified to apply to any traded asset $x \in M$. First, note that for the riskless asset x_0, $\text{cov}(R(x_0), R(m^*)) \equiv 0$; hence expression (15.10a) applies to it. Next, given any traded asset $x \in M$, by the finite basis set assumption (15.8)

$$x \equiv \sum_{j=0}^{K} \theta_j x_j \quad \text{for some shares } (\theta_0, \ldots, \theta_K)$$

So the real return on asset x is

$$R(x) = \frac{\sum_{j=0}^{K} \theta_j x_j / \rho_1 - \sum_{j=0}^{K} \theta_j p(x_j) / \rho_0}{\sum_{j=0}^{K} \theta_j p(x_j) / \rho_0} = \sum_{j=0}^{K} \eta_j R(x_j)$$

where $\eta_j = (\theta_j p(x_j) / \rho_0) / (\Sigma_{j=0}^{K} \theta_j p(x_j) / \rho_0)$ is the percentage of the portfolio in asset j for $j = 0, \ldots, K$, and $\Sigma_{j=0}^{K} \eta_j = 1$. So

$$\text{cov}(R(x), R(m^*)) / \text{var}(R(m^*)) = \text{cov}\left(\sum_{j=0}^{K} \eta_j R(x_j), R(m^*) \right) \bigg/ \text{var}(R(m^*))$$

$$= \sum_{j=0}^{K} \eta_j \, \text{cov}(R(x_j), R(m^*)) / \text{var}(R(m^*))$$

$$= \sum_{j=0}^{K} \eta_j \beta_j$$

This string of equalities implies that a portfolio's beta equals a weighted average of the individual component asset betas, where the weights correspond to the initial portfolio weights.

Finally, using this result

$$E(R(x)) = \sum_{j=0}^{K} \eta_j E(R(x_j)) = \sum_{j=0}^{K} \eta_j (R(x_0) + \beta_j (E(R(m^*)) - R(x_0)))$$

$$E(R(x)) = R(x_0) + \left(\sum_{j=0}^{K} \eta_j \beta_j \right) (E(R(m^*)) - R(x_0))$$

$$E(R(x)) = R(x_0) + \beta_x (E(R(m^*)) - R(x_0)) \quad \text{for all } x \in M \qquad (15.10c)$$

where $\beta_x = \text{cov}(R(x), R(m^*)) / \text{var}(R(m^*))$.

Expression (15.10c) is expression (15.10a) extended to all the traded assets. The extension follows directly from the linearity of returns, the covariance operator, and the expectations operator. A typical use of the market beta form of the CAPM, expression (15.10c), is discussed in Sec. 16.2 of the next chapter.

15.5. THE CONSUMPTION BETA

This section gives the consumption beta form of the CAPM. This form of the CAPM has generated considerable interest since, in this form, the single period CAPM generalizes most directly in the multiperiod models of Chap. 17.

Theorem 15.8: Aggregate Consumption and Traded Assets

Given assumptions 15.1–15.14, optimal aggregate consumption trades, i.e.

$$\sum_{i \in I} C_1^i \in M$$

Proof

$$\sum_{i \in I} C_1^i = \left[\sum_{i \in I} \overline{C}_1^i \right] + \sum_{i \in I} \left(\sum_{j=1}^{K} N_j^i x_j / \rho_1 \right)$$

$$= \left[\sum_{i \in I} \overline{C}_1^i \right] x_0 + \sum_{j=1}^{K} \left[\left(\sum_{i \in I} N_j^i \right) \frac{1}{\rho_1} \right] x_j \in M$$

by assumption 15.1. $\square$

This theorem asserts that aggregate consumption is a traded asset. Significant in the proof is the maintained assumption that the time 1 endowed units of consumption are constant, independent of the state of nature. This theorem is important, since if aggregate consumption trades, it has a price. The next theorem guarantees that it has a nonzero (positive) price.

Corollary 15.9: Pricing Aggregate Consumption

Given assumptions 15.1–15.15 and that $\{N_0^i, \ldots, N_K^i\}_{i \in I}$ and $\{p(x_0),$ $\ldots, p(x_K)\}$ is an asset market equilibrium, then

$$p\left(\sum_{i \in I} C^i \right) > 0$$

Proof

By theorem 15.4, $N_j^i > 0$ all i; hence $(\sum_{i \in I} N_j^i) 1/\rho_1 > 0$. Also, we have $(\sum_{i \in I} \overline{C}_1^i) > 0$. Combined, these give $p(\sum_{i \in I} C^i) = (\sum_{i \in I} \overline{C}_1^i) p(x_0) + \sum_{j=1}^{K} ((\sum_{i \in I} N_j^i) 1/\rho_1) p(x_j) > 0$. This last inequality also uses the fact that $p(x_0) > 0, \ldots, p(x_K) > 0$ since they are of limited liability (see theorem 8.1). $\square$

These two theorems in combination guarantee that the return on aggregate consumption, $r(\Sigma_{i \in I} C_1^i) = [\Sigma_{i \in I} C_1^i - p(\Sigma_{i \in I} C_1^i)]/p(\Sigma_{i \in I} C_1^i)$ is well defined. Given this observation, we can now state and prove the main theorem of this section.

Theorem 15.10: Consumption Beta Form of the CAPM

Given assumptions 15.1–15.15 and that $\{N_0^i, \ldots, N_K^i\}_{i \in I}$ and $\{p(x_0), \ldots, p(x_K)\}$ is an asset market equilibrium, then

$$E(R(x_j)) - R(x_0) = \frac{\text{cov}(R(x_j), R(C))}{\text{var}(R(C))}(E(R(C)) - R(x_0))$$

$$\text{for } j = 1, \ldots, K \qquad (15.11a)$$

where $C = \Sigma_{i \in I} C_1^i$ is aggregate consumption demand.

Proof

See Sec. 15.7. □

Theorem 15.10 contains the *consumption beta form* of the CAPM in expression (15.11a). Expression (15.11a) relates the excess expected return on asset j, $[E(R(x_j)) - R(x_0)]$, to the expected excess return on aggregate consumption, $[E(R(C)) - R(x_0)]$. They are proportional, where the proportionality factor is the *consumption beta*

$$\text{cov}(R(x_j), R(C))/\text{var}(R(C))$$

The interpretation of expression (15.11a) is analogous to the interpretation of the market beta. The consumption beta measures an asset's risk. The higher the consumption beta, the more expected return required on the asset in equilibrium to compensate for the increased risk.

The reasons why both the consumption beta and the market beta can simultaneously measure risk are clarified by examining expression (15.9) of the mutual fund theorem. Expression (15.9) combined with the time 1 budget constraint (15.4c) shows that the individual's time 1 consumption is proportional to (perfectly correlated with) the market return, i.e., $C_1^i = \overline{C}_1^i + (\overline{C}_0^i + \Sigma_{j=0}^{K} \overline{N}_j^i p(x_j)/\rho_0 - C_0^i)(1 + R(m^*))$. Hence aggregate consumption is proportional to the market return. The market beta (risk), therefore, will be proportional to the consumption beta.

Using an analogous argument to that in the preceding section, we can also extend expression (15.11a) to apply to all traded assets:

$$E(R(x)) = R(x_0) + \frac{\text{cov}(R(x), R(C))}{\text{var}(R(C))}(E(R(C)) - R(x_0)) \qquad (15.11b)$$

where $x \in M$.

The derivation of (15.11b) is left as an exercise for the reader.

15.6. EQUILIBRIUM PRICING
VERSUS ARBITRAGE PRICING

This section discusses the differences between the equilibrium pricing and arbitrage pricing methodologies. Arbitrage pricing theory requires fewer assumptions than does the equilibrium CAPM. The equilibrium CAPM requires assumptions 15.1–15.15. Arbitrage pricing theory requires only the market structure assumptions 15.1 and 15.2, a much weaker form of the homogeneous beliefs assumption 15.3 and the ideal market assumptions 15.5–15.8. Omitted are the preference-based assumptions 15.9–15.14, the concept of a competitive equilibrium, and the existence of a competitive equilibrium, assumption 15.15. Under these weaker assumptions, by the GAPT theorem 8.2, we have that (in nominal return form)

$$r(x) = r(x_0) + \sum_{j=0}^{K} \lambda_j(x)(r(x_j) - r(x_0)) \quad \text{for all } x \in M \quad (15.12)$$

where $\lambda_j(x)$ are constants dependent on x, with $\sum_{j=0}^{K} \lambda_j(x) = 1$.

To use this expression to price a traded asset x, in arbitrage pricing theory, we need as *exogenously* given the prices of *all* the basis assets $\{x_0, \ldots, x_K\}$. In expected return form, (15.12) becomes

$$E^i(r(x)) = r(x_0) + \sum_{j=0}^{K} \lambda_j(x)\{E^i(r(x_j)) - r(x_0)\} \quad (15.13)$$

where $E^i(\cdot)$ is the expectation operator for the ith investor. The risk interpretation of expression (15.13) is still appropriate. The expected excess return on asset x, $(E^i(r(x)) - r(x_0))$, is related to the expected excess returns on the basis assets, $(E^i(r(x_j)) - r(x_0))$, by a proportionality factor $\lambda_j(x)$ for $j = 0$, $\ldots, K$. Unfortunately, expression (15.13) is not very practical for pricing the traded assets in this economy. Too much information is required, i.e., all the prices of $\{x_0, \ldots, x_K\}$.[6]

In contrast, the CAPM obtains the market beta form of the CAPM, expression (15.10), or the consumption beta form of the CAPM, expression (15.11), which are similar in appearance to the GAPT, expression (15.13). The significant difference is that the CAPM determines the relative prices of the assets $\{x_0, \ldots, x_K\}$ endogenously within the model. They are not a given. Alternatively stated, to price *all* the traded assets in the CAPM, we require less information. We require only the price of the market portfolio or aggregate consumption. Given this price, all other prices are endogenously determined.

Yet the CAPM's result is only in an expectational sense. It does not hold on an ex-post basis, as does the GAPT expression (15.12). Further, the CAPM requires additional assumptions concerning homogeneous beliefs (15.4) and

---

[6]For Ross's APT (Chap. 9), M consists of an infinite number of assets. Recall that the idea in that model is to find K factors, $\{f_1, \ldots, f_K\}$, against which all the other traded assets could be *approximately* priced. Again, the approximate pricing in Chap. 9 is also in an expectational sense, not on an ex-post basis.

preferences (15.9–15.15), plus the concept of a competitive equilibrium. These additional assumptions provide us with a benefit [(15.10) or (15.11) versus (15.13)] but at a cost. The model is more restrictive and perhaps not reasonable as an approximation. The degree to which the CAPM is a reasonable approximation to the actual economy is discussed in Chap. 16.

The two approaches to pricing securities are better viewed as complements and not substitutes. They differ in the assumptions required (inputs) and the results generated (outputs). The choice of the pricing methodology should be dictated by the application at hand.

15.7. PROOFS OF THEOREMS 15.2, 15.4, 15.5, 15.6, AND 15.10

Proof of Theorem 15.2

Set up the Lagrangian

$$
L = v^i \left(C_0, \overline{C}_1 + \sum_{j=0}^{K} N_j E(x_j/\rho_1), \sum_{j=0}^{K} \sum_{k=0}^{K} N_j N_k \, \mathrm{cov}(x_j/\rho_1, x_k/\rho_1) \right)
$$
$$
+ \lambda \left(\overline{C}_0 + \sum_{j=0}^{K} \overline{N}_j p(x_j)/\rho_0 - C_0 - \sum_{j=0}^{K} N_j p(x_j)/\rho_0 \right)
$$

where λ is the Lagrangian multiplier. Necessary and sufficient conditions for the optimum are given by

$$
\frac{\partial L}{\partial C_0} = 0 \tag{15.14a}
$$

$$
\frac{\partial L}{\partial N_j} = 0 \quad \text{for } j = 0, \ldots, K \tag{15.14b}
$$

$$
\frac{\partial L}{\partial \lambda} = 0 \tag{15.14c}
$$

Performing the differentiation gives

$$
\frac{\partial v^i(C_0^i, EC_1^i, \mathrm{var}(C_1^i))}{\partial C_0} - \lambda = 0 \tag{15.15a}
$$

$$
\frac{\partial v^i(C_0^i, EC_1^i, \mathrm{var}(C_1^i))}{\partial EC_1} E(x_j/\rho_1) + \frac{\partial v^i(C_0^i, EC_1^i, \mathrm{var}(C_1^i))}{\partial \mathrm{var}(C_1)} \tag{15.15b}
$$
$$
\times \left[2 \sum_{k=1}^{K} N_k \, \mathrm{cov}(x_j/\rho_1, x_k/\rho_1) \right] - \lambda p(x_j)/\rho_0 = 0 \quad \text{for } j = 0, \ldots, K
$$

$$
\overline{C}_0 + \sum_{j=0}^{K} \overline{N}_j^i p(x_j)/\rho_0 - C_0^i - \sum_{j=0}^{K} N_j^i p(x_j)/\rho_0 = 0 \tag{15.15c}
$$

Condition (15.15b) uses the fact that

$$\frac{\partial}{\partial N_j}\left(\sum_{s=1}^{K}\sum_{k=1}^{K} N_s N_k \operatorname{cov}(x_s/\rho_1, x_k/\rho_1)\right) = 2\sum_{k=1}^{K} N_k \operatorname{cov}(x_j/\rho_1, x_k/\rho_1)$$

In (15.15b) we solve for λ by using the expression for the case $j = 0$. Note that $x_0(\omega) = 1$ for all ω, so $x_0/\rho_1 = 1/\rho_1$ is certain; hence $\operatorname{cov}(x_0/\rho_1, x_j/\rho_1) = 0$ for $j = 0, \ldots, K$. This gives

$$\frac{\partial v^i}{\partial EC_1}(C_0^i, EC_1^i, \operatorname{var} C_1^i)\frac{E(x_0/\rho_1)}{p(x_0)/\rho_0} = \lambda \qquad (15.16)$$

Noting that $(E(x_0/\rho_1)/p(x_0)/\rho_0) = (1 + R(x_0))$, substitution of (15.16) into (15.15a) gives (15.6b). To get (15.6a), substitute (15.16) into (15.15b) and divide by $p(x_j)/\rho_0$ and $\partial v^i(C_0^i, EC_1^i, \operatorname{var}(C_1^i))/\partial EC_1$. Finally, rewrite in terms of returns. This completes the proof. $\square$

Proof of Theorem 15.4

Define $\quad A^i \equiv -2\,\dfrac{\dfrac{\partial v^i(C_0^i, EC_1^i, \operatorname{var}(C_1^i))}{\partial \operatorname{var}(C_1)}}{\dfrac{\partial v^i(C_0^i, EC_1^i, \operatorname{var}(C_1^i))}{\partial EC_1}} > 0 \quad$ by assumption 15.13

From condition (15.6a) we have

$$[E(R(x_j)) - R(x_0)]$$

$$= A^i\sum_{k=1}^{K}[N_k^i p(x_k)/\rho_0]\operatorname{cov}(R(x_k), R(x_j)) \quad \text{for } j = 1, \ldots, K$$

In matrix form this is

$$\begin{bmatrix} E(R(x_1)) - R(x_0)] \\ E(R(x_K)) - R(x_0) \end{bmatrix}$$

$$= \begin{bmatrix} \operatorname{cov}(R(x_1), R(x_1)) & \cdots & \operatorname{cov}(R(x_1), R(x_K)) \\ \operatorname{cov}(R(x_K), R(x_1)) & \cdots & \operatorname{cov}(R(x_K), R(x_K)) \end{bmatrix}\begin{bmatrix} A^i N_1^i p(x_1)/\rho_0 \\ A^i N_K^i p(x_K)/\rho_0 \end{bmatrix}$$

Now by assumption 15.8, $x_1, \ldots, x_K$ are linearly independent. Hence the covariance matrix is nonsingular. To see this, note that the covariance matrix is singular if and only if the columns are linearly dependent; i.e., there exist α_1, $\ldots, \alpha_K$ not all zero such that

$$\sum_{j=1}^{K}\alpha_j\operatorname{cov}(R(x_k), R(x_j)) = 0 \quad \text{for } k = 1, \ldots, K$$

This is true if and only if there exist $\theta_1, \ldots, \theta_K$ not all zero such that

$$\sum_{j=1}^{K}\theta_j\operatorname{cov}(x_k, x_j) = 0 \quad \text{for } k = 1, \ldots, K$$

This implies

$$\text{cov}\left(x_k, \sum_{j=1}^{K} \theta_j x_j\right) = 0 \quad \text{for } k = 1, \ldots, K$$

Multiplying by θ_k and summing gives

$$\sum_{k=1}^{K} \theta_k \text{cov}\left(x_k, \sum_{j=1}^{K} \theta_j x_j\right) = 0 \quad \text{or} \quad \text{cov}\left(\sum_{k=1}^{K} \theta_k x_k, \sum_{k=1}^{K} \theta_k x_k\right) = 0$$

This is true if and only if there exists a constant c such that $\sum_{k=1}^{K} \theta_k x_k = c$ with probability one where not all θ_k equal zero. This contradicts the linear independence of $x_1, \ldots, x_K$ and $x_0 = 1$.

Define ψ_{ij} to be the (i, j)th element of the inverse of the covariance matrix; then

$$\left[\sum_{j=1}^{K} \psi_{kj}(E(R(x_j)) - R(x_0))\right] = N_k^i A^i p(x_k)/\rho_0 \quad \text{for } k = 1, \ldots, K \quad (15.17)$$

The left side of this expression depends only on Prob[ ], which is constant (homogeneous) across i. Hence the sign of $N_k^i A^i p(x_k)/\rho_0$ equals the sign of $N_k^q A^q p(x_k)/\rho_0$ for all i, q. Since A^q, A^i, $p(x_k)$, $\rho_0 > 0$ we have $N_k^i > 0$ if and only if $N_k^q > 0$ for all investors i, q. This is true for all assets $k = 1, \ldots, K$. Hence, *if* some investor holds asset k in positive amounts, then all investors hold it in positive amounts.

But, by the definition of an asset market equilibrium, for asset k, $0 < \sum_{i \in I} \bar{N}_k^i = \sum_{i \in I} N_k^i$. Hence, for some investor i, $N_k^i > 0$. Otherwise, the sum of aggregate demand would not be positive. This completes the proof. $\square$

Proof of Theorem 15.5

By expression (15.6a)

$$E(R(x_j)) - R(x_0) = A^i \sum_{k=1}^{K} (N_k^i p(x_k)/\rho_0) \text{cov}(R(x_k), R(x_j))$$

where

$$A^i \equiv -2 \frac{\dfrac{\partial v^i(C_0^i, EC_1^i, \text{var}(C_1^i))}{\partial \text{var}(C_1)}}{\dfrac{\partial v^i(C_0^i, EC_1^i, \text{var}(C_1^i))}{\partial EC_1}}$$

By theorem 15.4, $\sum_{k=1}^{K} N_k^i p(x_k)/\rho_0 > 0$, so we can rewrite this as

$$E(R(x_j)) - R(x_0) = A^i \left(\sum_{k=1}^{K} N_k^i p(x_k)/\rho_0\right) \sum_{k=1}^{K} w_k^i \text{cov}(R(x_k), R(x_j)) \quad (15.18)$$

where

$$w_k^i \equiv [N_{kp}^i(x_k)/\rho_0] \bigg/ \left[\sum_{k=1}^K N_{kp}^i(x_k)/\rho_0\right] \quad \text{and} \quad \sum_{k=1}^K w_k^i = 1$$

Note that

$$\sum_{k=1}^K w_k^i \, \text{cov}(R(x_k), R(x_j)) = \text{cov}\left(\sum_{k=1}^K w_k^i R(x_k), R(x_j)\right)$$

$$= \text{cov}(R(m), R(x_j)) \quad (15.19)$$

Multiply (15.18) by w_j^i and sum over $j = 1, \ldots, K$ to get (also using (15.19))

$$\sum_{j=1}^K w_j^i E(R(x_j)) - R(x_0)$$

$$= A^i \left(\sum_{k=1}^K N_{kp}^i(x_k)/\rho_0\right) \sum_{j=1}^K w_j^i \, \text{cov}(R(m), R(x_j)) \quad (15.20)$$

But

$$\sum_{j=1}^K w_j^i E(R(x_j)) = E(R(m))$$

and

$$\sum_{j=1}^K w_j^i \, \text{cov}(R(m), R(x_j)) = \text{cov}(R(m), R(m)) = \text{var}(R(m))$$

So expression (15.20) becomes

$$E(R(m)) - R(x_0) = A^i \left(\sum_{k=1}^K N_{kp}^i(x_k)/\rho_0\right) \text{var}(R(m)) \quad \text{i.e.}$$

$$\frac{E(R(m)) - R(x_0)}{\text{var}(R(m))} = A^i \left(\sum_{k=1}^K N_{kp}^i(x_k)/\rho_0\right) \quad (15.21)$$

Substitution of (15.21) into (15.18) yields (using (15.19))

$$E(R(x_j)) - R(x_0) = \frac{E(R(m)) - R(x_0)}{\text{var}(R(m))} \text{cov}(R(m), R(x_j)) \quad \square$$

Proof of Theorem 15.6

Step 1. Show that w_j^i is independent of i. From expression (15.17) we have

$$\sum_{j=1}^K \psi_{kj}(E(R(x_j)) - R(x_0)) = N_k^i A^i p(x_k)/\rho_0$$

From (15.21) we have

$$A^i = ([E(R(m)) - R(x_0)]/\text{var}(R_m)) \sum_{k=1}^K N_{kp}^i(x_k)/\rho_0$$

So

$$\sum_{j=1}^{K} \psi_{kj}(E(R(x_j)) - R(x_0)) = w_k^i[E(R(m)) - R(x_0)]/\text{var}(R_m)$$

$$\text{for } j = 1, \ldots, K \qquad (15.22)$$

where

$$w_k^i = (N_k^i p(x_k)\rho_0) \Big/ \left(\sum_{k=1}^{K} N_k^i p(x_k)/\rho_0 \right)$$

But $R(m) = \sum_{j=1}^{K} w_j^i R(x_j)$. So (15.22) represents K equations in the K unknowns w_k^i. Note that the solution, w_k^i, will be *independent* of i.

Step 2. Show $w_j^i = \text{mkt}_j$. This will be a manipulation of symbols.

$$\text{mkt}_j = \frac{\sum\limits_{i \in I} \overline{N}_j^i p(x_j)}{\sum\limits_{k=1}^{K} \sum\limits_{i \in I} \overline{N}_k^i p(x_k)} = \frac{\sum\limits_{i \in I} \overline{N}_j^i p(x_j)/\rho_0}{\sum\limits_{k=1}^{K} \sum\limits_{i \in I} \overline{N}_k^i p(x_k)/\rho_0}$$

$$= \frac{\sum\limits_{i \in I} N_j^i p(x_j)/\rho_0}{\sum\limits_{k=1}^{K} \sum\limits_{i \in I} N_k^i p(x_k)/\rho_0}$$

By the asset market equilibrium condition (ii)

$$\text{mkt}_j = \frac{\sum\limits_{i \in I} N_j^i p(x_j)/\rho_0}{\sum\limits_{i \in I} \left(\sum\limits_{k=1}^{K} N_k^i p(x_k)/\rho_0 \right)} = \frac{\sum\limits_{i \in I} w_j^i \left[\sum\limits_{j=1}^{K} N_j^i p(x_j)/\rho_0 \right]}{\sum\limits_{i \in I} \left(\sum\limits_{k=1}^{K} N_k^i p(x_k)/\rho_0 \right)}$$

$$= w_j^i \frac{\sum\limits_{i \in I} \sum\limits_{j=1}^{K} N_j^i p(x_j)/\rho_0}{\sum\limits_{i \in I} \sum\limits_{k=1}^{K} N_k^i p(x_k)/\rho_0} = w_j^i$$

The second to last quality is due to the fact that w_j^i is independent of i.

Step 3.

$$1 + \sum_{j=1}^{K} w_j^i R(x_j) = \frac{\sum\limits_{j=1}^{K} N_j x_j/\rho_1}{\sum\limits_{j=1}^{K} N_j p(x_j)/\rho_0}$$

$$= \left[\sum_{j=1}^{K} N_j x_j/\rho_1 \right] \Big/ \left(\overline{C}_0^i + \sum_{j=0}^{K} \overline{N}_j^i p(x_j)/\rho_0 - C_0^i \right)$$

By step 2

$$1 + \sum_{j=1}^{K} w_j^i R(x_j) = 1 + \sum_{j=1}^{K} \text{mkt}_j R(x_j)$$

Combining these two expressions gives the result. □

Proof of Theorem 15.10

From condition (15.6a) we have that

$$E(R(x_j)) - R(x_0) = A^i \sum_{k=1}^{K} N_k^i \, \text{cov}(x_k, R(x_j)) \quad \text{for } j = 1, \ldots, K \quad \text{or}$$

$$\left(\frac{1}{A^i}\right)[E(R(x_j)) - R(x_0)] = \text{cov}\left(\sum_{k=1}^{K} N_k^i x_k, R(x_j)\right) \qquad (15.23)$$

But

$$\text{cov}\left(\sum_{k=1}^{K} N_k^i x_k / \rho_1, R(x_j)\right) = \text{cov}(C_1^i, R(x_j))$$

since

$$C_1^i = \overline{C}_1^i + \sum_{k=1}^{K} N_k^i x_k / \rho_1$$

Substitution into (15.23) yields

$$\left(\frac{1}{A^i}\right)(E(R(x_j)) - R(x_0)) = \text{cov}(C_1^i, R(x_j))$$

Sum over all investors $i \in I$ to get

$$\left(\sum_{i \in I} \frac{1}{A^i}\right)(E(R(x_j)) - R(x_0)) = \text{cov}\left(\sum_{i \in I} C_1^i, R(x_j)\right)$$

So

$$\frac{\left(\sum_{i \in I} \dfrac{1}{A^i}\right)}{\dfrac{p\left(\sum_{i \in I} C_1^i\right)}{(1 + \Pi)}} (E(R(x_j)) - R(x_0)) = \text{cov}\left(\frac{\sum_{i \in I} C_1^i}{\dfrac{p\left(\sum_{i \in I} C_1^i\right)}{(1 + \Pi)}}, R(x_j)\right)$$

But

$$R(C) = \frac{\sum_{i \in I} C_1^i}{\dfrac{p\left(\sum_{i \in I} C_1^i\right)}{(1 + \Pi)}} - 1$$

where $C = \sum_{i \in I} C_1^i$, so we get

$$\frac{\left(\sum_{i \in I} \frac{1}{A^i}\right)(1 + \Pi)}{p\left(\sum_{i \in I} C_1^i\right)}(E(R(x_j)) - R(x_0)) = \text{cov}(R(C), R(x_j)) \qquad (15.24)$$

Using $C \in M$, we have $r(C) = \sum_{j=1}^{K} \psi_j r(x_j)$, where

$$\psi_j = \begin{cases} \sum_{i \in I} \overline{C}_1^i / p\left(\sum_{i \in I} C_1^i\right) & \text{for } j = 0 \\ \left(\sum_{i \in I} N_j^i / \rho_1\right) / p\left(\sum_{i \in I} C_1^i\right) & \text{for } j = 1, \ldots, K \end{cases}$$

and $\displaystyle\sum_{j=1}^{K} \psi_j = 1$

Note

$$1 + R(C) = [1 + r(C)]/[1 + \Pi] = \sum_{j=1}^{K} \psi_j(1 + r(x_j))/(1 + \Pi)$$

$$= \sum_{j=1}^{K} \psi_j(1 + R(x_j)) = 1 + \sum_{j=1}^{K} \psi_j R(x_j)$$

So multiplying (15.24) by ψ_j and summing over all j give

$$\frac{\left(\sum_{i \in I} \frac{1}{A^i}\right)\left(1 + \Pi\right)}{p\left(\sum_{i \in I} C_1^i\right)}(E(R(C)) - R(x_0)) = \text{var}(R(C)) \qquad (15.25)$$

Substituting (15.25) into (15.24) gives the result. $\quad\square$

15.8. SUMMARY

This chapter presents the single period capital asset pricing model. The model is developed as a restricted version of the arbitrage pricing theory of Chap. 8. It is a restricted version since the CAPM starts with the model of Chap. 8 and adds additional assumptions, plus the concept of a competitive equilibrium. In equilibrium, two forms of the CAPM are derived: the traditional market beta form of the CAPM and the newer consumption beta form. After the derivation, both models are contrasted with the arbitrage pricing theory of Chap. 8.

15.9. REFERENCES

1. Chamberlain, Gary, "A Characterization of the Distributions that Imply Mean-Variance Utility Functions," *Journal of Economic Theory*, 29 (1983), 185–201.

2. Hart, Oliver D., "On the Existence of Equilibrium in a Securities Model," *Journal of Economic Theory*, 9 (1974), 293–311.

3. Lintner, John, "The Valuation of Risk Assets and the Selection of Risky Investments in Stock Portfolios and Capital Budgets," *Review of Economics and Statistics*, 47 (1965), 13–37.

4. Mossin, J., "Equilibrium in a Capital Asset Market," *Econometrica*, 34 (1966), 768–783.

5. Rudin, Walter, *Principles of Mathematical Analysis*, 3rd ed. New York: McGraw-Hill, 1976.

6. Sharpe, W., "Capital Asset Price: A Theory of Market Equilibrium Under Conditions of Risk," *Journal of Finance*, 19 (1964), 425–442.

16

THE CAPM
Concluding Remarks

This chapter ties up some loose ends remaining with respect to the CAPM of Chap. 15. Since its origin, the CAPM has been studied in great detail and from numerous perspectives. It is one of the two leading models in financial economics, the other being the APT of Chaps. 9 and 18. This detailed analysis has generated some additional insights into the special structure of the CAPM. One of these is the concept of mean-variance efficiency. For this reason, Secs. 16.1 and 16.2 discuss this alternative approach to the CAPM. Also, one could not leave a discussion of the CAPM without mentioning its application to security analysis. A description and analysis of the standard approach are contained in Sec. 16.3. Finally, Sec. 16.4 gives a brief overview of Roll's critique on the testing of the CAPM.

16.1. EFFICIENT PORTFOLIOS

The CAPM of Chap. 15 is central to financial economics. Its preeminence has led to the development of terminology, specific to the CAPM, that needs to be understood in order to read the literature. We start with a definition. Let $R_m = \Sigma_{j=0}^{K} \text{mkt}_j R(x_j)$ be the return on the market portfolio. This notation will simplify much of the subsequent presentation. The market beta form of the CAPM (from expression (15.8)) is

$$E(R(x)) = R(x_0) + \beta_x[E(R_m) - R(x_0)] \quad \text{for any asset } x \in M \quad (16.1)$$

where $\beta_x = \text{cov}(R(x), R_m)/\text{var}(R_m)$.

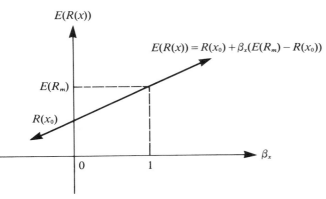

FIGURE 16.1: Graph of the security market line.

The symbol β_x in expression (16.1) is called the market *beta of asset x*. The graph of $(\beta_x, E(R(x)))$ for all assets $x \in M$ is called the *security market line*. The security market line is graphed in Fig. 16.1. The security market line is linear and passes through the market portfolio, which has a beta of 1, and is plotted as the pair $(1, E(R_m))$. The intercept with the vertical axis represents the riskless asset $(0, R(x_0))$. In equilibrium, all traded assets' (expected return, beta) pairs lie along this line.

In equilibrium, by the mutual fund theorem 15.6, we know that all investors hold a portfolio consisting of some percentage of the riskless asset and the remaining percentage in the market portfolio. The class of portfolios with this characteristic is called *efficient* portfolios. The meaning behind the term *efficient* will be clarified in the next section.

Definition: An Efficient Portfolio

An asset $x \in M$ is an *efficient portfolio* if asset x is a portfolio composed of $(1 - \phi)$ percent of the riskless asset and ϕ percent of the market portfolio for some $\phi \in \mathbb{R}$, i.e., $R(x) = (1 - \phi)R(x_0) + \phi R_m$.

The graph of an efficient portfolio in $(E(R(x)), \sqrt{\text{var}(R(x))})$ space is called the *capital market line*.

To get the equation for the capital market line, consider an efficient portfolio $x \in M$ with a positive amount invested in the market portfolio, i.e., $R(x) = (1 - \phi)R(x_0) + \phi R_m$, where $\phi > 0$. The variance of an efficient portfolio's return is

$$\text{var}(R(x)) = \phi^2 \text{var}(R_m)$$

so the standard deviation is

$$\sqrt{\text{var}(R(x))} = \phi \sqrt{\text{var}(R_m)}$$

This implies that ϕ, the percentage of the efficient portfolio invested in the market portfolio, can be identified as the ratio of the standard deviation of the efficient portfolio x to the standard deviation of the market portfolio, i.e.

$$\phi = \sqrt{\text{var}(R(x))}/\sqrt{\text{var}(R(m))}$$

Next, taking the expectation of the efficient portfolio's return gives

$$E(R(x)) = (1 - \phi)R(x_0) + \phi E(R_m)$$
$$= R(x_0) + \phi(E(R_m) - R(x_0))$$

Finally, substituting the expression for ϕ into this relationship generates the capital market line:

$$E(R(x)) = R(x_0) + [\sqrt{\text{var}(R(x))}/\sqrt{\text{var}(R_m)}](E(R_m) - R(x_0)) \qquad (16.2)$$

The capital market line is graphed in Fig. 16.2. The graph is linear, like the security market line; however, the x-axis on both graphs differ. The security market line plots the beta β_x on the x-axis, while the capital market line plots the standard deviation $\sqrt{\text{var}(R(x))}$ on the x-axis. The intercept of the capital market line with the y-axis represents the riskless asset with a standard deviation of 0 and expected return of $R(x_0)$. The market portfolio $(E(R_m), \sqrt{\text{var}(R_m)})$ also plots on this line, as shown.

It is important to recognize that the capital market line relationship, expression (16.2), is just a special case of the CAPM in expression (16.1). To see this, let us calculate an efficient portfolio's beta where the efficient portfolio's return is represented by $R(x) = (1 - \phi)R(x_0) + \phi R_m$. The beta is

$$\beta_x = \text{cov}(R(x), R_m)/\text{var}(R_m)$$
$$= \text{cov}((1 - \phi)R(x_0) + \phi R_m, R_m)/\text{var}(R_m)$$
$$= \phi$$

FIGURE 16.2: Graph of the capital market line.

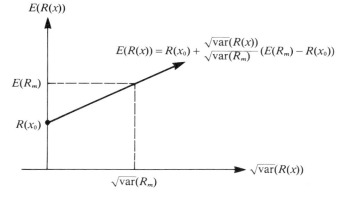

From the derivation of the capital market line, if the percent invested in the market portfolio is positive, $\phi > 0$, recall that

$$[\text{var}(R(x))/\text{var}(R_m)]^{1/2} = \phi = \beta_x \tag{16.3}$$

Substitution of this result into the security market line, expression (16.1), gives the capital market line, expression (16.2).

16.2. MEAN-VARIANCE EFFICIENCY

This section presents an alternate perspective on the CAPM and the capital market line that emphasizes the mean-variance efficiency of the investor's optimal portfolio of risky assets. This alternative derivation is studied because it enhances our understanding of the CAPM. This increased understanding highlights the special structure inherent in the mean-variance assumption 15.13. In addition, it underlies Roll's critique of the empirical testing of the CAPM, discussed in Sec. 16.4.

We start with some definitions. A *portfolio* of the risky assets $(x_1, \ldots, x_K)$ can also be represented as a vector of portfolio weights $(w_1, \ldots, w_K)$ such that the portfolio weights sum to one, i.e., $\Sigma_{j=1}^{K} w_j = 1$.

Given a portfolio $(w_1, \ldots, w_K)$, the portfolio's real return over the time period $(0, 1)$ is

$$\sum_{j=1}^{K} w_j R(x_j)$$

Some standard manipulation of expectation and covariance operators shows that

$$\text{var}\left(\sum_{j=1}^{K} w_j R(x_j) \right) = \sum_{j=1}^{K} \sum_{k=1}^{K} w_j w_k \, \text{cov}(R(x_j), R(x_k)) \quad \text{and}$$

$$E\left(\sum_{j=1}^{K} w_j R(x_j) \right) = \sum_{j=1}^{K} w_j E(R(x_j))$$

Definition: Mean-Variance Efficient Portfolio

A portfolio $(w_1, \ldots, w_K)$ of *risky* assets with an expected return of δ is said to be *mean-variance efficient* if it satisfies

$$\text{var}\left(\sum_{j=1}^{K} w_j R(x_j) \right) \leq \text{var}\left(\sum_{j=1}^{K} \eta_j R(x_j) \right) \tag{16.4}$$

for all portfolios $(\eta_1, \ldots, \eta_K)$ such that

$$\delta = E\left(\sum_{j=1}^{K} w_j R(x_j) \right) = E\left(\sum_{j=1}^{K} \eta_j R(x_j) \right)$$

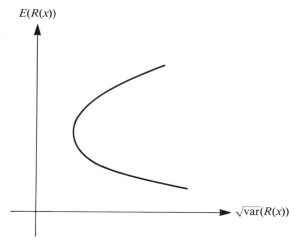

$E(R(x))$

$\sqrt{\text{var}(R(x))}$

FIGURE 16.3: Graph of the risky asset efficient frontier where $R(x)$ is the real return on a traded asset $x \in M$.

That is, for a given expected return of δ, a mean-variance efficient portfolio $(w_1, \ldots, w_K)$ minimizes the variance of the portfolio's return over all portfolios with the same expected return. If we let the expected return δ vary, we get a set of portfolios that are mean-variance efficient, each for a different expected return. Graphing the (expected return, standard deviation of return) pair for these portfolios yields the *efficient frontier of risky assets*, as shown in Fig. 16.3.

Theorem 16.1: Characterization of the Risky Asset Efficient Frontier

The risky asset efficient frontier is the set of coordinates $(\delta, \sqrt{\text{Var}} (\Sigma_{j=1}^{K} w_j(\delta)R(x_j)))$ for $\delta \in \mathbb{R}$ such that for a fixed δ, $(w_1(\delta), \ldots, w_K(\delta), t_0, t_1)$ is the unique solution to the following system of $K + 2$ equations:

$$2 \sum_{k=1}^{K} w_k(\delta) \, \text{cov}(R(x_k), R(x_j)) - t_0 - t_1 E(R(x_j)) = 0$$

$$\text{for } j = 1, \ldots, K \qquad (16.5a)$$

$$1 = \sum_{j=1}^{K} w_j(\delta) \qquad (16.5b)$$

$$\delta = \sum_{j=1}^{K} w_j(\delta)E(R(x_j)) \qquad (16.5c)$$

Proof

For a fixed δ, the mean-variance efficient portfolio $(w_1(\delta), \ldots, w_K(\delta))$ is the solution to: Choose $\{w_1, \ldots, w_K\}$ to

$$\text{Minimize} \quad \sum_{j=1}^{K} \sum_{k=1}^{K} w_j w_k \, \text{cov}(R(x_j), R(x_k))$$

subject to

$$\sum_{j=1}^{K} w_j = 1 \quad \text{and} \quad \sum_{j=1}^{K} w_j E(R(x_j)) = \delta$$

Using the Lagrangian

$$L = \sum_{j=1}^{K} \sum_{k=1}^{K} w_j w_k \, \text{cov}(R(x_j), R(x_k)) + t_0\left(1 - \sum_{j=1}^{K} w_j\right)$$

$$+ t_1\left(\delta - \sum_{j=1}^{K} w_j E(R(x_j))\right)$$

and solving for the first-order conditions yields expressions (16.5a–16.5c). Given the linear independence of assets $x_1, \ldots, x_K$, as in assumption 15.8, it can be shown that these conditions are both necessary and sufficient for a unique minimum. □

This theorem characterizes the risky asset efficient frontier as a set of (expected return, standard deviation of return) pairs such that the underlying portfolios solve a system of equations. Although we will not perform the algebra, a little more effort shows that the set of points characterized in theorem 16.1 is a hyperbola as graphed in Fig. 16.3 (see Merton [4]).

The next theorem relates the CAPM to mean-variance efficiency.

Theorem 16.2: Mean-Variance Efficiency of the Optimal Portfolio of Risky Assets

Given assumptions 15.1–15.15, the optimal portfolio of risky assets $w_j^i = (N_j^i p(x_j)/\rho_0)/(\sum_{j=1}^{K} N_j^i p(x_j)/\rho_0)$ for $j = 1, \ldots, K$ held by an individual is mean-variance efficient for the expected return $\delta = \sum_{j=1}^{K} w_j^i E(R(x_j))$.

Proof

Given the optimal consumption, C_0^i, and the optimal shares in the riskless asset, N_0^i, the first-order conditions (15.6a) uniquely identify the optimal shares held in the risky assets, N_j^i for $j = 1, \ldots, K$.

Define

$$t_0 \equiv R(x_0)\left(\frac{\partial v^i/\partial EC_1}{\partial v^i/\partial \text{var}(C_1)}\right) \bigg/ \left(\overline{C}_0^i + \sum_{j=0}^{K} \overline{N}_j^i p(x_j)/\rho_0 - C_0^i - N_0^i p(x_0)/\rho_0\right)$$

and

$$t_1 \equiv -\left(\frac{\partial v^i/\partial EC_1}{\partial v^i/\partial \text{var}(C_1)}\right) \bigg/ \left(\overline{C}_0^i + \sum_{j=0}^{K} \overline{N}_j^i p(x_j)/\rho_0 - C_0^i - N_0^i p(x_0)/\rho_0\right)$$

With this identification and condition (15.6c), condition (15.6a) rewritten in terms of w_j^i is equivalent to the necessary and sufficient conditions given in theorem 16.1, expression (16.5a). This completes the proof. $\square$

This theorem states that the optimal portfolio of risky assets held by an investor in the CAPM economy is mean-variance efficient, i.e., it lies on the risky asset efficient frontier. This is a direct implication of the mean-variance assumption 15.13. This theorem has an interesting corollary. Since in the equilibrium CAPM (by theorem 15.6) everyone's optimal portfolio of risky assets is equivalent to the market portfolio, theorem 16.2 implies that the *market portfolio is mean-variance efficient*.

One can also examine the mean-variance efficiency of portfolios that include the riskless asset, i.e., portfolios $(w_0, \ldots, w_K)$ such that $\Sigma_{j=0}^{K} w_j = 1$. The analogous definition of mean-variance efficiency to that contained in condition (16.4) applies but with the zeroth asset included. The graph of the (expected return, standard deviation of return) pairs generated by these mean-variance efficient portfolios is called the *efficient frontier*. The next theorem characterizes this set of points.

Theorem 16.3: Characterization of the Efficient Frontier

The efficient frontier is the set of coordinates $(\delta, \sqrt{\text{var}}(\Sigma_{j=0}^{K} w_j(\delta)R(x_j)))$ for $\delta \in \mathbb{R}$ such that for a fixed δ, $(w_0(\delta), \ldots, w_K(\delta), t_1)$ is the unique solution to the following system of $K + 2$ equations.

$$2 \sum_{k=1}^{K} w_k(\delta) \, \text{cov}(R(x_k), R(x_j)) - t_1(E(R(x_j)) - R(x_0)) = 0$$

$$\text{for } j = 1, \ldots, K \qquad (16.6a)$$

$$\sum_{j=0}^{K} w_j(\delta) = 1 \qquad (16.6b)$$

$$\sum_{j=0}^{K} w_j(\delta)E(R(x_j)) = \delta \qquad (16.6c)$$

Proof

For a fixed δ, the mean-variance efficient portfolio $(w_0(\delta), \ldots, w_K(\delta))$ is the solution to: Choose $\{w_0, \ldots, w_K\}$ to

$$\text{Minimize} \quad \sum_{j=0}^{K} \sum_{k=0}^{K} w_j w_k \, \text{cov}(R(x_j), R(x_k))$$

subject to

$$\sum_{j=0}^{K} w_j = 1 \quad \text{and} \quad \sum_{j=0}^{K} w_j E(R(x_j)) = \delta$$

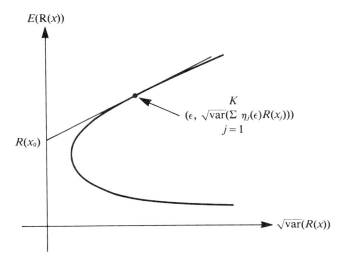

FIGURE 16.4: Graph of the efficient frontier where $(\epsilon, \sqrt{\text{var}}(\Sigma_{j=1}^{K} \eta_j(\epsilon)R(x_j)))$ represents the tangency point.

Setting up the Lagrangian under assumption 15.8

$$L = \sum_{j=0}^{K} \sum_{k=0}^{K} w_j w_k \, \text{cov}(R(x_j), R(x_k)) + t_0\left(1 - \sum_{j=0}^{K} w_j\right)$$
$$+ t_1\left(\delta - \sum_{j=0}^{K} w_j E(R(x_j))\right)$$

gives the following necessary and sufficient conditions for a unique minimum:

$$2\sum_{k=0}^{K} w_k(\delta) \, \text{cov}(R(x_j), R(x_k)) - t_0 - t_1(E(R(x_j)) = 0 \quad \text{for } j = 0, \dots, K$$

$$\sum_{j=0}^{K} w_j(\delta) = 1$$

$$\sum_{j=0}^{K} w_j E(R(x_j)) = \delta$$

Use of the first condition for $j = 0$ yields $t_0 = t_1 E(R(x_0))$. Substitution gives the desired result. □

The graph of the set of points characterized in theorem 16.3 is easily seen to be a straight line, passing through the points $(R(x_0), 0)$ and $(\epsilon, \sqrt{\text{var}}(\Sigma_{j=1}^{K} \eta_j(\epsilon)R(x_j))$ where $(\eta_1(\epsilon), \dots, \eta_K(\epsilon))$ is the mean-variance efficient risky asset portfolio with expected return ϵ, as in Fig. 16.4.[1]

---

[1]To see this, let $w_0(\delta) = (1 - w)$ and $w_i(\delta) = \eta_i(\epsilon)w$ for $i = 1, \dots, K$, where $\Sigma_{j=1}^{K} \eta_j(\epsilon) = 1$ is on the risky asset efficient frontier with expected return ϵ. Then to find the mean-variance efficient portfolio $(w_0(\delta), \dots, w_K(\delta))$ with expected return

A corollary to this theorem is that[2]

$$E(R(x_j)) = R(x_0) + \frac{\mathrm{cov}\left(R(x_j), \sum_{j=0}^{K} w_j(\delta)R(x_j)\right)}{\mathrm{var}\left(\sum_{j=0}^{K} w_j(\delta)R(x_j)\right)}(\delta - R(x_0))$$

$$\text{for } j = 0, \dots, K \qquad (16.7)$$

equal to δ is equivalent to solving

$$\underset{\{w, \epsilon\}}{\text{Minimize}} \quad w\sqrt{\mathrm{var}\left(\sum_{j=1}^{K} \eta_j(\epsilon)R(x_j)\right)}$$

subject to $\qquad\qquad\qquad\qquad\qquad\qquad\qquad\qquad\qquad\qquad$ (*)

$$\delta = (1 - w)R(x_0) + w\epsilon$$

Set up the Lagrangian

$$L = w\sqrt{\mathrm{var}\left(\sum_{j=1}^{K} \eta_j(\epsilon)R(x_j)\right)} - t((1 - w)R(x_0) + w\epsilon)$$

The necessary and sufficient first-order conditions for a minimum are

$$\frac{\partial L}{\partial w} = \sqrt{\mathrm{var}\left(\sum_{j=1}^{K} \eta_j(\epsilon)R(x_j)\right)} + tR(x_0) - t\epsilon = 0$$

$$\frac{\partial L}{\partial \epsilon} = \frac{wd\left(\sqrt{\mathrm{var}\left(\sum_{j=1}^{K} \eta_j(\epsilon)R(x_j)\right)}\right)}{d\epsilon} - tw = 0$$

Solving these simultaneously gives the result

$$1 \bigg/ \left[\frac{d\sqrt{\mathrm{var}\left(\sum_{j=1}^{K} \eta_j(\epsilon)R(x_j)\right)}}{d\epsilon}\right] = \frac{\epsilon - R(x_0)}{\sqrt{\mathrm{var}\left(\sum_{j=1}^{K} \eta_j(\epsilon)R(x_j)\right)}}$$

The left side of this expression is the slope of the risky asset efficient frontier at the portfolio $(\eta_1(\epsilon), \dots, \eta_K(\epsilon))$. The right side is the slope of the efficient frontier. This is the slope of the efficient frontier because the efficient frontier is the solution to (*) obtained by letting δ vary; i.e.

$$\sqrt{\mathrm{var}\left(\sum_{j=0}^{K} w_j(\delta)R(x_j)\right)} = w\sqrt{\mathrm{var}\left(\sum_{j=1}^{K} \eta_j(\epsilon)R(x_j)\right)}$$

where $\delta = (1 - w)R(x_0) + w\epsilon$.

To simplify, solving for w and substituting gives the equation for the efficient frontier:

$$\delta - R(x_0) = \frac{(\epsilon - R(x_0))}{\sqrt{\mathrm{var}\left(\sum_{j=1}^{K} \eta_j(\epsilon)R(x_j)\right)}} \cdot \sqrt{\mathrm{var}\left(\sum_{j=0}^{K} w_j(\delta)R(x_j)\right)}$$

This completes the proof of the statement in the text. $\qquad\square$

[2]To prove this expression, multiply expression (16.6a) by $w_j(\delta)$ and sum across $j = 0, \dots, K$. This gives

where $w_j(\delta)$ is as defined in theorem 16.3. This relationship between "risk" and expected return follows directly from mean-variance efficiency. Hence the form of the relationship between expected excess returns and risk measures derived in the preceding chapter is a property inherited from mean-variance efficiency. The market beta form of the CAPM merely identifies a particular portfolio $\{w_0(\delta), \ldots, w_K(\delta)\}$ on the efficient frontier, i.e., the market portfolio. This follows as a direct implication of the mean-variance assumption 15.13.

Analogous to theorem 16.2 we now have the following:

Theorem 16.4: Mean-Variance Efficiency of the Optimal Portfolio

Given assumptions 15.1–15.15, the optimal portfolio of assets held by an investor in the CAPM, $w_j^i = (N_j^i p(x_j)/\rho_0)/(\Sigma_{j=0}^{K} N_j^i p(x_j)/\rho_0)$ for $j = 0, \ldots, K$ is mean-variance efficient for the expected return $\delta = \Sigma_{j=0}^{K} w_j^i E(R(x_j))$.

Proof

Given the necessary and sufficient conditions of (16.6a)–(16.6c) for mean-variance efficiency, a glance at expression (15.6a) with $t_1 \equiv -((\partial v^i/\partial EC_1)/(\partial v^i/\partial \text{var}(C_1)))/(\Sigma_{j=0}^{K} N_j^i p(x_j)/\rho_0)$ yields the result. □

This theorem states that the optimal portfolio held by an individual in the CAPM lies on the efficient frontier. But, by Sec. 16.1, we know that it also lies on the capital market line. This is possible if and only if the capital market line and the efficient frontier coincide. Hence the tangency point of the efficient frontier with the risky asset efficient frontier in Fig. 16.4 is the market portfolio. This identification of $\delta = \Sigma_{j=1}^{K} \text{mkt}_j ER(x_j)$ in expression (16.7) completes this section.

16.3. SECURITY ANALYSIS

A popular use of the CAPM is for security analysis. The idea is to use the CAPM to identify underpriced securities for purchase and to identify overpriced securities to sell. This technique, modified in various ways, is in current use by professional investment managers today.

The technique employed is based on a quantity called the *alpha* or sometimes Jensen's alpha, named after its originator, Michael Jensen[1]. To use the alpha, the security analyst must obtain an independent estimate of the security's expected return, perhaps using historical price data or information obtained from

---

$$\text{var}\left(\sum_{j=0}^{K} w_j(\delta)R(x_j)\right) = (t_1/2)(\delta - R(x_0))$$

Solving for $t_1/2$ and substituting back into (16.6a) give this result.

traditional financial statements or firm fundamental analysis. Let $\overline{R(x)}$ be the analyst's estimate of the expected return on asset x.

Definition: The Alpha

Given an asset $x \in M$ and the estimated expected return, $\overline{R(x)}$, the *alpha*, α_x, is defined by

$$\alpha_x \equiv \overline{R(x)} - R(x_0) - \beta_x(E(R_m) - R(x_0)) \qquad (16.8)$$

The security evaluation rule is

If the alpha $\alpha_x > 0$, then buy asset x. $\qquad (16.9)$

If the alpha $\alpha_x = 0$, then asset x is priced properly.

If the alpha $\alpha_x < 0$, then sell asset x.

The idea underlying the rule can best be expressed by considering Fig. 16.5. First, plot the pair $(\beta_x, \overline{R(x)})$ on this graph. If when plotting the point $(\beta_x, \overline{R(x)})$ it lies above the security market line, asset x is expected to earn more return than it should (given its risk) in equilibrium. It is a good buy. If it plots on the line, it is priced as required by equilibrium. If it plots below the line, it earns less expected return than it should in equilibrium. In this case, it is a bad buy or a good sell.

Unfortunately, in a formal sense, this technique cannot be justified by the CAPM as developed in Chap. 15. There, the CAPM requires that $\overline{R(x)} =$

FIGURE 16.5: Security analysis using Jensen's alpha.

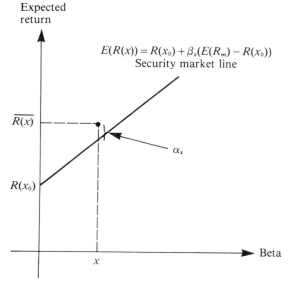

$E(R(x))$ for all investors—the homogeneous beliefs assumption 15.3. Hence the alpha is

$$\alpha_x = E(R(x)) - R(x_0) - \beta_x(E(R_m) - R(x_0))$$

which, in *equilibrium*, is always zero.

To utilize this technique, therefore, the economy must be allowed to experience "temporary" disequilibriums so that a nonzero alpha, $\alpha_x \neq 0$, is possible. The idea (perhaps) is that any disequilibrium situation is short-lived, and α_x will converge to zero fast. Although this is a standard technique for evaluating securities, the reader should be aware that its justification is beyond the CAPM as developed in Chap. 15.

16.4. TESTABILITY

The CAPM as developed in Chap. 15 has been the subject of considerable empirical testing. The accumulated evidence has not been very favorable (see Jensen [2] for a review). Even so, there is a strong argument that asserts that the CAPM is not testable. This criticism is most visibly leveled by Roll [4]. His criticism starts with the fact that the market portfolio's return is *not* observable. This is the case, since not all traded assets have easily accessible or published price data. For example, the price data on corporate bonds or private family housing are not readily available for short observation intervals. Given this fact, to test the model, we need to employ a proxy for the market portfolio. The proxy is often constructed as a large portfolio of common equity, for example, the S&P 500 index.

Along with this proxy, we collect data on individual traded assets' returns and then test the CAPM relationship (16.1). From the mean-variance analysis in Sec. 16.2, particularly theorem 16.3, we know that this is really equivalent to testing whether the market portfolio is mean-variance efficient. Now comes the difficulty. Given that we are using a proxy for the market portfolio and only a subset of the traded assets' returns, we are really testing only for the mean-variance efficiency of the proxy portfolio with respect to the sampled assets, not all traded assets. This testing leads to one of two results. We either accept the mean-variance efficiency of the proxy with respect to the sampled assets or we do not. However, this does not yield any information about the "true" market portfolio and whether it is mean-variance efficient. It is possible to "accept" the theory even if the CAPM is false, or "reject" the theory even if the CAPM is true. In either case, we are not testing the single period CAPM.

Roll's position is one extreme; counterarguments can be found in Mayers and Rice [3] and Shanken [6]. The counterarguments are based on the statistical notion of measurement error. First, they note that measurement error is a fact of life in all of economics (and statistical analysis), not just finance. But there are well-developed econometric techniques to confront this situation, usually involving the idea of instrumental variables. The crucial parameter in these techniques is the correlation of the proxy to the unobserved variable, in this case, the market portfolio. If the correlation is high, reliable asymptotic testing procedures are available. If the correlation is low, the tests are less reliable. Consequently, the counterargument shifts the focus to a discussion of the size of the correlation of the proxy to the true market and related statistical issues. Recent evidence suggests that this correlation coefficient is sufficiently high to provide a valid test (see Shanken [6]).

16.5. SUMMARY

This chapter discusses two topics closely associated with the CAPM: mean-variance efficiency and security analysis. The concept of a mean-variance efficient portfolio is defined and its relationship to the CAPM explored. This analysis leads to insights into the special structure of the mean-variance assumption 15.13. With respect to security evaluation, the alpha is defined and its flaws presented. The chapter ends with a reference to the testability of the CAPM and Roll's critique.

16.6. REFERENCES

1. Jensen, Michael C., "Risk, the Pricing of Capital Assets, and the Evaluation of Investment Portfolios," *Journal of Business* (April 1969), 167–247.
2. ———, "Capital Markets: Theory and Evidence," *Bell Journal of Economics and Management Science*, 2 (1972), 357–398.
3. Mayers, David, and Edward M. Rice, "Measuring Portfolio Performance and the Empirical Content of Asset Pricing Models," *Journal of Financial Economics*, 7 (1979), 3–28.
4. Merton, Robert C., "An Analytic Derivation of the Efficient Portfolio Frontier," *Journal of Financial and Quantitative Analysis* (September 1972), 1851–1872.
5. Roll, Richard, "A Critique of the Asset Pricing Theory's Tests. Part I: On Past and Potential Testability of the Theory," *Journal of Financial Economics*, 4 (1977), 129–176.
6. Shanken, Jay, "Proxies and Asset Pricing Relations: Living with the Roll Critique," unpublished, University of Rochester, 1986.

17

MULTIPERIOD CAPITAL ASSET PRICING MODELS*

Chapters 15 and 16 presented the single period capital asset pricing model. A brief summary of the empirical evidence, as related in Chap. 16, strongly suggests that the CAPM is not a good approximation for estimating security prices. This is especially true when considering corporate bonds or call options on common equity.

A reexamination of the model presented in Chap. 15 (especially assumptions 15.1–15.15) and the related discussion highlight two deficiencies. The first is the single period nature of the model. The second is the mean-variance assumption 15.13. It seems implausible that a model with only a single period can provide a reasonable approximation to the actual economy. If current decisions influence future decisions and planning is fundamentally multiperiod in nature, then the single period model will not suffice. Second, when discussing the mean-variance assumption 15.13, we argued that it is not a very realistic assumption. Sufficient conditions for its existence (normal returns or quadratic preferences) are contrary to alternative assumptions of the underlying model. In addition, the behavioral implication is also counterintuitive.

This chapter presents one approach to removing these deficiencies, the continuous time intertemporal CAPM as developed by Merton [12]. Related papers are by Breeden [1], Cox, Ingersoll, and Ross [3], Grossman and Shiller [5], Jarrow and Rosenfeld [7], and Williams [14]. This is not the only approach. Other discrete time multiperiod models exist (see Kraus and Litzenberger [9] or Long [11]). Furthermore, other deficiencies in the model of Chap. 15 have been highlighted and studied, for example, market frictions (assumption 15.5), the nonexistence of a risk-free rate (assumption 15.14), and the violation of the mean-variance assumption (see Jensen [8] for a review). All of these modifications are more consistent with the evidence. With the exception of the multiperiod generalizations, the modifications to the other assumptions are similar to the material studied in Chap. 15. For this reason, they are easily within the reader's grasp and left to independent reading. The multiperiod models, however, utilize new tools and provide new insights. These are studied here.

This chapter is starred because its material is more sophisticated from a mathematical perspective. The study of continuous time intertemporal CAPMs involves the use of stochastic calculus and stochastic control theory. The reader should have a brief familiarity with these topics prior to reading the chapter. An excellent introduction to this material is in Chow [2].

17.1. PRELIMINARIES

This section presents the notation and assumptions underlying a simplified version of Merton's [12] model. This model and the mathematical analysis employed are more difficult than the material elsewhere in this book. To facilitate the reader's understanding, we delegate technical details to footnotes wherever possible.

The model is a continuous time economy with a continuum of trading dates from time 0 to time T. At time T the uncertainty in the economy is characterized by the state space Ω with an arbitrary state denoted by $\omega \in \Omega$.

An asset is characterized by its *price* in units of the consumption good at each date $t \in [0, T]$ and at each state $\omega \in \Omega$. Hence an asset is a mapping x from $\Omega \times [0, T]$ into $\mathbb{R}$, denoted by $x(\omega, t)$. For much of the analysis, the functional dependence of x on $\omega \in \Omega$ will be ignored, and we will simply identify an asset as $x(t)$, where $x(t)$ is its (random) price in units of the consumption good at date t. We also assume that there are no cash flows from holding an asset over $[0, T)$.

This setup differs slightly from the multiperiod model employed in Chaps. 12 and 13. There, an asset was identified by its cash flows across dates and states, and the price was represented by a function mapping cash flows into dollars. This chapter identifies an asset with its (random) price across dates and states. An asset has no cash flows over $[0, T)$, and the price is denominated in units of the consumption good. These modifications are mainly imposed for notational and analytic convenience.

The set of assets that trade at each time $t \in [0, T]$ is denoted by M_t.

Assumption 17.1: Marketed Assets

If the assets $x(t), y(t) \in M_t$, then $\alpha x(t) + \beta y(t) \in M_t$ for all $\alpha, \beta \in \mathbb{R}$.

The marketed assets at any trading date t are closed under portfolios as indicated by assumption 17.1. The marketed assets generate an information set at each date t, denoted $\sigma(M_t)$. This set represents those events, subsets of Ω, which can be inferred from knowledge of the prices prior to and at date t. By assumption, more information becomes available over time so that the largest information set available is $\sigma(M_T)$ and the smallest information set is $\sigma(M_0)$.

Assumption 17.2: Resolution of Uncertainty

The information sets generated by the marketed assets at each date t are increasing, i.e., $\sigma(M_t) \subseteq \sigma(M_s)$ for $t \leq s$ and right continuous.[1]

The added phrase of right continuous in assumption 17.2 is imposed to make the information flow "smoothly" over time. It is a technical assumption included to facilitate the analysis.

The economy is populated by a finite number of investors whose beliefs satisfy the following assumption:

Assumption 17.3: Conditional Homogenous Beliefs

Given $x(t) \in M_t$, every investor agrees that $x(t, \omega)$ is the price in units of the consumption good to asset x at time t given state ω occurs.

Assumption 17.4: Homogeneous Beliefs

Given $H \in \sigma(M_T)$, $\mathrm{Prob}_i(H) = \mathrm{Prob}_j(H)$ for all investors i, j, where $\mathrm{Prob}_i(\cdot)$ represents investor i's subjective probability belief.

Investors are assumed to have homogeneous beliefs. This same assumption is utilized in the single period CAPM of Chap. 15. Since investor beliefs are identical, we will denote beliefs by $\mathrm{Prob}[\cdot]$ for each i.

Assumption 17.5: Finite Second Moments

For any asset $x(T) \in M_T$, $E[x(T)^2] < +\infty$.

This assumption is technical in nature, requiring a traded asset's price at time T to have a finite mean and variance. As usual, we assume that the markets are frictionless and competitive.

---

[1]A family of σ-fields $(F_t)_{t \in [0,T]}$ is right continuous if $F_t = \cap_{s>t} F_s$ for all $t \in [0, T]$ (see Ikeda and Watanabe [6, p. 20]).

Assumption 17.6: Frictionless Markets

The asset markets at each date have no transaction costs, no taxes, and no restrictions on short sales, and assets are divisible.

Assumption 17.7: Competitive Markets

Every investor acts as a price taker.

Now, since an asset is identified by its price at each date and state, we have implicitly defined a price functional. The price functional is really over the "liquidation" value of the asset at time T. By construction (assumption 17.1), these prices satisfy linearity in the sense of the no arbitrage opportunity assumption 8.6 of Chap. 8. We also require prices to satisfy another minimal condition, the same no arbitrage condition in Chap. 12.

Assumption 17.8: No Buy and Hold Strategy Arbitrage Opportunities

If $x(T) \in M_T$, $\text{Prob}[x(T) \geq 0] = 1$, $\text{Prob}[x(T) > 0] > 0$, then $x(t) > 0$ for all $t \in [0, T)$.

To interpret this assumption one should consider $x(T)$ as the "liquidating cash flow" to the asset at time T. The hypothesis in assumption 17.8 states that asset x is a limited liability asset. Recall that asset x has no cash flows over $[0, T)$. So the conclusion in assumption 17.8 is that any limited liability asset's price at time t is strictly positive.

This assumption is included for comparison with the no arbitrage opportunity assumption 15.7 of the single period CAPM in Chap. 15. It will not explicitly enter the analysis since it is an implication of additional assumptions later imposed upon preferences.

Assumption 17.9: Stochastic Structure of the Economy

The marketed assets M_t for $t \in [0, T)$ consist of the same $K + 1$ *limited liability* assets and all their portfolios, i.e., $M_t = \text{span}\{x_0(t), \ldots, x_K(t)\}$ for all $t \in [0, T]$, where

$$\frac{dx_j}{x_j} = \alpha_j(t, x_K(t)) \, dt + \sum_{i=1}^{K} \eta_{ij}(t, x_K(t)) \, dz_i(t)$$

for $j = 0, \ldots, K$ and $\{z_1(t), \ldots, z_K(t)\}$ is a standard K dimensional Brownian motion. The instantaneous covariance matrix $(dx_j/x_j, dx_k/x_k)$ is assumed to be nonsingular.[2] Furthermore, we set $\eta_{j0} = 0$ for all j so that $dx_0/x_0 = \alpha_0(t, x_K(t))\, dt$ is an instantaneous riskless return.

This assumption has two components. The first is that the same $K + 1$ limited liability assets trade at each date. The second describes the stochastic characteristic of asset returns. There is one "state" variable, $x_K(t)$, and it represents the price of a traded asset. For convenience, we will use the notation $\alpha_j = \alpha_j(t, x_K(t))$ and $\eta_{ij} = \eta_{ij}(t, x_K(t))$.

The stochastic characterization states that the return on the traded asset j, (dx_j/x_j), can be decomposed into a deterministic term, $\alpha_j dt$, plus K stochastic terms $\sum_{j=1}^{K} \eta_{ij}\, dz_i$. "Locally," these stochastic terms behave like the sum of K normal random variables. The implicit restriction in this characterization is the condition that the price process has a continuous sample path. This restriction is a "smoothness" condition that facilitates the use of a simpler analytic methodology. The instantaneous covariance matrix of the asset returns is assumed to be nonsingular, and the zeroth asset is assumed to have an instantaneous riskless return. The phrase a standard Brownian motion implies that $\{z_1(t) - z_1(0), \ldots, z_K(t) - z_K(0)\}$ are statistically independent normally distributed random variables with respect to $\text{Prob}[\cdot]$. Furthermore, the distribution of $(z_i(t) - z_i(0))$ for all i has mean 0 and variance t.

It is convenient to introduce some compact notation:

$$\left(\frac{dx_j}{x_j}\right)^2 = \sum_{i=1}^{K} \eta_{ij}^2\, dt \equiv \sigma_{jj}\, dt \tag{17.1a}$$

$$\left(\frac{dx_j}{x_j}\right)\left(\frac{dx_k}{x_k}\right) = \sum_{i=1}^{K} \eta_{ij}\eta_{ik}\, dt \equiv \sigma_{jk}\, dt \tag{17.1b}$$

Condition (17.1a) is the instantaneous variance of asset x_j and condition (17.1b) is the instantaneous covariance between asset x_j and asset x_k. These conditions define the symbols σ_{jj} and σ_{jk}. To obtain the expression $(dx_j/x_j)(dx_k/x_k)$, as in condition (17.1b), a formal algebraic manipulation of the symbols in assumption 17.9 is completed using the following rules:[3]

$$(dz_i)(dz_j) = \begin{cases} 0 & \text{for } i \neq j \\ dt & \text{for } i = j \end{cases}$$

$$(dz_i)(dt) = 0$$

$$(dt)(dt) = 0$$

---

[2]See Ikeda and Watanabe [6, p. 40] for a technical description of the phrase Brownian motion. This Brownian motion is with respect to $(\Omega, \sigma(M_T), \text{Prob}[\cdot])$, and it is adapted to the relevant information sets, $\sigma(M_t)$, across time. Furthermore, for these processes to be meaningful, the α_j and η_{ij} must satisfy certain regularity conditions (see Fleming and Rishel [4]).

[3]These rules can be rigorously justified (see Ikeda and Watanabe [6, p. 97]). The algebraic manipulation is

We embed this model into a consumption-saving framework similar to that in Chap. 14, on utility theory. There is a single consumption good available at all dates $[0, T]$. The ith consumer enters the economy with an endowment consisting of units of the consumption good at time 0, $\overline{C}_0^i$, and shares of the assets 0 through K, $\{\overline{N}_0^i, \ldots, \overline{N}_K^i\}$, where $\overline{N}_j^i$ is the number of shares of asset j held by individual i.

The consumer's preference structure is assumed to satisfy the following:

Assumption 17.10: Additive and Separable Preferences

The ith consumer's preference function is representable by

$$E\left(\int_0^T V^i(C(s), s) \, ds \right)$$

where $C(s)$ represents units of consumption at time s, $C(s) \in \mathbb{R}$ for all s, and $V^i(C(s), s)$ is a cardinal utility function defined over the certain outcomes $C(s, \omega)$ at time s given state ω occurs.

This assumption implies a special form for preferences. First, preferences are represented as an expectation of the utility function $\int_0^T V^i(C(s), s) \, ds$ defined over certain consumption flows. Second, the utility function $\int_0^T V^i(C(s), s) \, ds$ aggregates the utility of consumption $C(s)$ at any particular date s to obtain a utility function over the entire period $[0, T]$. In this aggregation, consumption at any date s does not directly influence the utility at an alternate date $t \neq s$ (except through the budget constraint). This preference function is therefore called additive and separable.

The ith consumer's consumption plan over time is constrained by his initial endowment of consumption goods and his initial endowment of portfolio shares. His time 0 constraints are

$$C(0) + \sum_{j=0}^K N_j(0)x_j(0) = \overline{C}^i + \sum_{j=0}^K \overline{N}_j^i x_j(0) \tag{17.2a}$$

$$(dx_j/x_j)(dx_k/x_k) = \left(\alpha_j \, dt + \sum_{i=1}^K \eta_{ij} \, dz_i \right)\left(\alpha_k \, dt + \sum_{i=1}^K \eta_{ik} \, dz_i \right)$$

$$= \alpha_j \alpha_k \, dtdt + \sum_{i=1}^K \eta_{ij}\alpha_k \, dz_i dt + \sum_{i=1}^K \alpha_j \eta_{ik} \, dtdz_i + \sum_{i=1}^K \sum_{\ell=1}^K \eta_{ij}\eta_{\ell k} \, dz_i dz_\ell$$

$$= \sum_{i=1}^K \eta_{ij}\eta_{ik} \, dt$$

The last step uses the rules provided in the text.

and at time t such that $T \geq t > 0$

$$\sum_{j=0}^{K} N_j(t)x_j(t) = \sum_{j=0}^{K} N_j(0)x_j(0) - \int_0^t C(s)\,ds + \int_0^t \sum_{j=0}^{K} N_j(s)\,dx_j(s) \qquad (17.2b)$$

Expression (17.2a) states that value of the time 0 consumption and the portfolio shares acquired, the left side, is equal to the value of the endowed time 0 consumption and endowed portfolio shares, the right side. This condition initializes the consumer's investment portfolio for future dates. After time 0, all consumption is financed internally by liquidating portfolio proceeds. This is implicit in expression (17.2b). Expression (17.2b) says that the value of the portfolio at time t, $\Sigma_{j=0}^{K} N_j(t)x_j(t)$, equals the value of the portfolio at time 0, $\Sigma_{j=0}^{K} N_j(0)x_j(0)$, minus the units consumed over $(0, t)$, $\int_0^t C(s)\,ds$, plus the capital gains on the portfolio received over $(0, t)$, $\int_0^t (\Sigma_{j=0}^{K} N_j(s)\,dx_j(s))$. The statement of condition (17.2b) makes explicit the assumption of continuous trading embedded in assumption 17.9.[4]

The consumer's decision problem is to choose a consumption $C(s)$ and portfolio shares $N_j(s)$ for $j = 0, \ldots, K$ and all times $s \in [0, T]$ to maximize

$$E\left(\int_0^T V^i(C(s), s)\,ds \right) \qquad (17.3a)$$

subject to

$$C(0) + \sum_{j=0}^{K} N_j(0)x_j(0) = \overline{C}^i + \sum_{j=0}^{K} \overline{N}_j^i x_j(0) \qquad (17.3b)$$

and

$$\sum_{j=0}^{K} N_j(t)x_j(t) = \sum_{j=0}^{K} N_j(0)x_j(0) - \int_0^t C(s)\,ds + \int_0^t \sum_{j=0}^{K} N_j(s)\,dx_j(s)$$

$$\text{for all } t \in (0, T] \qquad (17.3c)$$

This is a continuous time stochastic control problem. We assume

Assumption 17.11: Existence of Optimal Controls

For all investors, there exist optimal solutions to decision problem (17.3).[5] These solutions are such that

$$\sum_{j=0}^{K} N_j(t)x_j(t) > 0 \quad \text{for all } t \in [0, T)$$

[4]This expression assumes $C(s)$ is sufficiently regular such that $\int_0^t C(s)\,ds$ is well defined. Furthermore, the symbol $\int_0^t N_j(s)\,dx_j(s)$ is a stochastic integral (see Ikeda and Watanabe [6, p. 45]).

[5]These solutions are restricted to be from the class of admissible feedback controls (see Fleming and Rishel [4, p. 156]).

By hypothesis, we assume that optimal solutions exist to the stochastic control problem and that the investor never optimally goes bankrupt prior to time T. In addition, we impose the familiar assumptions of monotonicity, regularity, and concavity:

Assumption 17.12: Montonicity

Given $\delta > 0$, $C(s)$, $V^i(C(s) + \delta, s) > V^i(C(s), s)$ for all $s \in [0, T]$.

Assumption 17.13: Regularity of $E(\int_{\cdot}^{\cdot} V^i(C(s), s) \, ds)$

The function $V^i(C(s), s)$ and the beliefs Prob$[\cdot]$ are such that

(a) V^i has continuous second-order partial derivations of all orders, and
(b) differentiation up to the second order under the expectation operator is a valid operation.

Assumption 17.14: Concavity of V^i

For all investors, $V^i(C(s), s)$ is strictly concave in $C(s)$.

This completes the model's preliminary assumptions.

17.2. CHARACTERIZING THE OPTIMAL CONSUMPTION AND INVESTMENT DECISION

This section characterizes the optimal consumption and investment demands of an arbitrary investor. For convenience, we introduce notation for the investor's wealth at time t. Define

$$W(t) = \sum_{j=0}^{K} N_j(t)x_j(t) \tag{17.4}$$

and

$$w_j(t) = N_j(t)x_j(t)/W(t) \quad \text{for } j = 0, \ldots, K$$

The term $W(t)$ is the investor's portfolio wealth at time t, while $w_j(t)$ is the percentage of the investor's time t portfolio wealth in asset j. Note that the portfolio weights sum to one, i.e., $\Sigma_{j=0}^{K} w_j(t) = 1$. Expression (17.3) can now be rewritten using (17.4): Choose $C(s)$, $w_j(s)$ for $j = 0, \ldots, K$ to maximize

$$E\left(\int_0^T V^i(C(s), s) \, ds\right) \tag{17.5a}$$

subject to

$$C(0) + \sum_{j=0}^{K} N_j(0)x_j(0) = \overline{C}^i + \sum_{j=0}^{K} \overline{N}_j^i x_j(0) \qquad (17.5b)$$

$$dW(t) = \sum_{j=0}^{K} w_j(t)W(t)\, dx_j(t)/x_j(t) - C(t)\, dt \qquad (17.5c)$$

and

$$\sum_{j=0}^{K} w_j(s) = 1 \qquad (17.5d)$$

Condition (17.5c) is the stochastic differential equation form of condition (17.3c). Combining expressions (17.5c) and (17.5d) and assumption 17.9 yields another simplification:

$$dW(t) = \sum_{j=1}^{K} w_j(t)W(t)(\alpha_j(t, x_K(t)) - \alpha_0(t, x_K(t)))\, dt + W(t)\alpha_0(t, x_K(t))\, dt$$

$$+ \sum_{j=1}^{K} w_j(t)W(t)\left(\sum_{i=1}^{K} \eta_{ij}(t, x_K(t))\, dz_i(t)\right) - C(t)\, dt$$

Using this reduction of the system of constraints (17.5c) and (17.5d) gives the control problem in its final form: Choose $C(s)$, $w_j(s)$ for $j = 1, \ldots, K$ to maximize

$$E\left(\int_0^T V^i(C(s), s)\, ds\right) \qquad (17.6a)$$

subject to

$$C(0) + \sum_{j=0}^{K} N_j(0)x_j(0) = \overline{C}^i + \sum_{j=0}^{K} \overline{N}_j^i x_j(0) \qquad (17.6b)$$

$$dW(t) = \left[\sum_{j=1}^{K} w_j W(\alpha_j - \alpha_0) + W\alpha_0\right] dt + \sum_{j=1}^{K} w_j W\left(\sum_{i=1}^{K} \eta_{ij}\, dz_i\right) - C(t)\, dt$$

$$(17.6c)$$

Expression (17.6c) omits the functional dependence of the parameters α_j, η_{ij}, w_j, and W on time and the state variable $x_K(t)$.

To solve this problem, we set up the *Bellman* or *value function*

$$J(W(t), x_K(t), t) = \underset{\{C(s),\, w_j(s)\}}{\text{maximum}} \left\{E_t\left(\int_t^T V^i(C(s), s)\, ds\right)\right.$$

$$\text{subject to } (17.6c)\} \qquad (17.7)$$

for $t \in [0, T]$ where $E_t(\cdot)$ is the expectation operator conditional on the information set $\sigma(M_t)$.

To characterize the optimal solution, we need to assume that certain regularity conditions are satisfied by the value function.

Assumption 17.15: Existence of a Regular Value Function

$J(W(t), x(t), t)$ exists and has continuous second-order partial derivatives.[6]

Given this assumption, we can now prove the major theorem of this section.

Theorem 17.1: Optimal Consumption and Investment Demands

Under assumptions 17.1–17.15, the optimal consumption and investment demands of the ith investor $C^i(s)$, $w_j^i(s)$ for $j = 0, \ldots, K$ satisfy

$$\frac{\partial V^i(C^i(s), s)}{\partial C(s)} - \frac{\partial J(W^i(t), x_K(t), t)}{\partial W(t)} = 0 \qquad (17.8a)$$

$$\frac{\partial J(W^i(t), x_K(t), t)}{\partial W(t)} (\alpha_j(t, x_K(t)) - \alpha_0(t, x_K(t)))W(t) \qquad (17.8b)$$

$$+ \frac{\partial^2 J(W^i(t), x_K(t), t)}{\partial W(t)^2} \sum_{k=1}^{K} w_k^i(t)W^i(t)^2\sigma_{kj} + \frac{\partial^2 J(W^i(t), x_K(t), t)}{\partial W(t)\partial x_K(t)} W(t)\sigma_{Kj}x_K = 0$$

$$\text{for } j = 1, \ldots, K \quad \text{for all } t \in [0, T]$$

$$\sum_{j=0}^{K} w_j^i = 1 \qquad (17.8c)$$

$$C(0) + \sum_{j=0}^{K} N_j^i(0)x_j(0) = \overline{C}^i + \sum_{j=0}^{K} \overline{N}_j^i x_j(0) \qquad (17.8d)$$

where $N_j^i(t) = W^i(t)w_j^i(t)/x_j(t)$ and $W^i(t) = \Sigma_{j=0}^{K} N_j^i(t)x_j(t)$.

Proof

See Sec. 17.7. □

These conditions are analogous to those in theorem 15.2. Condition (17.8a) implicitly determines the optimal consumption decision at time s, while condition (17.8b) implicitly determines the optimal portfolio position at time s. This characterization involves the value function J and its first and second partial derivatives. Finally, conditions (17.8c) and (17.8d) reproduce the time 0 budget constraints.

---

[6]Additional technical conditions are needed to ensure the operations used in the proof of theorem 17.1 are valid. See Fleming and Rishel [4, p. 156] or Kushner [10, p. 326].

Corollary 17.2: Theorem 17.1

Under the hypotheses of theorem 17.1

$$w_j^i(t)W^i(t) = \left(-\frac{\partial J(W^i(t), x_K(t), t)/\partial W(t)}{\partial^2 J(W^i(t), x_K(t), t)/\partial W(t)^2} \right) \sum_{k=1}^{K} v_{jk}(\alpha_k(t, x_K(t)))$$

$$- \alpha_0(t, x_K(t))) \quad \text{for } j = 1, \ldots, K-1 \quad (17.9a)$$

$$w_K^i(t)W^i(t) = \left(-\frac{\partial J(W^i(t), x_K(t), t)/\partial W(t)}{\partial^2 J(W^i(t), x_K(t), t)/\partial W(t)^2} \right) \sum_{j=1}^{K} v_{Kj}(\alpha_j(t, x_K(t)))$$

$$- \alpha_0(t, x_K(t))) + \left(-\frac{\partial^2 J(W^i(t), x_K(t), t)/\partial W(t)\partial x_K(t)}{\partial^2 J(W^i(t), x_K(t), t)/\partial W(t)^2} \right) x_K \quad (17.9b)$$

where v_{kj} is the (k, j)th element of the inverse of the matrix $[\sigma_{ij}]_{i=1}^{K} {}_{j=1}^{K}$.

Proof

See Sec. 17.7. $\square$

This corollary gives the optimal investments in the risky assets $j = 1, \ldots, K$. This optimal investment in the zeroth asset follows from condition (17.8c).

17.3. COMPETITIVE EQUILIBRIUM

This section introduces the concept of a temporary asset market equilibrium. This is the analogue of the asset market equilibrium of Chap. 15 but in a multiperiod economy.

Definition: Temporary Asset Market Equilibrium

A *temporary asset market equilibrium* is a set of time 0 asset demands $\{N_0^i(0), \ldots, N_K^i(0)\}$ for all investors i and a set of time 0 prices $\{x_0(0), \ldots, x_K(0)\}$ such that

(i) $N_j^i(0)$ for $j = 0, \ldots, K$ satisfy conditions (17.8b), (17.8c), (17.8d), and

(ii) $\Sigma_{i \in I} \overline{N}_j^i = \Sigma_{i \in I} N_j^i(0)$ for $j = 0, \ldots, K$

A temporary asset market equilibrium is a set of optimal asset demands, condition (i), such that aggregate supply equals aggregate demand, condition (ii). The phrase temporary comes from the fact that the investors do not require the time t price of asset j, $x_j(t)$, to be an *equilibrium* price for times $t > 0$.

Investors are only concerned with the current or temporary prices, $x_j(0)$ (see Radner [13]).

As in Chap. 15, a temporary asset market equilibrium implies that the consumption goods market is also in equilibrium.

Theorem 17.2: Consumption Goods Market Equilibrium

If $\{N_0^i(0), \ldots, N_K^i(0)\}$ for all investors i and $\{x_0(0), \ldots, x_K(0)\}$ is a temporary asset market equilibrium, then

$$\sum_{i \in I} \overline{C}^i = \sum_{i \in I} C^i(0)$$

where the $C^i(0)$ satisfy condition (17.8a).

Proof

By condition (17.8d)

$$C^i(0) + \sum_{j=0}^{K} N_j^i(0)x_j(0) = \overline{C}^i + \sum_{j=0}^{K} \overline{N}_j^i x_j(0)$$

Summing across all investors and rearranging terms give

$$\sum_{i \in I} \overline{C}^i - \sum_{i \in I} C^i(0) = \sum_{i \in I} \sum_{j=0}^{K} N_j^i(0)x_j(0) - \sum_{i \in I} \sum_{j=0}^{K} \overline{N}_j^i x_j(0)$$

$$= \sum_{j=0}^{K} x_j(0) \left(\sum_{i \in I} N_j^i(0) - \sum_{i \in I} \overline{N}_j^i \right)$$

By the definition of a temporary asset market equilibrium, we get the stated result. $\square$

We assume that a temporary asset market equilibrium exists for the previous economy.

Assumption 17.16: Existence of a Temporary Asset Market Equilibrium

A temporary asset market equilibrium exists for the previous economy.

Some conditions for the existence of such an equilibrium in the above economy can be found in Cox, Ingersoll, and Ross [3]. Given this notion of an equilibrium, we next develop the multifactor beta and consumption beta forms of the intertemporal CAPM.

17.4. THE MULTIFACTOR BETA MODEL

This section derives the multifactor beta form of the intertemporal CAPM. It is the generalization of the market beta model of Chap. 15. To do this, we need a definition.

The *market portfolio* is defined to be any portfolio such that the percentage of the portfolio's value in asset j for $j = 1, \ldots, K$, denoted mkt_j, satisfies

$$\text{mkt}_j = \frac{\sum\limits_{i \in I} \overline{N}_j^i x_j(0)}{\sum\limits_{k=1}^{K} \left(\sum\limits_{i \in I} \overline{N}_k^i x_k(0) \right)} \tag{17.10}$$

where $\sum_{j=1}^{K} \text{mkt}_j = 1$.

The key step in deriving the multifactor beta model is a mutual fund theorem.

Theorem 17.3: Mutual Fund Theorem

Given assumptions 17.1–17.16 and that $\{N_0^i(0), \ldots, N_K^i(0)\}_{i \in I}$, $\{x_0(0), \ldots, x_K(0)\}$ is a temporary asset market equilibrium, there exist $\lambda^i \in \mathbb{R}$ such that

$$\frac{w_j^i}{(1 - w_0^i)} = \lambda^i \, \text{mkt}_j \quad \text{if } j = 1, \ldots, K - 1$$

and

$$\frac{w_K^i}{(1 - w_0^i)} = (1 - \lambda^i) + \lambda^i \, \text{mkt}_K$$

Proof

See Sec. 17.7. $\square$

To understand why theorem 17.3 is a mutual fund theorem, let us analyze the conditions. For risky assets $j = 1, \ldots, K - 1$ the optimal portfolio weight is seen to be $w_j^i = [(1 - w_0^i)\lambda^i] \, \text{mkt}_j$, some constant times the market portfolio weight. For risky asset K, the optimal portfolio weight is $w_K^i = (1 - w_0^i)(1 - \lambda^i) + (1 - w_0^i)\lambda^i \text{mkt}_K$. Let us compare this to the portfolio consisting of w_0^i percent of the wealth in the riskless asset, $(1 - w_0^i)\lambda^i$ percent of the wealth in the market portfolio, and $(1 - w_0^i)(1 - \lambda^i)$ percent of the wealth in asset K. These represent investing in the three mutual funds: the riskless asset, the market portfolio, and asset K. Since the market portfolio itself is composed of assets $j = 1, \ldots, K$, the decomposed positions in the separate assets from this aggregate portfolio are w_0^i in the riskless asset, $(1 - w_0^i)\lambda^i \text{mkt}_j$ in risky asset $j = 1, \ldots, K - 1$, and $(1 - w_0^i)[\lambda^i \text{mkt}_j + (1 - \lambda^i)]$ in risky asset K. This duplicates the portfolio weights in the optimal portfolio. Hence an investor can choose among three mutual funds and still obtain the same portfolio position (at her optimum) as with all the separate assets.

Theorem 17.4: Multifactor Beta Form of the CAPM

Given assumptions 17.1–17.16 and that $\{N_0^i(0), \ldots, N_K^i(0)\}_{i \in I}$, $\{x_0(0), \ldots, x_K(0)\}$ is a temporary asset market equilibrium

$$\alpha_j(t, x_K(t)) - \alpha_0(t, x_K(t)) = \beta_{jm}\left(\sum_{j=1}^{K} \text{mkt}_j \alpha_j(t, x_K(t)) - \alpha_0(t, x_K(t))\right)$$

$$+ \beta_{jK}(\alpha_K(t, x_K(t)) - \alpha_0(t, x_K(t))) \quad \text{for } j = 1, \ldots, K \quad (17.10)$$

where

$$\beta_{jK} = \frac{\sigma_{Km}\sigma_{jm} - \sigma_{jK}\sigma_{mm}}{\sigma_{Km}^2 - \sigma_{KK}\sigma_{mm}}$$

$$\beta_{jm} = \frac{\sigma_{Km}\sigma_{jK} - \sigma_{jm}\sigma_{KK}}{\sigma_{Km}^2 - \sigma_{KK}\sigma_{mm}}$$

$$\sigma_{Km} = \sum_{j=1}^{K} \text{mkt}_j \sigma_{Kj}, \quad \sigma_{mm} = \sum_{j=1}^{K}\sum_{k=1}^{K} \text{mkt}_j \text{mkt}_k \sigma_{jk}$$

Proof

See Section 17.7.   □

This theorem gives the multibeta form of the CAPM. The expected instantaneous excess return on asset j, $(\alpha_j - \alpha_0)$, is equal to the market beta, β_{jm}, times the excess expected return on the market portfolio $(\sum_{j=1}^{K} \text{mkt}_j \alpha_j - \alpha_0)$, plus the beta with respect to asset K, β_{jK}, times the excess expected return on asset K, $(\alpha_K - \alpha_0)$. There are two betas: β_{jm} and β_{jK}. An asset's "risk" has two components: the "risk" that is associated with movements in the market portfolio (represented by β_{jm}) and the "risk" that is associated with movements in the state variable (represented by β_{jK}). Both risks are systematic. The risk of the state variable x_K influences future asset returns and therefore future consumption flows. The investor adjusts her portfolio position in an attempt to hedge this "state variable" risk and smooth her consumption flows. It is important to emphasize that the expected returns in expression (17.10) are all instantaneous. This observation will be important later on when discussing the empirical testing of the intertemporal CAPM.

To aid our understanding of the single period CAPM, note that if the "investment opportunity" set $\{\alpha_j, \eta_{ij}\}$ is independent of x_K, then x_K is no longer needed as an additional state variable. In this case, reworking the previous analysis with x_K removed yields an instantaneous version of the single period CAPM, as in expression (17.10), but with only one beta, the market beta. This insight suggests that the conditions under which the "single period" CAPM results in the context of an intertemporal model are very restrictive. Essentially, the conditions require a statistical independence of the other "risks" in the economy to the traded assets' future investment opportunities, as represented in this model by the investment opportunity set $\{\alpha_j, \eta_{ij}\}$. In this case, investors will not use asset positions to hedge these "risks" and the single period form of the CAPM results.

17.5. THE CONSUMPTION BETA

This section presents the consumption beta form of the multiperiod CAPM. This model is a direct generalization of the consumption beta CAPM of Chap. 15.

Theorem 17.5: Consumption Beta Form of the CAPM

Given assumptions 17.1–17.16 and that $\{N_0^i(0), \ldots, N_K^i(0)\}_{i \in I}$, $\{x_0(0), \ldots, x_K(0)\}$ is a temporary asset market equilibrium, if aggregate consumption demand trades, $\Sigma_i C^i(t) \in M_t$, then

$$[\alpha_j(t, x_K(t)) - \alpha_0(t, x_K(t))] \, dt = \beta_{jc}(E(dc/c) - \alpha_0(t, x_K(t)) \, dt) \qquad (17.11)$$

where $c(t) \equiv \Sigma_{i \in I} C^i(t)$ is aggregate consumption demand at time t, and $\beta_{jc} = \mathrm{cov}(dc/c, dx_j/x_j)/\mathrm{var}(dc/c)$.

Proof

See Sec. 17.7 □

The consumption beta form of the CAPM is given in expression (17.11). The expected excess return on asset j, $\alpha_j - \alpha_0$, is proportional to a risk measure, β_{jc}, times the excess expected return on a portfolio perfectly correlated to aggregate consumption. The consumption beta β_{jc} represents the covariance of asset j to aggregate consumption, divided by the variance of the return on aggregate consumption. This expression is identical to the consumption beta form of the CAPM of Chap. 15, with the exception that it corresponds to the instantaneous returns (Chap. 15 corresponds to discrete returns). The risk interpretation of the consumption beta is identical. An investor attempts to smooth consumption over time and reduce its variability over states. The extent that an asset increases this variability, as measured by its consumption beta, is the extent to which it is considered risky.

17.6. TESTABILITY

The multiperiod CAPM has many of the same empirical problems associated with it as does the single period CAPM. For example, in the multibeta form of the model, expression (17.10), the return on the market portfolio appears. The market portfolio is not observable, and consequently the essence of Roll's critique of the single period CAPM can be applied to the multiperiod CAPM as well.

In addition, the multiperiod CAPM has another empirical difficulty. As derived, the multiperiod CAPMs, conditions (17.10) or (17.11), correspond to instants in time, that is, the return is over Δt as $\Delta t \to 0$. To test these expressions, the model needs to be transformed to a discrete time interval. This transformation introduces additional terms into the expression and must be accounted for in empirical investigations. In fact, they are consistent with many of the known violations of the single period CAPM.

To obtain these terms, let us examine a special case of the previous model. In assumption 17.9, assume that the investment opportunity set $\{\alpha_j, \eta_{ij}\}$ and therefore $\{\sigma_{ij}\}$ is constant. As discussed at the end of Sec. 17.4, this implies that the instantaneous "single period" CAPM holds, i.e.

$$\alpha_j = \alpha_0 + \beta_j(\alpha_m - \alpha_0) \quad \text{where } \alpha_m \equiv \sum_{j=1}^{K} \text{mkt}_j \alpha_j \qquad (17.12)$$

Let $dS_m/S_m \equiv \sum_{j=1}^{K} \text{mkt}_j \, dx_j/x_j$ be the random return on the market portfolio. Now, by applying Ito's lemma,[7] it can be shown that

$$\log (x_j(t + \Delta)/x_j(t)) = (\alpha_j - (1/2)\sigma_j^2)\Delta + \sigma_j[z_j(t + \Delta) - z_j(t)]$$

$$\text{for } j = 1, \ldots, K \qquad (17.13)$$

where $[z_j(t + \Delta) - z_j(t)]$ is normally distributed with mean 0 and variance Δ. So

$$E_t(\log (x_j(t + \Delta)/x_j(t)) = (\alpha_j - (1/2)\sigma_j^2)\Delta \qquad (17.14)$$

---

[7] Ito's lemma states that if $f(x_0, \ldots, x_n)$ is a twice continuously differentiable function of $(x_0, \ldots, x_n)$, then the stochastic differential of $f(x_0, \ldots, x_n)$ satisfies

$$df(x_0, \ldots, x_n) = \sum_{i=0}^{n} \frac{\partial f}{\partial x_i} dx_i + \frac{\partial f}{\partial t} dt + \frac{1}{2} \sum_{i=0}^{n} \sum_{j=0}^{n} \frac{\partial^2 f}{\partial x_i \, \partial x_j} dx_i \, dx_j$$

(see Ikeda and Watanabe [6, p. 99]).

To prove the statement in the text, let $y = \log x_j(t)$, by Ito's lemma $dy = (\partial y/\partial t) \, dt + (\partial y/\partial x_j) \, dx_j + 1/2 \, (\partial^2 y/\partial x_j^2) \, (dx_j)^2$. Using $dx_j^2 = = \sigma_j^2 x_j^2 \, dt$ yields $d \log x_j(t) = (dx_j/x_j) - (1/2) \, \sigma_j^2 \, dt$. In integral form this is

$$\log (x_j(t + \Delta)/x_j(t)) = \int_t^{t+\Delta} [\alpha_j - (1/2) \, \sigma_j^2] \, dv + \int_t^{t+\Delta} \sigma_j \, dz_j \, (v)$$

This is the expression in the text.

Similarly, we obtain

$$E_t(\log (S_m(t + \Delta)/S_m(t))) = (\alpha_m - (1/2)\sigma_m^2)\Delta \qquad (17.15)$$

where $\sigma_m^2 dt = \text{var } (dS_m/S_m)$.

Substitution of expressions (17.14) and (17.15) into (17.12) yields

$$E_t(\log [x_j(t + \Delta)/x_j(t)]) = \alpha_0\Delta + \beta_j(E_t(\log [S_m(t + \Delta)/S_m(t)]) - \alpha_0\Delta)$$
$$+ (1/2)\beta_j(\sigma_m^2 - \sigma_j^2)\Delta \qquad (17.16)$$

This is the discrete time form of the "single period" instantaneous CAPM. The expression is in terms of the logarithm of the price relatives and the discrete time interval $[t, t + \Delta]$ where $\Delta > 0$. Note that expression (17.16) is adjusted by the expression $(1/2)\beta_j(\sigma_m^2 - \sigma_j^2)\Delta$. This term is related to the nonsystematic risk σ_j^2 of asset j. If one utilizes expression (17.12) to test the CAPM, then the discrete time form would generate the appropriate regression model. The regression model contains an adjustment term that needs to be recognized in the estimation procedures.

17.7. PROOFS OF THE THEOREMS

Proof of Theorem 17.1

This proof is a sketch of a more detailed proof contained in Kushner [10, p. 326]. Write

$$J(W(t), x_K(t), t) = \max \{E_t \int_t^{t+\Delta} V^i(C(s), s) \, ds + E_t E_{t+\Delta} \int_{t+\Delta}^T V^i(C(s), s) \, ds\}$$

By Bellman's principle of optimality

$$J(W(t), x_K(t), t)$$

$$= \max \{E_t \int_t^{t+\Delta} V^i(C(s), s) \, ds + J(W(t + \Delta), x_K(t + \Delta), t + \Delta)\}$$

Use of the mean value theorem gives

$$\int_t^{t+\Delta} V^i(C(s), s) \, ds = V^i(C(t^*), t^*)\Delta \quad \text{for some } t^* \in [t, t + \Delta]$$

Combined, these two observations imply that

$$0 = \max \{E_t(V^i(C(t^*), t^*))\Delta + E_t(J(W(t + \Delta), x_K(t + \Delta), t + \Delta)$$
$$- J(W(t), x_K(t), t))\} \quad \text{for some } t^* \in [t, t + \Delta]$$

Next, write $J(W(t + \Delta), x_K(t + \Delta), t + \Delta) - J(W(t), x_K(t), t)$ using a multivariable Taylor series expansion, divide by Δ, and take the limit as $\Delta \to 0$.

Use of expression (17.6c) for $dW(t)$ and assumption 17.9 for $dx_K(t)$ in the resulting equation gives

$$0 = \underset{C(s),w_j(s)}{\text{maximum}}\left\{V^i(C(t), t) + \frac{\partial J}{\partial t}(W(t), x_K(t), t)\right.$$

$$+ \frac{\partial J}{\partial W(t)}(W(t), x_K(t), t)$$

$$\times \left(\sum_{j=1}^{K} w_j(t)W(t)(\alpha_j - \alpha_0) + \alpha_0 W(t) - C(t)\right)$$

$$+ \frac{\partial J}{\partial x_K(t)}(W(t), x_K(t), t)\alpha_K x_K + \frac{1}{2}\frac{\partial^2 J(W(t), x_K(t), t)}{\partial W(t)^2}\sum_{j=1}^{K}\sum_{\ell=1}^{K} w_j w_\ell W^2 \sigma_{j\ell}$$

$$+ \frac{\partial^2 J(W(t), x_K(t), t)}{\partial W(t)\partial x_K(t)}\sum_{j=1}^{K} w_j W \sigma_{jK} x_K + \frac{1}{2}\frac{\partial^2 J(W(t), x_K(t), t)}{\partial x_K^2(t)}\sigma_{KK}x_K^2\Big\}$$

The first-order conditions for this optimization problem imply

$$\frac{\partial V^i}{\partial C(t)}(C(t), t) - \frac{\partial J}{\partial W(t)}(W(t), x_K(t), t) = 0$$

$$\frac{\partial J}{\partial W}W(t)(\alpha_j - \alpha_0) + \frac{\partial^2 J}{\partial W^2}\sum_{k=1}^{K} w_k W^2 \sigma_{jK} + \frac{\partial^2 J}{\partial W \partial x_K}W\sigma_{jK}x_K = 0$$

$$\text{for } j = 1, \ldots, K$$

This completes the proof. $\square$

Proof of Corollary 17.2

From (17.8b)

$$\frac{\partial J}{\partial W}(\alpha_j - \alpha_0) + \frac{\partial^2 J}{\partial W^2}\sum_{k=1}^{K} w_k^i W^i \sigma_{kj} + \frac{\partial^2 J}{\partial W \partial x_K}\sigma_{Kj}x_K = 0 \quad \text{for } j = 1, \ldots, K$$

Dividing by $(\partial^2 J/\partial W^2)$ and rearranging terms give

$$\sum_{k=1}^{K} w_k^i W^i \sigma_{kj} = -\frac{\partial J/\partial W}{\partial^2 J/\partial W^2}(\alpha_j - \alpha_0) - \frac{\partial^2 J/\partial W \partial x_K}{\partial^2 J/\partial W^2}\sigma_{Kj}x_K$$

In matrix form this is

$$\begin{pmatrix} \sigma_{11} & \cdots & \sigma_{1K} \\ \vdots & & \vdots \\ \sigma_{K1} & \cdots & \sigma_{KK} \end{pmatrix}\begin{pmatrix} w_1^i W^i \\ \vdots \\ w_K^i W^i \end{pmatrix}$$

$$= -\frac{\partial J/\partial W}{\partial^2 J/\partial W^2}\begin{bmatrix} \alpha_1 - \alpha_0 \\ \vdots \\ \alpha_K - \alpha_0 \end{bmatrix} - \frac{\partial^2 J/\partial W \partial x_K}{\partial^2 J/\partial W^2}\begin{pmatrix} \sigma_{K1}x_K \\ \vdots \\ \sigma_{KK}x_K \end{pmatrix}$$

By assumption 17.9, the $[\alpha_{ij}]$ matrix is nonsingular.

Define v_{ij} to be the (i, j)th element of the matrix $[\sigma_{ij}]^{-1}$. This yields

$$w_j^i W^i = -\frac{\partial J/\partial W}{\partial^2 J/\partial W^2} \sum_{k=1}^{K} v_{jk}(\alpha_j - \alpha_0) - \frac{\partial^2 J/\partial W \partial x_K}{\partial^2 J/\partial W^2} \sum_{s=1}^{K} v_{js}\sigma_{sK}x_K$$

$$\text{for } j = 1, \ldots, K$$

But

$$\left(\sum_{s=1}^{K} v_{js}\sigma_{sK}\right) = \begin{cases} 1 & \text{if } j = K \\ 0 & \text{otherwise} \end{cases}$$

Substitution gives the result. $\quad\square$

We next prove theorem 17.4 before theorem 17.3.

Proof of Theorem 17.4

From (17.9a) and (17.9b)

$$x_j N_j^i(0) = w_j^i W^i = -\frac{\partial J^i/\partial W}{\partial^2 J^i/\partial W^2} \sum_{k=1}^{K} v_{jk}(\alpha_k - \alpha_0) \quad \text{for } j = 1, \ldots, K-1$$

$$x_K N_K^i(0) = w_K^i W^i = -\frac{\partial J^i/\partial W}{\partial^2 J^i/\partial W^2} \sum_{s=1}^{K} v_{Ks}(\alpha_s - \alpha_0) - \frac{\partial^2 J/\partial W \partial x_K}{\partial^2 J/\partial W^2} x_K$$

Next, sum over all i, and divide by $\sum_{j=1}^{K}[\sum_{i\in I} x_j N_j^i(0)]$ to get

$$\frac{\sum\limits_{i\in I} x_j N_j^i(0)}{\sum\limits_{j=1}^{K} \sum\limits_{i\in I} x_j N_j^i(0)} = A \sum_{k=1}^{K} v_{jk}(\alpha_k - \alpha_0)$$

$$\frac{\sum\limits_{i\in I} x_K N_K^i(0)}{\sum\limits_{j=1}^{K} \sum\limits_{i\in I} x_j N_j^i(0)} = A \sum_{s=1}^{K} v_{Ks}(\alpha_s - \alpha_0) - Hx_K$$

where

$$A \equiv \sum_{i\in I}\left(-\frac{\partial J^i/\partial W}{\partial^2 J^i/\partial W^2}\right) \bigg/ \sum_{j=1}^{K}\left(\sum_{i\in I} x_j N_j^i(0)\right)$$

$$H \equiv \sum_{i\in I}\left(-\frac{\partial^2 J^i/\partial W \partial x_K}{\partial^2 J^i/\partial W^2}\right) \bigg/ \sum_{j=1}^{K}\left(\sum_{i\in I} x_j N_j^i(0)\right)$$

Using the definition of the market portfolio, and the fact that the prices are equilibrium prices so aggregate demand equals aggregate supply, gives

$$\text{mkt}_j = A \sum_{k=1}^{K} v_{jk}(\alpha_k - \alpha_0) \quad \text{for } j = 1, \ldots, K-1$$

$$\text{mkt}_K = A \sum_{s=1}^{K} v_{Ks}(\alpha_s - \alpha_0) - Hx_K$$

$$(17.17)$$

In matrix form this is

$$
\begin{bmatrix} \mathrm{mkt}_1 \\ \vdots \\ \mathrm{mkt}_K + Hx_K \end{bmatrix} = A \begin{bmatrix} v_{11} & \cdots & v_{1K} \\ \vdots & & \vdots \\ v_{K1} & \cdots & v_{KK} \end{bmatrix} \begin{bmatrix} \alpha_1 - \alpha_0 \\ \vdots \\ \alpha_K - \alpha_0 \end{bmatrix}
$$

So

$$
\sum_{k=1}^{K} \mathrm{mkt}_k \sigma_{jk} + H\sigma_{jK} x_K = A(\alpha_j - \alpha_0) \quad \text{for } j = 1, \ldots, K
$$

Hence

$$
\sigma_{mj} + H\sigma_{jK} x_K = A(\alpha_j - \alpha_0) \quad \text{for } j = 1, \ldots, K \tag{17.18}
$$

We want to solve for Hx_K and A. First, for $j = K$, (17.18) becomes

$$
\sigma_{mK} + Hx_K \sigma_{KK} = A(\alpha_K - \alpha_0) \tag{17.19}
$$

Multiplying (17.18) by mkt_j and summing over $j = 1, \ldots, K$ yield

$$
\sum_{j=1}^{K} \mathrm{mkt}_j \sigma_{mj} + Hx_K \sum_{j=1}^{K} \mathrm{mkt}_j \sigma_{jK} = A\left(\sum_{j=1}^{K} \mathrm{mkt}_j \alpha_j - \alpha_0 \right)
$$

or

$$
\sigma_{mm} + Hx_K \sigma_{mK} = A\left(\sum_{j=1}^{K} \mathrm{mkt}_j \alpha_j - \alpha_0 \right) \tag{17.20}
$$

Rearranging (17.19) and (17.20) gives

$$
(\alpha_K - \alpha_0) = \frac{1}{A}\sigma_{mK} + \left(\frac{Hx_K}{A} \right)\sigma_{KK}
$$

$$
\left(\sum_{j=1}^{K} \mathrm{mkt}_j \alpha_j - \alpha_0 \right) = \frac{1}{A}\sigma_{mm} + \left(\frac{Hx_K}{A} \right)\sigma_{mK}
$$

Solving for $(1/A)$ and (Hx_K/A) yields ($A > 0$ by assumption 17.14).

$$
\frac{1}{A} = \frac{\sigma_{mK}(\alpha_K - \alpha_0) - \sigma_{KK}\left(\sum_{j=1}^{K} \mathrm{mkt}_j \alpha_j - \alpha_0 \right)}{\sigma_{mK}^2 - \sigma_{mm}\sigma_{KK}}
$$

$$
\frac{Hx_K}{A} = \frac{-\sigma_{mm}(\alpha_K - \alpha_0) + \sigma_{mK}\left(\sum_{j=1}^{K} \mathrm{mkt}_j \alpha_j - \alpha_0 \right)}{\sigma_{mK}^2 - \sigma_{mm}\sigma_{KK}}
$$

Substitution into (17.18) gives

$$
\sigma_{mj}\left(\frac{\sigma_{mK}(\alpha_K - \alpha_0) - \sigma_{KK}\left(\sum_{j=1}^{K} \mathrm{mkt}_j \alpha_j - \alpha_0 \right)}{\sigma_{mK}^2 - \sigma_{mm}\sigma_{KK}} \right)
$$

$$
+ \sigma_{jK}\left(\frac{-\sigma_{mm}(\alpha_K - \alpha_0) + \sigma_{mK}\left(\sum_{j=1}^{K} \mathrm{mkt}_j \alpha_j - \alpha_0 \right)}{\sigma_{mK}^2 - \sigma_{mm}\sigma_{KK}} \right) = (\alpha_j - \alpha_0)
$$

Simplification gives the result. Note that

$$\sigma_{mK}^2 - \sigma_{mm}\sigma_{KK} \leq 0 \quad \text{if and only if}$$

$$\sigma_{mK}^2 \leq \sigma_{mm}\sigma_{KK} \quad \text{if and only if}$$

$$\frac{\sigma_{mK}^2}{\sigma_{mm}\sigma_{KK}} \leq 1$$

This says that the correlation of $(\Sigma_{j=1}^{K} \text{mkt}_j \, dx_j/x_j, \, dx_K/x_K) \leq 1$. This last result is always true.

Proof of Theorem 17.3

Define

$$\lambda^i = -\frac{\dfrac{\partial J^i\,(W^i(t),\, x_K(t),\, t)}{\partial W\,(t)}}{\dfrac{\partial^2 J^i(W^i(t),\, x_K(t),\, t)}{\partial W^2(t)}} \frac{1}{W^i(t)A} \frac{1}{(1 - w_0^i)}$$

where

$$A = \sum_{i \in I}\left(-\frac{\partial J^i/\partial W}{\partial^2 J^i/\partial W^2}\right) \Bigg/ \sum_{j=1}^{K}\left(\sum_{i \in I} x_j N_j^i(0)\right)$$

From the proof of theorem 17.4, expression (17.17)

$$\frac{\text{mkt}_j}{A} = \sum_{k=1}^{K} v_{jk}(\alpha_k - \alpha_0) \quad \text{for } j = 1, \ldots, K - 1$$

$$\frac{\text{mkt}_K}{A} + \frac{Hx_K}{A} = \sum_{j=1}^{K} v_{Kj}(\alpha_j - \alpha_0)$$

so substitution of these results into (17.9a–b) yields

$$w_j^i/(1 - w_0^i) = -\frac{\partial J^i/\partial W}{\partial^2 J^i/\partial W^2} \frac{\text{mkt}_j}{A} \frac{1}{W^i} \frac{1}{(1 - w_0^i)} = \lambda^i \, \text{mkt}_j$$

$$\text{for } j = 1, \ldots, K - 1$$

$$w_K^i/(1 - w_0^i) = -\frac{\partial J^i/\partial W}{\partial^2 J^i/\partial W^2} \frac{1}{W^i} \frac{1}{(1 - w_0^i)}\left(\frac{\text{mkt}_K}{A} + \frac{Hx_K}{A}\right)$$

$$- \frac{\partial^2 J/\partial W \partial x_K}{\partial^2 J/\partial W^2} x_K \frac{1}{W^i} \frac{1}{(1 - w_0^i)}$$

$$= \lambda^i \, \text{mkt}_K + \left[\lambda^i H x_K - \frac{\partial^2 J/\partial W \partial x_K}{\partial^2 J/\partial W^2} x_K \frac{1}{W^i} \frac{1}{(1 - w_0^i)}\right]$$

Note that

$$1 = \frac{\sum_{j=1}^{K} w_j^i}{(1 - w_0^i)} = \lambda^i \sum_{j=1}^{K} \text{mkt}_j + \left(\lambda^i H x_K - \frac{\partial^2 J/\partial W \partial x_K}{\partial^2 J/\partial W^2} \frac{x_K}{W^i} \frac{1}{(1 - w_0^i)}\right)$$

Hence

$$1 - \lambda^i = \left(\lambda^i H x_K - \frac{\partial^2 J / \partial W \, \partial x_K}{\partial^2 J / \partial W^2} \frac{x_K}{W^i} \frac{1}{(1 - w_0^i)} \right)$$

This completes the proof. $\square$

Proof of Theorem 17.5

$$C^i(t) = C^i(t, W^i(t), x_K(t))$$

so by Ito's lemma (see footnote 7)

$$dC^i(t) = \frac{\partial C^i}{\partial t} + \frac{\partial C^i}{\partial W^i} \, dW^i(t) + \frac{\partial C^i}{\partial x_K} \, dx_K + \frac{1}{2} \frac{\partial^2 C^i}{\partial x_K^2} \, dx_K^2$$

$$+ \frac{\partial^2 C^i}{\partial x_K \, \partial W^i} \, dx_K dW^i + \frac{1}{2} \frac{\partial^2 C^i}{\partial W^{i2}} \, (dW^i)^2$$

Hence

$$\mathrm{cov}\left(\frac{dx_j}{x_j}, \, dC^i \right) = \frac{\partial C^i}{\partial W^i} \, \mathrm{cov}\left(\frac{dx_j}{x_j}, \, dW^i(t) \right) + x_K \frac{\partial C^i}{\partial x_K} \, \mathrm{cov}\left(\frac{dx_j}{x_j}, \, \frac{dx_K}{x_K} \right)$$

$$= \left[\frac{\partial C^i}{\partial W^i} \sum_{k=1}^{K} w_k^i W^i \sigma_{kj} + x_K \frac{\partial C^i}{\partial x_K} \sigma_{jK} \right] dt \qquad (17.21)$$

From (17.8b)

$$(\alpha_j - \alpha_0) = -\frac{\partial^2 J / \partial W^2}{\partial J / \partial W} \sum_{k=1}^{K} w_k^i W^i \alpha_{kj} - \frac{\partial^2 J / \partial W \, \partial x_K}{\partial J / \partial W} \sigma_{Kj} x_K$$

$$\text{for } j = 1, \ldots, K$$

From (17.8a)

$$\frac{\partial V^i}{\partial C} = \frac{\partial J}{\partial W}$$

at the optimum. Therefore

$$\frac{\partial^2 V^i}{\partial C^2} \frac{\partial C}{\partial W} = \frac{\partial^2 J}{\partial W^2} \quad \text{and}$$

$$\frac{\partial^2 V^i}{\partial C^2} \frac{\partial C}{\partial x_K} = \frac{\partial^2 J}{\partial W \, \partial x_K}$$

Substitution gives

$$(\alpha_j - \alpha_0) = -\frac{\dfrac{\partial^2 V^i}{\partial C^2}}{\dfrac{\partial V^i}{\partial C}} \left(\frac{\partial C}{\partial W} \sum_{k=1}^{K} w_k^i W^i \sigma_{kj} + \frac{\partial C}{\partial x_K} \sigma_{Kj} x_K \right) \quad \text{for } j = 1, \ldots, K$$

From (17.21)

$$(\alpha_j - \alpha_0)\, dt = -\frac{\dfrac{\partial^2 V^i}{\partial C^2}}{\dfrac{\partial V^i}{\partial C}} \operatorname{cov}(dx_j/x_j,\, dC^i)$$

Hence

$$\left(-\frac{1}{\dfrac{\partial^2 V^i/\partial C^2}{\partial V^i/\partial C}}\right)(\alpha_j - \alpha_0)\, dt = \operatorname{cov}(dx_j/x_j,\, dC^i) \qquad (17.22)$$

Next sum over all i

$$\sum_{i\in I}\left(-\frac{\partial V^i/\partial C}{\partial^2 V^i/\partial C^2}\right)(\alpha_j - \alpha_0)\, dt = \operatorname{cov}\left(\frac{dx_j}{x_j},\, d\left(\sum_{i\in I} C^i\right)\right)$$

Since $\Sigma_i C^i \in M_t$, take the portfolio ψ_j for $j = 1, \ldots, K$ such that

$$\sum_{j=1}^{K} \psi_j\, dx_j/x_j = \frac{d\left(\displaystyle\sum_{i\in I} C^i\right)}{\displaystyle\sum_{i\in I} C^i}$$

then

$$\sum_{i\in I}\left(-\frac{\partial V^i/\partial C}{\partial^2 V^i/\partial C^2}\right)\left(\sum_{j=1}^{K}\psi_j\alpha_j - \alpha_0\right) dt = \operatorname{cov}\left(\sum_{j=1}^{K}\psi_j\, dx_j/x_j,\, d\left(\sum_{i\in I} C^i\right)\right)$$

or

$$\frac{\left(\displaystyle\sum_{j=1}^{K}\psi_j\alpha_j - \alpha_0\right) dt}{\operatorname{cov}\left(\displaystyle\sum_{j=1}^{K}\psi_j dx_j/x_j,\, \dfrac{d\sum_{i\in I} C^i}{\sum_{i\in I} C^i}\right)} = \sum_{i\in I}\left(-\frac{\dfrac{\partial V^i/\partial C}{\partial^2 V^i/\partial C^2}}{\displaystyle\sum_{i\in I} C^i}\right)$$

or

$$\frac{E(dc/c) - \alpha_0\, dt}{\operatorname{var}(dc/c)} = \sum_{i\in I}\left(-\frac{\dfrac{\partial V^i/\partial C}{\partial^2 V^i/\partial C^2}}{\displaystyle\sum_{i\in I} C^i}\right)$$

where $c \equiv \Sigma_{i\in I} C^i$. Substitution into (17.22) yields

$$(\alpha_j - \alpha_0)dt = \frac{E(dc/c) - \alpha_0 dt}{\operatorname{var}(dc/c)} \operatorname{cov}(dx_j/x_j,\, dc/c)$$

This completes the proof. $\square$

17.8. SUMMARY

This chapter presents the multiperiod capital asset pricing model, which generalizes the material contained in Chap. 15. The multiperiod CAPM relaxes the unrealistic mean-variance assumption of the single period CAPM. It accomplishes this feat by introducing continuous trading and continuous sample path stochastic processes for stock price movements. These continuous sample path stock price movements imply (through Ito's lemma) that preferences "locally" or "instantaneously" satisfy the mean-variance assumption. This observation explains the consumption beta form of the multiperiod CAPM. This "local" analysis *nearly* collapses the multiperiod CAPM to the single period analysis. The remaining difference is the ability of portfolio choice to hedge changes in the future "investment opportunity" set, i.e., changes in expected returns and the covariance of returns. This planning or foresight aspect of the model results in the *multibeta* form of the CAPM as opposed to the single market beta form of Chap. 15.

With respect to empirical testing, the multiperiod CAPM still suffers from Roll's critique. In addition, since the models hold instantaneously, to test them the models must be transformed to a discrete time form. This discrete time form contains additional terms, which must be recognized in empirical testing.

17.9. REFERENCES

1. Breeden, Douglas, "An Intertemporal Asset Pricing Model with Stochastic Consumption and Investment Opportunities," *Journal of Financial Economics*, 7 (1979), 265–296.

2. Chow, Gregory C., "Optimum Control of Stochastic Differential Equation Systems," *Journal of Economic Dynamics and Control*, 1 (1979), 143–175.

3. Cox, John, Jonathan Ingersoll, and Stephen Ross, "An Intertemporal General Equilibrium Model of Asset Prices," *Econometrica*, 53 (March 1985), 363–384.

4. Fleming, Wendell, and Raymond Rishel, *Deterministic and Stochastic Optimal Control*. New York: Springer-Verlag, 1975.

5. Grossman, Sanford, and Robert Shiller, "Consumption Correlatedness and Risk Measurement in Economics with Non-Traded Assets and Heterogeneous Information," *Journal of Financial Economics*, 10 (1982), 195–210.

6. Ikeda, Nobuyuki, and Shinzo Watanabe, *Stochastic Differential Equations and Diffusion Processes*. Amsterdam: North-Holland, 1981.

7. Jarrow, Robert, and Eric Rosenfeld, "Jump Risks and the Intertemporal Capital Asset Pricing Model," *Journal of Business*, 57 (July 1984), 337–351.

8. Jensen, Michael C., "Capital Markets: Theory and Evidence," *Bell Journal of Economics and Management Science*, 3 (1972), 357–398.

9. Kraus, Alan, and Robert Litzenberger, "Market Equilibrium in a Multiperiod State Preference Model with Logarithmic Utility," *Journal of Finance*, 30 (December 1975), 1213–1227.

10. Kushner, Harold, *Introduction to Stochastic Control*. New York: Holt, Rinehart & Winston, 1971.

11. Long, John, "Stock Prices, Inflation, and the Term Structure of Interest Rates," *Journal of Financial Economics*, 1 (1974), 131–170.

12. Merton, Robert C., "An Intertemporal Capital Asset Pricing Model," *Econometrica*, 41 (September 1973), 867–887.

13. Radner, Roy, "Equilibrium Under Uncertainty," in *Handbook of Mathematical Economics*, vol. II, ed. K. J. Arrow and M. D. Intriligator. Amsterdam: North-Holland, 1982.

14. Williams, Joseph, "Capital Asset Prices with Heterogeneous Beliefs," *Journal of Financial Economics*, 5 (1977), 219–239.

18

AN EQUILIBRIUM VERSION OF ROSS'S APT

This chapter presents an equilibrium pricing version of Ross's APT. As an equilibrium pricing model, additional assumptions on preferences are required beyond those in the model of Chap. 9. These additional assumptions, however, strengthen the implications of the model in two ways. First, they generate a tighter approximation result for an asset's expected return than the relationship in Chap. 9. Second, implications for investor portfolio behavior are generated. These differences delineate the equilibrium pricing version from the arbitrage pricing version. The testable implications for asset expected returns are also discussed. The derivation here is partially adapted from Grinblatt and Titman [3]; related models are those of Dybvig [2] and Conner [1].

18.1. PRELIMINARIES

This section presents the model's assumptions and notation. The basic structure follows the asset model in Chap. 9, Ross's APT. This asset model will be embedded within the consumption-saving framework developed in Chap. 14, on utility theory, in order that the equilibrium pricing methodology can be employed. There is one major adjustment. The model in Chap. 9 contains a countably infinite number of assets (see assumption 9.8)). This section approximates the countably infinite asset economy of Chap. 9 with a sequence of finite economies. This sequential approach simplifies the mathematics employed and allows the use of the utility theory developed in Chap. 14. For an alternative approach using Hilbert space theory, see Conner [1].

The model has two time periods, times 0 and 1. At time 1, the uncertainty in the economy is characterized by the state space Ω with an arbitrary state denoted by $\omega \in \Omega$. An asset x is defined by its dollar cash flows across all states at time 1, $x(\omega)$, where $x:\Omega \to \mathbb{R}$.

A sequence of economies indexed by $n = 1, 2, 3, \ldots$, is identified by the set of assets that trade at time 0. The set of assets that trade at time 0 in the nth economy is denoted by M^n. The following assumptions parallel those in Chap. 9. Modifications are identified by daggers and discussed in greater detail; the reader is referred to the complete description in Chap. 9.

Assumption 18.1: Marketed Assets

For all economies n, if assets $x, y \in M^n$ and $\alpha, \beta \in \mathbb{R}$, then $\alpha x + \beta y \in M^n$.

Each economy along the sequence is closed under finite portfolios. As before, the marketed assets generate an event set at time 1, denoted by $\sigma(M^n)$. This set of events are the subsets of Ω that can be inferred using only the knowledge of the cash flows at time 1. The economy consists of a finite number of investors whose beliefs satisfy the following assumption:

Assumption 18.2: Conditional Homogeneous Beliefs

For all economies n, given an asset $x \in M^n$, every investor agrees that $x(\omega)$ is the cash flow in dollars to asset x at time 1, given state ω occurs.

Assumption 18.3: Homogeneous Beliefs

For all economies n, given an event $H \in \sigma(M^n)$, $\text{Prob}_i(H) = \text{Prob}_j(H)$ for all investors i, j where $\text{Prob}_i(\cdot)$ represents investor i's probability beliefs.

This assumption imposes considerably more structure on investor beliefs than the unconditional beliefs assumption 9.3. Assumption 9.3 only requires investors to agree on zero probability events, while assumption 18.3 requires investors to have *identical* probability beliefs across all events. This implies that investors agree on the expectations and variances of asset cash flows. This is a very strong assumption.

A possible justification for this assumption (as an approximation) is based on the dominance of institutional trading in the securities markets. If professional investment managers (e.g., mutual fund managers) make the market for securities *and* they have similar beliefs, then assumption 18.3 is a good first approximation. One might expect professional investment managers to have similar beliefs since they have access to the same information sources. Whether or not one accepts this argument, assumption 18.3 is utilized below. This same assumption is also contained in the capital asset pricing model of Chaps. 15 to 17. Chapter 19, on market efficiency, explores the relaxation of this assumption.

For convenience, we drop the i subscript on beliefs and write $\text{Prob}_j(\cdot) = \text{Prob}(\cdot)$ for all j. This is without loss of generality since all investors have identical beliefs. We need to ensure that the assets' time 1 cash flows have finite variances—hence we add

Assumption 18.4: Finite Second Moments

For all economies n and for any asset $x \in M^n$

$$E(x^2) < +\infty$$

The markets are assumed to be frictionless and competitive.

Assumption 18.5: Frictionless Markets

The asset market has no transaction costs, no taxes, and no restrictions on short sales, and asset shares are divisible.

Assumption 18.6: Competitive Markets

Every investor acts as a price taker.

We define a price functional over the traded assets in M^n, $p:M^n \to \mathbb{R}$, where $p(x)$ gives the time 0 price in dollars of the asset $x \in M^n$. In principle, the price functional p should also have an n subscript because it is dependent on the particular economy in the sequence. For notational simplicity, we omit the n subscript; however, this should not cause any confusion.

The price functional is assumed to preclude the existence of arbitrage opportunities.

Assumption 18.7: No Finite Asset Arbitrage Opportunities

For each economy n, the asset market contains no finite asset arbitrage opportunities as defined in Chap. 8; i.e., the price functional p satisfies value additivity and all limited liability assets have strictly positive prices.

We next identify the set of assets available in the sequence of economies. Let $\{x_j\}_{j=0}^{\infty}$ be a countable set of *limited liability* assets, where asset x_0 is the (nominal) riskless asset, i.e., $x_0(\omega) = x_\Omega = 1$ for all $\omega \in \Omega$.

Assumption 18.8: Sequencing of Economies[†]

M^n consists of all finite portfolios using the primary assets $\{x_j\}_{j=0}^n$, where $x_j : \Omega \to \mathbb{R}$ are limited liability assets with $x_0(\omega) = 1$ for all $\omega \in \Omega$.

This assumption clarifies how the sequence of markets $\{M^n\}_{n=1}^{\infty}$ approaches the market economy of Chap. 9. The market economies change through the introduction of additional primary assets. For example, M^{n+1} contains an additional limited liability asset, x_{n+1}, that the market M^n does not include. In the limit, as more and more assets are included, M^n approaches the economy studied in Chap. 9.

Recall that for any traded asset $x \in M^n$, if its time 0 price $p(x) \neq 0$, then the return on asset x is defined by $r(x) = (x - p(x))/p(x)$. The return is a random variable mapping states, Ω, into the real line. Since the primary assets are all of limited liability, their returns are well defined by the no arbitrage opportunity assumption 18.7. Here, again, returns should actually be subscripted by an n. We omit this subscript to simplify the notation.

Given assumptions 18.1–18.8, by the GAPT of Chap. 8, we know there exists a finite basis set of traded assets $\{z_j\}_{j=0}^m \in M^n$, where $m \leq n$ such that

$$r(x_j) = \sum_{k=0}^{m} \lambda_{jk} r(z_k) \text{ for } j = 0, \ldots, n \qquad (18.1)$$

where $\sum_{k=0}^m \lambda_{jk} = 1$.

Because the riskless asset trades, we can rewrite this expression as

$$r(x_j) = r(x_\Omega) + \sum_{k=0}^{m} \lambda_{jk}(r(z_k) - r(x_\Omega)) \quad \text{for } j = 0, \ldots, n$$

Without loss of generality, let $z_0 = x_\Omega$. Define

$$r(z_k) = f_k \qquad \text{for } k = 1, \ldots, K \quad \text{and}$$

$$r(z_k) = u_{k-K} \quad \text{for } k = K + 1, \ldots, m$$

The first K basis assets correspond to the factors, while the remaining basis assets correspond to the residual returns. With this new notation, expression (18.1) is equivalent to

$$r(x_j) = r(x_\Omega) + \sum_{k=1}^{K} \lambda_{jk}(f_k - r(x_\Omega)) + \sum_{s=1}^{m-K} \lambda_{j, K+s}(u_s - r(x_\Omega))$$

$$\text{for } j = 1, \ldots, n \qquad (18.2)$$

We now add an additional assumption.

Assumption 18.9: Linear Factor Hypothesis[†]

For any economy $n \geq K + 1$

$$r(x_j) = r(x_\Omega) + \sum_{k=1}^{K} \lambda_{jk}(f_k - r(x_\Omega)) + \lambda_{j, K+j}(u_j - r(x_\Omega))$$

$$\text{for } j = 1, \ldots, n \qquad (18.3a)$$

where

$$f_k, u_i, u_j \quad \text{are statistically independent[1] for all } i, j, k \qquad (18.3b)$$

and

$$\text{var}(\lambda_{j, K+j}(u_j - r)) \leq \overline{\sigma}^2 \text{ for } j = 1, \ldots, n \qquad (18.3c)$$

This assumption differs from the linear factor hypothesis, assumption 9.9, in the restrictions contained in condition (18.3b). For each market in the sequence, this new assumption requires the residual returns u_i to be statistically independent of each other and to be statistically independent of the factor returns f_k for $k = 1, \ldots, K$. This is stronger than assumption 9.9. In assumption 9.9, the residuals were just uncorrelated, not statistically independent. Furthermore, no additional restriction was imposed on the factor returns f_K. Otherwise, the linear factor hypothesis assumption is identical.

Formally the number of basis assets m is a nondecreasing function of n, i.e., $m = m(n)$. We will not use this explicit notation unless absolutely necessary. As the sequence of economies $n \to \infty$, the number of basis assets need not approach infinity. The basis assets $m \to \infty$ as long as the number of linearly independent primary assets approaches infinity. A sufficient condition for this is that an infinite number of the coefficients in expression (18.3a), $\lambda_{j, K+j} \neq 0$. Otherwise, for some economy n, all assets x_j for large enough j would be linearly dependent on the remaining primary assets. This implies that for the linearly dependent assets with nonzero coefficients $\lambda_{j, K+j}$, the corresponding residual u_j is linearly dependent on the factors $\{f_1, \ldots, f_K\}$ and the remaining residuals, contradicting condition (18.3b).

We now embed this model into the consumption-saving framework. This construction is contained in Chap. 14, Sec. 14.1. For ease of reference, we review the relevant features. There is a single consumption good available in both times 0 and 1. Consumers enter with an endowment consisting of units of the consumption good in both times 0 and 1, i.e., $(\overline{C}_0^i, \overline{C}_1^i(\omega))$ for all $\omega \in \Omega$, where $\overline{C}_0^i > 0$ or $\overline{C}_1^i(\omega) > 0$ all $\omega \in \Omega$.[2]

---

[1]Two random variables x, y are statistically independent if $\text{Prob}[x \leq \alpha, y \leq \beta] = \text{Prob}[x \leq \alpha]\text{Prob}[y \leq \beta]$ for all $\alpha, \beta \in \mathbb{R}$. This implies, in particular, that $E[xy] = E[x]E[y]$ and therefore that $\text{cov}(x, y) = 0$. It also implies that $E[g(x)y] = E[g(x)]E[y]$ where g is a Borel measurable function such that $E[|g(x)|] < +\infty$.

[2]It is assumed that for some n^*, $\overline{C}_1^i$ are $\sigma(M^n)$ measurable for all $n \geq n^*$.

The basis assets are used for the construction of portfolios in the nth economy, $\{z_j\}_{j=0}^m$. This is without loss of generality, since the redundant assets can be priced using value additivity as implied by the no arbitrage opportunity assumption 18.7. The consumer is endowed with shares of these basis assets $\{\overline{N}_0^i, \ldots, \overline{N}_m^i\}$, where $\overline{N}_j^i$ represents the number of shares of basis asset j held by individual i. We assume that $\Sigma_{i \epsilon I} \overline{N}_j^i > 0$ for $j = 1, \ldots, m$, i.e., the total supply of asset j shares outstanding is positive.

To convert dollars into units of the consumption good there is a price level at time 0, $\rho_0 > 0$, and a price level at time 1 under each state $\omega \epsilon \Omega$, $\rho_1(\omega) > 0$.

Given this structure, as developed in Chap. 14, the consumer's decision problem is to choose

$$\{C_0, N_0, \ldots, N_m\} \quad \text{to maximize}$$

$$E(V^i(C_0, C_1)) \quad \text{subject to} \tag{18.4a}$$

$$\overline{C}_0^i + \sum_{j=0}^m \overline{N}_j^i p(z_j)/\rho_0 = C_0 + \sum_{j=0}^m N_j p(z_j)/\rho_0 \tag{18.4b}$$

$$\overline{C}_1^i(\omega) + \sum_{j=0}^m N_j z_j(\omega)/\rho_1(\omega) = C_1(\omega) \quad \text{for all } \omega \epsilon \Omega \tag{18.4c}$$

The utility function $V^i(C_0, C_1)$ is assumed to satisfy assumptions 14.1–14.4 of Chap. 14:

Assumption 18.10: Monotonicity

Given $\delta > 0$, C_0 and C_1, $V^i(C_0, + \delta, C_1) > V^i(C_0, C_1)$ and $V^i(C_0, C_1 + \delta) > V^i(C_0, C_1)$. This is true for all investors.

Assumption 18.11: Existence of an Optimal Distribution for Consumption

For all investors, there exists an optimal solution to the decision problem (18.4).

Assumption 18.12: Regularity of $E(V'(C_0, C_1))$

For all investors

(a) $V^i(C_0, C_1)$ has continuous second-order partial derivatives, and
(b) differentiation (up to the second order) under the expectation operator is a valid operation.

Assumption 18.13: Concavity of V

For all investors, $V^i(C_0, C_1)$ is strictly concave.

This last assumption implies that all investors are risk averse. Given assumptions 18.10–18.13, by theorems 14.2 and 14.4 of Chap. 14, we know there exists a unique solution to the investor's decision problem given by condition 18.4. This solution can be characterized using calculus. Before proceeding to this analysis, however, we add one additional assumption.

Assumption 18.14: Uniformly Bounded Risk Aversion

For all investors, there exists a constant ψ^i, independent of the economy n, such that

$$-\frac{\dfrac{\partial^2 V^i(C_0^i, \alpha)}{\partial C_1^2}}{E\left(\dfrac{\partial V^i(C_0^i, C_1^i)}{\partial C_1}\right)} \le \psi^i \tag{18.5}$$

for all $\alpha \in \mathbb{R}$, where

$$C_0^i = \overline{C}_0^i + \sum_{j=0}^m \overline{N}_j^i\, p(z_j)/\rho_0 - \sum_{j=0}^m N_j^i\, p(z_j)/\rho_0$$

and $(C_0^i, N_0^i, \ldots, N_0^i)$ are the optimal solutions to the decision problem (18.4).

In utility theory (Chap. 14), we know that a local measure of the ith investor's risk aversion is

$$-\frac{E\left(\dfrac{\partial^2 V^i(C_0^i, C_1^i)}{\partial C_1^2}\right)}{E\left(\dfrac{\partial V^i(C_0^i, C_1^i)}{\partial C_1}\right)}$$

(see theorem 14.1). Hence condition (18.5) implies that the investor's risk aversion is uniformly bounded by a constant ψ^i, which is independent of the particular economy n.

This assumption is included so that as the sequence of market economies changes, the investors do not become more and more risk averse. To see why this condition is important, suppose the contrary. That is, as the sequence of economies increases, suppose that investors become more risk averse. If the number of basis assets also approaches infinity, we know that in a large portfolio the residual return's risk can be diversified away. But although the residual risk is more diversifiable in an absolute sense, it need not be relative to an investor's preferences. Investor preferences can change faster than the risk can be diversified, so that the investor always considers a large portfolio to contain significant residual risk. In this case, the residual expected return will always exceed the risk-free rate and the APT approximation result will not occur.[3] Assumption 18.15 excludes this possibility.

In order to make real returns proportional to nominal returns, we assume that the inflation rate is a known quantity.

Assumption 18.15: Constant Inflation

$$\rho_1(\omega) = \rho_1 > 0 \quad \text{for all } \omega \in \Omega$$

The model's results can be restated without this assumption. To obtain this alternate model, set the price levels $\rho_0 = \rho_1 = 1$, and interpret all cash flows as denominated in units of the consumption good. Under this interpretation, dollars never enter the analysis. The subsequent analysis proceeds unchanged with this alternate interpretation.

18.2. CHARACTERIZING THE OPTIMAL CONSUMPTION AND INVESTMENT DEMANDS

This section utilizes Lagrangian multiplier techniques to characterize the optimal consumption and investment demands of an arbitrary consumer. To do this, we need some additional notation. Define the *inflation rate* at time 1 for a given state $\omega \in \Omega$ as

$$\Pi(\omega) = [\rho_1(\omega) - \rho_0]/\rho_0 \tag{18.6}$$

By the constant inflation assumption 18.15, this is a constant.

Next, define the *real return* on asset $x \in M$ by

$$R(x) = [1 + r(x)]/[1 + \Pi] - 1 \tag{18.7}$$

The real return on asset x is a random variable mapping M^n into state contingent returns. Formally, we should subscript the real return by n; however, to simplify the notation, we will omit this dependence.

Theorem 18.1: Optimal Consumption and Investment Demands

Given assumptions 18.1–18.15, $(C_0^i, C_1^i, N_0^i(m), \ldots, N_m^i(m))$ are optimal demands if and only if they are the solutions to

---

[3] For a detailed example of preferences becoming risk averse faster than the diversifiability of residual risk, see Ross [5, p. 345].

$$E\left(\frac{\partial V^i(C_0^i, C_1^i)}{\partial C_1}(r(z_j) - r(x_\Omega))/(1 + \Pi)\right) = 0$$

$$\text{for } j = 1, \ldots, m \qquad (18.8a)$$

$$\frac{E\left(\dfrac{\partial V^i(C_0^i, C_1^i)}{\partial C_1} \cdot \dfrac{1}{1 + \Pi}\right)}{E\left(\dfrac{\partial V^i(C_0^i, C_1^i)}{\partial C_0}\right)} = \frac{1}{[1 + r(x_\Omega)]} \qquad (18.8b)$$

$$\overline{C}_0^i + \sum_{j=0}^{m} \overline{N}_j^i p(z_j)/\rho_0 = C_0^i + \sum_{j=0}^{m} N_j^i(m)p(z_j)/\rho_0 \qquad (18.8c)$$

$$C_1^i(\omega) = \overline{C}_1^i + \sum_{j=0}^{m} N_j^i(m)z_j(\omega)/\rho_1(\omega) \quad \text{for all } \omega \in \Omega \qquad (18.8d)$$

Proof

See Sec. 18.7. ☐

This theorem characterizes the optimal consumption and portfolio decisions of the ith consumer as the implicit solution to a system of equations. The system of equations is conditions (18.8a)–(18d). Expression (18.8a) states that for asset j, the marginal change in the optimal utility level from investing one more dollar in asset j and financing it with one additional dollar of borrowing at the riskless rate is zero.[4] If the marginal change were positive, utility could be increased by making the revision. If the marginal change were negative, reversing the strategy would create a utility-increasing revision. Either of these possibilities contradicts (C_0^i, C_1^i) being optimal. Condition (18.8a) holds for all risky assets $j = 1, \ldots, m$.

Condition (18.8b) says that, at the optimum, the marginal change in utility from increasing time 0 consumption by one more unit and financing this change

[4]This statement says that

$$\left.\frac{\partial E(V^i(C_0^i, C_1^i(\epsilon)))}{\partial \epsilon}\right|_{\epsilon = 0} = 0 \quad \text{where}$$

$$C_1^i(\epsilon) = C_1^i + \frac{\epsilon(1 + r(z_j))}{(1 + \Pi)} - \frac{\epsilon(1 + r(x_\Omega))}{(1 + \Pi)} \quad \text{where } z_0 = x_\Omega$$

This represents the portfolio

$$N_k^i(\epsilon) = \begin{cases} N_k^i(m) & \text{for } k \neq j \\ N_j^i(m) + \epsilon\rho_0/p(z_j) & \text{for } k = j \\ N_0^i(m) - \epsilon\rho_0/p(z_0) & \text{for } k = 0 \end{cases}$$

by decreasing time 1 consumption through borrowing at the riskless rate is zero.[5] If the marginal change were positive, utility could be increased by making the revision. If the marginal change were negative, reversing the strategy would create a utility-increasing revision. Either of these possibilities contradicts (C_0^i, C_1^i) being optimal. This condition equates the marginal trade-off between consumption today and consumption tomorrow. Finally, condition (18.8c) is the time 0 budget constraint, while condition (18.8d) is the definition of the optimal time 1 consumption.

Note that the functional dependence of the asset demands on the particular market economy M^n is made explicit through the notation for asset shares demanded, $N_j^i(m)$. Recall that the number of basis assets m itself is a function of the sequence in the economy n such that as $n \rightarrow \infty$, m increases or stays constant. Given this theorem, we now investigate the concept of a competitive equilibrium.

18.3. COMPETITIVE EQUILIBRIUM

This section defines the meaning of a competitive equilibrium for the economy of Secs. 18.1 and 18.2. This notation generalizes the definition of a competitive equilibrium of Chap. 6 and it is analogous to the definition in Chap. 15.

Definition: Asset Market Equilibrium

An *asset market equilibrium* is a set of asset demands $\{N_0^i(m), \ldots, N_m^i(m)\}$ for all investors $i \in I$ and asset prices $\{p(z_0), \ldots, p(z_m)\}$ such that

(i) $N_j^i(m)$ for $j = 0, \ldots, m$ satisfy conditions (18.8a) and (18.8c), and

(ii) $\sum_{i \in I} \overline{N}_j^i = \sum_{i \in I} N_j^i(m)$ for $j = 0, \ldots, m$

[5]This statement says that

$$\left. \frac{\partial E(V^i(C_0^i(\epsilon), C_1^i(\epsilon)))}{\partial \epsilon} \right|_{\epsilon = 0} = 0 \quad \text{where}$$

$$C_0^i(\epsilon) = C_0^i + \epsilon \quad \text{and}$$

$$C_1^i(\epsilon) = C_1^i - \epsilon(1 + R(x_\Omega))$$

This represents $C_0^i + \epsilon$ in time 0 consumption and a portfolio of

$$N_k^i(\epsilon) = \begin{cases} N_k^i & \text{for } k \neq 0 \\ N_0^i - \epsilon p_0/p(x_\Omega) & \text{for } k = 0 \end{cases}$$

The time 0 budget constraint is still satisfied.

A competitive equilibrium is defined to be a set of optimal asset demands, condition (i), and prices such that the aggregate supply of shares equals the aggregate demand, condition (ii). Condition (ii) contains $m + 1$ equations in the $m + 1$ unknowns $(p(z_0), \ldots, p(z_m))$. The solution yields the equilibrium prices. A detailed interpretation of a competitive equilibrium is given in Sec. 6.3 of Chap. 6.

We note that an asset market equilibrium implies a competitive equilibrium in the consumption goods market at times 0 and 1. This is a consequence of the Walras law, and it represents a generalization of theorem 6.3.

Theorem 18.2: Consumption Goods Market Equilibrium

If $\{N_0^i(m), \ldots, N_m^i(m)\}_{i \in I}, \{p(z_0), \ldots, p(z_m)\}$ is an asset market equilibrium, then

$$\text{(i)} \quad \sum_{i \in I} \overline{C}_0^i = \sum_{i \in I} C_0^i, \quad \text{and}$$

$$\text{(ii)} \quad \sum_{i \in I} \overline{C}_1^i + \sum_{i \in I} \left(\sum_{j=0}^{m} \overline{N}_j^i z_j / \rho_1 \right) = \sum_{i \in I} C_1^i$$

where C_0^i and C_1^i satisfy conditions (18.8b) and (18.8d).

Proof

By the time 0 budget constraint (18.4b), we have

$$\overline{C}_0^i + \sum_{j=0}^{m} \overline{N}_j^i p(z_j) / \rho_0 = C_0^i + \sum_{j=0}^{m} N_j^i(m) p(z_j) / \rho_0$$

Summing across all investors and rearranging terms give

$$\sum_{i \in I} \overline{C}_0^i - \sum_{i \in I} C_0^i = \sum_{i \in I} \sum_{j=0}^{m} N_j^i(m) p(z_j) / \rho_0 - \sum_{i \in I} \sum_{j=0}^{m} \overline{N}_j^i p(z_j) / \rho_0$$

$$\sum_{i \in I} \overline{C}_0^i - \sum_{i \in I} C_0^i = \sum_{j=0}^{m} p(z_j) \left[\sum_{i \in I} N_j^i(m) - \sum_{i \in I} \overline{N}_j^i \right] / \rho_0$$

By the definition of an asset market equilibrium, the second term is zero—hence we get condition (i).

The condition for consumption at time 1 follows from (18.4c) in an analogous manner.   □

Before proceeding to Sec. 18.4, we need to ensure that an asset market equilibrium exists for the previous economy. The additional assumptions necessary for the existence of an asset market equilibrium can be found in Hart [4]. A complete discussion of these conditions and their subtleties is outside the scope of this text. For our purposes, the following assumption will suffice.

Assumption 18.16: Existence of an Asset Market Equilibrium

An asset market equilibrium exists for the previous economy.

18.4. THEOREMS

This section presents four theorems that characterize investor demands and approximate the risk-return trade-off in equilibrium. The first theorem shows that, in equilibrium, every investor holds a portfolio containing *all* the traded basis assets $j = 1, \ldots, m$; i.e., investors hold *diversified* portfolios.

Theorem 18.3: Diversification

Under assumptions 18.1–18.16, for each n, given that $\{N_0^i(m), \ldots, N_m^i(m)\}_{i \in I}$ and $(p(z_0), \ldots, p(z_m))$ is an asset market equilibrium, $N_j^i(m) > 0$ for all assets $j = 1, \ldots, m$ and all investors i.

Proof

See Sec. 18.7. □

This theorem provides an implication for investor portfolio behavior. In equilibrium, an arbitrary investor will hold every basis asset. The optimal portfolio is said to be diversified. Yet differences in portfolio choice across investors still exist. The absolute magnitudes of the assets held by different investors are not identical in the above model. These differences in portfolio composition persist due to differences in preferences. This contrasts with the CAPM in Chap. 15, where, in equilibrium, by the mean-variance assumption all investors hold some combination of the market portfolio and the riskless asset. Portfolio choice in the CAPM is therefore more restricted than in the APT.

The next theorem gives a bound on the risk-return trade-off in equilibrium. To motivate this theorem, recall the linear factor hypothesis assumption 18.9. This assumption states that

$$r(x_j) = r(x_\Omega) + \sum_{k=1}^{K} \lambda_{jk}(f_k - r(x_\Omega))$$

$$+ \lambda_{j,K+j}(u_j - r(x_\Omega)) \quad \text{for } j = 1, \ldots, n \qquad (18.9a)$$

Taking expectations, we have

$$E(r(x_j)) = r(x_\Omega) + \sum_{k=1}^{K} \lambda_{jk}(Ef_k - r(x_\Omega))$$

$$+ \lambda_{j,K+j}(Eu_j - r(x_\Omega)) \quad \text{for all } j \qquad (18.9b)$$

Since all investors hold a diversified portfolio (theorem 18.3), and the residual returns u_j are statistically independent, one might expect that due to the ability to diversify, the excess expected return on the residual component, $E(\lambda_{j,K+j}(u_j - r(x_\Omega)))$, should be approximately zero. Unfortunately, this need not be true in general. The next two theorems provide insights into these issues.

First, recall the definition of the *risky asset market portfolio*. It is the portfolio with weights

$$\text{mkt}_j(m) = \frac{\sum_{i \in I} \bar{N}^i_j p(z_j)/\rho_0}{\sum_{j=1}^{m} \left(\sum_{i \in I} \bar{N}^i_j p(z_j)/\rho_0 \right)}$$

where $0 < \text{mkt}_j(m) < 1$ for $j = 1, \ldots, m$ and $\sum_{j=1}^{m} \text{mkt}_j(m) = 1$.

The market portfolio consists of all risky basis assets in proportion to the percentage of the total market value their value represents. We can now state the theorem.

Theorem 18.4: Bounds on the Residual Excess Expected Return

Under assumptions 18.1–18.16, given that for each economy n, $\{N^i_0(m), \ldots, N^i_m(m)\}_{i \in I}$ and $(p(z_0), \ldots, p(z_m))$ is an asset market equilibrium, then

$$0 < |\lambda_{j,K+j}E(u_j - r(x_\Omega))| \leq \phi(\text{mkt}_{j+K}(m))/|\lambda_{j,K+j}|$$

$$\text{for } j = 1, \ldots, (m - K)$$

where ϕ is a constant.

Proof

See Sec. 18.7.   □

This theorem implies two results. First, the excess expected return on the residual component is *nonzero*. This is true for *all* assets along any particular economy on the sequence. Second, the excess expected return on the residual component is bounded above by a constant, which is related to the market portfolio weight of the basis asset $j + K$. The index starts with $K + 1$ since the $(K + 1)$st basis asset corresponds to the first residual return [see expression (18.2)]. This bound provides the final step in the derivation of the next theorem. Recall that, by construction, as the number of assets in the economy n increases, m is a nondecreasing function of n.

Theorem 18.5: The Equilibrium Version of the APT

Under assumptions 18.1–18.16, for each economy n, given that $\{N^i_0(m), \ldots, N^i_m(m)\}_{i \in I}$ and $(p(z_0), \ldots, p(z_m))$ is an asset market equilibrium

$$\text{if} \quad \lim_{n \to \infty} \text{mkt}_j(m) = 0 \quad \text{for } j = K + 1, \ldots, \infty$$

$$\text{then} \quad \lim_{n \to \infty} |\lambda_{j,K+j} E(u_j - r(x_\Omega))| = 0 \quad \text{for } j = 1, \ldots, \infty$$

Proof

Direct application of theorem 18.4. Note that by assumption 18.9, $\lambda_{j,K+j}$ is independent of n. $\quad \square$

This theorem provides the main implication of the equilibrium version of the APT. It is true both for a limit economy with a finite number of basis assets and a limit economy with an infinite number of basis assets. Of course, the power of the theorem is for the case of an infinite number of basis assets. Recall that the basis assets $\{z_1, \ldots, z_K\}$ represent the factors and $\{z_{K+1}, \ldots\}$ represent the residual returns. This explains why the condition in the theorem is only for the basis assets $j = K + 1, \ldots, \infty$. The basis assets $j = K + 1, \ldots, \infty$ are indexed $\{u_{j-K}\}$ and they are in one-to-one correspondence with the primary assets $\{x_j\}$; see expression (18.3).

Using expression (18.9b), the result of theorem 18.5 can be rewritten as

$$\text{if} \quad \lim_{n \to \infty} \text{mkt}_j(m) = 0 \quad \text{for } j = K + 1, \ldots$$

$$\text{then} \quad \lim_{n \to \infty} \left| E(r(x_j)) - r(x_\Omega) - \sum_{k=1}^{K} \lambda_{jk}(Ef_k - r(x_\Omega)) \right| = 0 \quad \text{for all } j \quad (18.10)$$

In words, if the jth basis asset composes an insignificant part of the market portfolio ($\text{mkt}_j(m) \approx 0$), then its residual risk is "diversifiable" and it receives approximately zero excess expected return in equilibrium. For every primary asset j, therefore

$$E(r(x_j)) \approx \left(r(x_\Omega) + \sum_{k=1}^{K} \lambda_{jk}(Ef_k - r(x_\Omega)) \right) \quad (18.11)$$

If the market weight of the basis asset corresponding to the primary asset j satisfies $\text{mkt}_{j+K}(m) \geq \epsilon > 0$ for some positive constant ϵ, then the above limiting argument will not work. Since by theorem 18.3 this asset must be held, in equilibrium, one would expect the asset's residual excess expected return to be nonzero. This is true because the residual risk cannot be diversified away. A partial result in this direction is given by the following converse of theorem 18.5.

Theorem 18.6: Partial Converse of Theorem 18.5

Under the hypothesis of theorem 18.5

$$\text{if} \quad \lim_{n \to \infty} |\lambda_{j,K+j}(E(u_j - r(x_\Omega)))| = 0 \quad \text{for } j = 1, \ldots, \infty$$

$$\lim_{n \to \infty} E\left(\sum_{j=1}^{m} \text{mkt}_j(m)r(z_j) - r(x_\Omega) \right) \Bigg/ \text{var}\left(\sum_{j=1}^{m} \text{mkt}_j(m)r(z_j) \right) > 0$$

and the returns z_j are normally distributed

$$\text{then} \quad \lim_{n \to \infty} \text{mkt}_j(m) = 0 \quad \text{for } j = K + 1, \ldots, \infty$$

Proof

See Sec. 18.7. $\square$

This theorem states that if the jth asset's residual expected excess return is approximately zero, i.e.

$$\lambda_{j,K+j} E(u_j - r(x_\Omega)) \approx 0$$

the market excess expected return per unit variance is nonzero, and returns are normally distributed, then the jth basis asset is an insignificant part of the market portfolio, i.e., $\text{mkt}_j(m) \approx 0$. In summary, if the market portfolio weight for the jth basis asset, $\text{mkt}_j(m) \neq 0$, then the excess expected return on the jth residual is nonzero,

$$\lambda_{j,K+j} E(u_j - r(x_\Omega)) \neq 0$$

This theorem will be referred to again in the next section.

18.5. COMPARISON OF THE APT TO THE CAPM

Given the results of the preceding section, we are now in a position to compare the CAPM of Chap. 15 to the equilibrium version of Ross's APT. The two models are very similar. Both models utilize the market structure and preference assumptions 18.1–18.8 and 18.10–18.13. The CAPM utilizes the mean-variance assumption 15.13, while the APT replaces this with the linear factor hypothesis, assumption 18.9, and uniformly bounded risk aversion, assumption 18.14. These differing assumptions are not inconsistent. Both sets can hold simultaneously. The differing assumptions provide alternative approaches to attaining an equilibrium restriction on an asset's excess expected return.

If we assume (for the sake of argument) that the three assumptions 15.13, 18.9, and 18.14 hold simultaneously, then we can write an asset's expected return in two ways:

$$E(r(x_j)) \approx r(x_\Omega) + \sum_{k=1}^{K} \lambda_{jk}(Ef_k - r(x_\Omega)) \quad \text{and}$$

$$E(r(x_j)) = r(x_\Omega) + \beta_j \left(E\left(\sum_{k=1}^{m} \text{mkt}_j(m)z_j \right) - r(x_\Omega) \right)$$

where

$$\beta_j = \text{cov}\left(\sum_{k=1}^{m} \text{mkt}_j(m)z_j, x_j \right) \Big/ \text{var}\left(\sum_{k=1}^{m} \text{mkt}_j(m)z_j \right)$$

Both models provide different characterizations of an asset's expected return. By theorems 18.5 and 18.6, we know that the APT and CAPM hold if and only if

$\text{mkt}_j(m) \approx 0$ for the basis assets $K + 1, \ldots, \infty$; i.e., the market portfolio's proportion due to the residual asset's component is insignificantly different from zero.

18.6. COMPARISON OF THE APT TO THE EQUILIBRIUM VERSION OF ROSS'S APT

The equilibrium version of the APT extends the APT of Chap. 9 by adding additional restrictions on beliefs (assumptions 18.3, 18.9), preferences (assumptions 18.10–18.14), and an equilibrium concept (assumption 18.16). To the extent that they are not reasonable approximations to the actual economy, this additional structure limits the applicability of the model.

The major implication of the APT of Chap. 9 is that

$$\lim_{n \to \infty} \sum_{j=1}^{n} (\lambda_{j,K+j} E_i(u_j - r(x_\Omega)))^2 < +\infty \quad \text{for all } i \text{ investors} \quad (18.12)$$

while the major implication of this chapter's model is that

$$\lim_{n \to \infty} |\lambda_{j,K+j} E(u_j - r(x_\Omega))| = 0 \quad \text{for all } j \quad (18.13)$$

The latter result holds *uniformly* across all assets, while condition (18.12) holds only on *average*. Hence, in this sense, the APT condition (18.12) is a weaker result. There is a second difference as well. Condition (18.12) allows beliefs to differ across investors, while in condition (18.13) they must be identical.

In terms of testability, the models differ. To test the APT condition (18.12), one needs to test the hypothesis that

$$1 \Big/ \sum_{j=1}^{n} (\lambda_{j,K+j} E_i(u_j - r(x_\Omega)))^2 \approx 0 \quad \text{for } \textit{large } n$$

If we reject this hypothesis, we accept the model. To test the equilibrium APT condition (18.13), one needs to test the hypothesis that

$$\lambda_{j,K+j} E(u_j - r(x_\Omega)) \approx 0 \quad \text{for } \textit{all assets } j = 1, \ldots, \infty$$

If we reject the hypothesis, we reject the model. To make a precise test of condition (18.13), just as with condition (18.12), we must examine all assets $j = 1, \ldots, \infty$, an infinite number. Obviously this is an impossible task.

Yet, the equilibrium version of the APT has a finite asset economy analogue, as represented by theorem 18.4. The upper bound in this theorem is (in theory) potentially testable, providing a uniform bound for a *finite* number of assets. Evidence consistent with theorem 18.4 would support the finite asset equilibrium version of the APT.

The empirical validity of these models is still an unanswered question. The evidence is inconclusive because numerous statistical problems plague the literature. See Sec. 18.9 for suggested references.

18.7. PROOFS OF THE THEOREMS

Proof of Theorem 18.1

First, set up the Lagrangian based on condition (18.4)

$$L(C_0, C_1) = E\left(V^i\left(C_0^i, \overline{C}_1^i + \sum_{j=0}^{m} N_j z_j / \rho_1\right)\right)$$

$$+ \delta\left(\overline{C}_0^i + \sum_{j=0}^{m} \overline{N}_j^i p(z_j)/\rho_0 - C_0 - \sum_{j=0}^{m} N_j p(z_j)/\rho_0\right)$$

where δ is the Lagrangian multiplier.

Necessary and sufficient conditions for the optimum C_0^i, N_j^i for $j = 0, \ldots, m$ are

$$\frac{\partial L(C_0^i, C_1^i)}{\partial C_0} = 0 \qquad (18.14a)$$

$$\frac{\partial L(C_0^i, C_1^i)}{\partial N_j^i} = 0 \quad \text{for } j = 0, \ldots, m \qquad (18.14b)$$

$$\frac{\partial L(C_0^i, C_1^i)}{\partial \delta} = 0 \qquad (18.14c)$$

Performing the partial differentiation yields

$$E\left(\frac{\partial V^i(C_0^i, C_1^i)}{\partial C_0}\right) - \delta = 0 \qquad (18.15a)$$

$$E\left(\frac{\partial V^i(C_0^i, C_1^i)}{\partial C_1} z_j / \rho_1\right) - \delta p(z_j)/\rho_0 = 0 \quad \text{for } j = 0, \ldots, m \qquad (18.15b)$$

$$\overline{C}_0^i + \sum_{j=0}^{m} \overline{N}_j^i p(z_j)/\rho_0 - C_0^i - \sum_{j=0}^{m} N_j^i(m) p(z_j)/\rho_0 = 0 \qquad (18.15c)$$

In condition (18.15b), for $j = 0$ solve for δ to get

$$\delta = E\left(\frac{\partial V^i(C_0^i, C_1^i)}{\partial C_1} \frac{(1 + r(z_0))}{(1 + \Pi)}\right) \qquad (18.15d)$$

Substitution of (18.15d) into (18.15a) gives

$$E\left(\frac{\partial V^i(C_0^i, C_1^i)}{\partial C_0}\right) - E\left(\frac{\partial V^i(C_0^i, C_1^i)}{\partial C_1} \frac{(1 + r(x_\Omega))}{(1 + \Pi)}\right) = 0$$

which directly implies (18.8b). Substitution of (18.15d) into (18.15b) gives

$$E\left(\frac{\partial V^i(C_0^i, C_1^i)}{\partial C_1} z_j / \rho_1\right) - (p(z_j)/\rho_0) E\left(\frac{\partial V^i(C_0^i, C_1^i)}{\partial C_1} \frac{(1 + r(x_\Omega))}{(1 + \Pi)}\right) = 0$$

which, after some algebra, implies (18.8a). $\square$

Proof of Theorem 18.3

Condition (18.8a) is

$$E\left(\frac{\partial V^i(C_0^i, C_1^i)}{\partial C_1}(r(z_j) - r(x_\Omega))/(1 + \Pi)\right) = 0$$

Using the fact that $\text{cov}(x, y) = E(xy) - E(x)E(y)$, this transforms to

$$0 = E\left(\frac{\partial V^i(C_0^i, C_1^i)}{\partial C_1}\right)E(r(z_j) - r(x_\Omega))/(1 + \Pi)$$

$$+ \text{cov}\left(\frac{\partial V^i(C_0^i, C_1^i)}{\partial C_1}, (r(z_j) - r(x_\Omega))/(1 + \Pi)\right)$$

By monotonicity, $E(\partial V^i(C_0^i, C_1^i)/\partial C_1) > 0$, so

$$E[r(z_j) - r(x_\Omega)]/(1 + \Pi) = -\text{cov}\left(\frac{\frac{\partial V^i(C_0^i, C_1^i)}{\partial C_1}}{E\left(\frac{\partial V^i(C_0^i, C_1^i)}{\partial C_1}\right)}, \frac{r(z_j)}{(1 + \Pi)}\right) \quad (18.16)$$

This last expression uses the fact that $\text{cov}(x, \alpha) = 0$, where α is a constant to show that $\text{cov}(\partial V^i(C_0^i, C_1^i)/\partial C_1/E(\partial V^i(C_0^i, C_1^i)/\partial C_1), r(x_\Omega)/(1 + \Pi)) = 0$. Multiplying (18.16) by $(1 + \Pi) > 0$ and substituting in for C_1^i give

$$E(r(z_j) - r(x_\Omega)) = -\text{cov}\left(\frac{\frac{\partial V^i\left(C_0^i, \overline{C}_1^i + \sum_{k=1}^{m} N_k^i(m)z_k/\rho_1\right)}{\partial C_1}}{E\left(\frac{\partial V^i(C_0^i, C_1^i)}{\partial C_1}\right)}, r(z_j)\right) \quad (18.17)$$

Recall that

$$r(z_0) = r(x_\Omega)$$

$$r(z_j) = f_j \qquad \text{for } j = 1, \ldots, K$$

$$r(z_j) = u_{j-K} \quad \text{for } j = K + 1, \ldots, m$$

where f_j, u_k are statistically independent.

Now $r(z_j) = (z_j - p(z_j))/p(z_j)$; hence $z_j = p(z_j)(1 + r(z_j))$ and $r(z_K)$ are statistically independent for $k \neq j$. So, in (18.17), the covariance term is zero if $N_j^i(m) = 0$ since z_k for $k \neq j$ are statistically independent of z_j. If $N_j^i(m) > 0$, then since $(\partial^2 V^i/\partial C_1^2) < 0$ by risk aversion (assumption 18.14), the covariance term is strictly negative. Similarly, if $N_j^i(m) < 0$, then the covariance term is strictly positive. Summarizing:

if $N_j^i(m) = 0$, then $E(r(z_j) - r(x_\Omega)) = 0$,

if $N_j^i(m) > 0$, then $E(r(z_j) - r(x_\Omega)) > 0$, and

if $N_j^i(m) < 0$, then $E(r(z_j) - r(x_\Omega)) < 0$.

Given homogeneous beliefs, assumption 18.3, if $E(r(z_j) - r(x_\Omega)) = 0$ for some i, it is zero for all i. Hence $N_j^i(m) = 0$ for some i implies $N_j^i(m) = 0$ for all i. Similarly, $N_j^i(m) > 0$ for some i implies $N_j^i(m) > 0$ for all i.

Now, in equilibrium, $\Sigma_{i \epsilon I} \overline{N}_j^i(m) = \Sigma_{i \epsilon I} N_j^i(m)$. Since aggregate supply $\Sigma_{i \epsilon I} \overline{N}^i(m) > 0$, this implies that for some i, $N_j^i(m) > 0$. Therefore by the above assertion this must be true for all i. This completes the proof. $\square$

Proof of Theorem 18.4

First, consider $(\partial V^i(C_0^i, C_1^i)/\partial C_1)$. By a Taylor series expansion (Rudin [6, p. 110])

$$\frac{\partial V^i(C_0^i, C_1^i)}{\partial C_1} = \frac{\partial V^i(C_0^i, x)}{\partial C_1} + \frac{\partial^2 V^i}{\partial C_1^2}(C_0^i, y)N_j^i(m)z_j/\rho_1$$

where

$$x(\omega) = \overline{C}_1^i + \sum_{\substack{k=0 \\ k \neq j}}^{m} N_k^i(m)z_k(\omega)/\rho_1$$

and

$$y(\omega) \epsilon [x(\omega), x(\omega) + N_j^i(m)z_j(\omega)/\rho_1] \quad \text{for all } \omega \epsilon \Omega$$

or

$$\frac{\partial V^i(C_0^i, C_1^i)}{\partial C_1} = \frac{\partial V^i(C_0^i, x)}{\partial C_1} + \frac{\partial^2 V^i(C_0^i, y)}{\partial C_1^2}[N_j^i(m)p(z_j)/\rho_0]\frac{(1 + r(z_j))}{(1 + \Pi)}$$

Substitution into (18.17) gives

$$E(r(z_j) - r(x_\Omega)) = -\text{cov}\left(\frac{\dfrac{\partial V^i(C_0^i, x)}{\partial C_1}}{E\left(\dfrac{\partial V^i(C_0^i, C_1^i)}{\partial C_1}\right)}\right.$$

$$\left. + \frac{\dfrac{\partial^2 V^i(C_0^i, y)}{\partial C_1^2}}{E\left(\dfrac{\partial V^i(C_0^i, C_1^i)}{\partial C_1}\right)}[N_j^i(m)p(z_j)/\rho_0]\frac{(1 + r(z_j))}{(1 + \Pi)}, r(z_j)\right) \quad (18.18)$$

But $\text{cov}((\partial V^i(C_0^i, x)/\partial C_1), r(z_j)) = 0$ since x is statistically independent of $r(z_j)$. Also, $-(\partial^2 V^i(C_0^i, y)/\partial C^2)/(E(\partial V^i(C_0^i, C_1^i)/\partial C_1)) \leq \psi^i$ by assumption 18.15. These observations change (18.18) to

$$E(r(z_j) - r(x_\Omega)) \leq \psi^i\frac{N_j^i(m)p(z_j)/\rho_0}{(1 + \Pi)} \text{ cov }(r(z_j), r(z_j))$$

Recall that $r(z_j) = u_{j-K}$ for $j = K + 1, \ldots, m$. Premultiply by $|\lambda_{j,K+j}|$ to get

$$E(|\lambda_{j,K+j}|(u_j - r(x_\Omega))) < \psi^i\left(\frac{N_j^i(m)p(z_j)/\rho_0}{(1 + \Pi)}\right)\left(\frac{\text{var}(\lambda_{j,K+j}u_j)}{|\lambda_{j,K+j}|}\right)$$

By assumption 18.9 we have var $(\lambda_{j,K+j}u_j) \leq \bar{\sigma}^2$, so define

$$\phi \equiv \frac{\bar{\sigma}^2}{1 + \Pi} \max_{i \in I}\left[\psi^i \sum_{j=1}^{m} N_j^i(m)p\,(z_j)/\rho_0\right]$$

then

$$E(|\lambda_{j,K+j}|(u_j - r(x_\Omega))) \leq \frac{\phi}{|\lambda_{j,K+j}|}\left[\frac{N_j^i(m)p\,(z_j)/\rho_0}{\sum\limits_{j=1}^{m} N_j^i(m)p\,(z_j)/\rho_0}\right]$$

Multiply both sides by $\sum_{j=1}^{m} N_j^i(m)p\,(z_j)/\rho_0$ and sum over all investors i to get

$$\left[\sum_{i \in I}\sum_{j=1}^{m} N_j^i(m)p\,(z_j)/\rho_0\right]E(|\lambda_{j,K+j}|(u_j - r(x_\Omega))) \leq \frac{\phi}{|\lambda_{j,K+j}|}\sum_{i \in I} N_j^i(m)p\,(z_j)/\rho_0$$

Divide by $[\sum_{i \in I}\sum_{j=1}^{m} N_j^i(m)p\,(z_j)/\rho_0]$, to get

$$E(|\lambda_{j,K+j}|(u_j - r(x_\Omega))) \leq \frac{\phi}{|\lambda_{j,K+j}|}\frac{\left(\sum\limits_{i \in I} N_j^i(m)\right)p\,(z_j)/\rho_0}{\sum\limits_{j=1}^{m}\left(\sum\limits_{i \in I} N_j^i(m)\right)p\,(z_j)/\rho_0}$$

Substituting in the definition of an equilibrium gives the right-hand side of theorem 18.4.

In the proof of theorem 18.3 we show that

$$E(u_j - r(x_\Omega)) > 0$$

Premultiply by $|\lambda_{j,K+j}|$ to get

$$0 < |E(\lambda_{j,K+j}(u_j - r(x_\Omega)))|$$

This gives the left-hand side of theorem 18.4 and completes the proof. □

Proof of Theorem 18.6

Suppose $\lim_{n \to \infty} \mathrm{mkt}_j\,(m) \neq 0$ for some $j \geq K + 1$. Then there exists an $\epsilon > 0$ such that $\lim_{n \to \infty} \inf \mathrm{mkt}_j\,(m) = \epsilon > 0$. Hence there exists $\alpha > 0$ such that $\mathrm{mkt}_j\,(m) \geq \epsilon/2$ for all $n \geq \alpha$. So $\mathrm{cov}(u_j, \sum_{j=1}^{m} \mathrm{mkt}_j\,(m)r(z_j)) \geq [\epsilon/2]^2$ $\mathrm{var}(u_j) > 0$ for $n \geq \alpha$. This uses the statistical independence of z_j for $j = 1,$ ..., m.

If all returns are normally distributed (which is consistent with assumptions 18.1–18.16), then assumptions 18.1–18.16 generate the CAPM for any n, so

$$E(u_j) = r(x_\Omega) + \frac{\mathrm{cov}\left(u_j, \sum\limits_{j=1}^{m} \mathrm{mkt}_j\,(m)r(z_j)\right)}{\mathrm{var}\left(\sum\limits_{j=1}^{m} \mathrm{mkt}_j\,(m)r(z_j)\right)}E\left(\sum_{j=1}^{m} \mathrm{mkt}_j\,(m)r(z_j) - r(x_\Omega)\right)$$

$$\geq r(x_\Omega) + \left(\frac{\epsilon}{2}\right)^2 \text{Var}(u_j) \left(\frac{E\left(\sum_{j=1}^{m} \text{mkt}_j(m)r(z_j) - r(x_\Omega)\right)}{\text{var}\left(\sum_{j=1}^{m} \text{mkt}_j(m)r(z_j)\right)} \right)$$

$$> r(x_\Omega) \text{ for all } n \geq \alpha$$

This contradicts $\lim_{n\to\infty} |\lambda_{j,K+j}| |E(u_j) - r(x_\Omega)| = 0.$ □

18.8. SUMMARY

This chapter uses equilibrium pricing to provide an equilibrium version of Ross's APT from Chap. 9. To obtain this equilibrium pricing version, additional restrictions on preferences and beliefs are required. These restrictions are embodied in assumptions 18.3, 18.9, and 18.10–18.14. The additional restrictions give stronger implications about investor portfolio behavior and prices. With respect to portfolio behavior, we obtain a diversification theorem 18.3, which states that, in equilibrium, all investors hold all risky assets. With respect to prices, we obtain theorem 18.5, which states that the residual excess expected return is approximately zero, *uniformly* across all assets. This result differs from theorem 9.1, which states that this same result holds only on *average*.

18.9. REFERENCES

1. Conner, Gregory, "A Unified Beta Pricing Theory," *Journal of Economic Theory*, 34 (1984), 13–31.
2. Dybvig, P., "An Explicit Bound on Individual Assets' Deviations from APT Pricing in a Finite Economy," *Journal of Financial Economics*, 12 (1983), 483–496.
3. Grinblatt, Mark, and Sheridan Titman, "Factor Pricing in a Finite Economy," *Journal of Financial Economics*, 12 (1983), 497–507.
4. Hart, Oliver, "On the Existence of Equilibrium in a Securities Model," *Journal of Economic Theory*, 9 (1974), 293–311.
5. Ross, Stephen, "The Arbitrage Theory of Capital Asset Pricing," *Journal of Economic Theory*, 13 (1976), 341–360.
6. Rudin, W., *Principles of Mathematical Analysis*, 3rd ed. New York: McGraw-Hill, 1976.

A partial listing of the references related to the testing of Ross's APT follows:

Brown, S., and M. Weinstein, "A New Approach to Testing Asset Pricing Models: The Bilinear Paradigm," *Journal of Finance*, 38 (1983), 711–743.

Chen, N., "Some Empirical Tests of the Theory of Arbitrage Pricing," *Journal of Finance*, 38 (1983), 1393–1414.

Dhrymes, Phoebus, Irwin Friend, and N. Bulent Gultekin, "A Critical Reexamination of the Empirical Evidence on the Arbitrage Pricing Theory," *Journal of Finance*, 39 (1984), 323–346.

Dyvbig, Philip, and Stephen Ross, "Yes. The APT Is Testable," *Journal of Finance* (September 1985), 1173–1188.

Roll, Richard, and Stephen Ross, "An Empirical Investigation of the Arbitrage Pricing Theory," *Journal of Finance,* 35 (1980), 1073–1103.

————, "A Critical Reexamination of the Empirical Evidence on the Arbitrage Pricing Theory: A Reply," *Journal of Finance,* 39 (1984), 347–350.

Shanken, Jay, "The Arbitrage Pricing Theory: Is it Testable?" *Journal of Finance,* 37 (1982), 1129–1140.

————, "Multi-beta CAPM or Equilibrium APT: A Reply," *Journal of Finance* (September 1985), 1189–1196.

19

MARKET EFFICIENCY

Up to this point, when examining equilibrium prices and allocations, we restricted ourselves to economies consisting of investors with homogeneous beliefs and homogeneous information sets. Trading strategies based on "insider" information were not considered, and only "consumption" or "liquidity" based trading takes place. This is the case with the capital asset pricing model (Chaps. 15, 16, and 17) and the equilibrium version of Ross's APT (Chap. 18). Market efficiency, on the other hand, is the study of equilibrium prices and allocations in economies consisting of investors with heterogeneous beliefs and heterogeneous information sets. In other words, market efficiency is the study of trading based on differential information. This is a broad area of research. Our focus will be limited to introducing the concept of an efficient market and understanding some of its implications. In particular, the concept of market efficiency will be related to the CAPM and the equilibrium version of the APT.

Introducing differential information into the previous economies necessitates the use of conditional expectations from probability theory. This is the only new mathematical concept employed beyond those of Chaps. 15 and 18. The basic ideas for the following material come from the microeconomics literature on various equilibrium concepts under differential information. In particular, the idea of a rational expectations equilibrium will play a key role in the subsequent analysis.

19.1. PRELIMINARIES

This chapter uses the economy presented in Chap. 14, on utility theory, with those modifications necessary to include heterogeneous beliefs and heterogeneous information sets into the analysis. An interesting twist with respect to the price functional is also needed. Modifications of the familiar assumptions will be isolated with a dagger and discussed in greater detail.

The economy has two dates, times 0 and 1. At time 1 the uncertainty in the economy is characterized by a state space Ω with an arbitrary state denoted by $\omega \in \Omega$. An asset x is identified by its dollar cash flows across all states ω at time 1, $x(\omega)$, where $x: \Omega \to \mathbb{R}$. The set of assets that trade at time 0 is denoted by M. We assume that the market is closed under composition of portfolios.

Assumption 19.I: Marketed Assets

If assets x, $y \in M$, then $\alpha x + \beta y \in M$ for all α, $\beta \in \mathbb{R}$.

The marketed assets generate a set of events, subsets of Ω, denoted by $\sigma(M)$. These represent those events that can be inferred using only knowledge of the assets' time 1 cash flows. The economy is populated by a finite number of investors whose beliefs satisfy the following assumption:

Assumption 19.2: Conditional Homogeneous Beliefs

Given $x \in M$, every investor agrees that $x(\omega)$ is the cash flow in dollars to asset x at time 1, given state ω occurs.

Investors in the economy enter at time 0 with probability beliefs $\text{Prob}_i(\cdot)$ defined over the event set $\sigma(M)$. Investors also enter the economy at time 0 with different information about the time 1 value of the traded assets. This different information can be attributed to different levels of research by the investors into the assets' fundamentals. We denote the information available to an investor i at time 0 by F_i. Since the events of concern at time 1 are $\sigma(M)$, we assume that F_i is a subset of $\sigma(M)$.[1] This limits investor information to signals about the assets' time 1 cash flows. This information could potentially be traded upon at time 0 to generate greater wealth at time 1. Formally, at time 0, the ith investor knows which event in F_i occurred. This knowledge gives the investor insights into the time 1 prices of the assets trading in M. We formalize this discussion with an assumption.

---

[1] F_i is a σ-algebra over Ω, and $F_i \subset \sigma(M)$ for all i.

Assumption 19.3: Differential Information[†]

At time 0, the ith investor has available the information set F_i, which is a subset of the event set $\sigma(M)$. Probability beliefs $\text{Prob}_i[\cdot]$ are defined over $\sigma(M)$.

An example will help to clarify this concept.

Example 1   Differential Information

The purpose of this example is to clarify how private information is modeled in the previous assumption. Consider the diagram below.

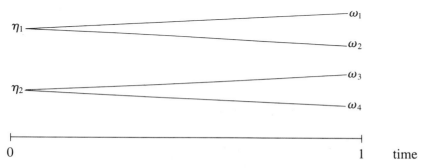

The state space at time 1, Ω, consists of four states, $\{\omega_1,\ \omega_2,\ \omega_3,\ \omega_4\}$. For simplicity, we assume that the market consists of a single traded asset, x, which has the following cash payoffs at time 1:

$$x(\omega) = \begin{cases} 1 & \text{if } \omega = \omega_1 \\ 2 & \text{if } \omega = \omega_2 \\ 3 & \text{if } \omega = \omega_3 \\ 4 & \text{if } \omega = \omega_4 \end{cases}$$

The highest cash flow to asset x occurs under state ω_4; the worst cash flow occurs under state ω_1. Since the cash flow to asset x at time 1 reveals the state, $\sigma(M)$ consists of the events $\{\omega_1\}$, $\{\omega_2\}$, $\{\omega_3\}$, $\{\omega_4\}$, and all unions and intersections of these sets. The investors' probability beliefs are defined over the event set $\sigma(M)$. Since there are only four "basic" events, the ith person's probability beliefs are completely specified by $\text{Prob}_i(\omega_j)$ for $j = 1,\ 2,\ 3,\ 4$.

The ith investor's private information is represented by assuming that he knows at time 0 whether the event η_1 or η_2 has occurred. This tells him at time 0 that either $\{\omega_1,\ \omega_2\}$ or $\{\omega_3,\ \omega_4\}$ will occur at time 1. This is valuable information, and he knows this at time 0. His information set F_i is therefore

$$F_i = \{\{\omega_1,\ \omega_2\},\ \{\omega_3,\ \omega_4\},\ \phi,\ \{\omega_1,\ \omega_2,\ \omega_3,\ \omega_4\}\}$$

When making decisions at time 0, the ith investor will condition his probability beliefs on the information contained in F_i. □

This example motivates our next assumption on probability beliefs.

Assumption 19.4: Heterogeneous Unconditional Beliefs[†]

Given $H \in \sigma(M)$, for a fixed $\omega \in \Omega$, $\text{Prob}_i(H|F_i)(\omega) = 0$ if and only if $\text{Prob}_j(H|F_j)(\omega) = 0$ for all i, j, where $\text{Prob}_i[\cdot|F_i](\omega)$ is the ith investor's conditional probability belief given the information set F_i.[2]

Given their information sets, investors agree on zero probability events. This is the conditional version of the standard unconditional beliefs assumption introduced in Chap. 8. For fixed $\omega \in \Omega$, the conditional probability distributions $\text{Prob}_i[\cdot|F_i](\omega)$ are still defined over the event set $\sigma(M)$, but they utilize the additional information contained in the private information sets F_i.

Assumption 19.5: Frictionless Markets

The asset market has no transaction costs, no taxes, and no restrictions on short sales, and asset shares are divisible.

Assumption 19.6: Competitive Markets

Every investor acts as a price taker.

At time 0 the prices of the assets are represented by a price functional. This time, however, we assume that this price functional is *random*; i.e., the price also depends on the state of nature ω through the mapping $p:M \times \Omega \to \mathbb{R}$. The price of asset $x \in M$ at time 0, given state $\omega \in \Omega$, is denoted $p(x, \omega)$.[3] The state enters the price at time 0 through the information sets F_i of the different investors. Given their differential information, and partial knowledge of the state $\omega \in \Omega$ at time 0, they will desire different portfolio holdings. This in turn will generate different time 0 prices through the trading process, making the price functional dependent on the state ω. This complication was not present in the previous equilibrium models.

---

[2]For fixed $\omega \in \Omega$, we assume that $\text{Prob}_j(\cdot|F_j)(\omega)$ is a regular probability, as defined in Breiman [1, p. 77].

[3]We assume that $p(x, \omega)$ is $\sigma(M)$ measurable.

The price functional $p(x, \omega)$ represents an aggregation or filtering of all the investors' private information sets, F_i for $i = 1, \ldots, I$. This filtering utilizes more information than any single investor may possess. If an investor is *sophisticated* in his understanding of the market process, he may be able to infer the functional form of $p(x, \omega)$—perhaps through repeated observations of the market price over time, or perhaps by understanding the equilibrium price mechanism well enough to perform the necessary calculations (using preferences, information sets, and so on to determine the equilibrium prices directly). In either case, observing prices at time 0 (before trading) will enable a sophisticated investor to infer additional information (above F_i) about asset cash flows at time 1. Prices are said to reflect information. If an investor is *naive*, and does not know the functional form $p(x, \omega)$, observing prices at time 0 will provide no additional information. We assume that all investors are sophisticated.

Assumption 19.7: Sophisticated Investors

Each investor knows the functional form $p(x, \omega)$ at time 0.

Assumption 19.8: No Finite Asset Arbitrage Opportunities

The asset market contains no arbitrage opportunities, as defined in Chap. 8, with the exception that all probability statements for the ith investor are based on $\mathrm{Prob}_i(\cdot \mid F_i)(\omega)$ for a fixed $\omega \in \Omega$.

For convenience, we add the following:

Assumption 19.9: Finite Asset Economy

The marketed assets M consist of $K + 1$ limited liability assets and all their portfolios, i.e., $M = \mathrm{span}\{x_0, \ldots, x_K\}$, where $x_j : \Omega \to \mathbb{R}$ for $j = 0, \ldots, K$, and the x_j are linearly independent.

We embed this model into the consumption-saving framework, as in Chap. 14, Sec. 14.1. Recall that there is a single consumption good available in both dates 0 and 1. The ith consumer enters the economy with an endowment consisting of units of the consumption good $(\overline{C}_0^i, \overline{C}_1^i(\omega))$ for all $\omega \in \Omega$ and an endowed portfolio $\{\overline{N}_0^i, \ldots, \overline{N}_K^i\}$. We assume that the endowed consumption at time 1 is constant at $\overline{C}_1^i(\omega) = \overline{C}_1^i$ for all $\omega \in \Omega$. To convert dollars into units of the consumption good there is an exogenous price level of $\rho_0 > 0$ at time 0 and $\rho_1(\omega) > 0$ for all $\omega \in \Omega$ at time 1.

Assumption 19.10: Certain Inflation

$$p_1(\omega) = p_1 \quad \text{for all } \omega \in \Omega$$

This assumption is equivalent to specifying all asset prices in units of the consumption good and excluding dollars from the analysis. This alternate interpretation follows by setting $p_0 = p_1 = 1$.

Given this structure, as demonstrated in Chap. 14, the consumer's decision problem is to choose

$$\{C_0, N_0, \ldots, N_K\}$$

to maximize

$$E^i[V^i(C_0, C_1) \mid F^i, p(x)](\omega) \tag{19.1a}$$

subject to

$$\overline{C}_0^i + \sum_{j=0}^{K} \overline{N}_j^i p(x_j, \omega)/p_0 = C_0 + \sum_{j=0}^{K} N_j^i p(x_j, \omega)/p_0 \tag{19.1b}$$

$$\overline{C}_1^i + \sum_{j=0}^{K} N_j x_j(\omega)/p_1 = C_1(\omega) \tag{19.1c}$$

for all $\omega \in \Omega$.

Note that the expectation operator over the investor's utility function is conditional upon the information set F_i and prices $p(x)$. This is due to the differential information assumption 19.3 and the sophisticated investor assumption 19.7.

The utility function $V^i(C_0, C_1)$ is assumed to satisfy assumptions 14.1, 14.2, and 14.3:

Assumption 19.11: Monotonicity

Given $\delta > 0$, C_0, C_1, then $V^i(C_0 + \delta, C_1) > V^i(C_0, C_1)$ and $V^i(C_0, C_1 + \delta) > V^i(C_0, C_1)$. This is true for all investors.

Assumption 19.12: Existence of an Optimal Distribution over Consumption

For all investors, for fixed $\omega \in \Omega$, there exists an optimal solution to the decision problem (19.1).

Assumption 19.13: Concavity of V

For all investors, $V^i(C_0, C_1)$ is strictly concave.

19.2. RATIONAL EXPECTATIONS EQUILIBRIUM

This section defines the concept of a competitive equilibrium for the economy of Sec. 19.1, where investors are sophisticated and use prices to infer information possessed by other investors. This is the concept of a *rational expectations equilibrium*.

To define a rational expectations equilibrium, we need to introduce some notation. For a fixed state $\omega \in \Omega$, let the solution to the decision problem (19.1) for the ith investor be $N_j^i(\omega, F_i, p(\cdot))$ for $j = 0, \ldots, K$. The notation indicates that the investor's optimal demand depends on the state $\omega \in \Omega$, his information set F_i, and the form of the price functional $p(\cdot)$.

Definition: Rational Expectations (RE) Asset Market Equilibrium

An *RE asset market equilibrium* is a set of asset demands $\{N_0^i(\omega, F_i, p(\cdot)),$ $\ldots, N_K^i(\omega, F_i, p(\cdot))\}$ for all investors $i = 1, \ldots, I$ and a price functional $p(x, \omega)$ defined for all $x \in M$ and $\omega \in \Omega$ such that for all $\omega \in \Omega$

(i) $N_0^i(\omega, F_i, p(\cdot))$ are the optimal solutions to the decision problem (19.1), and

(ii) $\sum_{i \in I} \overline{N}_j^i = \sum_{i \in I} N_j^i(\omega, F_i, p(\cdot))$ for $j = 0, \ldots, K$

The distinction between this definition of an equilibrium and that used in Chap. 15 is the conditioning with respect to private information and the price functional in the asset demands. By the sophisticated investor assumption 19.7, investors formulate a *conjecture* about the price functional, $p(\cdot, \omega)$, and condition their probability beliefs on it in the decision problem (19.1). An equilibrium occurs when the price functional investors' conjecture exists is actually true and it clears the market for all asset shares. The equilibrium price functional is said to confirm the investors' conjecture.

If the asset market is an RE equilibrium, the consumption goods market is also in equilibrium. The same proof as that used for theorem 15.3 can be used to validate the following theorem.

Theorem 19.1: Consumption Goods Market Equilibrium

If $\{N_0^i(\omega, F_i, p(\cdot)), \ldots, N_K^i(\omega, F_i, p(\cdot))\}_{i \in I}$, $p(x, \omega)$ for all $x \in M$, $\omega \in \Omega$ is a RE asset market equilibrium, then

$$\sum_{i \in I} \overline{C}_0^i = \sum_{i \in I} C_0^i$$

where C_0^i is the optimal solution to the decision problem (19.1).

The previous concept of an asset market equilibrium captures the notion of rationality in the asset markets. For the concept to be of any use, however, such a set of equilibrium demands and prices needs to exist for the economy under consideration. Extensive research has been devoted to examining sufficient conditions such that RE equilibrium exist. These conditions are reviewed in Jordan and Radner [4]. Given there are economies for which these RE equilibria exist, we are guaranteed the next assumption is not vacuous.

Assumption 19.14: Existence of an RE Asset Market Equilibrium

An RE asset market equilibrium exists for the previous economy.

19.3. THE DEFINITION OF MARKET EFFICIENCY

This section presents the definition of market efficiency with respect to an information set. We restrict ourselves to RE asset market equilibrium allocations when defining market efficiency. In an RE asset market equilibrium, the price functional $p(x, \omega)$ reveals information about the economy. The quality and extent of the information revealed by prices are what the concept of an efficient market attempts to characterize.

Definition: Market Efficiency with Respect to an Information Set ψ

The market is said to be *efficient with respect to the information set* ψ, which is a subset of $\sigma(M)$ if and only if given the RE asset market equilibrium price functional, $p(\cdot, \omega)$, the information set ψ satisfies $\psi \subset \{F_i \cup p(\cdot, \omega)\}$ for all i where $\{F_i \cup p(\cdot, \omega)\}$ represents the information set containing F_i and the information reflected by the price functional.[4]

Some observations are in order. Consider the information set $\psi = \cap_i F_i$, which represents the *common* information across all investors. This set is common because it includes those event sets that all investors agree upon at time 0—hence the intersection symbol. An RE asset market equilibrium price is by definition efficient with respect to this information since $\cap_i F_i \subset \{F_i \cup p(\cdot, \omega)\}$ for all i.

The largest information set for which the market can be efficient with respect to is the set $\{(\cap_i F_i) \cup p(\cdot, \omega)\}$. This set consists of the common knowledge information and the information revealed by prices. This information

---

[4] $\{F_i \cup p(\cdot, \omega)\}$ is the smallest σ-algebra containing both F_i and $\sigma(p(\cdot, \omega))$, where $\sigma(p(\cdot, \omega))$ is the smallest σ-algebra for which $p(\cdot, \omega)$ is measurable.

set is called *public* information since it is available using only price data and common information sources. For special economies, it is possible that the public information $\{(\cap_i F_i) \cup p(\cdot, \omega)\} = \cup_j F_j$, i.e., prices reveal *all* the information available to private investors (see Jordan and Radner [4]). Such an equilibrium is called a *fully revealing* RE asset market equilibrium, since the price functional reveals every investor's private information.

A fully revealing RE asset market equilibrium implies the market is efficient with respect to all available private information. This is a very special economy. If this were true in an economy with costly markets for information, there would be no incentives for any investor to search for additional information about asset prices. But if there is no incentive to search for information, then investors would have no private information available.This would, in turn, imply the nonexistence of an equilibrium for such a market (see Grossman and Stiglitz [3]).

The more probable RE equilibrium is one where prices reveal partial, but not total, information. It is an empirical question the extent to which this is true. Some conventional terminology should be mentioned at this point. If the market is efficient with respect to common information, $\cap_i F_i$, it is said to be *weak-form* efficient. If the market is efficient with respect to partial information, $\psi \neq \cap_i F_i$, $\psi \subset \cup_i F_i$, $\psi \neq \cup_i F_i$, it is said to be *semistrong-form* efficient. Finally, if the market is efficient with respect to all private information, $\cup_i F_i$, it is said to be *strong-form* efficient.

19.4. THE CAPM AND MARKET EFFICIENCY

This section relates the concept of market efficiency to the CAPM studied in Chap. 15. The CAPM implicity assumes that all investors have homogeneous information sets, i.e., F_i equals $\{\phi, \Omega\}$ for all i, and homogeneous beliefs (see assumption 15.3 in contrast to assumption 19.4). Given this interpretation, it is easy to see that it is trivially true that the CAPM economy is efficient with respect to all available private information (of which there is none).

The CAPM economy can be given another interpretation, however, consistent with an economy containing differential information. Here we let investors have differential information, i.e., $F_i \neq F_j$ for $i \neq j$, but investors are sophisticated and condition on prices. This is consistent with assumption 15.3, homogeneous beliefs, if and only if $p(x, \omega)$ reveals all the private information $\cup_j F_j$ so that $\{(\cap_i F_i) \cup p(\cdot, w))\} = \cup_j F_j$. Hence the beliefs $\text{Prob}_i[\cdot]$ in Chap. 15 are really conditional on the same information, $\cup_j F_j$, which is all the private information available. The CAPM is efficient with respect to all available information, but this time because it is a fully revealing RE asset market equilibrium.

Given the homogeneous beliefs assumption 15.3, the CAPM of Chap. 15 is seen to imply that the market is efficient with respect to *all private information*. This is a strong implicit implication of the CAPM. It needs to be emphasized that since the assumptions underlying the CAPM of Chap. 15 imply the market is strong-form efficient, strong-form efficiency is not an added restriction to the model. This statement is emphasized since there appears to be some confusion in the literature on this point. It is, therefore, not possible for the market to be inefficient and the CAPM true. This observation implies that all the empirical anomalies of recent years (see Jensen [2]) should only be interpreted as rejections of the CAPM and not a rejection of market efficiency.

Although this discussion has pertained to the CAPM, it should also be noted that the equilibrium version of Ross's APT requires the homogeneous beliefs assumption 18.3. Consequently, the equilibrium version of the APT also has the same implication for market efficiency, i.e., it implies that the market is strong-form efficient.

19.5. SUMMARY

This chapter introduces information economics through a discussion of market efficiency. Market efficiency revolves around the concept of an asset market equilibrium in an economy where investors have heterogeneous information and heterogeneous beliefs and can learn from prices. The concept of a rational expectations (RE) equilibrium captures these notions. In turn, an RE equilibrium leads to the concepts of weak-form, semistrong-form, and strong-form efficiency. The relationship between these concepts of efficiency and the CAPM is also discussed.

19.6. REFERENCES

1. Breiman, Leo, *Probability*. Reading, Mass.: Addison-Wesley, 1968.
2. Jensen, Michael, "Some Anomalous Evidence Regarding Market Efficiency," *Journal of Financial Economics*, 2 (June 1978), 95–102.
3. Grossman, Sanford, and Joseph Stiglitz, "On the Impossibility of Informationally Efficient Markets," *American Economic Review*, 3 (June 1980), 393–408.
4. Jordan, James S., and Roy Radner, "Rational Expectations in Microeconomic Models: An Overview," *Journal of Economic Theory*, 26 (1982), 201–223.

INDEXES

AUTHOR INDEX

293

SUBJECT INDEX